The History of the
KAREN PEOPLE
of Burma

Angelene Naw

Edited by Jerry B. Cain

JUDSON PRESS
PUBLISHERS SINCE 1824
VALLEY FORGE, PA

Interior design by Crystal Devine.
Cover design by Danny Ellison.

Library of Congress Cataloging-in-Publication data

Library of Congress Control Number: 2022942982

Printed in the U.S.A.

First printing, 2023.

To

My parents, Saw Yankee Myint Oo and Naw Khu Paw,
who nurtured six children to love Jesus and cherish Karen culture;

My son Dominic and wife, Htoo Tha Shee, who shared
my daily vicissitudes with patience;

and

for my grandchildren Uriel, Skye, and Praise
to embrace and carry on the legacy of their great-grandparents
even if they were not born in the land called Kawthoolei

Contents

Online Materials

Maps

1. The British Annexation of Burma (1824–1886)
2. Force 136 and Karen Levies' Operation Character in World War II
3. Karen National Defence Organization Toungoo Brigade Operation—Objective Maymyo in Upper Burma (February to May 1949)
4. Karen National Defence Organization-Controlled Areas (1949)

Photographs

1. T. Thanbyah, founder of Karen National Asssociation and first graduate (1870) from an American university
2. Sir San C. Po (CBE, MD), the first Karen and the first from Burma to become a citizen of the United States of America
3. Karen Goodwill Mission in the United Kingdom (1946)
4. Saw Ba U Gyi, founder of Karen National Union
5. Mahn Ba Zan, Karen National Union first general
6. General Bo Mya

Text

Hta about the Foundation of Karendom (chapter 2)

Karen National Anthem (chapters 3 and 4)

Karen New Year Day Recognition Bill, 1937 (chapter 4)

The Humble Memorial of the Karens of Burma to His Britannic Majesty's Secretary of State for Burma (chapters 5 and 6)

Chart of Refugee Resettlement (chapter 9)

The Twenty-First-Century Karen Diasporas: Australia, Canada, Norway, and Singapore

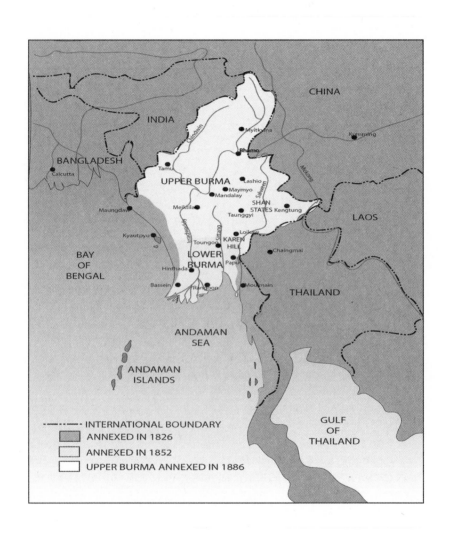

CHINA

INDIA

BANGLADESH

Calcutta

Tamu

Chindwin

Myitkyina

Kunming

Bhamo

UPPER BURMA

Lashio

Maungdaw

Meiktila

Maymyo
Mandalay

Salween

Mekong

LAOS

SHAN
STATES Kengtung

Taunggyi

Kyautpyu

Irrawaddy

Toungoo

Sittang

Loikaw

KAREN
HILL

Chaingmai

LOWER
BURMA

Papun

BAY
OF
BENGAL

Hinthada

Bassein

Rangoon

Moulmain

THAILAND

ANDAMAN
SEA

ANDAMAN
ISLANDS

INTERNATIONAL BOUNDARY

ANNEXED IN 1826

ANNEXED IN 1852

UPPER BURMA ANNEXED IN 1886

GULF
OF
THAILAND

Preface

My first six years were spent in a war zone where guns, bullets, and soldiers were my inescapable companions. We followed my military officer father, Saw Yankee Myint Oo, who joined the Karen national movement soon after World War II. With the sounds of roaring tigers and the crawling poisonous snakes around at night, we had to shift from one campsite to another, sometimes on elephants and sometimes on foot. At age seven, we settled in a war-free zone where my maternal great-grandfather had been the church pastor for more than thirty years. I enjoyed accompanying my great-grandmother to every home and church service. Through reading the Bible with her day and night, I learned how to read and write the Karen language. As a little girl, my first dream was to become a pastor or missionary who preached God's Word.

After moving to Insein, we lived next to Nanthagone Karen Baptist Church, where I developed more dreams. Our church was celebrating its golden jubilee in 1961 and the Sunday school children had to participate in the concert. There, behind the stage, I met Naw Louisa Benson, Miss Burma, an actress and famous singer. I praised her beauty incessantly, but my father reminded me that I should also admire her brain because she was teaching English at Rangoon University. Deeply inspired, I was determined to do the work necessary to become a university teacher. Two years later, my church sent me to a women's Bible study workshop. Its program included a dramatic contest of the women in the Bible. I was assigned to act as Queen Esther, who saved her people from Persian captivity. I began to dream of doing similar work for my Karen people who were in a struggle for self-determination. It was a dream too big to talk about for a teenager.

These young dreams originated from the faith that my parents implanted in me since my terrifying childhood years in the war-weary jungles of Burma. Had it not been for my academic career, my intention to become a missionary, and my wish to contribute time and energy to the Karen cause would not have been fully realized. God opened that opportunity for me after I became a history faculty member at Judson University in Elgin, Illinois.

In 2007, Karen refugees were relocating to Illinois. Since most of these Karen families came from the refugee camps on the border of

Thailand and Burma, they spoke only Karen or the Thai language. I was contacted by organizations involved in the refugee resettlement program and became a volunteer in the Karen interpreting service not only in Illinois but also all over the United States. Then I began to concern myself with the spiritual growth of these Karen families and felt it was vital to organize a regular worship service in the Karen language. We were able to start a Karen Christian worship service in June 2007. With the support of Dr. Jerry Cain, the president of Judson University, and Dr. Richard Clossman, emeritus professor of history, the Karen Baptist Church of Western Chicago was formed and became a member of the American Baptist Churches of the Great Rivers Region. For this church without a pastor, it became my responsibility to lead the church services and deliver weekly church messages.

As I became closer to my Karen people through our church activities, I began to have a concern for the future of the Karen children. Would they be able to remember their roots and even speak the Karen language? My father from Burma heard about my work with the Karen people and reminded me of my dream to be like Queen Esther helping her people. I had now earned a PhD in history and was teaching in America, and if I truly wanted to help my Karen people preserve their culture, my duty was to write a history of the Karens. Following my father's advice, I started to work on Karen history in 2009.

The Judson University Surbeck Summer Award in 2009 was a great help to travel and start my research work on my Karen history project. My colleagues in the history department at Judson University have always been a source of encouragement. Dr. Jim Halverson and Dr. Craig Kaplowitz set the bar high not only for teaching and student engagement but also for scholarly achievement. Their true colleagueship allowed me to take a sabbatical leave in 2010 and do my research in Thailand. My personal friends from the Judson community, Dr. Charles DeRolf, Judy DeRolf, and Dr. Sharon Kim, have pushed me to put the story I knew from experience and study to paper so others could grasp it also. I wish to thank them and all my colleagues at Judson University for their constant support and for showing me how to engage the Judson University community standards, which are based on Galatians 5:22-23.

My dreams as a little girl all became true at Judson University: teaching, preaching, and especially my vision to preserve the Karen national identity through writing the history of my Karen people. For all this, I am indebted to Dr. Jerry Cain, who took a risk and hired me to teach the history of Asia at Judson University, even though I had no teaching experience in an American university. One of my dreams came true because Dr. Cain went beyond his duty and supported me in forming the Karen Baptist Church of Western Chicago. Above all, I have to admit that this book never would have come to existence without the encouragement and hard work of Dr. Cain. I stopped writing for a few years, but he pushed me to finish the book. As I wrote again, he read every word and reread every sentence to make it readable and user-friendly.

It takes a long time and a lot of work to reduce a story of the ages down to a single volume one person can hold in their hand. Thus, I am very grateful for those who helped me tell this story that you are about to engage. I am indebted to General Oliver of the Karen National Liberation Army and his brother Orlando, who are the sons of Karen National Association leader Saw Tha Din. (You will learn about his goodwill mission to London with Saw Ba U Gyi in chapter 6.) Through interviews they provided lots of information and, in addition, gave me books and other materials which are invaluable resources for this manuscript. I also owe Kawthoolei Lahpoe, who now lives in Norway, for driving me to Karen villages in remote areas of northern Thailand. Without her help, I would not be able to include the lives of the Karen people who now live in Norway. I am also indebted to Dr. Mark Tamthai, director of the Institute of Religion, Culture, and Peace at Payap University in Chiangmai, Thailand. He provided a place to work as a research scholar, with a resourceful Karen assistant, Miss Kansinee Jirekun (Noonu), from January to July 2010. Conducting research at Payap University was very convenient and productive because of Dr. Tamthai's wonderful arrangement and the hospitality of the faculty of the institute.

Since it is impossible to write Karen history without Karen Christian organizations and Christian leaders, I wish to thank all the following Christian leaders, pastors, and friends who provided valuable input and information to make this work complete: the late Rev. Dr. Clifford Kyaw Dwe, Professor Tun Aung Chain, former Karen Affairs Minister Saw Tun Aung Myint, Dr. Anna May Say Pa, Rev. Dr. Doh Say, Rev. Dr. Yaha Lay Lay La, Rev. Dr. Say Lwai Wah, Rev. Saw Ywa Hdut Moo, Marcia and Duane Binkley, Saw Bla Htoo Po, Dr. Rebecca Yah, Rev. Dr. Saw Ler Htoo, Rev. Hsa Moo, Rev. Hsi Mu, Pastor Sa Ba Taw, Rev. Gail Moe, Pastor Winsome Paul, Saw Michael Thaw Tha, Saw Paul Kyaw, Naw Pla Hset, and Naw Tansy Kadoe. Last but not least, my heartfelt gratitude to my niece Sally Myint Oo, granddaughter of World War II soldier Saw Yankee Myint Oo, for drawing the maps; Mie Tha La for the photo of his great-grandfather T. Thanbyah; and readers Naw Helen Pe, Annasue McCleave Wilson, and Rebecca Ryanne Cain.

I want to acknowledge my parents as the impetus that made this happen. They raised me in a Christian community in a minority culture where the majority gave us no advantages. My parents were happy people who raised six children in the nurture and admonition of the Lord. They encouraged education and dreamed of big things for their children. I promised my father I would write this book and am proud to dedicate it to him.

Angelene Naw (Maku Oo)
Professor Emerita, Judson University
Elgin, Illinois

Editor's Introduction

On February 1, 2021, the bedroom radio awakened me with the morning news from NPR. The military armed forces of Myanmar, often called the Tatmadaw, had overthrown the elected government of the National League for Democracy led by Nobel Prize winner Aung San Suu Kyi. Shocking though not unexpected, this news reminded me of my several trips to Myanmar.

For some reason that morning, I recalled movies about Burma and the Karens. For example, *Rambo* (2008) was about John Rambo, portrayed by Sylvester Stallone—a soldier of fortune who fought to protect Karens and rescue their missionary helpers from the attacking Tatmadaw. Then I saw images of *Beyond Rangoon* and the Karens helping the female doctor escape the events of 8-8-88. That portrayal ignited thoughts of *The Lady*, a film about Aung San Suu Kyi, whose home compound I visited several times when staying in the Sedona Hotel in Yangon. And, of course, the movie *All Saints* that accurately portrays the refugee Karens with whom I worship each Sunday at Grace Baptist Church in Kansas City.

But my overriding concern on that morning was for Dr. Angelene Naw, who had previously started writing a history of the Karen people of Burma but had been distracted from the project by life and the declining health of her parents. Thus, the embers were warmed again, and together, we felt the call to tell the world about *The History of the Karen People of Burma*. This is an exhilarating yet sad story of the best and worst of humanity lived out on the left side of the map of Southeast Asia. Though officially called Myanmar today, Burma is the stage upon which this tale is told. This is the story of an ancient civilization that has been handed the proverbial dirty end of the stick for centuries. Known as the Karens (Cah-REN, pronounced with the emphasis on the second syllable), this group of some five million Sino-Tibetans has experienced the underbelly of human nature but, in most instances, has responded with the best in human nature.

The Karens met the western world in the sixteenth century while they were farmers in Burma, who fed the hungry mouths of the Burmese majority yet did not enjoy the fruits of the dominant culture. Beginning in the nineteenth century, they faithfully served the British colonialists yet did not get to enjoy the independence they were promised. These Karens were key in defeating the Japanese in Burma during World War II, yet they were denied the reward that enticed them to fight alongside the Burmese, who had been their oppressors. Though the Christian Karens were the objects of genocide in war-torn Burma, they fought on the side of their Burmese abusers to prevent communists from taking over the government after World War II. The Karens have endured the longest civil war in modern history, now lasting more than sixty years.

The crucial lens through which this story of suffering and forbearance must be understood is from the context of an ancient fable of a white man with a book and the ministry of missionary Adoniram Judson, who served in Burma from 1813 to 1850. The humanitarian impact of the modern mission movement is wonderfully exemplified here in *The History of the Karen People of Burma*.

Dr. Naw is uniquely qualified to record this story, which is most often retold as oral history. She was born during the time of the Karen nationalist movements and spent the first six years of her life hiding in the jungles of Burma, where her father was a front-line communications officer with the Karen insurgents. She finished two degrees at the University of Rangoon before completing her PhD at the University of Hawaii. Though a minority Karen, she had a career with the Burmese government before coming to the United States to teach Asian history at Judson University in Elgin, Illinois.

Dr. Naw fulfilled her academic role in an admirable fashion and has now turned her attention to honoring her Karen culture by scribing their first history in ninety years. Her voice in this book will faithfully convey not only the saga of the Karens but also the visions of the dominant Burmans, the colonizing British, and the evangelizing Americans. She has lived in all these worlds and is equipped from personal experience and formal education to tell the story of the Karen people.

Why serve as an editor? Motivated by the events in Myanmar on February 1, 2021, I made a covenant with Dr. Naw to help her finish the manuscript and tell the story of the Karens. The first half of the manuscript had been completed but had been laid aside, because she was caught in the sandwich generation between her son and his new family in Illinois and her aging parents and their health concerns in Yangon, Myanmar. She was flying back and forth twice each year, spending extended time with each side of the family—both needing her full-time attention.

Exhausted after the death of her mother in 2018, then her father in 2020, and the worldwide coronavirus pandemic, it seemed time to settle in the US and help raise her grandchildren. But the events of February 1,

2021, called us to action. I agreed to be her editor if she could now finish the manuscript as she had promised her parents. And so, Angelene started writing again, and I started reading.

Dr. Naw is conversant in many languages and fluent in four, as will be evident to the insightful reader of *The History of the Karen People of Burma*. Her native heart language is Karen, but she had to learn Burmese because daily trade and social contacts were done in that language. But she had to master British English since government and education were conducted in the language of the Empire. Then, she mastered American English because of her Christian background and eventual studies in Hawaii.

In her lithe way Dr. Naw can tell you about her language learning experiences, as excerpted from a November 4, 2021, email:

> My teachers from 1st grade all grew up under British rule. I think the influence is more from my father. He learned English under British rule and his bosses were British military officials. Since I was four, he started to teach me English when he was home. Then after we settled in Insein, he taught me English at home after school every day until 10th grade. At the University when I wrote on Kachin Hill Tracts Administration for my M.A. thesis, I had to read all documents and records compiled by British officers. Thanks to my Sunday school classes and Karen church, I can still write and read Karen.

Frequently, her original sentences show elements of Karen, Burmese, and/or English all in one line. My role as the first editor was to make the text readable to all our audiences without losing Dr. Naw's unique voice and experience. Word order in Karen or Burmese might occasionally sound strange to the western reader. As an editor, I helped reorder words, employing punctuation and capitalization throughout the manuscript to communicate more clearly. I made some long sentences shorter and merged some fragments into complete sentences. My involvement helped Dr. Naw carry her heavy load of research, scholarship, and communication.

The reader will notice hints from all of Dr. Naw's backgrounds throughout the book. We have left those identifiers in their original form when they do not destroy the flow of the story. Nor did we change the quoted material from its original form. Thus, British and Karen materials will include the spellings "defence" and "centre" while American materials will use the spellings "defense" and "center." We hope you see flavorings from both the East and the West in this history.

The intellectual property herein is entirely the work of Dr. Angelene Naw. She researched every book and wrote the first draft of every sentence. I assisted only with readability and helped make connections with sources, publishers, proofreaders, and now the general public. It has been a true joy to work with this phenomenal scholar.

Readers of world history and of Christian missions will find this book riveting, as will students interested in Southeast Asia or minority cultures. But *The History of the Karen People of Burma* will be a must-read for the Karen diaspora spread throughout the US and the rest of the world who will never return to Myanmar to experience their cultural and historical impact on Burma. And for the general reader, it is an exciting and well-told saga revealing the best and the worst in all of us.

Jerry B. Cain
Chancellor, Judson University
Elgin, Illinois

Abbreviations

ABCUSA – American Baptist Churches USA

ABFMS – American Baptist Foreign Mission Society

ABIM – American Baptist International Ministries

ABFSU – All Burma Federation of Students Union

ABKO – All Burma Karen Organization

ABSDF – All Burma Students' Democratic Front

AFO – Anti-Fascist Organization

AFPFL – Anti-Fascist People's Freedom League

AKF – Australian Karen Foundation

AKO – Australian Karen Organization

ASEAN – Association of Southeast Asian Nations

AUSCO – Australian Cultural Orientation

BCP – Burma Communist Party (White Flag)

BDA – Burma Defence Army

BIA – Burma Independence Army

BKNA – Buddhist Karen National Association

BNA – Burma National Army

BPF – Burma Patriotic Forces

BSM – British Service Mission

BSPP – Burma Socialist Programme Party

CAS (B) – Civil Affairs Service (Burma)

CAS-K – Civilian Affairs Service-Kawthoolei

CCCA – Christian Consortium of Christian Agencies

CBF – Cooperative Baptist Fellowship

CPB – Communist Party of Burma (Red Flag)

DAA – Dobama Asi-Ayon

DAB – Democratic Alliance of Burma

DDS(I) – Directorate of Defence Service (Intelligence)

DNUF – Democratic Nationalities United Front. Karen, Mon, Karenni, Pa'O, 1956

DKBA – Democratic Kayin Buddhist Army

DSI – Defence Service Institute

FACE – Frontiers Areas Committee of Enquiry, February 21, 1947

FBC – Free Burma Coalition

FOB – Friends of Burma

GAR – Government Assisted Refugees

GCBA – General Council of Burmese Association

IM-ABCUSA – International Ministries of the American Baptist Churches USA

IOM – International Organization for Migration

IOR – India Office (Record) in London

JBCS – Judson Baptist Church of Singapore

KACF – Karen American Community Foundation

KBC – Karen Baptist Convention

KBCA – Karen Baptist Churches of Australia

KBCC – Karen Baptist Churches of Canada

KBCS – Karen Baptist Church of Singapore

KBC-USA – Karen Baptist Churches, United States of America

KBN – Karen Baptist Norway

KBTS – Karen Baptist Theological Seminary

KCC – Karen Canadian Community

KCN – Karen Community Norway

KCO – Karen Central Organization

KCOM – Karen Culture Organization of Minnesota

KGB – Karen Governing Body (formed in 1955)

KHRG – Karen Human Rights Group

KIA – Kachin Independence Army

KIO – Kachin Independence Organization

KKBC – Kawthoolei Karen Baptist Convention

KMA – Kawthoolei Military Administration (another name of CAS-K)

KMT – Chinese Nationalist Party; Kuomintang

KNA – Karen National Association

KNDO – Karen National Defence Organization

KNLA – Karen National Liberation Army

KNLC – Karen National Liberation Council

KNLP – Karen New Land Party

KNPP – Karen National Progressive Party

KNU – Karen National Union

KNUF – Karen National United Front (Bo Mya and Mahn Ba Zan), 1968

KNU/KNLA PC – National Union/ Karen National Liberation Army Peace Council

KNUP – Karen National United Party (communist model in 1953)

KOA – Karen Organization of America

KOM – Karen Organization of Minnesota

KPLA – Kaawthoolei Peoples Liberation Army

KPG – Kawthoolei People's Guerrilla Force

KPMG – Karen Peace Mediator Group

KPLA – Kawthoolei People's Liberation Army

KRC – Karen Revolutionary Council (replaces KGB)

KYN – Karen Youth Norway

KYO – Karen Youth Organization

MIS – Military Intelligence Service (aka DDSI/Directorate Defense Services Intelligence)

MIT – Myanmar Institute of Theology

NCGUB – National Coalition Government of the Union of Burma

NCUB – National Council of the Union of Burma

NDUF – National Democratic United Front (merger of KNUP, NMSP, and BCP)

NDF – National Democratic Front

NLA – National Liberation Alliance 1960 (Karen, Shan, Karenni)

NLD – National League for Democracy

NMSP – New Mon State Party

NUF – National United Front

NULF – National United Liberation Front

PP, C – Parliament, House of Commons, Sessional Papers

PBF – Patriot Burmese Force (previously known as BNA)

PKBC – Pwo Karen Baptist Convention

PRO – Public Record Office, in London

PVO – People's Volunteer Organization

SLORC – State Law and Order Restoration Council

SNLD – Shan National League for Democracy

SPDC – State Peace and Development Council

TCI – Dr. T. Thanbyah Christian Institute

UNHCHR – United Nations High Commission for Human Rights

YMBA – Young Men's Buddhist Association

1

Christianity in Pre-Colonial Burma (Before 1824)

An Introduction to Peoples and the Land

Like other world river valley civilizations, the Pyu people developed the first city-states in central Burma along the Irrawaddy River valley in the second century BCE. They adopted Hinduism and Buddhism, which arrived through trade with India. In the ninth century CE, the Mon established the first prominent Buddhist kingdom in the Thaton area in lower Burma. When King Anawratha of Bagan conquered the Mon country in 1057, he carried the Mons' Theravada Buddhism to Bagan. Thousands of pagodas that spread over sixteen square miles in today's Bagan city attest to how deep-seated Buddhist culture has been in this region since. In protecting the Buddhist faith, these kings persecuted foreign missionaries and their subjects who contacted them. Despite such obstructions, Christian missionaries tried to enter the forbidden land of the Buddhist kings.

Amongst the people in this land are the Karens. The origin of the name *Karen* is uncertain, but they called themselves *Pwa K' Nyaw*, which means "human." They were the earliest inhabitants of Burma (Myanmar), after the Mon. The Chin, Burman, Arakanese, Shan, and Kachin followed later in chronological order. However, from the twelfth century CE, the Burmans dominated the land, building Buddhist empires—Bagan, Toungoo, and Konbaung—before the British annexation. According to records, the Burmans called "Kayin" (transliteration of the word *Karen*) "wild people" and "aborigines," and treated them as the inferior caste, making them slaves. To be free from such ferocity, the Karens lived as far away as possible from the Burmans in the remote hilly zone.

The Karen situation drastically changed after they met American Baptist missionaries in the first quarter of the nineteenth century. The Old Karen legend of the Lost Book brought by the white brothers and the similarities between the Karen traditional old tales and Old

Testament stories convinced thousands of Karens to convert to Christianity. The missionaries devised a Karen script, translated the Bible, and provided education. The educated Karens further spread the gospel among the Chins and the Kachins. The Burmese rulers were infuriated and persecuted the Karens. The missionaries had to set up refugee camps for the Karen refugees in the Arakan Mountains, which became British territory after the first Anglo-Burmese war.

In 1851, the Burmese viceroy in Rangoon threatened to shoot instantly the first Karen he found capable of reading.[1] Amidst the punishment, Karens studied modern education from their missionaries and prospered. Christian education promoted upward mobility. It also aroused the Karen nationalist sentiment with the dream of building a Karen national state. This Christian-oriented Karen nationalism posed a threat to the Buddhist Burmans, making the Karens objects of genocide in Burma from 1942 and continuing in the twenty-first century. Several years ago, a Burmese military general publicly proclaimed that the Karens would be eliminated, until in the future, no Karen would be found except in the museum. When the British occupied the country, they named it "Burma" after the ruling people who called themselves "Bama." Subsequently, the "Burman" referred to the major ethnic group in Burma. Currently, they form 68 percent of the total population, followed by the Shan (10 percent), Karen (7 percent), Rakhine (4 percent), Mon (2 percent), Kachin (1.5 percent), Chin (1 percent), and others less than 1 percent. Remarkably, the Karens, who are the third largest ethnic group in Burma, constitute 90 percent of the refugee population from Burma in the United States, indicating the Karens are the main target of persecution to flee for their lives. Afraid of losing their identity, the Karens did not like to be called "Burmese" refugees. They preferred their ethnic name, "the Karen refugees." The term "Karens" applied to several subgroups, but this book deals mostly with the Baptist Karen Christians, whose legacies promise the future Karen national heritage.

The Beginnings of Christianity in Burma

Baptist Christians outnumber other Christian denominations in today's Myanmar, but Baptist missionaries were not the first Christians to step on the land known for its golden pagodas. The first documented record of Christians in Burma comes from the account of an Italian traveler, Ludovico di Varthema (Lewes Vertomannus). He reported, "The city of Pego is on the mainland, and is near the sea. . . . The king is extremely powerful in men, both foot and horse, and has with him more than a thousand Christians."[2] He described these Christians as people who "write after the manner of Armenia" and "are as white as we are,"[3] suggesting that they were not locals but foreigners residing in Burma. We surmise they were Oriental Orthodox Christians.

Next came the Portuguese Catholic Christians. When Vasco da Gama was asked about his interest in sailing around the Cape of Good Hope to India in 1498, the legendary Portuguese adventurer reportedly said, "Christianity and spices." This was arguably the reason that the Roman Catholic mission came to Burma, though Burma was not a land of spices. Alfonso de Albuquerque captured Goa in 1510 and made it the first Portuguese naval base in India. Throughout the sixteenth century, Portuguese expansion continued in India, and Christianity was introduced to the conquered peoples. However, these colonists could not penetrate the Burma ports, as the Burmese kingdom was too powerful. After its disintegration in 1581, an internal civil war followed. In 1596, the Arakan king defeated the Mon kingdom but returned to his capital. He left a garrison to protect Pegu city and Syriam (Thanlyin), then the principal seaport of Burma. He sent a Portuguese adventurer, Philip de Brito, to take charge of the customs house in Syriam and to represent the king to European traders.[4]

De Brito's local power grew. After some political, marital, and military entanglements, he was named king of Pegu by his loyal followers.[5] After accepting both the title and the power, de Brito erected fortifications, marked out the limits of the city, and built a church (probably the first in Burma).[6] In 1612, de Brito's army marched to Toungoo where they conquered and plundered the city. The Burmese king, Maha Dhamma Raja, retaliated in 1613 and, after the fall of Syriam, executed de Brito and all the leading Portuguese. The remaining foreigners and those of mixed race, including de Brito's wife, were taken as captives to Ava.[7]

When the first Christian community in Syriam collapsed, Christian mission activities in Burma ceased for about eighty years. Late in the seventeenth century, Christian missionary activity resumed when French Catholics, Father Jean Genoud and Father Jean Joret, arrived in Pegu in 1692. Within a few months, they successfully built a Christian community that consisted of the foreigners residing in Pegu plus a good number of native people. The conversion of the natives made the Buddhist monks unhappy, so the monks appealed to the king to act. The king responded with an order of execution preceded by a period of physical torture. Father Genoud and Father Joret were stripped naked and exposed to the scorching sun in the daytime and mosquitoes at night before they were sewn into sacks and drowned in the Pegu River on February 12, 1693, within a year of their arrival.[8]

After the Armenians, Portuguese, and French Christians, the subsequent century saw the arrival of the Barnabite order (Congregation of Clerks Regular of St. Paul) from Italy, representing the Roman Catholic Church. The Barnabite Christian missionaries came to Burma through their mission work in China. In 1719, the pope sent Father Monsignor Mezzabarba with five others of the Barnabite order as an ambassador to the emperor of China. When the mission failed, some of them were sent to Cochin-China, including Sigismond Calchi, who later was reassigned to the Pegu mission in Burma. Calchi was accompanied to Pegu by another priest, Joseph Vittoni. When they arrived in 1721, the king of Ava received them cordially and gave Father Calchi permission to preach and circulate freely. The king sent Father Vittoni back to Italy with gifts for the pope, but no record of his return to Burma exists. Calchi continued to work in Ava until his death in 1728. Before he died, Calchi composed a small dictionary to facilitate the study of the Burmese language for the priests who would succeed him.[9]

Father Gallizia arrived two months after the death of Father Calchi. He first worked in Ava but later moved to Syriam, where he built a church and cultivated the Christian faith among the local people. Gallizia recruited four Italian helpers for his Barnabite mission. The ruler of the Mon kingdom of Pegu gave them permission to preach and even provided a plot of land to build a church.[10] The mission's progress was interrupted by the Dutch in 1745 when the Dutch governor, accompanied by six ships, came from Serampore to Syriam with the intention of making it a European factory. As the Dutch marched to Pegu, Bishop Gallizia served as an interpreter, but the situation quickly deteriorated. The king of Pegu ordered the execution of all foreigners, including the Christian priests. Bishop Gallizia was among those killed.

Two of Bishop Gallizia's helpers, Father Paolo Nerini and physician Angelo Capello, returned to Syriam together in 1749. The king of Pegu approved of their continuing mission among Christians. Both local and foreign Christians joined Nerini and Angelo in rebuilding the church, with an Armenian named Nicholas de Aguilar as their main financial supporter. Adjoining the church, they built a large house for orphan girls. The locals and numerous wealthy Armenians involved in international trade respected Father Nerini highly for the advancement of the Catholic religion. In addition to his evangelistic efforts, Father Neirni found time to revise and perfect the grammar and dictionary of the

Burmese language that Father Calchi had started. Additionally, he composed a catechism and prayer book.[11]

Father Nerini's mission progress was disrupted by changing political leadership in the country. In 1751, the king of Pegu's armed forces advanced north to the capital of Ava. By March 1752, Ava was captured.[12] However, a military officer from Ava, Alaungpaya, gained many followers and was recognized as the new leader. He organized troops and recaptured Ava in December 1753. The king of Pegu fled to Syriam where his allies, the French and the Dutch, resupplied his armies in the struggle against Alaungpaya. However, in May 1757, the king of Pegu lost the war, thus inaugurating the Konbaung dynasty, the last Burman kingdom in history, with Alaungpaya as king. In the wars between Ava and Pegu, the French assisted the king of Pegu, hoping for future trading benefits. King Alaungpaya suspected that Father Nerini assisted the French, and so he ordered the priest beheaded. Father Nerini was executed in 1756.[13]

Most political incidents during the first 250 years of Catholic ministry either weakened or stopped mission activities. However, the war with King Ayutthaya of Siam during the Konbaung dynasty seemed to strengthen the Catholic mission in Burma. After the conquest of Ayutthaya in 1768, Hsin Byu Shin returned to Burma with thousands of captives, including the Christians and their bishop, Monsignor Brigot, the Vicar Apostolic of Siam. With Bishop Brigot in Burma, Father Marcia Percoto, who had arrived in Burma in 1761, was consecrated and designated Bishop of Maxula. In 1776, Bishop Percoto passed away in Ava at the age of forty-seven after working for fifteen years in Burma. He was thoroughly acquainted with the Burmese language, and he produced a dictionary plus translations of Genesis and the epistles of the apostle Paul.[14] One of his significant contributions was the *Book of Controversy*, which consisted of a dialogue between a Christian and a Burman. He composed this book with the assistance of a Burmese scholar.[15]

The Konbaung kings tolerated foreign religions more than previous rulers had.[16] By the end of the eighteenth century, three Roman Catholic mission centers were well established in Amarapura, Rangoon, and Mergui. Due to thriving trade, Rangoon attracted more foreigners, and the number of Christians also increased. The total number of Christians, both native and foreigners, reached nearly three thousand attending the two Roman Catholic churches in Rangoon.[17] However, the Burmese destroyed both churches in 1824 at the beginning of the first Anglo-Burmese war.

Judging by the number of native Christians, the work of early Catholic missionaries probably yielded insignificant results, despite their zeal and sacrifices. However, some substantial contributions are notable. They established several schools and a college. Native priests graduating from these schools enabled churches to function when few foreign missionaries were available for leadership. When Father Vincentiues Sangermano left Burma in 1806, only two European priests remained in the Burma Catholic mission. The mission's work continued, however, with two native priests, Father Ignatius de Britto and Father John Koo.[18]

The translation work initiated by these priests was significant. Father Calchi, the first Barnabite priest in Burma, composed a small dictionary during his six years of service (1722–1728). Later, Bishop Percoto continued the dictionary work, while also translating the Bible. Bishop Caejetan Montegazza further advanced the literacy work by traveling to Europe in 1784 with two Burmans including one named Tsau, a former Buddhist monk. With the help of these companions in Rome in 1786, Montegazza printed an alphabet, a small prayer book, and a catechism in Burmese characters with the Latin translation.[19]

Obviously, the first Christian church in Burma was established by the priests imported by the Portuguese governor, Philip de Brito. Those Christians were principally Portuguese and people from West India. The growing number of Catholic Christian missionaries and practicing Christians in the eighteenth century can be attributed to the religious tolerance of King Alaungpaya and his Konbaung kings who ruled the country during that period.

Arrivals of the First Baptist Missionaries

Though initiated by the Portuguese and Italian Catholics, the growth of Christianity in Burma can be attributed primarily to American Baptist missionaries. However, English Baptist missionary William Carey (1761–1834) prepared the way for the Americans in Burma. William Carey was a pioneer missionary who, in 1800, established a mission center in Bengal in the small Danish colony of Serampore. He created newspapers and journals and translated the Bible into twenty-four languages.[20] The successful mission in Serampore motivated Carey to expand his mission field to neighboring areas including Burma. For his numerous contributions, he earned several titles including "the Father of the Second Reformation through Foreign Missions."[21]

Political scientists indict Christianity as an imperialist tool. Paradoxically, the British policy in India forbade all missionary activities.

Though William Carey's Serampore mission was under Danish rule, the British East India port at Calcutta controlled access to the mission. When two new British missionaries arrived in 1806, the British authority deported them. One missionary, James Chater, was sent to Burma, where he stayed for four years. He was able to learn the language and made a preliminary translation of the Gospel of Matthew into Burmese. Upon Chater's request for reinforcements, William Carey encouraged his son Felix Carey (1786–1822) to join this mission. Felix Carey arrived in Rangoon in December 1807. He began learning the language immediately and revised Chater's translation work. He married a local woman of Portuguese descent in 1811, which made it convenient for him to establish relationships with local authorities. In 1812, after setting up a printing press in the capital of Ava, Chater left the Burma mission.[22]

Meanwhile, William Carey's zeal and success attracted many young missionaries. One such missionary was an American, Adoniram Judson. Judson's interest in India's mission field was fanned by Rev. Claudius Buchanan's famous sermon, "The Star of the East."[23] Ultimately, the Congregational Church established the American Board of Commissioners for Foreign Missions and appointed the young enthusiast as their first missionary. Along with seven companions, Judson traveled to India to proclaim the Christian message.

The American missionaries, including Judson and his wife Ann Hasseltine Judson, arrived at the port of Calcutta on June 17, 1812. There, they were greeted by bad news—Britain and America were at war. The British East India Company ordered that no American missionary was to stay in any part of the territory that belonged to the company. Without choice, on November 30, Adoniram and his wife sailed for Port Louis, four thousand miles away, to the Isle of France (Mauritius), where they pondered other mission fields in Asia.[24]

After reading *An Account of an Embassy to the Kingdom of Ava* by Michael Symes,[25] Judson became interested in Burma. The news, however, from Felix Carey, who was representing the English Baptist Mission in Burma, was not encouraging. According to their earlier experience in Rangoon, mission work was impossible in Burma since the Burmese people were not permitted to accept a new religion. The Burmese were so hostile to foreigners that, a year earlier, outsiders residing in Rangoon sought refuge for fifty days on a British frigate in the Rangoon harbor.[26] With such gloomy news about Burma, the Judsons considered Penang, an island of Malaysia, as their new mission field. To find their way to Penang, they sailed back to India in May 1813. Again, the British authorities forced them to leave. On June 22, 1813, Adoniram and Ann boarded the only available ship, *Georgiana*, which took them to Rangoon.[27] The Judsons arrived in Rangoon on July 13, 1813. They worked closely with Felix Carey until Carey accepted a position as Burmese ambassador to the British government in Calcutta and prepared to leave missionary work.[28] On August 20, 1815, Carey and his family left for Ava. Tragically, the vessel that carried them capsized in the Irrawaddy River, drowning his family and destroying his property.[29] On November 15, 1815, he resigned from the mission at Serampore, which had sent him to Burma.[30]

By the end of 1815, both Adoniram and Ann Judson were fluent in daily conversational Burmese, though the former knew more about the nature and construction of the language.[31] With her linguistic skills, Ann started a school for girls in 1816. There, she wrote a catechism for the children while sharing the Bible with their mothers.[32] George Hough, a missionary printer from America, arrived in October 1817. He brought a printing press and other equipment as a gift from William Carey. The press printed one thousand copies of a summary of Christian doctrine entitled "The Way to Heaven" prepared by Adoniram. In addition, three thousand copies of Ann's children's catechism were printed.[33]

In 1818, two new American missionary couples, Edward and Eliza Wheelock and James and Elizabeth Colman, arrived in Rangoon to reinforce the Judsons' mission. Meanwhile, Adoniram reaped the first fruit of his work with the baptism of a Burman, Maung Nau, on June 27, 1819.[34] Hoping to build a cordial relationship with the king of Burma, Judson and Colman traveled to Ava, 350 miles up the Irrawaddy River, on December 21, 1819. King Bagyidaw granted them an audience on January 27, 1820, but nothing significant came from that interview.[35]

Judson's efforts to reach the court of Ava were ongoing when another new missionary couple, Dr. and Mrs. Jonathan Price, arrived in December 1821. Dr. Price's skills in cataract surgery opened the door for Judson and Price to gain the favor of the king. The king invited Dr. Price to his palace. Since Price was not able to speak the language, Judson accompanied him as an interpreter. The king, Price, and Judson met formally in September 1822. This time, the king encouraged them to stay in Ava, even granting them a piece of land on the riverbank just a mile from the king's palace.[36] On January 23, 1823, leaving Price in Ava, Judson returned to Rangoon, where he completed the translation of the entire New Testament into Burmese by July. By then, Judson had baptized eighteen Burmese including two women, but the Burmese authorities began to chase and punish the new church members.

Ann departed Burma for the USA on August 21, 1821, because of severe liver issues. She returned on December 5, 1823, bringing with her a new missionary couple, Jonathan and Deborah Wade. Ann started teaching them the Burmese language during their six-month voyage from Bradford, Massachusetts, to Rangoon.[37] However, all the mission activities ceased in 1824 when war between the British East India Company and the king of Burma began.

Early Encounters between the Missionaries and the Karens

Although records of Roman Catholic priests in Burma from the early sixteenth to eighteen centuries exist, they did not appear to have a continuing relationship with the Karen people. In the *Life of Monsignor Percoto*, Father Nerini, who was in Burma from 1743 to 1755, mentioned "wild populations styled Cariani (Karens) living separately from others, and in full liberty."[38] This may be the first reference to Karens from the western lens.

The journal of Captain Michael Symes describes another encounter between an Italian priest, Father Vincentiues Sangermano, and the Karens. In 1775, Symes had been sent to the court of Ava to investigate a serious frontier issue that occurred between the British East India Company and the Burmese king. Symes recorded the information about the Karens he learned from Father Sangermano:

> [H]e told me of a singular description of people called Carayners, or Carianers [Karens], that inhabit different parts of the country, particularly the western provinces of Dalla and Bassein, several societies of whom also dwell in the districts adjacent to Rangoon. . . . A great part of the provisions used in the country is raised by the Carianer, and they particularly excel in gardening. They have of late years been heavily taxed and oppressed by the Burman landholders, in consequence of which numbers have withdrawn into the mountains of Arracan.[39]

Arguably, the first non-Roman Catholic missionary who encountered the Karens in Burma was Rev. Claudius Buchanan, chaplain of the East India Company, who accompanied Symes on his visit to Ava in 1795. Symes reported their visit to a Karen village near Rangoon as follows:

Dr. Buchanan interrogated one of the men, who admitted their want of knowledge and assigned as the reason, that God once wrote his laws and commands on the skin of a buffalo, and called upon all nations of the earth to come and take a copy; a summon which all obeyed except the Carianers [Karens], who had not leisure, being occupied in the business of husbandry; and that is the consequences of this neglect, they remained ever since in a state of ignorance, without any other cares, than those which related to their pastoral employment.[40]

This "state of ignorance" probably kept the early Christian missionaries from engaging the Karens, because these newcomers were trying to engage the political and cultural leaders.

Like early Catholics, both British and American Baptist missionaries worked hard to establish mission centers in the cities. After their arrival in 1806, British missionaries James Chater and Felix Carey sought the ruler's favor to gain approval to develop a mission center in the royal capital, where they might convert Burmese social elites. Adoniram Judson and his early team members followed suit and established their missions in Rangoon and Ava. Little evidence exists of encounters between Felix Carey and the Karen people.

In contrast, Adoniram Judson was attracted by "small parties of strange, wild-looking men, clad in unshapely garments, who from time to time straggled past his residence." Upon inquiry, Judson learned that "they were called Karens; that they were more numerous than any other similar tribe in the vicinity, and untamable as the wild cows of the mountains."[41] It took more than a decade for the pioneer American Baptist missionary to discover Karendom and invest in those people who were as untamable as the wild cows of the mountains.

Notes

1. Henry I. Marshall, *Burma Pamphlets No. 8: The Karens of Burma* (New York: Longmans, Green & Co., 1945), 32.

2. John Winter Jones and George Percy Badger, eds., *The Travels of Ludovico de Varthema: in Egypt, Syria, Arabia Deserta and Arab Felix, in Persia, India and Ethiopia, A.D. 1503–1508*, translated from the original Italian edition of 1510 (London: Printed for the Hakluyt Society, 1863), 215–18.

3. Klaus Koschorke, Ludwig Frieder, Delgado Mariano, and Spliesgart Roland, eds., *A History of Christianity in Asia, Africa, And Latin America, 1450–1990: A Documentary Sourcebook* (Grand Rapids, MI: Eerdmans, 2007), 4–5. See also Arthur Purves Phayre, *History of Burma* (London, 1885; reprint, Bangkok: Orchid Press, 1998), 262–63.

4. Phayre, 124–25. Phayre's footnote on page 125 stated that De Brito was mentioned in the letters of the Jesuit fathers Bowes and Fernandes. One of the fathers stated that he went to Pegu with De Brito in 1600. Phayre cited from, *Purchas' Pilgrims*, vol. ii, 1746 (no publisher and date provided).

5. *An Outline of the History of the Catholic Burmese Mission from the Years 1720–1887*, comp. the Head of the Mission (Rangoon: Hanthawaddy Press, 1887), 6.

6. Phayre, 126–27.

7. Ibid., 129.

8. Aung Hla, *The Karen History* (Rangoon: self-published, 1939), 234; Samuel Moffett, *A History of Christianity in Asia*, vol. 2 (Maryknoll, NY: Orbis Books, 2005), 43, cited from Joseph Schmidlin, *Catholic Mission History* (Techny, IL: Mission Press, 1933), 309–10.

9. *Outline of the History of the Catholic Burmese Mission*, 14.

10. Ibid.

11. Ibid., 16–17.

12. Phayre, 147–48.

13. *Outline of the History of the Catholic Burmese Mission*, 18.

14. Ibid., 21.

15. Ibid., 19, 22. Father Joseph D'Amatto continued the translation work after Bishop Percoto died.

16. Michael Symes, *Journal of His Second Embassy to the Court of Ava in 1802* (London: George Allen & Unwin, 1955), 203–4.

17. Schmidlin, 309–10.

18. *Outline of the History of the Catholic Burmese Mission*, 25.

19. Ibid., 23.

20. Allen Yeh and Chris Chun, eds., *Expect Great Things: William Carey and Adoniram Judson, Missionary Pioneers* (Eugene, OR: Wipf & Stock, 2013), 4.

21. George Smith, *The Life of William Carey, D.D.: Shoe Maker and Missionary* (London: John Murray, 1885), 439.

22. Sharon James, *My Heart in His Hands: Ann Judson of Burma* (Darlington, Durham, England: Evangelical Press, 2012), 66.

23. Francis Wayland, *A Memoir of the Life and Labors of the Rev. Adoniram Judson*, 2 vols. (Boston: Philips, Sampson, 1853), 1:29. Also see Courtney Anderson, *To the Golden Shore* (Boston: Brown and Company, 1972), 52.

24. Wayland, 1:115–17.

25. Michael Symes, *An Account of an Embassy to the Kingdom of Ava, sent by the governor-general of India, in the year 1795* (London: W. Bulmer and Co., 1800).

26. Bertie Reginald Pearn, *Judson of Burma* (London: Edinburgh House Press, 1939), 105.

27. Wayland, 1:118.

28. D. G. E. Hall, "Felix Carey," *Journal of Religion* 12, no. 4 (October 1932): 473–92.

29. Wayland, 1:170.

30. Sumil Kumar Chatterjee, *Felix Carey: A Tiger Tamed* (Calcutta: Hoogly Chatterjee, 1991), cited in James, 75.

31. James D. Knowles, *Memoir of Mrs. Ann H. Judson Late Missionary to Burmah* (London: Lincoln & Edmands, 1831), 146.

32. Ibid., 155.

33. James, 91.

34. Ibid., 104.

35. Christie Vance, *Into All the World: Four Stories of Pioneer Missionaries* (Uhrichsville, OH: Barbour, 2004), 89–90.

36. Anderson, 274–75.

37. *Baptist Missionary Magazine* 4 (July 1824), 376.

38. Donald Mackenzie Smeaton, *The Loyal Karens of Burma* (London: Kegan Paul, Trench & Co., 1887), 69.

39. Symes, *Journal of His Second Embassy to the Court of Ava*, 207.

40. Ibid., 465-66.

41. Emily Chubbuck Judson [Fanny Forester], *Memoir of Sarah B. Judson, Member of the American Mission to Burmah* (New York: L. Colby and Company, 1848), note 8, 17, cited by Wayland, 1:543.

2

The American Baptist Missionaries and the Foundation of Karendom

When American missionaries arrived in Burma, the Karens lived in the wild with little knowledge of affairs beyond their villages. Donald Mackenzie Smeaton, the British commissioner residing in Burma from 1879 to 1884, studied the development of the Karens. He said, "Up to 1828, they were, as a separate nation, unknown. They were looked upon as a mixed horde of aboriginal savages."[1] His observation was similar to other accounts, but why did he emphasize the year 1828 as the turning point? That was the year that the first Karen, Ko Tha Byu, whom Adoniram Judson had purchased from slavery, was baptized by Rev. George Dana Boardman.

The First Encounter and the First Karen Converts

Adoniram Judson arrived in Burma with his wife, Ann Hasseltine Judson, in 1813 as the first American missionaries. He eventually became the key person in civilizing the wild Karens. What intervened in these fifteen years "up to 1828"? This story requires us to trace the work of Adoniram Judson and his early team of missionaries, especially Jonathan Wade, George Dana Boardman, and Francis Mason. These men left the population centers and boldly journeyed into the tiger-infested jungles of the early nineteenth-century Karen wilderness.

As with the Roman Catholic priests, American missionaries initially had no interest or intention to work among the wild Karen people. Their emphasis was to enter the court of Ava and gain the favor of the rulers. To accomplish this strategy, Judson met the king of Burma twice, first in 1820 with James Colman and then in 1822 with Dr. Jonathan Price.

The first Anglo-Burmese war (1824–1826) altered the political life of the country and brought suffering to Judson and his colleagues. Both Judson and Jonathan Price were arrested and incarcerated for nineteen months. The king released them only when negotiations for peace with the British began, and he needed interpreters who could speak both English and Burmese. Their role was important during the negotiations and the signing of the treaty in Yandabo, February 12–24, 1826:

> The king was prepared to fly northward, but at last authorized a treaty to be concluded. The American missionaries, Messrs. Price and Judson, were sent down with the senior *Wungyi* [minister]. . . . The Burmese commissioners . . . announced their readiness to accept the general terms before proposed. The treaty was now signed. . . . By its provisions, Asam, Arakan, and the coast of Tenasserim, including the portion of the province of Martaban lying east of the Salween River were ceded to the British government.[2]

Judson's service as interpreter and translator was invaluable, and both the Burmese court and the British authority recognized his contribution. The Burmese king requested that Judson remain in Ava with promises of honors and rewards. However, the American Baptist mission was placed in a region controlled by the Union Jack.[3] Contrary to the hostile reception in India in 1812 and 1813, British authorities now treated Adoniram Judson with respect and gave full support to his missionary endeavors. For a brief time, the British and the Baptists settled in the new capital, named Amherst in honor of the governor general of the East India Company.[4] But within two years, both had moved to Moulmein, situated twenty miles up the Salween River from Amherst, for strategic reasons.[5]

Although a short-lived mission center, Amherst was key in connecting American missionaries with the Karen people. Additionally, Amherst became the town of memorial for Mrs. Ann Hasseltine Judson, who died on October 24, 1826,[6] and her daughter, little Maria Elizabeth Butterworth Judson, who passed away on April 24, 1827. For the Christian Karens, Amherst is analogous to Paul's Damascus. In this town, the first Karen was bought from slavery and learned about Jesus. Amherst was where the first encounter between the missionary Adoniram Judson and his first Karen convert, Ko Tha Byu, occurred.

Adoniram Judson and Ko Tha Byu

On April 22, 1827, Judson's journal mentioned three inquirers for the day with one being "Moung Thah-pyoo [Ko Tha Byu], a poor man, belonging to Moung Shwa-bay."[7] Initially, Ko Tha Byu was a slave of U Shway Bay, who bought him from the slave market in 1826. U Shway Bay expressed his intention for buying Ko Tha Byu in these words:

"We had before felt an interest in the Karens, as a people who had not adopted the systems of idolatry exhibited by the more civilized nations around them; and this being the first opportunity we had enjoyed presenting to their minds the religion of the Bible."[8]

Judson happened to be visiting U Shway Bay's family. So, he purchased Ko Tha Byu and set him free from slavery.

From that point, Ko Tha Byu was under the close tutelage of Judson, who took him from Amherst to Moulmein. In October 1827, Judson commented, "Moung Thah-byoo, a Karen by nation, imperfectly acquainted with the Burman language, and possessed of very ordinary abilities . . . has been about us several months."[9] Clearly, Ko Tha Byu could speak limited Burmese, and Judson had no knowledge of the Karen language. Because of Judson's missionary zeal, patience, hope, wisdom, and faithful mentoring, Ko Tha Byu was open to becoming a true Christian. A century later another missionary recorded the first encounter between Ko Tha Byu and Adoniram Judson:

> Ko Tha Byu was the name of the slave. He had been a robber bandit. He could remember having taken part in some thirty murders. A thoroughly darkened criminal he was, dull and heavy of eye, lazy and indolent of mind. Most unpromising material on which to build a new society or with which to win the confidence of a new race. However, after months of patient teaching the dull mind began to open and the hard heart to soften. He looked upon his awful past with repentant eyes and threw himself upon the regenerating blood of Christ. He is a new creature. He asked for baptism, but it is withheld.[10]

George Boardman and the Civilizing Mission in the Tavoy Karen Wilderness

As events unfolded, Ko Tha Byu waited a long time for baptism, as it did not occur in either Amherst or Moulmein. After settling in Moulmein, Judson and his colleagues proposed a new mission in the south with George Boardman in charge. During the March 1828 meeting, a Burmese pastor, U Ing, suggested that Tavoy would be a good location for the new station. He reported that many Karens lived in the jungles to the east of Tavoy. This led to the appointment of Ko Tha Byu as Boardman's assistant.[11]

The Boardmans and Ko Tha Byu left Moulmein on March 29 and arrived in Tavoy on April 9. Boardman commenced his mission duty with the baptism of Ko Tha Byu on May 16, 1828. This event, which Christian Karens continue to commemorate every year as a historic day, was detailed in these words:

Repaired early in the morning to a neighboring tank, and administered Christian baptism to Ko Thah-byu, the Karen Christian who accompanied us from Maulmain. May we often have the pleasure of witnessing such scenes! The three Karen visitors were present. . . . They have urged Ko Thah-byu to accompany them, so that I have left it for him to choose whether he will go or stay. He has concluded to go. Perhaps God has a work for him to do among his countrymen. He is very zealous in the cause of declaring what he knows.[12]

With the blessing of Boardman, Ko Tha Byu left Tavoy immediately after his baptism with two Karen witnesses to visit the Karens in the hills and valleys of the Tavoy and Mergui areas. Aflame with new faith, Byu soon traveled beyond the British territory where the American missionaries were not free to go. His preaching led many Karens to embrace Christianity in Hmawbi near Rangoon, the Irrawaddy delta region, and along the foothills of the Pegu Yoma.

Ko Tha Byu's preaching tours brought Karens to George Boardman as early as September 1828. This encouraged Boardman to expand his mission field to Karen villages beyond Tavoy. On February 5, 1829, Boardman followed Ko Tha Byu and made his first trip to preach among the Karens.[13] From then until the day he died, except for a few months in 1830 during his time in Moulmein, Boardman dedicated his mission work to the Karens. His wife, Sarah, wrote to a friend in June 1830, "My dear husband is suffering from a distressing cough, . . . by the hardship he endured in his village-preaching at Tavoy. He used to sometimes walk twenty miles in a day preaching and teaching as he went, and at night have no shelter . . . , and no bed, but a straw mat spread on the cold, open bamboo floor."[14]

Boardman eventually became ill with tuberculosis and too frail to perform baptisms. A month before he died, in December 1830, his Karen students carried him to the pond to observe their baptisms conducted on his behalf by U Ing, a Burmese pastor from Rangoon who had initially suggested Tavoy as the mission site.[15] Among the eighteen immersed was Saw Quala, who later was known as the second Karen apostle.

George Dana Boardman and his wife, Sarah, were the first missionaries to live among the Karens. Sadly, Boardman did not live long enough to see the Karen's additional accomplishments and advancements following his teachings. After fewer than three years in Tavoy, on February 11, 1831,[16] Boardman died at the age of thirty while traveling in the Karen jungle. His student, Saw Quala, along with other Karens, laid him to rest.[17] Within his short service, Boardman gained seventy Karen converts to Christianity who were baptized by others.

As the first missionary who journeyed in the Karen wilderness, George Boardman was concerned with the needs of the Karen people. In a letter dated September 9, 1828, he wrote to Dr. Daniel Sharp, corresponding secretary for the General Missionary Convention of the Baptist Denomination in the United States of America for Foreign Missions, "I have lately been visited by a company of Karens, in whose history I trust you will feel an interest. The Karens are a race of wild people, inhabiting the interior, dwelling on mountains and in valleys, at a distance from cities, and living in the most rural and simple style. They have no written language, no schools, no religion, no temples, no object of worship, no priests, none who even profess to know the way of truth."[18]

In conclusion, George Boardman suggested that a missionary be sent specifically to the Karens: "There are more than two thousand Karens in this province, and Karen villages are dispersed all over the wildernesses of Burmah, Pegu, Arracan and Siam. Is it not exceedingly desirable that at least one Missionary should be sent to them immediately? Such a Missionary should be acquainted with the modern improvements for forming a written language."[19]

On January 23, 1831, Rev. Francis Mason, another linguist missionary, joined the Tavoy mission. After waiting for more than two years, Boardman's wishes had finally materialized just three weeks before he passed away. The dying Boardman took great comfort in knowing that his beloved Karen people would not be ignored.

From Untamed Wild to the Gentle Apostles: Ko Tha Byu and Saw Quala

Among the earliest Karen converts in Tavoy, Saw Quala, or "Mr. Hope" in the Karen language, was "led to Christ by Ko Tha Byu's first sermon."[20] He wanted to learn more from the message that Ko Tha Byu brought, but he did not know Burmese. With great enthusiasm, Saw Quala worked hard to learn how to read and write the Burmese language, and in 1830, Saw Quala went to George Boardman to learn more about the Scripture.[21]

Francis Mason, who came to reinforce the mission work among the Karens, noticed Saw Quala just a few days after his arrival and reported their first encounter:

> I first met him three or four weeks after his baptism when a party of Karens came in to Tavoy to accompany Mr. and Mrs. Boardman out to

the jungle. They were the first Karens I had seen. Whenever we met, in town, by the way, and at our encampment, I improved the leisure moments by asking the Karen nearest to me the names of objects in his language, and noted down the answers. I soon found that one young man was always near me to reply to my queries, and on asking his name was told, "Maung Shatoo". This proved to be the Burman name for Saw Quala, and the only name [by which] he was known in the mission for several years.[22]

Soon after this meeting, Saw Quala became Mason's assistant as well as his language teacher. In 1833, he was sent to Adoniram Judson in Moulmein to learn Karen scripts, which were just invented by Jonathan Wade. After his return to Tavoy, he helped with Mason's translation work. When Mason traveled to Taungoo to start a new mission in October 1853, Saw Quala accompanied him. Due to health problems, Mason and his wife went on leave in 1854, during which Quala, who was already ordained, became a great missionary. He baptized 741 Karens in the first year alone, and by 1855, he had built twenty-eight churches with 1,860 members in Taungoo and the surrounding hill areas.[23]

About one hundred years later a missionary wrote, "Of the Karens who were the right hand men of the missionaries as they explored new fields and spread the glad tidings in districts hitherto forbidden, we cannot stop to speak the length. The outstanding man perhaps was Thra Saw Kwa La, the first convert of Ko Tha Byu's preaching. . . . He became the apostle of Toungoo."[24] Judson not only led Ko Tha Byu to become the first Karen Christian but also transformed him to be one of the most effective preachers in the Karen mission.

From Tavoy, Ko Tha Byu sowed the seeds. His mission field was extensive, covering the Irrawaddy delta, Bassein, Rangoon, and even Thailand. By 1833, Judson recognized Ko Tha Byu as a missionary. In his report on December 31, 1833, Judson stated, "Ko Thah-byoo, the missionary pioneer among the Karens at Tavoy and this place [Moulmein], was sent to Maubee, a Karen district north of Rangoon."[25] In 1836, when the American missionaries Justus Vinton, Hosea Howard, and Elisha Litchfield Abbott toured that area, they baptized 173 Karens who had become Christians, chiefly "through the instrumentality of Ko Thabbyu."[26]

When British troops left Rangoon and the delta following the agreements in the Yandabo Treaty of 1826, Burmese troops returned to resume their rule. Because the Mons and the Karens supported the British in fighting the Burmese during the first Anglo-Burmese war, the Burmese retaliated and took revenge upon their return. Many Mon and Karen villages were destroyed, Those Karens who were captured were either killed or tortured in prison.[27] Ko Tha Byu's last days were with Rev. E. L. Abbott, who initially was stationed in Bassein but later moved his headquarters to the British territory in Sandoway, Arakan division. There, he helped resettle Karen refugees who were being persecuted by Burmese officials.

By the early 1830s, severe persecution by Burmese officials made it impossible for the Christians to live in Rangoon. So, Ko Tha Byu had no choice but to follow Missionary Abbott. They took refuge in a little village near Sandoway, where Ko Tha Byu died on September 8, 1840. One missionary noted, "By the time of his death at the age of sixty-two, he had broken the ground for the great ingathering of Karens, which Boardman, Abbott, and Vinton were to witness during their service in Burma."[28]

For all that Ko Tha Byu had done, Rev. Mason honored him with the title "the Karen Apostle" and said, "The baptism of Ko Thah Byu, in 1828, was the commencement of the mission; for not till this period was any effort made for the Karens, as a people. . . . At the end of these twelve years, one thousand two hundred and seventy Karens are officially reported as members of the churches in good standing."[29] Clearly, the dawn of the Karen civilization and the development of Karendom began with the first encounter of Adoniram Judson and Ko Tha Byu.

Jonathan Wade and the Karen Written Language

"When I first stood by the grave of my husband, I thought that I must go home with George. But these poor, inquiring, and Christian Karens . . . would then be left without any one to instruct them."[30] With these words, Sarah Boardman expressed her concern for the Karens, even though she was in sadness. She was left with her three-year-old son, George Dana Boardman, after the death of her husband in February 1831. She continued in Tavoy and dedicated herself to the mission work of teaching and preaching. She wrote to a friend, "Every moment of my time is occupied, from sunrise till ten o'clock in the evening. . . . The Karens are beginning to come to us in companies."[31]

Sarah's note signaled the critical need for the Karens to read the Bible in their own language. Her husband had observed this need as well, and requested help from the mission headquarters two years previously. Illiterate Saw Quala had to learn Burmese before he could study the Bible. Rev. Francis Mason arrived for the purpose of translating the

Bible into Karen, but he needed time to study the language before starting the translation work.

Jonathan Wade also noticed the urgent need for a Karen written
language. He learned Burmese from Ann Judson on a ship bound for
Burma in 1823. Then, the Boardmans learned Burmese from the Wades
while they sheltered in Calcutta, India, during the first Anglo-Burmese
war. When the Boardmans moved to Tavoy, Jonathan Wade and his wife
worked at the Moulmein mission where they encountered the Karens,
came to know the Karen language, and grew to love the Karen people.

After a short sojourn in Rangoon, Wade decided to visit the Karens
living north of Moulmein up the Gyaing River, where no missionary
had yet explored. He was accompanied by Cephas Bennett, a missionary from the printing department,[32] and Ko Myat Kyaw as interpreter.[33]
Wade found not only the S'gaw Karens and Pwo Karens but also other
ethnic groups of Burma, specifically the Mon, Shan, and Pa'Os. He had
made his second trip to the area in February 1831 and baptized his first
Karen, Tau-nah. These two tours in this jungle resulted in the formation
of one Karen church of fourteen members. A village named Wadesville
(also known as Newville) came into existence in honor of Jonathan
Wade, who first preached there.[34] Although Tavoy was the first mission
center that brought Christianity to the Karens, the Wadesville area was
where the concept of inventing a written language for the Karens originated. During his tour in early 1831, a Karen chief came to Wade and
said, "Teacher, give us the Karen books."[35] When Wade said he was not
able to do so because Karens had neither books nor written language,
the chief told him this story of the Karen Lost Book:

> The Karens once had books. God gave them his word, written on
> leather, and the Karens lost it; but our ancestors have told us that the
> white foreigner also had God's word, and would come and give it to the
> Karens. The white foreigners have come, but where are the books? Give
> us God's book, that happiness may return to the Karens, for our ances-
> tors said, 'when the white foreigners come and restore God's book to
> the Karens, they will again be prosperous.'[36]

Jonathan Wade could not ignore the plea. In his attempt to satisfy
the request, he took the challenge of codifying both the S'gaw Karen
and Pwo Karen spoken languages to writing. He chose the Burmese
alphabet, which he found had all but two of the Burmese characters
necessary to reach the understanding of the Karens.[37] Having lived in
Burma since 1823, Wade's Burmese was proficient, and linotype was

already available with Burmese characters. For Wade, S'gaw Karen was easier to translate to writing than Pwo Karen because it had no final consonants and every syllable ended in an open vowel sound. With great zeal and scholarly ability, Jonathan Wade produced the first written Karen script. In 1832, a six-page tract and a spelling book of thirty-three pages in the Karen language were in print.[38]

THE FIRST KAREN LANGUAGE INSTRUCTOR IN AMERICA: SAW CHET THAING

Initially, Judson's major focus had been on converting the Burmans. By the 1830s, he stridently worked for the expansion of the Karen mission field. His mission was to train teachers and open schools for the universal use of the new written Karen script. In his journal on September 28, 1831, he recorded, "Three of the Karens whom I have selected from all baptized, namely, Tau-nah, Pan-lah, and Chet-thing, have arrived. . . . It is our intention to place the men in the adult school, and qualify them to read and interpret the Scriptures to their countrymen."[39]

By the end of 1832, Chet Thaing and Pan La could write the language and were competent to teach. In search of more Karens to train as instructors, Judson wrote to Francis Mason on December 30, 1832, asking him to send his two best Karen converts from Tavoy to Moulmein to learn the new script and start teaching it in the Tavoy field. In response, Saw Quala and Saw Kaw La Paw were sent to Moulmein in January 1833.[40] After three months of training, Judson recognized their success and identified in his April report that these two were "the most important students who became qualified to teach their countrymen."[41]

Jonathan Wade's hard work was soon disrupted by a serious attack of neuralgia of the stomach. Hoping that a cold climate would help his recovery, Judson arranged for the Wades to return to the United States in November 1832. He sent Saw Chet Thaing and Ko Shwe Maung to the United States with the intention that they teach the Karen language to new missionary appointees in America.[42]

Judson's effort was not in vain. Arriving in America in May 1833, just after the Baptist Board of Foreign Missions' annual meeting, Wade and his team presented their case. The personal presentation of the Wades and the two natives from Burma aroused a new wave of interest in missions. The board members proposed that the persons who were under appointment as missionaries were to begin stateside study of the languages of the people to whom they were appointed. On June 20, the board decided that the Baptist Education Society (now Colgate University) in Hamilton, New York, was to be the seat for the new missionary training school.[43]

In fewer than six weeks from the day of their arrival in Boston, the Wades and their two assistants had eight students learning the Burmese and Karen languages. Among those who studied the Karen language were two couples who eventually became missionaries in Burma, Justus Hatch Vinton and Calista Vinton, and Hosea and Theresa Howard.[44] Although the program did not become permanent, the training continued for nine months.

Saw Chet Thaing was the first Karen in America, teaching his language and culture to the missionaries who were to serve in Burma. In 1847, Mr. Vinton took two Karens with him, Mya Aye, a S'gaw Karen, and Koh Lok, a Pwo Karen, to America to assist in translation work.[45] By 1871, nine Karens were studying in the United States.[46] With this exposure and training, the minds of the Karens were opened and their outlook broadened. They were no longer the Karens who were scared to travel outside their village. They left the shores of Burma, crossed oceans and continents, and toured foreign lands that even the Burmese court officials had never trod.[47] Christianity brought the Karens new privileges that advanced them ahead of the people living around them. The transformation of the Karens from uncivilized to civilized people had begun.

THE FIRST KAREN MISSION CENTER AND PUBLICATIONS OF KAREN LITERATURE

Jonathan Wade planned to translate the Bible directly from Hebrew and Greek into the Karen language, but Francis Mason took over the task when Wade left Burma due to his health problems. When Mason needed a Karen to assist in translation work, he selected Saw Quala for the task. Mason sent Saw Quala and Saw Kawla Paw to Moulmein for training. Rev. Mason finished the translation, and the New Testament was published in Karen in November 1842. Saw Quala was so efficient in assisting Rev. Mason in translation work that Rev. Mason stated that Saw Quala was "like a Karen dictionary for him."[48]

On December 6, 1834, after 157 days onboard the *Cashmere*, the Wades arrived back at Amherst accompanied by new missionaries. Justus Vinton and his wife, Calista, became the first of three Vinton generations who would spend their lives in Burma for the Karens leading a separate Karen mission department that was established in Moulmein.[49]

Understanding the need to assist Mason in the translation work into the S'gaw Karen language, the Wades went to Tavoy, where Mason and his assistant, Saw Quala, were working. The mission center for the Karen people was set up at Matah, which is situated over the mountain from Tavoy. From there, Mason and Wade traveled on foot preaching in all the Karen villages between Matah and Megui. During the rainy season, Wade and Mason returned to Tavoy and provided leadership training to the Karens, many of whom came from Matah. When the monsoon season was over, they visited Matah again. Mrs. Deborah Wade served as teacher and leader at Matah, supervising the distribution of tracts and the evangelistic work carried on by the Karen Christians. She also taught housekeeping habits, which were revolutionary but instrumental in civilizing the Karens.[50] In 1835, a Karen boarding school with sixty students was established under the supervision of Mrs. Wade.[51]

Though they devoted much time to fieldwork, Wade and Mason also made progress in their translation work. In 1836, manuscript copies of the Gospel of Matthew and a hundred hymns were translated.[52] As Tavoy became the center for Karen literary work, a second printer with Burmese type arrived on October 12, 1831.[53] In 1837, Cephas Bennett went to Tavoy and set up a mission press to print Christian literature that was translated into S'gaw Karen by Jonathan Wade and Francis Mason.[54]

By the end of 1838, items printed in the Karen language included the Gospels of Matthew, John, and Luke; a hymn book of 320 pages, followed a year later by a supplement also of 320 pages; a *Vade Mecum* or book of Scripture and hymns for family and public worship of 312 pages; and at least nine other items. By 1843, the list of books in the S'gaw Karen language included the New Testament; an *Epitome of the Old Testament* of 840 pages; and another supplement to the hymn book of 128 pages. Ten years later, in 1853, Mason completed the translation of the entire Bible, both the Old and New Testaments. This first published S'gaw Karen Holy Bible had 1,040 pages.[55]

Karen language publications were not limited to religious matters. Books printed prior to 1843 included a *Child's Book* of 154 pages; a *Church History* of 468 pages; a *Catalog of Plants*; a *Key to Astronomy*; and school texts varying from *Infant's Readers* to *Trigonometry*. The monumental *Karen Thesaurus*, a vernacular encyclopedic dictionary of language and customs in four volumes of 3,243 pages written by Saw Kaw-Too and compiled by Wade, was published in 1850.[56] In 1855, the number of pages printed had reached a total of 20,933,800, almost all in S'gaw Karen.[57]

Without Jonathan Wade's invention of the written language for the Karens, no such publications in the Karen language would have happened. From the time he was first among the Karens in 1831 until his death in Rangoon on June 10, 1872, Wade dedicated his life to the growth of Karen literature. He promoted the Karen language by writing

The Grammar of the Sgaw and Pgho Karen Language, published in 1842, as well as *A Dictionary of the Sgaw Karen Language* (Karen into English), which was later revised by Rev. E. B. Cross in 1896. Wade also began *The Anglo-Karen Dictionary*, although it was completed after his death by Mrs. J. G. Binney in 1883.[58]

Having the Bible in their own language, the Karens felt that the Lost Book was returned, and their prosperity would soon be restored. In addition, with written language and published literature, the term "the wild savage" could no longer apply to the Karens. Certainly, with the eager cooperation of the Karen pastors and leaders, Jonathan Wade gave the Karen people the opportunity to read and write. Proud of their written literature, the Karens consumed this canon with great passion. According to mission records, the New Testament, which was first printed in 1843 with two thousand copies, was so in demand that they entirely sold out within a few years. In 1851, four thousand additional copies were printed. Out of these, only seventy-four copies remained in 1853.[59]

One of the most important publications during this period was the monthly Christian magazine called *The Morning Star* (*Hser Tu Gaw*), published in both the Karen and English languages. It is considered one of the oldest vernacular periodicals in Southeast Asia and was started by Rev. Francis Mason in 1841.[60] The Karen *Morning Star* lasted for more than a century until the press was burned down in World War II. The last editor was a Karen Baptist pastor, Rev. Htoo Saw.[61]

The dedication and literacy contributions of Wade and Mason transformed the lives of the Karens, who embraced Christianity and built schools, opening the passage for them to cross the boundary from the uncivilized to the civilized world. T. Thanbyah, the first Karen graduate from an American university (1870), wrote in 1904, "Rev. Wade who gave us the Karen written language and Rev. Mason who gave us the Bible in our Karen language, both their names will live forever among our Karen people."[62] Such words of gratitude come from the hearts of nineteenth-century Karen leaders. These missionaries' names will ever be engraved in the memoirs of the Christian Karens, if not all Karens around the world: Judson, Boardman, Wade, Mason.

Shaping the Identity of the Karen People: Francis Mason and the Karen Hta

When Francis Mason arrived in January 1831 at Tavoy, a town of about six thousand people, George Boardman had already won the hearts of seventy Karen people with fifty-one yet to be baptized. Mason began his duty by baptizing these converts while the ailing Boardman watched from his couch. The transfer of the mission work upon Boardman's death in 1831 left Mason with a very important task—to study and master the Karen language. Once the Karen alphabets were ready, Mason started to translate the Bible for the Karens. Additionally, he studied everything that he found in the Karen wilderness from plants to insects to Karen traditions.

Mason traveled extensively in the Karen villages preaching and teaching aided by his Karen assistants. In September 1831, Judson wrote, "On looking at the result of the past year, I find that seventy-six persons have been baptized at Tavoy, one hundred and thirty-six at Maulmain, [Moulmein], and five at Rangoon; two hundred and seventeen in all; of whom eighty-nine are foreigners, nineteen Talings or Burmans, and one hundred and nine Karens."[63] With this report, Karens comprised 50 percent of the Christian population in Burma.

The same pattern continued during the following years. The total number baptized through Judson's Burma Baptist Mission in 1836 was 358, among which 323 were exclusively Karens.[64] Comparing his labor between the Karens and the Burmans, Mason made this remark: "When I laboured among the Karens at the commencement of this mission, I baptized about one hundred converts and the whole of them did not cost me as much labour as it has to bring in these two Burmans."[65]

The missionaries questioned, "Why did the Karens accept the Christian gospel far more readily than the Burmans or Mons in Burma?" They found their answer in the oral traditions of the Karen religious teachers as transmitted by their ancestors. One of these stories was the Lost Golden Book, with which Wade became familiar in his early explorations among the Karens north of Moulmein. The return of the Lost Book by the white brother promised not only prosperity but also an end to suffering. According to the legend,

> the original father of the peoples of Burma had three sons. To his eldest son, the Karen, he gave a golden book; to his second son, the Burman, a palm-leaf book; to his youngest son, who was white, a book of leather. The father, from his home in the far north, sent his sons down into Burma. The Burman's palm-leaf book was eaten by white ants, the white brother's leather book by pigs. Then the Burman began to quarrel with the Karen for possession of the golden book. To preserve it the Karen entrusted it to his young white brother. The latter was skilled in sailing boats and he sailed away with it across the sea.

The Karen believed that one day the young brother would return bringing with him the golden book. Then the sufferings of the Karens would cease.[66]

The Lost Book was not the only story that made the Karens eagerly convert to Christianity. Wade and Mason discovered the tradition of Karen bard literature, encompassing hundreds of legends, folklore, mythical stories, epics, poems, idioms, proverbs, riddles, and rhymes. Many of these stories were in the form of poetic verses called *hta* in Karen and were usually recited at weddings, funerals, and joyful occasions, often accompanied by a harp. The learned elders orally taught hta to selected youths whom they considered reliable enough to transmit them exactly to the next generation.[67]

From these hta, Mason discovered the Karen traditional religious beliefs and the *Ywa* legend, which was very similar to the story in Genesis. The following is Mason's translation of the Karen hta about an all-powerful God, which the Karen called Ywa, the creator of the world, and Ywa's instructions for humans to follow:[68]

> *God (Ywa)*
> God is unchangeable eternal;
> He was in the beginning of the world,
> God is endless and eternal;
> He existed in the beginning of the world.
> God is truly unchangeable and eternal;
> He existed in ancient time, at the beginning of the world.
> The life of God is endless;
> A succession of worlds does not measure his existence;
> Two successions of worlds do not measure his existence.
> God is perfect in very meritorious attribute,
> And dies not in succession on succession of worlds.
> . . .
> God created men anciently;
> He has a perfect knowledge of all things,
> God created man at the beginning;
> He knows all things to the present time.

According to the Karen tradition,

> Father God said, my son and daughter, Father will make and give you a garden. In the garden are seven different kinds of trees, bearing seven

different kinds of fruits. Among the seven, one tree is not good to eat. Eat not of the fruit. If you eat you will become old, you will die. Eat not. All I have created I give to you. Eat and drink with care. Once in seven days I will visit you. All I have commanded you, observe and do. Forget me not. Pray to me every morning and night.

The creation story continued with the temptations and fall and ended with the curse for their sins. This Karen legend made the missionaries conclude that the monotheistic tradition, with its narratives about creation, temptation, and the fall of humankind that were all identical to the book of Genesis, had prepared the Karen people to accept the Christian Bible.

Mason's collection of Karen traditional legends and his translation work on the Ywa tradition ignited curiosity about the story's roots and authenticity. Eventually, the Ywa legend itself incepted major debate among scholars who were interested in the Karen people. In his letter to the Baptist Missionary Society in October 1832, Mason wrote that he thought the Karen Ywa traditions came from the Portuguese priests who had earlier come to the east.[69] Mason's innovative theory on the Karens' creation story as being infused by the earlier Catholic priests caught the attention of others whose responses led to further investigation of Karen religious beliefs.

Inspired by Mason's work, Donald Mackenzie Smeaton, the British financial commissioner of Burma, argued against Mason and the influence of Catholic priests on the Karen traditional religious beliefs. His argument was based on the names of the progenitors of humanity—Adam would not have been *Tha-nai* and Eve would not have been *E-u*. Smeaton stressed the story of the creation and the relation of God to man could not have become a national bard tradition within the short period since the recent contact with western Christians. In his opinion, the Karen traditional beliefs dated from the time when the Karens had not yet entered Burma. He further suggested that these beliefs "were derived from the colony of Nestorian Jews who made their way by land from Armenia to China in the early Middle Ages, and whose track the Karens must have crossed in their journey northwards."[70]

From the middle of the nineteenth century, Mason's interpretation of the roots of the Karen Ywa traditions brought the Karen people to the attention of scholars and to the public eye. In his communication to the government from the "Headquarters of the Tenasserim" dated December 6, 1833, Mason wrote that he had come to believe that the traditions were indigenous to the Karens, whom he thought to be the lost Hebrew tribes.[71] By 1860, after doing further research and observing other social and cultural elements, he refuted this early view and formulated a new interpretation.[72] About these later conclusions of Mason, A. R. McMahon wrote, "He [Mason] argues that the affinities of the Karen language are strongest with Tai and Chinese, and when we know more of the Chinese languages as spoken in the south of China, he [Mason] thinks that the Karen will be found to be an off-shoot of Chinese."[73]

Some scholars reinforced the idea that Karens were descendants of the Jews, but others argued against it, conveying new ideas and theories. A missionary in China, Miles Justice Knowlton, was one of the contributors, and he made these remarks in the *Baptist Missionary Magazine* in September 1857:

> We have discovered evidence of the existence of a Jewish colony in Chingtu, not far from Lushau, nor yet from the original seat of the Karens, a century before our era. Now, as the Jews of Chingtu seem to have disappeared about the period when the Huns were expelled from China, we are of opinion that they fled to the mountains, and if they are not the progenitors of the Karens, the latter are at least indebted to them for their remarkable scriptural tradition.[74]

Another respondent to Mason's theory on the Karen people's origins was John Hackney, who was also a missionary. He claimed that the native land of the Karen people was Mesopotamia, but he did not agree with Mason that Karens were one of the lost tribes of Israel. Hackney observed that the Karens left Babylonia long before the children of Abraham and Isaac morphed into Israelites. He further asserted that before the Karens left Babylon, they lived with the Acadians, with whom they shared many similar words. God in Acadian is *Ho-a* and in Karen *Ywa*. Both share the same word for master, *Kissar* in Acadian, in Karen *Kasa*.[75]

The early nineteenth-century theories about Karen origins became obsolete, but Francis Mason's pioneer work collecting and translating the Karen traditional bard literature was the best resource for the study of the Karen people. Without other reliable sources, the words from the Karen traditional hta articulating the Karen legends stood as the centerpiece for scholarly studies. McMahon confirmed that "the Karens cannot boast of historical records, but their oral traditions are far more reliable and trustworthy, and consequently of much more ethnological value, than the pretentious productions of their more civilized neighbor."[76]

Among these traditions, the most outstanding story is the one that relates to their journey into Burma. The Karen original homeland, according to these hta, was somewhere in the north, near *Thaw Thi Ko* (the peak of a mountain called *Thaw Thi*). Due to overpopulation, they left that place and followed the father of the Karen race, *Htawt Meh Pa* (literally Father of Wild Boar's Tusk). They crossed a river, *Htee Hset Meh Ywa* (the river of flowing sand), where the Karen children lost their leader. There, they waited for his return. The location of the river of flowing sand, Htee Hset Meh Ywa, became the center of interest for scholars as an actual geographical landmark of the Karens.

Because of their significant role in the debates of nineteenth-century scholars, three Karen hta that describe these stories are presented for observation.

Thaw Thi Ko[77]

Verse 1:

Karen: သီသံၣ်ခိၣ်ကစၢၣ်ထိၣ်ထီ, ယွၤအိၣ် ဒၣ် လၢပျၢၤလၢသီ
          သီသံၣ်ခိၣ်ကစၢၣ်စီဆှံယွၤအိၣ် ဒၣ် လၢပျၢၤလဲၤ လဲၤ,

Karen Transliteration: Thaw thi koh, K'hser htau htaw, Ywa O dar,
          ler blur ler thaw,
          Thaw thi koh k'hser saw hsri, Ywa O dar, ler blur lee lee.

English: Thaw Thi Koh, mountain peak high, God lived there since
          ancient time
          Thaw Thi Koh, Mountain holy, God lived there since the
          beginning

Verse 4:

Karen: လၢ်သီသံၣ် လၢပှၢ်ကိၢ်ခိၣ်, အိၣ်ဝဲလၢပျၢၤသးပှၢ် ခိၣ်,
          အိၣ် ဒီး ဖိ ဒီး လံၤအါကှၣ်,ဖုၣ်ခုးဖဲၣ်သံၣ် တၢကတၢ်

Karen Transliteration: Ler thawthi ler bwar gaw koh, O weh ler blur
          tha bwar doh,
          O dau po dau lee ah kugh, peh ku peh thi ta ka dur.

English: At "*Thawthi*" on country high, lived an old man ancient
          time
          He had children, grandchildren, never ending farming land.

Htee Hset Meh Ywa[78]

Verse 1, Question:

Karen:　ပထံတၢ်ပကိၢ်အတီ,မှၢ်အအိၣ်ဖဲလဲၣ်တခီ, ပထံတၢ်ပကိၢ်မိၢ်ပှၢ်, အိၣ်ဖဲလဲၣ်နပိၣ် ဦး ကွၢ်

Transliteration: P'tee D p'kaw ah taw, may ah O peh leh ta kaww,
p'tee D p'kaw moh bywar, O peh leh
Ner poh dau kwar.

English:　Our roots, our real country, location right by which side
Our roots, our main country, location where, would you tell?

Verse 4, Answer:

Karen:　ထံဆဲးမဲးယွၤအိၣ်အမျၣ်, မှၢ်ပထံပကိၢ်မိၢ်ပှၢ်, ထံဆဲးမဲးဘီအိၣ်အလိၢ်, မှၢ်ပထံနိၢ်ပကိၢ်နိၢ်

Transliteration: Htee Hset Met ywa, O ah mlah, may p'tee p'kaw
moh byaw,
Htee hset met baw O a'lau, may p'tee nau p'kaw nau

English:　By river of water flowing with sand, was our country our
mainland.
By river of water flowing with yellow sand, was our true
native land

The answer, "River of water flowing with sand," in Karen was found in
every hta relating to the original country of the Karens.

The following Karen hta is a good example of the river *Htee Hset
Meh Ywa*, and the mythical father of the Karens, *Htaw Meh Pa*.

Hpu Htawt Meh Pa[79]

Verse 1:

Karen:　လၢပျၢၤသးပှၢ်အိၣ်တဂၤ, အမံၤမှၢ်ဝဲထိးမဲပၢ်, အိၣ်ဝဲ ဦး အဖိအလံၤမၤအိၣ်ဝဲလၢခုးလၢသံၣ်

Transliteration: Ler bler tha bywa O ta ghar, ah mee may weh htoke
meh pa, O weh dau ah po a lee, mar au weh ler kukh ler the

English:　In ancient days, lived an old male, "Father Boar Tusk" was
his name
He had children, grandchildren, cultivating his farmland

Verse 2:

Karen:　ဖုအဘုအသၣ်ဂ့ၤမး, ထိးဟဲမၤဟးဂီၤအတၢ်, ဖုးဆဲးထိးတၢ်အံၤလၢဘၢ, ထိးမဲလီၤတံၥ်တဘ့ၣ်လီၤ

Transliteration: Hpu a bu a thar ghay ma, htoke heh mar ha ghau a tar,
hpu hset htoke de au ler baw, htoke meh lauh tae ta bay lau

English:　Grandpa's rice grains grew abound, Boar came and ruined
his farm ground
Grandpa stabbed Boar hard with spear, One Boar tusk out
dropping there

Verse 3:

Karen: ထိးတၢ်မဲၢကၢ်ဝါဆ့, ဖုထၢထိၣ် ဒီး ကွၢဆူဟၣ်,ဘိၣ်ဝဲ ဒၣ် သ့သ့တနၤ,ထိးမဲကဲထိၣ်လၢသံၣ်ခွဲ

Transliteration: Htoke D meh kabaw wah hsree, hpu ter htaw dau gay
hsu he, bwa weh dar thay thay ta nee, htoke me keh htaw ler
thi kwee.

English: Boar tusk curvy, crystal white clean, Grandpa seized and
homeward lean
Working day whole creating own, from boar tusk turned a
lovely comb

Verse 4:

Karen သံၣ်ခွဲဖိစိကမီၤ ဒိၣ်, ပှၤသးပှၢ်မှၢ်ခွဲအဒိၣ်, အသးစၢ်လီၤဝဲ ဒၣ် လီၤ,သးဖှံဝဲတဘိယူၢ်ယီ

Transliteration: thi kwee po so kamaw doh, bwa tha bwa may kwee
ah kho,
ah tha sar lau weh dar lau, tha pwee ta boh yu kghaw.

English: Comb tiny power mighty, once old man combed his hair
string
Youthful look of younger age, happy ever joyful bliss

Verse 5:

Karen: ဖုအဖိအလံၤအါထိၣ်,တၢ်လိၢ်တအိၣ်လၢအကိၢ်,ထံၣ်န့ၢ်တၢ်လိၢ်တကဝီၤ,မှၢ်ထံဆဲးမဲးယွၤန့ၣ်လီၤ

Transliteration: hpu ah po ah lee ah taw, tar lau ta O ler ah kaw,
T nay tar lau ta k'war, may htee hset met ywa nay lau.

English: Grandpa's offspring much increased, fewer space in country
petite,
Found a site for dwelling land: "River of water flowing with
sand"

Verse 6:

Karen: ဖုတုၤလၢထံဆဲးမဲးယွၤ,ကွၢ်လၢ်ဖိကီးနံၤကိးနၤ, ဖိတတုၤဖုသ့ၣ်ညါဝဲ, ဖုသးပှၢ်ကဟဲက့ၤ ၤး

Transliteration: Hpu tu ler htee hset met ywa, kwa lar po koh nee koh
nar, po ta du hpu thay nyar lee, hpu tha Bwa ka heh gay dee.

English: Grandpa reached river of water running with sand, waiting
children each day end.
Children couldn't reach once he found; grandpa surely would
turn around

Gleaned from three hta, except for a slight variation, the story of Hpu
Htaw Meh Pa,[80] the founder of the Karens, goes as follows. Once there
was a leader with the name Htaw Meh Pa,[81] meaning "the grandfather."
He owned a magical comb that was made from the tusk of a boar that he

had hunted. Whoever used this boar-tusk comb became eternally young and healthy. This leader, Htaw Meh Pa, had to seek new land for his ever-increasing population. They all traveled together until they arrived at a river called Htee Hset Meh Ywa. There, the leader, Htaw Meh Pa, traveled ahead of his people, who spent time relishing the food they had found. When they resumed the journey, they were unable to trace the footsteps of Htaw Meh Pa and decided to settle at the last stopover where food was plentiful. They believed that this leader would come back to lead them again once he realized that his offspring were unable to reach him.[82] The wait at Htee Hset Meh Ywa for the leader Htaw Meh Pa with his magic comb received the attention of Francis Mason, who tried to find the religious traditions or origins of the Karen people.

Mason initiated the study of the Karen hta, and others followed through the middle of the nineteenth century. The missionaries and scholars were divided in their views on the home of the Karens before migrating to Burma. Some believed that the mountain Thaw Thi Ko was in Tibet, but some considered it to be in western China. For Mason, the term "Htee Hset Meh Ywa" meant "River of Running Sand." Referring to the records of Marco Polo and the Chinese Buddhist pilgrim Faxian, Mason chose the Gobi Desert as the location of Htee Hset Meh Ywa.[83] Opposing this theory was American Baptist missionary and scholar David C. Gilmore, who had a deep affection for the Karens. By retranslating the Karen term "Htee Hset Meh Ywa" as "the river of water running with sand," he claimed that the Salween River was the location and thus Burma was the Karen native home.[84]

From his exploration, Mason suggested that the Karens had a connection with Tibet, referring to the way Tibetans and Karens designated the months in their calendar. He reasoned:

> The names of the months in Karen are usually significant, each designating some circumstance or labor indicative of the season; but the two months corresponding to June and July are exceptions, being designated numerically. June is called the seventh month, and July the eighth month; by which enumeration, the first month would be December. Now no people of whom I have read, commence their year in December but the Thibetans; and they also denominate their months numerically.[85]

Referring to language as his evidence, Mason added, "The connection of the Karens with the north-western tribes is furnished by their language. Of a vocabulary of seventy words, published in the periodicals to illustrate the language of those tribes, about fifty, with slight

modifications, are found in one or other of the Karen dialects."[86]
Through his study of Karen religious traditions and bard literature, Rev.
Mason provoked the academic world to join his search for the origins
of the Karen people. The next missionary generation remembered Francis Mason as "a name ever honored both in mission and scientific circles
in Burma."[87]

The Influence of Missionaries and Karens in the Making of Karen History

Starting with Mason, American missionaries translated the Karen
bard literature, or hta, into English, thus escorting the previously unknown Karen people into the academic arena. These translations have
become a rich source for scholars in their attempts to describe the historical, social, and cultural patterns of the Karens. As the hta continued to play a key role as a scholar's repository, several native-educated
Karens became proud of their nationality and joined the debate in their
own language. One of these Karen scholars was Saw Aung Hla, who
published his Karen History in his native language in 1939. It is one of
the most treasured Karen history books of all time for the Karen people.
   Aung Hla devised his own theory concerning the birthplace of his
Karen people. As a Karen, Saw Aung Hla tried to explain how and why
the Karens called themselves *Bwa K'Nyaw* based on the four verses of
a hta named "Origins of the Karens."

ပှၤကညီအထူအထဲ; Origins of the Karens[88]
Karen transliteration: Bwa K'Nyaw A'Htoo A'Hteet

Verse 1:
Karen: ဒူလီၢ်ခိာ်စၢ်ယွၤတၢ့လီၤ,တၢ့လီၤဝဲ ဒီး ပှၤကညီ,ကလုၢ်ကတိၤသိာ်ကညီၢ်,ယှၢ်အမံၤလၤပှၤကညီၢ်
Transliteration: Du lau koh ywa tay lau, tay weh dau bwa k'nyor,
          k'lu k'toh thor k'nyor, yu ah mee ler bwa k'nyor,
English: Ancient great world, was God made, with people of might
          and grace
          Voice powerful humming roared, was named people mighty
          force

Verse 2:
Karen: ဟိာ်ခိာ်ကဲသီသဘ့ဝး.မ့ၢ်လၢယွၤတ့ ဒီး ယွၤမၤ,ဟိာ်ခိာ်ကဲသီသဘ့ဖိ.မ့ၢ်လၢယွၤတ့ ဒီး ယွၤဘိ
Transliteration: Hor-ko keh thaw tha bweh pa, may ywa tay dau ywa
          mar,
          hor ko keh thaw tha bweh paw, may ywa tay dau ywa bwar.

English: The World beginning, burst bubbling, God's creating, God's making,
The World beginning, bloom blossoming, God's creating, God's mending

Verse 3:

Karen: ဟီၣ်ခိၣ်လၢပျုၤယွၤဟ်လီၤ,ဟ်လီၤ၀ဲ ဒီး အိၣ် ဒီး အီ,တၢ်အီၣ်ဝဲၤအံၤမ့ၢ်ယွၤတ့,အိၣ်ဟ်ဝဲကိးမံၤကိးစှ

Transliteration: Hor-ko ler blur ywa par lau, par lor weh dau or dau ore, ta or e, may ywa tay, O par weh koke me koke say

English: The World in ancient days, was God made, with food and drink all in it.
Abundant food God supplied, prepared and placed for a while.

Verse 4:

Karen: မိၢ်ပၢ်လၢပျုၤမ့ၢ်ယွၤတ့, ယွၤမၤလိာ်ကိးမံၤကိးစှ, မိၢ်ပၢ်လၢပျုၤမ့ၢ်ယွၤဘိ, ယွၤဘိအီၤအကျၢ်အဂီၤ လိၤကဟှ ဒီး လိၤကညီၢ်, ယုၢ်အမံၤလၢပုၤကညီၢ်

Transliteration: Mo par ler blur may ywa tay, ywa mar loke koh me koh say,
Mo par ler blur may ywa bwar, ywa bwar ywa ah gay ah ghaw,
Lau K'hu dau Lau K'nyor, Yu ah mee ler bwar k'nyor

English: Mother Father, ancient days, God made and gave rules to play
Mother Father ancient days, God fixed and formed His own way
Strong and powerful appeared in sight, named them people powerful might

This hta in Karen emphasized *Bwa K'Nyor*, not *Bwa K'Nyaw*, as the Karen people call themselves today. According to this hta, Bwa K'Nyor was the original name given to the Karen people by God. In Karen, *Bwa* means "people" and *Nyor* means "powerful" or "mighty." In this hta, the word *Nyor* was repeatedly used in defining a group of people with might and strength plus a powerful humming voice. The hta has eight verses, and the details of the four omitted verses were widely quoted by the missionaries in the early days.[89] With a slight variation to the story in the book of Genesis, the fall of man, according to this poem, came from eating a forbidden fruit that made them forget the rules set by God. Later, they repented and were full of sorrow, thinking of how Satan had easily tempted them and how they easily allowed it to happen. The Karen word *Nyaw* literally means "easy" and thus instead of *K'Nyor* they called themselves *K'Nyaw*. Thus, *Bwar K'Nyor* (people of might) became *Bwar K'Nyaw* (people at ease or simplicity).[90]

Combining Karen hta sources with the earlier scholarly theories, Aung Hla began his history of the Karen people with the creation and a mountain called Thaw Thi. The creator God became so angry with the people's misdemeanors that he let a flood destroy everything except birds, animals, and one family. When the flood receded and land began to appear, there on the mountain peak was a tiny *Thi Kwee Koh* or comb. It was later ornamented with boar tusk, gold, and silver, and was called *Thi Htawt Meh*. After the flood story, Aung Hla depicted Karens as the descendants of one of Noah's three sons, who lived in Babylonia with the Arcadians and the Iranians. Due to unrest and turmoil in Babylonia, the Karens, like their cousins of the distant past, left Babylonia at the time of its collapse.[91]

The chronology of the Karen migration in time immemorial was divided into four major parts in Aung Hla's book, starting from 2234 BCE. The first migration began when they moved northwards along the Euphrates to its source at the foot of Mount Ararat, at the bank of Lave Van in Persia (today Iran). They cultivated the land and grew crops while they stayed there temporarily. Then they crossed over Mount Ararat and settled on the northern side of Lake Urimia, located east of Ararat. From there, they turned eastwards, passing through rivers, valleys, and mountains until they reached and settled at a place on the south coast of the Caspian Sea. Not very long thereafter, the Karens headed to the east of the Caspian Sea and journeyed along the Atrek River to its source. After crossing vast plains and ranges, they entered Turkistan, from which they moved to Lake Issyk Kul Nor, after following the river Sir Daria and crossing the Tian Shan Mountains. They continued their journey to the northeast when in 2197 BCE they reached Mongolia and settled at Ugro Altaic or Liral Altaic, until 2017 BCE.[92] The first migration of the Karens from Babylonia to Mongolia, according to this source, took thirty-seven years.

They settled for 180 years in Mongolia, where the Karen population grew to the extent that the ruler became threatened and treated them harshly. Adding to their misery was the degradation of the soil, which made it hard to survive. Thus began their second journey of migration. The Karens left Mongolia and wandered for three years before settling in 2013 BCE at a place they called Law-ber-nor. Though located in Turkistan, many lives were lost struggling around the fringe of the Gobi Desert. The hard life in Turkistan made them search for a new place, and in 1866 BCE, they traveled to a place called *Thi Baw Thi Mu* or Tibet, where they lived until 1388 BCE. From Tibet, the Karens marched eastward into China and settled in their new home, Sichuan, in 1385 BCE.

With little archeological evidence, earlier migrations from Babylonia to Mongolia can be little more than legendary folklore. Scholars however have a consensus that the Karens lived in Tibet and China, referring to the two words *Htee Hset Meh Ywa* and *Thaw Thi*. Notably, Aung Hla's approach to Karen history was based on what Mason had claimed almost a century before:

> "the Karens are emigrants from the border of China and Tibet" because their customs and traditions pointed strongly that way . . . the [Karen] nation is divided into two parties, one of these is in the constant practice of making offerings to the departed spirits of their ancestors—a custom which could not well be derived from any but the Chinese. The other sect denounces this practice, and is careful to avoid it, as they say their ancestors were; which further goes to show that the practice has been engrafted on their ancient customs. Again, *Teen*, the Chinese name for God, exists in Karen poetry as the name of a false god, which they regard as having been worshiped by a people with whom they were formerly in contact; though they have not the most distant idea that that people were the Chinese.[93]

Referring to the work of William Edward Soothill and Charles Gutz-laff, Aung Hla suggests that the Karens began to move southward from Yunan, China, during the reign of the oppressive king Chaw Hsin (1134–1122 BCE). The first migration started with ninety clans who left China in 1128 BCE and arrived in Burma, where they found the land uninhabited, in 1125 BCE.[94] The second Karen migration of thirty-three families occurred in 741 BCE and arrived in Burma in 739 BCE.

According to Aung Hla, the first batch of Karens left China in three groups following three routes with an interval of three years. They followed *Gaw Lo* River (Mekong) and first stayed in a place called *TawGee*. They then moved to Thailand and eventually moved down to Cambodia, ending at the seaside called *Gaw EhNa*. However, soon they were forced to move further south by the Thai living in China, who came down the same route in large numbers. Blocked by the Thai and the sea, the Karens turned around and followed the Menam River toward its source to the river *MehPi*. From there, they followed its source and settled in a place called *GeeMeh* (Chiang Mai). *GeeMeh* was their great capital city where various clans of Karens assembled. However, the Karens living in *GeeMeh* frequently fought with the *Yoh* (Thai) people. The Karens eventually lost the battle and were dispersed into the hill areas of Mu Yu, Mu Dror, Luu Thaw Koh, and Ler Mu Htit. They also settled near the rivers of HkoWa—HkoBahr and in the mountains where they live today. Some Karens even migrated down to Borneo.[95]

The second batch of Karens left Yunnan, China, in 741 BCE and followed *M'Oh* River (Shweli) and entered *Kaw Thoo Lei* because the Thai people dominated the Shweli plains. With increasing numbers, the Karens further moved down the *Plai* River (Irrawaddy) towards the plains where they built their city *Pwo*. The people of Sittagaung and the Arakanese could not pronounce the name Pwo and thus called it Pyay (Prome). Some Karens who lived in the upper reaches of the Irrawaddy River turned to the west to the Arakan (Rakkine) country where they established villages and a city called Sgaw City. It is pronounced in Karen *Sgaw Wei* or SaDweh, morphing to Sandoway in English and is today known as Thandwe.[96]

Aung Hla's approach to his Karen history was somewhat different from that of western scholars. With information from the bard literature, he gave in detail the different Karen groups. He used a Karen hta to demonstrate the division of the Karen family.[97]

Karen:

> ၁. မိၢ်တၢ်လၢပျπလီၢ်နံၣ်ခီ, ပၢ်ကီၤလၢပျπ လီၢ်နံၣ်ခီ, လီၤလၢနီၢ်ဘိကျိၣ်တခီ, လီၤလၢစီၤပကူတနီၤ, လီၤဖးယုၢ်ဟဲဝံၣ်ကလီၤ,ကီၢ်တဖုၢ်ယွၤထိၣ်ယွπလီၤ.

> ၂. လၢပျπမိၢ်ဖိတ ဒုၣ် ယီ, လၢပျπပၢ်ဖိတ ဒုၣ် ယီ, လီၤလၢနီၢ်ပ ဒး တ ဒုၣ်, လီၤလၢမိၣ်နုၢ်ပုၤတ ဒုၣ်, လၢပျπမုၤ ဒီး ပုၢ်စံၣ်ဖး, အိၣ်ဂုၢ်ဂီၤလၢအံၤလၢဘး

> ၃. မိၢ်စၢၤလၢပျπတထၢဃီ, ပၢ်စၢၤလၢပျπတထၢဃီ, လီၤလၢနီၣ် အၣ်တထၢ, လီၤလၢပွဲၣ်, ၀ုၤၐီၤခံထၢ, ၀ၣ်ကလီၤယုၢ်ဟဲလီၤဖး, ကီၢ်ဟားၐီၤလီၤမုၢ်လီၤဖး

> ၄. မိၢ်ဖိလၢပျπအိၣ်နံၤဂπ, ပၢ်ဖိလၢပျπအိၣ်နံၤဂπ, ထံတမုၣ်လီၤမုၢ်လီၤဖး, ကီၢ်တမုၣ်လီၤမုၢ်လီၤဖး, ထိၣ်ကွπတဲၣ်ကွπထံတၢ်ခီ, နံၣ်ပ ဒုး တခီခီ

> ၅. မိၢ်တၢ်လၢပျπအိၣ်နံၣ်ခီ, ပၢ်ကီၤလၢပျπအိၣ်နံၣ်ခီ, လီၤလၢပိၢ်လၢစီၤတခီ, လီၤလၢစီၤလၢပိၢ်တနီၤ, ထိၢ်ကွπတဲၣ်ကွπဟၣ်ကွπပၢၤဟၢခီ, နံၣ် ဒုး တခီခီ.

> ၆. လၢပျπပၰ ဒုၣ် နံၣ်, နၰ ဒုၣ် နံၣ်ခီတခိၣ်ဃီ, ထိၣ်ကွπတဲၣ်ကွπထံတၢ်ခီ, ထိၣ်ကွπအဆၢမုၢ်ဘၣ်လံ, ပနံၣ် ၐ ချၣ်ထိၣ်ဘဲ

English:

  1. Mother's offspring, in ancient time, seven parts belong the line
     Father's ground, in ancient time, seven parts belong the line
     Falling on side, Naw BawKlor, falling on side, Saw Pa Ku

Torn apart then, came the rats, falling of the bamboo shafts
Nation in strife, up to flow and down to slide

2. In ancient time, mother-children one family line,
   In ancient time, father-children one family line
   Making Naw Pa Det a kind, making MawNayBwar a kind
   In ancient time, in-laws split, wandering here there made to
   live
3. In ancient time, mother children one family line,
   In ancient time, father children one family line
   Making Naw PaAar a kind, making Saw Way War two kinds
   Bamboo falling, rats coming, nation torn and parts in time
4. In ancient time, Mother had seven children, in ancient time,
   Father had seven children,
   Nation torn and drifting apart, guessing pieces and counting
   the seven to start.
5. Mother's children, in ancient time, seven parts belong the line
   Father's ground, in ancient time, seven parts belong the line
   Making Pwo's children one kind, making Saw children one
   kind
   Measure made by steaming pot, seven parts found would
   bring one source

The hta told the story of how the Karens split into different groups although originally they came from one family, the father Pa S'Gaw and mother Naw Pa Oh. Initially, this couple had seven children, three daughters and four sons. The daughters were Naw Pa Det, Naw Baw Klaw, and Naw Pa Aar, and the four sons, Saw Pa Ku, Saw Maw Nay Bwar, Saw Way War, and Saw Chaw. One day Pah S'Gaw and Naw Pa Oh quarreled and separated. The three daughters, in consideration of the fact that they were female with their roots from the maternal side, took the mother's name and called themselves PaOh, the name with time morphing to Pwo. This maternal clan or Moh Hteet (Naw Pa Oh = Pwo) in the Karen language had been divided into three groups following the names of the three sisters: Pwo Baw Klor, Pwo Pa Det, and Pwo Pa Aar (Tawthu).

The name of Tawthu was said to have derived from the following incident. One day, Pwo Pa Aar's family caught and killed an elephant. Following a family tradition, the elephant was cut into pieces, and the meat was distributed to other siblings and relatives, both Pwo and S'gaw. Soon after, the Sgaws caught a large porcupine or *Da Thu* in the Karen language, which means "black." They also cut the meat into small pieces and shared it with others, as the Pwo Pa Aar did. However, the Pwo Pa Aar, seeing the big hairs on the meat, reasoned that the animal must be bigger than the elephant, and yet, the portion of meat given was smaller. With that, the family felt that the S'gaws were not sharing appropriately as they did. They decided not to eat the meat and threw it away. Because they did not eat porcupine meat (meat of Thu), they were called by S'gaw, *TaAwThu* (*TaAw* means "not eating," *thu* means "black"). Not understanding the Karen language, the Burmese called TaAwThu "Taungthu." The Pwo Pa Aar people do not refer to themselves as Taungthu, but they called themselves Pa O, which is Pwo, according to Aung Hla.[98]

Like the three daughters, when the parents were separated, the four sons considered themselves descendants of the paternal line. They took their father's name (S'Gaw), but with the passing of time, it changed to Sgaw. In the Karen language, they are called *Pah Hteet*, which means "paternal origin." Thus, the paternal lines of the four sons of Pa S'Gaw are Sgaw (Paku), Sgaw (Maw Nay Bwa), Sgaw (Way War), and Sgaw (Cheir or Chaw).

This old poem located Karen settlements in different parts of Burma and Thailand. It is said that after a time, the children of Pwo and the children of Sgaw married, and their children came to be called Bwe, which formed another Karen family. The descendants of all these Karen families took separate journeys and soon spread over the region.[99]

The descendants of Saw PaKu, the eldest brother, grew and became the largest group who built their cities in today's Chiang Mai and Taungoo areas. Due to political turmoil, they later had to move from Chiang Mai further south to the Mergui and Tavoy areas. The Karens called their Toungoo city *Wei Cger* (*Wei* in Karen means "city"). The second brother, Saw Maw Nay Bwa, also grew a large family. The Maw Nay Bwa clan built cities in regions that are today called Shwegyin in Toungoo. They had rulers/kings called *Hsawdee* or *Zawti*. The descendants of their brother Saw Wei War settled in lower Burma in the Pegu and Hanthawaddy regions, Insein, Tharrawaddy, and Prome, all lands that silted up or shoaled up the delta area to the sea. Saw Wei War and Saw Chaw families were said to have even founded Sandoway city or Sandoway, now called Thandwe city, in which they had lived for years. The Saw Chaw (the Chin) clan lived in western Burma, from Arakan State in the south to the Naga country north of Kachin State.[100]

Although the Karens may be split into various groups, Smeaton found "the division . . . never stands in the way of combination for a common object by the entire nation . . . the power and willingness to combine as a nation for a common land is a characteristic which stands out in the Karens most prominently, and is the main ground of hope for the stability of their national existence."[101]

Probably, the instructions left by the elders through their hta hold the Karens together. According to one hta, before their separation, father Pa Sgaw and mother Naw Pa Oh broke a kettle or steaming pot into seven pieces and gave one piece each to each of their children. Then, they told the seven children that, although they were heading in different directions and far apart from each other, they could be back together again to build a big nation. Their task to make that happen was to bring their seven pieces back together and match the pieces until the kettle is restored its original form. The interpretation has been that the seven siblings would be separated, but if they work hard to meet again for reunion, they will be able to reestablish a country with their own rulers and kings.

Even if parts of Aung Hla's story were considered speculation, the territory where the Karens prevailed and dominated was obvious. In 1887, the acting chief commissioner of British India wrote that the S'gaw Karens were the sole settlers in the hills along the Pegu Yoma range but spilled over the plains below, occupying the hills and jungles of the Irrawaddy district, a large part of the Shwegyin, Prome, and Henzada districts. According to him, the Pwos occupied the seaboard belt from Mergui and Tavoy to Moulmein. He further claimed that both S'gaw and Pwo "are found in Siam."[102] The 1881 census of British Burma reported that the population of Karens was 557,000,[103] and by 1930, the Karens, numbering 1.2 million, stood out as the most numerous indigenous ethnic group after the Burmans.[104]

Whether a Karen history written by Karens in the Karen language was entirely accurate or not, the fact that the Karens, who had no written language and were illiterate up to the 1830s, were able to join the intellectual community boasting of their culture and history in their own language seventy years later was undeniably the fruit of American Baptist missionaries. Through their evangelical zeal, they discovered Karendom and unknowingly shaped the foundation for the Karen national identity. Indeed, Adoniram Judson was the first American missionary to bring the first Karen into Christendom, while George Boardman and his wife, Sarah, were the first to live with the Karens and made the Karen jungle their home. With his linguistic skills, Jonathan Wade was the first to codify the language and elevate the status of the Karen people from illiterate to literate. Francis Mason, by his startling theories and ideas of the Karen genesis, triggered global interest in the

Karen people, orchestrating a monumental step in the creation of the Christian-oriented Karen national identity.

Notes

1. Donald Mackenzie Smeaton, *The Loyal Karen of Burma* (London: Kegan Paul Trench & Co., 1887), 192.

2. Arthur Purves Phayre, *History of Burma* (London, 1885; reprint, Bangkok: Orchid Press, 1998), 257. See the complete document signed by both parties in Colonel W. F. B. Laurie, *Our Burmese Wars and Relations with Burma*, 2nd ed. (London: W. H. Allen & Co., 1885), 56–59.

3. Francis Wayland, *A Memoir of the Life and Labors of the Rev. Adoniram Judson*, 2 vols. (Boston: Phillips, Sampson, 1853), 1:401.

4. Ibid., 1:402, 425. Judson believed that Amherst was a better location because of its navigational position, whereas Moulmein, which was situated twenty-five miles up the river, was not navigable for vessels of any size.

5. P. E. Jamieson, *Burma Gazetteer, Amherst District*, Vol. A. (Rangoon: Government Printing, 1913), 11.

6. Wayland, 1:415.

7. Ibid., 1:427. See Francis Mason, *The Karen Apostle, or Memoir of Ko Thah-Byu, the First Karen Convert with Notes Concerning His Nation*, rev. H. J. Ripley (Boston: Gould, Kendall, and Lincoln, 1861), 10.

8. Mason, *Karen Apostle*, 12. Like all other Karens of that time, there was no record of Ko Tha Byu's exact date of birth, but the assumption was that he was born about the year 1778 and lived with his parents in his native village, called Oo-twau, north of Bassein until he was fifteen. Several years later, he became a slave for committing various types of crimes. He had even confessed that he had murdered around thirty people. At the time of the end of the first Anglo-Burmese war, Ko Tha Byu was sold to Ko Shway-bay.

9. Wayland, 1:442–43.

10. Henry I. Marshall, *On the Threshold of the Century: An Historical Sketch of the Karen Mission, 1828–1928* (Rangoon: American Baptist Mission Press, 1929), 6.

11. Mason, *Karen Apostle*, 10.

12. Ibid., 14.

13. Robert G. Torbet, *Venture of Faith: The Story of the American Baptist Foreign Mission Society and the Women's American Baptist Foreign Mission Society, 1814–1954* (Philadelphia: Judson Press, 1955), 45–46.

14. Emily Chubbuck Judson [Fanny Forester], *Memoir of Sarah B. Judson, Member of the American Mission to Burmah* (New York: L. Colby and Company, 1848), 115.

15. Ibid., 118.

16. Ibid., 5.

17. Joseph Chandler Robbins, *Boardman of Burma: A Biography* (Philadelphia: Judson Press, 1940), 148.

18. James D. Knowles, *Memoir of Mrs. Ann H. Judson, Late Missionary to Burmah*, 4th ed. (Boston: Lincoln & Edmands, 1831), 382.

19. Ibid., 386.

20. Walter Newton Wyeth, *The Wades: Jonathan Wade, D. D., Deborah B. L. Wade: A Memorial* (Philadelphia: Published by the author, 1891), 140.

21. Francis Mason, "Saw Quala, 'The Second Karen Convert,'" *Baptist Missionary Magazine* (1856), 36; Maung Shwe Wa, *Burma Baptist Chronicle*, ed. Genevieve and Erville Sowards (Rangoon: Burma Baptist Convention, 1963), 69–72.

22. Ibid., Maung Shwe Wa, 72

23. T. Thanbyah, *Karen People and Development* (Rangoon: American Baptist Mission Press, 1906; republished by Global Karen Baptist Fellowship, 2010), 5.

24. Marshall, *On the Threshold of the Century*, 9.

25. Wayland, 2:88.

26. Chapin Howard Carpenter, *Self-Support, Illustrated in the History of the Bassein Karen Mission from 1840–1880* (Boston: The Franklin Press, 1883), 9.

27. John F. Cady, *A History of Modern Burma* (Ithaca, NY: Cornell University Press, 1960), 74–75.

28. Torbet, 44.

29. Mason, *Karen Apostle*, 75.

30. Judson, 149.

31. Ibid., 153.

32. Knowles, 389. Cephas Bennett arrived in Moulmein on January 15, 1830.

33. Wyeth, 82.
34. Ibid., 84.
35. Ibid., 82.
36. Ibid., 83.
37. Ibid.
38. Maung Shwe Wa, 312.
39. Wayland, 2:12.
40. Ibid., 2:59, 63.
41. Ibid., 2:66–67.
42. Wyeth, 56–57.
43. Ibid., 97.
44. Ibid., 97–104. Those who studied the Burmese language were Grover Comstock, William Dean, and Sewall M. Osgood, plus their wives and Miss Ann P. Gardner.
45. P'doh Tha Bwa Oo Zan, *History of the Baptist Mission among the Karen in Burma* (Rangoon: Go Forward Press, 1961), 50.
46. *Baptist Missionary Magazine* (February 1871), 62.
47. The earliest diplomatic mission sent out by King Mindon to America arrived in New York on February 18, 1857. This delegation was headed by an American Baptist missionary, Dr. Eugenio Kincaid, who arrived in Burma in 1837. See Maung Maung, *Burma in the Family of Nations* (Amsterdam: Djambatan Ltd., 1958). 49.
48. Oo Zan, 18–19.
49. Marshall, *On the Threshold of the Century*, 13.
50. Wyeth, 112-32; Torbet, 64.
51. *Baptist Missionary Magazine* 17, no. 2 (February 1837), 30–35.
52. Maung Shwe Wa, 312–13.
53. Knowles, 387, 408.
54. Maung Shwe Wa, 313.
55. Ibid.
56. Ibid. *Thesaurus of Karen Knowledge, Native Karen Dictionary*, Vols. 1-4, was written by Saw Kaw-Too and compiled by J. Wade, Tavoy: Karen Mission Press, C. Bennett, 1850)
57. Ibid.
58. Thanbyah, 102.
59. Maung Shwe Wa, 313.
60. James Lee Lewis, "The Burmanization of the Karen People: A Study in Racial Adaptability" (Unpublished Master of Arts Dissertation Presented to the Department of Practical Theology, University of Chicago, 1924), 126 (microfilm).
61. Maung Sin Kyeh, *Kayin Bawa Dalay* (Rangoon: Padaytha Sarbay, 1967), 174.
62. Thanbyah, 107.
63. Wayland, 2:16–17.
64. Ibid., 113 (207 were Burmans and Mons; 107 were foreigners).
65. Mason, *Karen Apostle*, 102.
66. Ian Morrison, *Grandfather Longlegs: The Life and Gallant Death of Major H. P. Seagrim, G.C., D.S.O., H.P.* (London: Faber and Faber, 1947), 26–27.
67. Henry I. Marshall, *The Karen People of Burma: A Study in Anthropology and Ethnology* (Columbus: The Ohio State University, 1922), 33–34. "The Karens used words in pairs, even pairing the verbs to emphasize the expression and force of the ideas, these Karen *hta* were full of repetitions of words by using such words of pairs."
68. Mason, *Karen Apostle*, 97–98.
69. *Baptist Missionary Magazine* (December 1833), 469.
70. Smeaton, 188-89.
71. *Baptist Missionary Magazine* (December 1833), 469; (October 1834), 382.
72. Francis Mason, *Burmah, Its People and Natural Productions* (London: Trubner & Co., 1860), 72, 135.
73. A. R. McMahon, *The Karens of the Golden Chersonese* (London: Harrison, 1876), 66.
74. Ibid., 96. *Baptist Missionary Magazine* (September 1857), 325.
75. Aung Hla, 64. For the Karen word *Kasa* see *Thesaurus of Karen Knowledge, Native Karen Dictionary*, vol. 2, written by Sau Kau-Too and compiled by J. Wade (Tavoy: Karen Mission Press, 1850), verse 1, 1355.
76. McMahon, 29.
77. Aung Hla, 62; English translations by Angelene Naw.
78. Ibid., 27. There are eight verses in total.
79. *Karen Folk Songs*, 4 (N.p.: private publication, n.d); English translations by Angelene Naw.

80. *Hpu* or *Pu* in Karen means "grandfather," but this word is used by the Karen as a title for the leader of the community.

81. *Hpu* means "grandfather"; *htawt* means "wild boar"; *meh* means "tooth" or "tusk"; *Pa* means "father."

82. Marshall, *Karen People of Burma*, 6; Smeaton, 66–67, Morrison, 23.

83. Mason, *Burmah*, 71–72.

84. David Gilmore, "The Karen Traditions," *Journal of the Burma Research Society* 1, part 2 (1911), 36.

85. Mason, *Karen Apostle*, 96–97.

86. Ibid.

87. Marshall, *Karen People of Burma*, 8.

88. Aung Hla, 48. English translation by Angelene Naw.

89. Marshall, *Karen People of Burma*, 32–33.

90. Aung Hla, 49.

91. Ibid., 61.

92. Ibid., 63.

93. Mason, *Karen Apostle*, 97.

94. Aung Hla, 80; William Edward Soothill, *A History of China* (1929; New York: Contemporary Books, 1951), 8-9; Karl Friedrich August (Charles) Gutzlaff, *A Sketch of Chinese History, Ancient and Modern* (New York: J. P. Haven, 1834), 3, 162–66.

95. Aung Hla, 81.

96. Ibid.

97. Ibid., 75, English translations by Angelene Naw.

98. Ibid., 92.

99. Ibid., 91.

100. Ibid., 94.

101. Smeaton, 73.

102. Ibid., 70–71.

103. F. S. Copleston, *Census Report of British Burma*, August 1881 (Rangoon: Government Printing, 1881), 70.

104. India Statutory Commission, Vol. 11: *Memorandum Submitted by the Government of Burma to the Indian Statutory Commission* (London: His Majesty's Stationery Office, 1930), 10.

3

Christian Education and the Great Leap Forward for the Karen People of Burma

The Missionaries' Zeal for Education

> We have a complete education system in Burma including kindergartens, primary and secondary schools, high schools for boys and girls, a college of standard English grade, an agricultural school, two theological seminaries, and two women's training schools, one each for the Burman and for the Karen.[1]

The quote above was the proud report of the American Baptist Convention in 1929—one hundred years after the first Karen, Ko Tha Byu, converted to Christianity.

Adoniram Judson's pioneer zeal went beyond religious evangelism. To grow the mission, he started schools, trained preachers, and translated the Bible. Among other accomplishments, *Judson's English-Burmese Dictionary* could stand alone as his most significant enduring legacy in Burma. The British government announced in 1876 that "the adoption of Dr. Judson's Dictionary as the standard of orthography has been finally determined on, which it is hoped, will eventually result in some general systematization of Burmese spelling."[2] The British colonizers' decision sealed the name of Adoniram Judson with the advancement of western education in Burma.

Ann Judson also set a benchmark by sowing seeds for female education. The report of the American Baptist Convention in 1929 noted the advancement of "two women's training schools, one each for the Burman and for the Karen." These schools blossomed because of Ann's innovative ideas and strenuous efforts for the education of girls in Burma. Ann Hasseltine Judson's idea of a school for children was conceived before she married Adoniram Judson. While teaching in Bradford, Massachusetts, she noticed the influence of Christian educators. By opening a school for children, she felt that she could not only educate them but also mentor them toward conversion. During her short stay in India in

1812 and prior to her journey to Burma, she visited the school in Calcutta for mission children operated by the Baptist wives. That experience compelled her to pursue her dream. In a letter to her sisters dated August 23, 1812, she expressed her vision of the role of missionary wives and scribed, "Good female schools are extremely needed in this country. I hope no Missionary will ever come out here without a wife, as she, in her sphere, can be equally useful with her husband."[3]

Ann's letter revealed two of her visions: education is for girls, and missionaries' wives should be educators. Although Ann did not have the opportunity to realize her idea of educating girls in India, she was quick to instill the idea in Burma. Once she was fluent in Burmese, Ann formed a Sabbath Society with a group of women and taught them the Bible. She started a Christian school for boys and girls in 1821. Ma Min Lay was one of Ann Judson's pupils in the women's Bible group and accepted the story of Jesus. She is noted as the first Burmese female convert and the first Burmese female member of the first Burmese Church in Rangoon when it was established with ten members.

In February 1824, when the Judsons moved from Rangoon to Ava, the capital city of the Burmese king, Ann started a Christian school with three girls enrolled. Through her connections in Massachusetts and because of her talks during her 1823 visit there, this fledgling Burmese school was supported by American gifts from "the Judson Association of Bradford Academy."[4] The establishment of a girls' school by Ann Hasseltine Judson in the capital city of Burma was a revolutionary movement for her time. Until then, education in Burma was reserved only for boys through the instruction from monks at Buddhist monasteries.[5]

As the wife of the first American missionary in Burma, Ann Judson set a pattern for future missionaries' wives to be educators. Her extraordinary accomplishments in the mission field added to her legacy, including her ability as a linguist. During her thirteen years in Burma, Ann translated the Old Testament books of Daniel and Jonah into Burmese; the Gospel of Matthew into Thai; and wrote a book, *A Particular Relation of the American Baptist Mission to the Burman Empire.*[6]

In addition to her outstanding ideas and talents, compounded by her suffering and adventures as the wife of the first American missionary in Burma, Ann became a social activist of her time. The deaths of her children, plus the painful adventure of traveling to two prisons with baby Maria to save her husband from torture and starvation, captured the hearts of American Christians when her biography was published in October 1826. Ann's ideas about education were adopted by later missionaries. Ann's word to her sister in 1812, "I hope no Missionary will ever come out here without a wife," became a requirement for American missionaries. The American Board of Commissioners for Foreign Missions (ABCFM) prohibited unmarried persons from entering the mission fields in 1830. The ABCFM helped young male missionary candidates find "young, pious, educated, fit and reasonably good-looking" women to marry them and accompany them to the mission field.[7] Even before the prerequisite was officially announced, the Massachusetts Baptist Missionary Society arranged to find an intelligent missionary-minded bride for twenty-three-year-old George Boardman, who had been appointed to join the mission field in Burma. They found twenty-year-old Sarah Hall, an admirer of Ann Judson, who accepted the match and was married to George Boardman on July 3, 1825. Two weeks after their wedding, the young missionary couple left for Burma.[8]

Many young, educated American women married missionaries and took the responsibility of becoming Christian educators in Burma. Karen day schools and boarding schools came into existence and thrived because of the good services of these missionary wives: Mrs. Sarah Hall Boardman, Mrs. Deborah Lapham Wade, Mrs. Calista Holman Vinton, Mrs. Ellen Huntly Bullard Mason, Mrs. Stella Kneeland Bennett, Mrs. Juliette Patterson Binney, Mrs. Louisa Hooker Van Meter, and Mrs. Martha Foote Beecher.

The Origins of Christian Education in British Burma

The first Anglo-Burmese war ended with the signing of the Yandabo treaty on February 24, 1826, at which Adoniram Judson played a pivotal role as interpreter and translator. Article 4 of this treaty required Bagyidaw, king of Burma, to cede the provinces of Ye, Tavoy, Mergui, and Tenasserim to the British East India Company "taking the Salween River as the line of demarcation on that frontier."[9] Despite the agreement, the two countries remained in dispute due to robberies and crimes on the Martaban-Moulmein frontier, marked by the Salween River. Until his retirement in 1829, the chief commissioner for Tenasserim, Major-General Archibald Campbell, struggled with the political and commercial issues related to the two nations. Finally, in 1830, the pacification of Tennasserim was completed by Campbell's successor, A. D. Maingy.[10] In his letter to the British government dated January 12, 1830, Maingy stated that the commercial activities which passed between the two countries along the banks of Salween became safe for the first time since the occupation of Moulmein.[11]

Just before total peace was installed on April 9, 1828, George and Sarah Boardman arrived in Tavoy and were received by the British Resident Henry Burney.[12] The Boardmans immediately tried to start schools based on their experience in Amherst. Sarah had worked there with Deborah Wade in the school started by Ann Judson.[13] Sarah Boardman oversaw starting a new school in Tavoy, and records report that she opened a day school for girls while others established schools for boys.[14]

Missionary George Boardman traveled extensively in the rough Karen wilderness with his Karen assistant, Ko Tha Byu, while Sarah devoted her time to schoolchildren. The schools functioned regularly, except for a time of revolt in Tavoy in August 1829. By January 21, 1830, the Tavoy church had ten native converts of which seven were Karens. There was a school for boys, consisting of thirty scholars, part of whom were boarders. In addition, there were three schools for girls.[15]

In late 1831, Sarah Boardman wrote from Tavoy to her family in the United States that "we have sixty scholars in town, and about fifty among the Karens in the jungle."[16] The number of schools increased after a new missionary couple, Mr. and Mrs. Francis Mason, joined the Tavoy mission center. Mr. Mason supported vernacular education, since he believed that by using their own language children learned better, whereas the Boardmans believed in teaching in both English and Burmese.[17]

Despite differences in pedagogical approach, both the Masons and the Boardmans dedicated their time and energy to the growth of education in Tavoy. On January 19, 1832, Sarah wrote about herself and her fellow missionaries, Mr. and Mrs. Mason:

> We meet with much encouragement in our schools, and our number of day-scholars is now about eighty. These with the boarding schools, two village schools and about fifty persons who learn during the raining season in the Karen jungle, make upwards of one hundred and seventy under our instruction. The scholars in the jungle cannot of course visit us often; but a great many have come to be examined in their lessons, and we are surprised and delighted at the progress they have made.[18]

In the same letter, she mentioned "the day-schools are entirely supported at present by the Honorable Company's allowance [East India Company], and the civil commissioner, Mr. Maingy appears much interested in their success."[19]

British Commissioner Maingy had succeeded in establishing order, ending slavery, and curbing divorce, thievery, and rape in the territory under his rule.[20] After attaining peace and stability, his interest turned to developing an educational system that would meet the needs of the new British administration and its inhabitants. Public education began in Tenasserim province in 1833, with a government sanction of five hundred rupees per month for the education of children. But the British government in India did not approve of teaching Christian Scriptures in schools that received grants. Because of that prohibition, on August 24, 1833, Sarah Boardman wrote a substantial letter to Commissioner Maingy detailing her view with the following conclusion:

> With this view of things, you will not, my dear sir, be surprised at my saying, it is impossible for me to pursue a course so utterly repugnant to my feelings, and so contrary to my judgment, as to banish religious instruction from the schools in my charge. It is what I am confident you yourself would not wish; but I infer from a remark in your letter that such are the terms on which Government affords patronage. It would be wrong to deceive the patrons of the schools and if my supposition is correct, I can do no otherwise than request that the monthly allowance be withdrawn.[21]

The commissioner's response is fully reproduced here not only because it provides information on the teaching effectiveness of Sarah Boardman, but also it marks the central role of this American Baptist missionary in setting the platform for the early education system in British Burma.

> My Dear Madam,
>
> I cannot do otherwise than honor and respect the sentiments conveyed in your letter, now received. You will, I hope, give me credit for sincerity, when I assure you, that in alluding to the system of instruction pursued by you, it has even been a source of pride to me, to point out the quiet way in which your scholars have been made acquainted with the Christian religion. My own government in no way proscribes the teaching of Christianity. The observations in my official letter are intended to support what I have before brought to the notice of the Government, that all are received, who present themselves for instruction at your schools, without any stipulation as to their becoming members of the Christian faith.
>
> I cannot express to you how much your letter has distressed me. It has been a subject of consideration with me, for some months past, how I could best succeed in establishing a college here, the scholars of

which were to have been instructed in the same system, which you have so successfully pursued. Believe me.

Yours very faithfully,

A. D. Maingy

Before the end of the year, the commissioner issued an order to government schools throughout the province that they were "to be conducted on the plan of Mrs. Boardman's school at Tavoy."[22]

Commissioner Maingy went further by inviting the American Baptist missionaries to join him in setting up government schools. In 1830, Mr. and Mrs. Cephas Bennett and their two children arrived in Burma to take over the printing ministry abandoned by George Hough when he resigned to enter government work in 1824. In 1834, Bennett was asked to start a government English school on Maingy Street in Moulmein. With the approval of his fellow missionaries, Bennett accepted the offer and became the founder of the government school in Burma.[23] When Mr. Bennett eventually resigned, former American Baptist missionary George Hough, who came to Burma as a printer in 1816 but who had been in British service since 1827, became the head of the Moulmein government school. In 1845, Hough accepted the role as inspector of schools for all Tenasserim province, where he prepared vernacular textbooks for government schools and was assisted by many missionaries who participated in the project.[24] American Baptist missionaries and their wives played a pivotal role in setting up the platform for public education in British Burma, in addition to the development of their own system of Christian education.

Early Forms of Education for the Karen People in Tavoy and Moulmein (1830–1852)
The missionaries produced the written scripts for the Karens and proposed that education was imperative for the Christianization of the Karen people. With the view that Christianity and education are inseparable, the missionaries imparted literacy skills to individuals of promise who would become missionaries' assistants. Qualified assistants recieved further training to serve as preachers at church as well as teachers at schools.

Theological Education: Training Preachers and Teachers
Before the written Karen script was available in 1831, Judson selected three Karen individuals—Tau-nah, Pan-Lah, and Chet Thiang—and

trained them in the Burmese language in Moulmein. Mason also sent Saw Quala and Kaw La Paw to be trained in the Burmese script. After the script was ready for Karens in 1832, these trained individuals began to assist the missionaries by teaching Karen scripts and the Bible in the Karen schools and churches. Chet Thiang became an efficient assistant to Jonathan Wade, who eventually took him to America in 1833 as a translator and language teacher. Tau-nah and Pan-Lah became assistants to Miss Sarah Cummings, the first single American woman missionary to arrive in Burma. Assigned to Chummerah, Miss Cummings and her assistants conducted worship, received inquiring visitors, instructed school, and prepared elementary works in the Karen language.[25] Saw Quala, the first and only assistant to Rev. Mason in Tavoy, took the leadership role among Karens in the Toungoo area once that region came under British rule in 1852, after the second Anglo-Burmese war.

While their wives were teaching the children at day and boarding schools, missionaries Wade, Mason, and Vinton conducted theological classes. In 1835 in Moulmein, Justus Vinton conducted the first Karen language instruction provided by a missionary. Vinton offered no regular class or regular syllabus but rather used an apprentice system of theological education. Students gathered in the classrooms of the boarding schools during the monsoon months, June to October, when two hundred inches of heavy rainfall prevented them from traveling. Once the rain stopped, both teacher and students went for preaching tours, where they learned through hands-on experiences. All the preachers who worked in Moulmein and Rangoon until 1846 were trained by this system.[26]

Plans for a more permanent theological school for all ethnic groups were made at the first convention of missionaries in 1836, which was held in Moulmein during the visit of Mr. Howard Malcom from the Baptist Mission Board in America. Jonathan Wade was responsible for locating a theological institution temporarily at Tavoy. The course of study was to be drawn up by the missionaries, based on their firsthand knowledge of the students' needs. The syllabus was to include a general exposition of the Bible, beginning astronomy, geography, chronology, and an outline of church history. Other courses added later included public health and medicine, English, and arithmetic.[27]

Following the plan, Wade started the new central seminary in Tavoy with twenty students—seven Burmans and thirteen Karens—coming from Moulmein, Bassein, and Tavoy. Most of them had already worked for some time as mission assistants.[28] In 1839, this central seminary was relocated to Moulmein.

One recommendation from the first convention was to conduct separate classes for the Karens in consideration of those who had limited knowledge of the Burmese language.[29] As converts were coming into the church more rapidly than could be assimilated, missionaries began to consider establishing a training school for larger numbers of pastors. At the Eleventh Triennial convention of American Baptists held in Philadelphia in 1844, a committee was appointed to consider "the expediency of the establishment of the Karen Theological Seminary at Moulmein." This study resulted in a call to a prominent pastor in Savannah, Georgia, Rev. Joseph Getchell (J.G.) Binney, to go to Moulmein and take charge of the new pastor-training seminary for the Karens.[30]

In May 1845, Rev. Binney started the Central Karen Theological School in Moulmein. The curriculum included reading and writing; arithmetic with some plane geometry and geology; and land surveying, with practical lessons measuring the mission compound so the Karens would learn to protect their lands. The students completed monthly assignments including monthly original compositions in their mother tongue and monthly sermons to be preached and critiqued. Besides these general education courses, "their principal study was theology, with the Bible as their textbook. The whole of the New Testament was studied verse by verse."[31]

Reports from Rev. Binney on his class of 1847 included

Phrahai, whose "peculiarity is that he preaches with great point and power to the heart and to the conscience";

Kyahpah, a man who has manifested a deep interest "in all that affects the welfare of the churches"

Aupaw, "Tried in the fire of persecution and pronounced to be pure gold"; and

Tahoo, a man who has "too much attachment to the plain, simple gospel as he first learned it ever to go astray."[32]

After serving five years, Mr. Binney returned to America in April 1850 because of his wife's health. Norman Harris took temporary charge of the institution until Rev. Justus Vinton assumed responsibility in 1851. The school in Moulmein closed when Vinton moved to Rangoon after the second Anglo-Burmese war in 1852.[33]

During its seven years of operation, the Karen Theological School met about eight months per year with an average student body of twenty-eight. Sixty students, of which one-third came from Moulmein and two-thirds from Rangoon and Bassein, trained there.[34] Among its students were Thra Maung Yin, Thra Shwe Pu, Thra Nga Lay, Thra Kleh Po, Thra Lu Tu, Thra Thar Pan, Thra Pu Kaw, Thra Yo Pho, Thra Dar Pu, and others who became not only pastors but also leaders of their Karen communities.[35]

GENERAL EDUCATION FOR THE KARENS

Following Ann Judson's model, nineteenth-century American missionary wives enthusiastically engaged in the development of Christian education. Deborah Wade accompanied Ann on her return to Burma from sick-leave furlough in 1823. She became the earliest educator for the Karen people in the Moulmein and Tavoy areas.[36] Schools were started in Tavoy, and Sarah Hall Boardman's schools became the model for British government schools in their educational system.

In his letter dated October 11, 1831, Adoniram Judson spotlighted how Calista Bennett was overloaded with the school operations, and how it was difficult to sustain the female boarding school in Moulmein due to the transfer of Mrs. Mason to Tavoy, Mrs. Jones to Rangoon, and Mrs. Wade to Mergui.[37] In another letter dated April 12, 1833, Judson complimented Miss Sarah Cummings, who devoted herself to the Karens in the Chummerah school that she was supervising.[38] She passed away from an unnamed fever only sixteen months after arriving in Burma.

The two basic formats that offered general education were day schools and boarding schools. The desire to read the Bible for themselves and the hope of securing for their children an education motivated the Karens to make sacrifices to support teachers and schools. From the early days, Karens in Tavoy established a reputation for self-support in building their own village chapels and schools. In 1836, Rev. Howard Malcolm, who was sent by the American Mission Board to visit missions in Asia, made a thorough study of the American Baptist work in Burma, visiting every station, including Ava and Arakan. He remarked on the Karen Christians in the Tavoy field:

> A greater evidence of Christian generosity is seen in their missionary zeal. . . . Assistants or schoolmasters . . . are ever ready to part with their families, and go wearisome journeys of six months at a time, among distant villages where they are utterly unknown, carrying on their back tracts and food . . . and enduring many privations. Young men whose services are very important to their aged parents in clearing jungle and planting paddy are readily spared, and go to various points during the rainy season teaching schools, for which their salary is two or three dol-

lars a month—half what they could earn in other employ. About twenty
school masters and assistants are now thus employed.[39]

Due to the hard work of these missionaries and their wives, the Karen day schools and boarding schools thrived in the mission fields of Amherst, Moulmein, Tavoy, and Mergui in the Tenasserim division since 1835. The British government encouraged the development of schools by giving grants-in-aid to qualified private schools.

In Moulmein, Rev. Justus Vinton oversaw the theological training school for the Karens. His wife, Calista, who had learned the Karen language before coming to Burma, started schools immediately upon her arrival in December 1834. The emergence of the Karen normal schools in Moulmein was a result of the good work of two Vintons, Mrs. Calista Vinton and Miss Miranda Vinton, wife and sister of Rev. Justus Vinton.[40] Rev. and Mrs. Vinton were well-known for their extensive tours in the Karen jungle with their native Karen assistants. One of Vinton's Karen leaders was Thra Papoo, who was highly praised for his success in raising contributions. In 1849, Thra Papoo brought in five hundred baskets of paddy (pre-threshed rice) for the schools and raised contributions amounting to an average of twenty-two cents per member, the largest contribution at that time in the history of self-support.[41]

For Pwo Karen children north of Moulmein, Miss Eleanor Macomber started a school in Dohn Yahn village after her arrival in 1836.[42] Impressed with her outstanding service among the Pwo Karens, Adoniram Judson wrote to the American Baptist Mission Board explaining the need for more single female missionaries like her. In his letter, he admitted his awareness of the board's rule not to appoint single women to missionary work.[43] Regrettably, Miss Macomber passed away in 1840 after serving for only four years. Durlin L. Brayton and Mary H. arrived in Moulmein in 1838 and worked among the Pwo Karens. From 1839 to 1854, they were assigned to Tavoy and Mergui, where they opened a school during the rainy seasons and traveled to the villages to carry out their evangelistic work during the dry seasons.[44]

By 1847, more than twenty schools in the Tenasserim province were founded, with four of these schools in Tavoy:

English and Burmese school under Rev. Cephas Bennett with
    thirty students;
Karen day school under Rev. Francis Mason with twelve students;
Karen boarding school under Mrs. Bennett and Mrs. Wade with
    twenty-five students; and

Karen theological school under Rev. E. B. Cross with twenty-three students.

In addition, eleven village schools were established in the Tavoy district, supervised by the missionaries and their wives.[45]

In Moulmein and Amherst, seven Baptist schools operated; four were taught in the Karen language:

The S'gaw Karen boarding school under the supervision of Rev. Justus Vinton had 154 students;
Pwo Karen boarding school under Rev. E. E. Bullard had 40 students;
Karen normal school under Mrs. Juliette Pattison Binney had 17 students; and
Karen theological school under Rev. J. G. Binney had 36 students.

There were additional district schools in the Karen areas to the south and east of Moulmein, where Judson and Vinton toured and worked during this period. These included Chet Thiang's village on the Salween; Newville on the Dagyaing; Bootah on the Ataran; and Dohn Yahn on the Gyaing.[46]

A boarding school for both Pwo and S'gaw Karens was established in 1848 in Moulmein, using both Pwo and S'gaw dialects. This was one of the first schools for the general education of Karens, as the only other Karen schools at that time were those in Buddhist monasteries. An early principal of the Pwo Karen boarding school in Moulmein was Sra Kon Luht, who was the first Pwo Karen to be ordained and the first to travel to America in 1848.[47]

Karen students outnumbered others in theological, boarding, and day schools, a reflection of the Karen hunger for formal education. The opening of these mission schools by the American Baptist missionaries not only opened the eyes of the Karens but also uplifted the status of many Karens. An article in the *Calcutta Review* made it obvious that the Karens began to take leading roles in the distribution of knowledge: "Their [American Baptist Mission] schools are far more superior in every respect to the government schools at Moulmein and Mergui, and producing among the Karens very remarkable effects. . . . The progress has been wonderful; their pupils have gone forth into the villages and have imparted to their brethren the seed of knowledge."[48] The effectiveness of the educational system operated by the American missionaries was measured by the progress of the Karen.

Sandoway: The First Karen Refugee Settlements and Training Center (1840–1852)

Karen Christian schools and publications started in Tavoy and Moulmein in Tenasserim province, the locations from whence the first Karen mission fields were inaugurated. Equally important is the Sandoway mission center from 1840 to 1850, in Arakan province, where the first Karen refugee camps were established. Under the able direction of American Baptist missionary Elisha L. Abbott, many able Karens learned leadership skills, becoming not only effective preachers and schoolteachers but also developers of Karen communities in the Irrawaddy delta area after the second Anglo-Burmese war in 1852.

Elisha Abbott arrived in Burma in 1835 with Eugenio Kincaid. Together, they worked among the Karens in Baluegyun village near Moulmein. In 1837, Abbott married another missionary, Ann P. Gardner. The couple were assigned to Tavoy but were eventually shifted to the Rangoon area.[49] By then the mission in Rangoon was in progress, having been originally organized by Adoniram Judson. Back on November 10, 1833, the first five Karens in the Rangoon area were baptized by U Tha Aye, but they soon were thrown into prison. All who converted to Christianity during that time were penalized by the Burmese government. Nevertheless, the church continued to grow. When Abbott arrived in early 1835, the Rangoon mission sported a Burmese-language church, an English-language church, and a Karen-language church.[50]

Due to continuing persecution in areas controlled by the Burmese king, mission work became more difficult. In 1836, church members were scattered throughout the Rangoon area. Ko Tha Byu, the first Karen convert, stayed in the area, preaching among the Karen villages in the Irrawaddy delta area until he had to move to Hmawbi, about twenty miles north of Rangoon.[51] When the Abbotts arrived in Rangoon, they invested time in the Karens, traveling often to Hmawbi and Pandanaw. Within a year, Rev. Abbott had baptized 110 people. Together with his wife Ann, Abbott conducted a school for pastors with 25 students. However, in November 1838, all foreign missionaries were forced to leave Rangoon when King Tharrawaddy's restrictive policies went into force. Burma proper, not under the control of Great Britain, was closed to all missionary activities. The churches were left under the charge of their local pastors.[52]

As punishments became more severe on those who converted to Christianity, Karens from Bassein had to hide throughout the jungles to meet missionaries. Many were seized and thrown into prison because of their Christian faith. Some were fettered with their legs and necks drawn up until only their buttocks rested on the ground. Others were "pierced with swords and spears and others had incisions made over their bodies, then rubbed with salt and tortured to death." Christian chiefs were imprisoned, and their villages were stripped of everything including food. Faithful Karens were driven to beg for their rice or were compelled to work as pagoda slaves.[53]

Since missionaries' presence made it worse for the converts, both Rev. Kincaid and Rev. Abbott, together with their families, were transferred to British territory in Arakan.[54] Without missionaries and amid numerous persecutions, however, the Karen churches continued to grow. When Kincaid and Abbott visited Rangoon in 1839, the Karen churches had a membership of 387 with several hundred waiting to be baptized.

Arakan, situated in the western coastal area, is separated from the rest of Burma by the Arakan Mountains or Pegu Yoma. It is covered with dense forest. Until the twentieth century, this region was labeled "the home of peacocks, tigers, elephants and gigantic serpents."[55] It shares a border with Bangladesh in the north. Many Karens from Bassein and the delta areas fled across the mountain and took refuge around the Sandoway area of Arakan, where Rev. Abbott helped them resettle. The journey was expressed in the following manner: "Desiring freedom to worship God, and finding no rest from the Burman oppressor in the Bassein District, Karens cross the mountains to the sandy soil and sickly climate of Arracan. There under the British Raj they need not fear death for reading the Bible."[56]

From the start, the Abbotts almost entirely spent their time helping these Karen refugees settle along the coastal villages from Sandoway on the north down through Gwa, Satthwa, Magezin, Bawmi, Onchaung, Chaungtha, Sinma, Great Plains, Phaungdo, and Thay Rau. Both husband and wife conducted training for fifty young men who were Karen pastors and evangelists from the Rangoon, Pantanaw, and Bassein areas. The first two Karen pastors, Thra Myat Kyaw and Thra Tway Po, were ordained in the Sandoway district in 1842. They became the leaders of the Karen Christian communities in the delta region. Records show that by 1845, Thra Myat Kyaw alone had baptized more than two thousand converts, and Thra Tway Po almost equaled that number.[57]

Sandoway Karen mission center training was so effective that many Karen pastors and evangelists who studied there became leaders in other refugee resettlements. Their management skills brought forth the remarkable development of self-supporting churches and schools. New, self-sufficient village settlements such as Great Plains and Thay Rau were led by these Karen pastors. Pastor Thra Wah Dee led the Great Plains village development, with houses built in rows and built with care. The ground under and around the homes was cleared of shrubs and rubbish. Each home had cultivated and fruitful garden plots with thriving nurseries. The streets were straight and wide, neatly ordered with fruit trees and flowers, all planned and directed by Thra Wah Dee.[58]

Similarly, under Thra Tway Po's leadership, Thay Rau village was carved out of the jungle. The land that the wild elephants were roaming in the early 1840s became rice fields in the latter years of the 1840s. Residents were encouraged to take initiative and began to take pride in their progressive and cooperative accomplishments.[59] The success of the Karen preachers' and pastors' leadership in the Arakan province refugee resettlements served as a role model for future Karen communities, as well as for Karen refugees who resettled in Bassein and Rangoon from their hiding places after the second Anglo-Burmese war in 1852.

Another achievement of the Sandoway mission during this time was the deputation of evangelists to other groups outside the Karen communities. In many of the new villages, Karens built their own church and supported their own pastor out of the meager resources they had at their disposal. A Karen Home Mission Society was formed, making it cooperatively possible to send home missionaries to other regions. The first three Karen evangelists trained by Rev. Abbott, Thra Myat Kyaw, Thra Tway Po, and Thra Shwe Bo, were sent to the Bassein area by 1852.[60]

Sandoway mission center provided good experience and training for the Karen refugees who were forced to leave their villages in the delta areas. Now that they were well-equipped with knowledge to develop their communities, they prepared to impart these new ideas and apply them in their own villages once the situation permitted them to go home. Following the pattern set in Sandoway, the Karens would build new churches and schools in Bassein, when the area came under British control in 1852 after the second Anglo-Burmese war.

The Second Anglo-Burmese War (1852) and the Restructuring of Mission Centers

The training and educational progress in Tennasserim and Arakan was changed by the impending second Anglo-Burmese war in 1852. The British invasion began with the occupation of Martaban on April 4, Rangoon on April 14, Bassein on May 19, followed by Prome in

November and Pegu in December. The new treaty line that divided British and Burmese territories ran east-west across the country from Arakan through a point fifty miles north of Prome to Toungoo and the Karenni area. Major Arthur Phayre was appointed the first commissioner of the new British Burma in 1852.[61]

The second Anglo-Burmese war brought lower Burma under British control, paving the way for new mission fields. However, Adoniram Judson's death on April 12, 1850, was a great loss to the mission. At the end of the Judson era, there were 8 mission stations, 52 outstations, 74 churches with 7,904 members, 48 American missionaries and wives, 114 preachers and assistants, and a publication office that had printed 5,095,180 pages. In addition, 12 boarding schools and 44 day schools operated.[62] Judson's passing in 1850 and the second Anglo-Burmese war beginning 18 months later played topsy-turvy with missionary and political relationships in Burma.

Though new opportunities and mission fields opened under British colonialism, the years following the war were full of drastic changes with a growing division between the American Baptist Mission Union (ABMU) in Boston and the missionaries in Burma. Many missionaries could not wait for specific mission board permissions when the British re-established order in areas where mission work was needed. Before receiving specific approval from the board in Boston, Elisha Abbott and H. L. Van Meter, who needed to move the Sandoway Karen mission to Bassein, left Moulmein on July 10, 1852, to travel to Bassein.[63] They did not wait the expected six to eight months for approvals from Boston to move. Concurrently, Mr. and Mrs. Vinton were in Rangoon by May 1852, taking care of the desperate needs of seventeen Karen churches without receiving the ABMU's blessing.

Another serious issue that split the ABMU in Boston and missionaries in Burma was the opening of schools and the teaching of English. Because of these disagreements in 1856, several missionaries and their wives resigned, including Rev. Justus H. Vinton, Rev. John Sydney Beecher, Rev. Norman Harris, Rev. Durlin L. Brayton, and Rev. A. T. Rose. Except for Rose, the four other missionaries went to work among the Karens.[64] Their dedication to the Karen people called these missionaries to continue their service without thinking of the consequences. The abolitionist American Baptist Free Mission Society, which was formed in 1845, stepped in as the financial agent and sponsor for these five families after their resignations from the ABMU.[65]

After the war ended, and missing the iconic leadership of Adoniram Judson, the 1853 Burma ABMU Convention transferred missionaries to newly opened towns in the Irrawaddy and Sittang deltas. The missionaries from Sandoway, Elisha Abbot and Henry Van Meter, were assigned to work among the Karens in Bassein. The return of all the Karen refugees to their home villages in the delta zone ended the need for the mission in Sandoway. Under the leadership of the missionaries and the remarkable efforts and sacrifices of the Karen themselves, many Karen Christian communities were established in Bassein, from whence Christian education thrived and reached heights undreamed of in the past.

BASSEIN: DEVELOPMENT OF SELF-SUPPORTING KAREN MISSION AND EDUCATION CENTER

British annexation of Bassein was officially announced on January 8, 1853, although British troops had occupied the town since May 19, 1852. In a letter dated June 5, 1852, the governor general of India praised the ability of General Henry Thomas Godwin and his command for the successful capture of Bassein and appointed Godwin to see to the restoration of peace and resettlement matters in Bassein.[66] Godwin's support enabled the resettlement and development of the Karen Christian community.

During the transition period, the situation was unstable, but the Karens who had been compelled to live in Sandoway rushed to return home. In his letter from Moulmein dated May 12, 1852, Abbott described the situation of the war and his future task:

> Bassein will become the center of our mission operations, hitherto conducted from Sandoway. The war will throw everything into confusion. Villages and churches will be broken up and scattered, pastors killed, and everything in desolation. The work of years is to be done over again—villagers are to be gathered, churches to be re-organized, a station to be built up, provision made to meet the increased demand for trained preachers and school teachers; and the Home Mission Society, on which so much depends, to be resuscitated.[67]

The war had noticeably created confusion and desolation. Since the beginning of the second Anglo-Burmese war, Karen villages were attacked, villagers were tortured, and some were even crucified. The first of those who suffered on the cross until death was Thra Klaw Meh at Thra Tha Gay pastor of Kyar-Inn Gone village. In early 1852, he and another forty villagers were arrested by the Burmese chief of Yegyi. After paying ransom money asked by the captors, all were released except Thra Klaw Meh. While keeping the old pastor and demanding more money, the Burmese chief demanded the pastor vow that he would never preach the gospel again. The faithful pastor's refusal enraged the chief, and the torture began. He was eventually nailed to the cross, and his abdomen was ripped open. While he suffered helplessly on the cross, the crows pecked at his hanging intestines. A Burmese soldier rubbed his gun with the pastor's blood and shot Thra Klaw Meh to death.[68] There were numerous incidents of atrocities and sufferings during the war.

American Baptist missionaries Abbott and Van Meter arrived in Bassein on July 12, 1852, before the official proclamation of annexation. They brought with them several young Karens including Saw Dahbu, Shahshu, Pu Goung, Yo-hpo, and Thah-ree. Among the welcoming crowd was Shwe Waing, a Karen who had taken the risk in December 1841 to join Abbott at the missionary meeting at Magezzin, eighty miles south of Sandoway.[69] Shwe Waing was among the four Karen Christians who were offered positions in the new British township, after the official annexation of Bassein was announced on January 8, 1853.[70] As Shwe Waing sent people to spread the news of the missionaries' arrival, additional Karens, including ordained pastors Thra Myat Keh, Thra Po Kway, and Thra Shwe Bo, arrived in Bassein.

The British commanding officers, General Godwin and Major Roberts, provided land near the Bassein south gate, on which stood a deserted and roofless monastery, to build a new mission center. The failing health of Mr. Abbott left Mr. Van Meter to take charge in the renovation work.[71] Without hesitation, Van Meter started the repairs upon the arrival of the Karen pastors. The monastery was made of timber, and after careful demolition, sufficient materials were secured to divide it into three rooms. These became a chapel (30 x 50 feet) and a room each for Mr. Abbott and Mr. Van Meter.[72] A significant meeting took place in this new mission center on Sunday, July 21, 1852, at which twelve native preachers, including Tway Poh, Mau Yeh, Myat Keh, and Poh Kway, were appointed as a committee to ask all the assistants about their losses during the recent troubles and to present their pressing needs.[73]

Because of his failing health, in September 1852, Abbott had to return to America, leaving Van Meter to carry on alone for several weeks until John Sydney Beecher, formerly stationed in Kyaukpyu in Arakan, joined him. They were fully occupied with the resettlement of more Karen refugees, who returned in bulk from the Arakan coast despite the warning to postpone their return due to the desolate conditions.[74] The Karen preachers who had trained earlier in Tavoy, Moulmein, and Sandoway worked strenuously along with their mentors, the American Baptist missionaries.

Challenged by the insatiable desire to uplift their community, Karen pastors took the initiative to establish a school in Bassein. Each village in the surrounding area was asked to select three or four promising boys who were eager to learn and submit their applications.[75] The response was overwhelming for the limited prepared space. Amid this difficult situation, the schools were established. By 1854, 330 pupils enrolled in village schools and 150 in the boarding schools in Bassein.[76]

In their eagerness to obtain better education for their children, the Karen Christian community decided to make further educational progress. In 1854, a proposal was made to establish a more advanced school at Kozu, which would be called an academy. Mr. Beecher recorded the Karen leaders' reaction to this idea:

> For them to support their children at school in their own village, or to send them to the missionary to be supported from foreign sources, are ideas which they can understand and appreciate; but to send their children to another Karen village to be taught by a Karen teacher, at the expense of their parents, is an idea which must be explained and urged again and again, before they will be half as ready to pay five rupees for tuition as they are to pay the same amount for tobacco. Whether we see anything like an academy this year or not, we expect to see common schools of a higher order, and in larger numbers, than we should have seen otherwise, and we hope for the day when academies worthy of the name, taught and supported by the Karens, shall enlighten and adorn these provinces.[77]

A major issue encountered for the full operation of the school was a teacher shortage. Appointing female teachers resolved the issue, which was a revolutionary idea, contrary to the Karen customs.[78]

The high energy and self-supporting spirit among the Karens ignited the great forward leap in the Bassein mission field. At the third quarterly meeting of the Ministerial Conference and Home Mission Society at Naw-p'eh in October 1854, it was decided that the church would undertake the entire support of native preaching, both in the churches and among non-Christians. This marked a new era in the mission's history. A committee that studied the matter carefully brought the following resolution: "We, brethren Myat Keh, Shwe Baw, U Sah, and Tutanu, are agreed that for preachers and ordained ministers we should expend no more of the money of our American brethren. So far as there is occasion to help support them, we will do it ourselves. But for books and schools we greatly need help, and we request that our dear brethren in America will continue to aid us in these things."[79]

Because of their determination and hard work, the academy at Kozu started with fifty students in the first term. Two other advanced schools started a year later in the villages of Naw-p'eh and P'nah-thein. The Karens also assumed the financial support of the pastors in their fifty churches and among the non-Christians around them. Except for the expenses for books and three or four teachers, the Karens supported the education of more than eight hundred pupils.[80]

Since the American Baptist Missionary Union never approved Beecher for work in Bassein, he was dismissed from his post in 1856. He came back to Bassein in 1858 under the sponsorship of the Baptist Free Mission Society when the Karen Christian community in Bassein paid his return fare to get back their teacher.[81] During this period, the Bassein S'gaw Karens supported their own evangelists plus the American missionaries, as they rebuilt houses that had been burned along with everything they possessed. In addition to bearing the expenses for Mr. Beecher's return fare, they contributed two hundred rupees to the ABMU to help them out of debt that was caused by the global financial panic.[82]

Upon his return, Beecher focused on improving Christian education. He and his Karen leaders agreed that their duty was not merely to Christianize the Karens but also to raise their intellectual and religious culture. With great determination, they started the project of building a Christian institution of higher education. The British government granted sixteen acres of land free as a reward for their service in the second Anglo-Burmese war. Later, they received more donations and bought the adjacent ten acres from various owners. Mrs. Beecher selected the location for the project in a village known as Lee Wah Lu, meaning "White Book Hill," which was far from town and came with danger from tigers, other wild animals, and robbers. In addition, it was near an old Burmese cemetery, and many Karen leaders were afraid of ghosts.

They cleared land and built the school with minimal resources on hand. It was not possible to receive money from the United States due to the imminent American Civil War. Amidst the difficulties, the building was completed in 1858, and Mr. Beecher named the school Bassein Sgaw Karen Normal and Industrial Institute.[83] It was built with no American financial involvement. Today it is known as the Sgaw Karen Ko Tha Byu Compound.

Beecher wanted to ensure that the Karen students learned the Bible comprehensively and were equipped with strong writing skills. In addition, a variety of courses such as history, geography, mathematics, civics, and hygiene were included in the course syllabi, along with Bible and Christian literature.

One major issue of disagreement between the American Baptist Missionary Union and several missionaries in the Karen mission field centered on the teaching of the English language. The Karens insisted that their children be taught English. One of their leaders, Thra Kway, was compelled to make a strong proposal to the missionaries. As a result, an English department was established in May 1860, with Mrs. Beecher as the program head. She taught the thirty students enrolled in her class with the help of two Karen teachers, San Tha and Sahnay. San Tha had studied in America for seven years before he came back to Bassein to assist Mrs. Beecher.[84]

From its founding, the Sgaw Karen Normal and Industrial Institute placed an emphasis on industry. Thus, all the students were assigned to work three hours each day. Ten of the vernacular students trained as carpenters, joiners, and wheelwrights. Fifteen to twenty students were assigned to pound and clean rice for the school, and the mills they used were set up by the students. Six boys were trained to make bamboo and cane furniture each year. There were sixteen women and girls studying sewing. The younger boys had the task of clearing and grading the school compound.[85] The success of these early self-supporting schools, Kozu Academy and the Normal Institution, contributed not only to the development of the Karen Christian community in Bassein but also to the whole of the country for years to come.

Mr. Beecher, who initiated and contributed to the advancement of Karen education beyond religious teachings, died on October 22, 1866. When he died, in Bassein there were 40 S'gaw Karen schools, 816 S'gaw Karen scholars, 209 churches with 83 pastors and preachers, 12 Pwo Karen schools with an attendance of 186 students, and 2 Burmese schools with 73 enrolled.[86] The Karens were serious about pursuing their new educational system.[87]

The missionaries laid the foundation for the education, and the Karen leaders in the 1850s and 1860s were raised even higher by another missionary, Mr. Chapin Howard Carpenter. He was with the Karen Seminary in Rangoon for more than five years before being assigned to Bassein in 1868.[88] When he started in Bassein, there were 1,321 Karen students,[89] but within a year, enrollment increased to 2,857.[90]

At a meeting held on March 18, 1875, a resolution was adopted to build a church, and donations were collected during the succeeding years.[91] The church building was completed on May 16, 1878, and the dedication worship service of the Ko Tha Byu Memorial Church was held. Together with the American missionaries, Karen pastors and preachers, plus an additional two thousand participants, Ko Tha Byu's wife, Mah A, and son Yaw Tha (Joseph) commemorated the faithful service of Ko Tha Byu, exactly on the fiftieth anniversary of his baptism.[92]

Mr. Charles A. Nichols and his wife Jennie Root Nichols came in 1879 after Carpenter's retirement and continued to strengthen the mission field. During this period, the wooden structure of the Ko Tha Byu School was rebuilt in brick. The Sgaw Karen Normal and Industrial Institute was rebranded as Nichols High School. Other academies opened in several villages in the Bassein district under the Nichols' leadership. These academies were the hosts in Bassein when American missionaries and Karens celebrated the Ko Tha Byu centennial in 1928. A witness to that ceremony said, "The school has the finest educational plant in Burma, built entirely by the Karens and costing about eight lakhs of rupees."[93]

Meanwhile, the Pwo Karen community was also progressing in Bassein, Tharrawaddy, and the delta areas, though at a lesser momentum, under the leadership of Mr. Van Meter. Sarah "Sally" Higby was a key player in the operation of the Pwo Karen mission schools first in Moulmein and Bassein and from 1895 in Tharrawaddy. According to the reports in 1866, there were 17 Pwo Karen churches with 28 pastors and preachers, 12 schools, and 186 scholars.[94] After Mr. Van Meter, other missionaries joined the field and continued the work developing the school, establishing new buildings, and strengthening the village churches.

The Karen advancement in the field of education went beyond the territory of Burma and into international venues. In 1833, the first Karen, Saw Chet Thiang, came to America and assisted Rev. Jonathan Wade in teaching the Karen language to new missionaries. Rev. Justus Vinton took two Pwo Karens, Mya Aye and Kong Lonk, to America in 1848 for Bible translation work.[95] From the time the schools in Bassein developed and the Karen Christian community began to thrive, Karen scholars began studying in America. When they returned to Burma, they taught in Karen schools with great enthusiasm and dedication. San Tha in 1853 and Sahnay in 1856 went to America for advanced studies.[96] On their return, they both assisted Mrs. Beecher in teaching English when the English department was established in 1860 in Bassein. That same year, Ka Ser and Pa Gaw Htoo accompanied Rev. Harris to study in America.[97] Ya Ba Hto Lo, a student of Mrs. Beecher, in 1860 went to America and came back to teach after obtaining his degree.[98] Another Karen, Bokanaung, followed the Beecher family to America in 1866, where he received his medical degree from the University of Chicago.[99]

By 1875, Yaba Hto Lo, Maung Htwe, and Bokannaung were all teaching at Ko Tha Byu School.[100] T. Thanbyah was the first Karen to obtain his bachelor's degree in America in 1871. He originally was a student of Mr. Beecher in 1852, but he later went to study at missionary Vinton's school in Rangoon. When he came back from America, he taught first at the Karen Theological Institute in Rangoon, and in 1885 he became the principal of Ko Tha Byu School.[101]

The collaborative work of the American Baptist missionaries and the Karens in the development of educational opportunities was well established by the close of the nineteenth century. The Karens originally learned through religious education in the missionary schools, then through general education, and eventually from studies abroad. In only fifty years, they were equipped with new ideas and skills which would allow them to shape their own civilization.

The Great Leap Forward for the Karen People

The training received from the missionaries in Tavoy, Moulmein, and Sandoway produced capable Karen preachers and teachers, who in turn passed their religious beliefs and knowledge to their own people. In the 1850s, many trained pastors and teachers expressed interest in spreading Christianity among other ethnic groups in Burma. The Bassein Karen Home Mission Society was formed to facilitate this calling. In 1853, the Home Mission Society sent two men to the Henzada district and two others to Shwedaung on the east bank of the Irrawaddy below Prome. When Francis Mason and Saw Quala started the new mission field in Taungoo, six additional Karen missionaries came from Bassein to help. In 1855, a group of fifteen Karen bachelors went to Taungoo to work as missionaries.[102] The Home Mission Society fully supported ten Karen missionaries from Bassein along with workers in their own district.[103]

In 1858, Thra Po Kway and two young men volunteered to go to the little-known area north of Ava to explore the country as far north as Bhamo in search of their kinsmen and other Karen people. He reported at the general meeting in February 1859 that he did not leave any of his team members since they did not find any Karens, but they did discover the Kachins.[104] After a slow beginning, Francis Mason prompted the Karens to go to the Kachin people in the far north of Burma. After penetrating the area in 1873, he confirmed, "Bhamo is the earliest bit of solid ground we have on which to found Karen history." Always the anthropologist, Mason found striking similarities: "The Kachins carry baskets on their backs, like the Karens. The Karens, like the Kachin women, use a very peculiar kind of loom in weaving; and the look of the Kachin women is precisely the same. Like the Karen, the Kachins chew the betel-leaf."[105]

Tempted by Mason's theory of kinship, pastor Bogalay and American Baptist missionary Josiah Cushing wanted to spread the gospel north beyond Mandalay. They reached Bhamo in 1876, but Bogalay left the mission. He was replaced by Thra S'Peh, whose name is forever sealed in the heart of the Kachin Christian community. Because of his labor, the first seven Kachin converts were baptized by W. H. Roberts in 1882.[106] In the early twentieth century, Thra Sein Nyo and his wife joined the Kachin hill mission and went up to the Triangle, which was a two-week journey beyond Myitkyina.[107]

Evangelistic work among the Chin people began in 1859 when Thra Goompany, also from the delta region, successfully opened a mission among the Chin in Thayetmyo of the Prome district.[108] From there, the first Chins converted to Christianity. When Englishman Arthur E. Carson was invited by the British colonial officer Captain Dury in 1896 to start mission work among the Haka Chin, three Karen preachers from Bassein accompanied him.[109] An American missionary in the Chin Hills, Mr. Cope, said that these early Karen preachers went out to strange villages where no preparations had been made for them and where they were threatened directly.[110] The first Christian was a Zomi Chin, Thuam Hang, who was baptized by Dr. East Johnson in 1906. It was, however, a Karen, Thra Shwe Zan from Henzada, who spent time with Thuam Hang and his family earning their confidence in preparation for their conversion. Since Thuam Hang was the chief of a village that was a seven-day journey from Haka, he worked alone for an entire year without seeing the missionary.[111]

The spread of Christianity among the Shan, Lahu, and Wa people was also the work of the Karen preachers. Although most of the Lahu people live in China and Thailand, they are also scattered throughout the villages in Burma's eastern Shan states. Saya Ba Te and Thra Po Tun were well known for their work for the Lahu mission. Thra Po Tun's New Testament translation was available for Lahu Christians in 1932.[112] Rev. Telford wrote in 1927: "A historical sketch of the Kengtung Mission would not be complete if we failed to make mention of the great part the Karen Christian workers have had in the development of the Lahu Church. Much of the success . . . has been largely due to their splendid consecration."[113]

The recognition of the excellent contribution of the Karen preachers went beyond the religious arena. As they worked to convert different groups of people, they became good teachers, dedicated to the people they reached. They learned native languages, learned about the people with whom they engaged, and helped solve their problems.

The mission schools in the Chin Hills were established by Christian missionaries with the assistance of the Karens from the delta mission. By 1930, these schools came under the British government, and yet, the inspector and almost all the teachers were Christians. The popularity of the Karen teachers in the field of education was expressed by Mr. Cope as follows:

> We owe everything to the Karens. . . . For a long time they [the Karens] were the only evangelists here. . . . In the first literary work I did, it was Karens who helped me. In the school as well, we had Karen headmasters and they proved as valuable there as in the evangelistic work. . . . When the new educational scheme was inaugurated, the D.C. [deputy commissioner] promptly asked for the Karen Headmaster of the Haka school, placing him as headmaster of the most important school in the district. . . . Then the D.C. asked for Karen teachers for his other schools and now three headmasters along with some assistants are Christian Karens. As the D.C. said, in an official letter, a Burma would not come on the salary we offer but the Karens look on this as missionary work. Only the other day the D.C. said he would not have anyone but a Karen in his schools in spite of their Christian zeal.[114]

It was not only among the hill people that the Karen teachers were highly appreciated. Their services were in great demand among the Burmese community in the Prome district. Thonze, the headmistress of the Burman girls' school in Prome, was a Karen. In the Okkan School with 135 students, all the teachers including the headmasters were Karens.[115] Undeniably, many Karen leaders, both secular and religious, were the products of the self-support mission schools that developed in Bassein during the nineteenth century.

The Vinton Family and the Development of the Karen People in Rangoon

The second Anglo-Burmese war of 1852 left the Karen villages around Rangoon in such desperate conditions that people were short of food and shelter. The Vintons helped those Karens who came to them from their hiding places. In addition to caring for refugees, Mrs. Vinton started a school for some two hundred pupils, consisting of both old and young students with parents and children studying together on the same bench and learning to read the Bible.[116] The mission's success is reported in a letter written by Rev. Kincaid: "During the rains 250 Karens learned to read the word of God, who could not read before. Over thirty young men received biblical instruction preparatory to labor in the distant villages, some as preachers, and some as schoolteachers."[117]

The Vintons originally lived and worked in temporary accommodations in a large *zayat* close to the pagoda. After peace was declared, the British government ordered the evacuation of all religious buildings that had been occupied during and after the war. The Vintons moved to facilities in Ahlone, which Rev. Vinton acquired from the British authorities without having time to wait for the approval of the mission board in Boston. Misunderstandings developed with the American Mission Board, but Vinton's work of love and service to the people who were suffering from postwar trauma turned the hearts of both Burmans and Karens toward Christ. They said, "This is the man who saved our lives and the lives of our little ones: his religion is the one we want."[118] With more converts, the Vintons organized more churches and built more chapels and schools.

In 1854, on Mr. Vinton's suggestion, the Rangoon Karen Home Mission Society formed on lines like the societies already started in Tavoy, Sandoway, and Bassein. They raised 600 rupees in the first year for sending out 8 evangelists, and 200 rupees were given to the town school where 600 children were under instruction. They raised an additional 3,830 rupees to match the amount from America for the building of Franc's Chapel, which was constructed on the Vinton compound in Rangoon.[119] By 1856, there were 36 village schools and 42 Karen churches with more than 2,000 members working together under the leadership of 39 Karen preachers.[120]

The Vintons were great missionaries, not only because of their preaching and praying but also because they helped the oppressed and healed the sick. Under their guidance, the Karens learned to work together for their own needs during times of crisis. Unfortunately, in 1853, when the Baptist Convention stipulated that English was not to be taught at school, the Vintons had already started a large school, which included the teaching of English. And when the missionaries agreed to have only a single theological school located in Moulmein, the Vintons had already conducted training for pastors and teachers in Rangoon. All these efforts were considered refusals to follow the board's policy. This misunderstanding led to Mr. Vinton's withdrawal from the mission in 1856. Despite that, the Vintons, both husband and wife, worked with vigor for the Karen people living beyond Rangoon.

In 1858, Mr. Vinton died suddenly after a long and difficult jungle trip by elephant in the Shwegyin hills. His wife, Calista, remained to carry on the work. Soon, two missionaries joined her. One was Rev. Durlin

L. Brayton, who also left the ABMU but came back from Danubyu to continue the Pwo Karen mission work in Rangoon. Additionally, Dr. J. G. Binney returned from America in 1859 with the intention of bringing the theological school from Moulmein to Rangoon. In 1862, Calista Vinton's son, J. Brainerd Vinton, and his wife Julia, the daughter of Dr. and Mrs. James Haswell of the Burmese mission, joined her mission work.[121] Two years later, her daughter, Mrs. Calista Vinton Luther, and her husband, Mr. R. M. Luther, joined her and worked in Rangoon until 1870.

Like his father, Brainerd Vinton spent his time and energy for the Karen people. Through his leadership, the Karens were able to protect themselves from the chaos of lawlessness during the close of the third Anglo-Burmese war in 1885. After his death in 1889, his daughter Alice and her husband, Mr. Albert E. Seagrave, continued the mission work in the area stretching from the delta to the Pegu hills and from Tharrawaddy to Papun. The Vintons rendered their services both in the school and in district observation. In addition, the third Vinton generation, Dr. Grace Vinton Seagrave, and her husband, Dr. Gordon Seagrave, served in the medical field at Namhkam and Moulmein respectively.[122] The hospitals they set up during their time lasted for more than a century until the Burmese socialist government nationalized them in 1965.

Christian Education and the Advancement of the Karen People in Toungoo

When Toungoo became British territory after the second Anglo-Burmese war, Rev. Francis Mason wrote to the deputation in America in September 1853. Rev. Mason stated his view of Toungoo as the most important Karen station in Burma and asked permission to transfer to that place. He and his assistant, Saw Quala, the second Karen convert, who had become a pastor by then, had long been interested in the Toungoo area. According to tradition, it was the principal seat of their forefathers and the fountain from which the Karens flowed before historic times into Thailand, the delta of the Irrawaddy, and Tenasserim.[123] The political turbulence had left Toungoo almost deserted when Mason first arrived in October 1853.

As they started their mission work, Rev. and Mrs. Mason discovered additional Karen tribes to the S'gaw and Pwo Karens to whom they were accustomed in the Tenasserim and delta areas. Among these included the people who called themselves *Maw Nay Pwa* (*Mophgas*), the *Pakus*, and the *Bwes*, who were again divided into three subtribes known as *Bwe-pho* or little Bwes. Many of these Karen villagers visited the Masons and soon embraced Christianity. Saw Quala, who joined Mason in December 1853, worked among the Maw Nay Pwa and baptized hundreds of them.[124]

The Toungoo mission field would not have developed successfully without the unusual leadership of Ellen Huntley Mason. During the first few months in Toungoo, Mrs. Mason, like other wives of the missionaries, started a normal school for the training of village teachers in addition to raising funds from English residents. Many of the students later became workers in all parts of the hills. Due to health problems, Mr. and Mrs. Mason left Burma for a short period, but upon her return from America in 1857, Mrs. Mason worked to launch education for girls, which was a revolutionary idea to these Karen villagers. Although the plan was not favorable in the beginning, she was later able to persuade the Karen chiefs to materialize her plan. More than 200 villagers came to cut timber and construct the buildings. The Karen Education Society organized to take charge of the Female Institute for all tribes. This society included some 260 chiefs from 6 different tribes.[125]

Like Karen communities in other parts of Burma, the missionary schools in Toungoo uplifted the area Karens. Donald Smeaton, the British finance commissioner of lower Burma from 1879 to 1884, wrote,

> In a minute by the Chief Commissioner of British Burma, dated May 1, 1863, I find the following: . . .The district of Toungoo was occupied by British troops early in 1853. . . . At that time nearly the whole of the Karen tribes on the mountains east of Toungoo—that is over an area of more than two thousands square miles—were in a savage state. The Burmese Government never had authority over any of the tribes living more than a day's journey from the city and river. In process of time, from the constant labour of the [American] missionaries, many thousands of the mountain Karens were instructed in Christianity, abandoned their savage mode of life and their cruel wars and lived as Christian men and women. . . . I assert, from long experience among similar tribes, that such results could not be obtained by the civil administration, unaided by missionary teaching.[126]

Besides educating the Karens, missionary teaching sowed the seed for the rise of Karen nationalism. Ellen Mason reported in *Great Expectations Realized; or Civilizing Mountain Men*, how the Karen national consciousness began. According to her record, Saw Quala, by then an ordained pastor, made the first nationalist gesture in his suggestion that the Karen nation should have a flag. "Let us erect the National banner, as other book nations have done."[127]

Mrs. Mason's work for the development of Karen education in the Toungoo area was directly connected to Saw Quala's idea of a Karen national banner. After obtaining some financial support from the British commissioner, Ellen Mason was able to build the Karen Female Institute for the six Karen clans—the Sgaus (S'gaws), Pakus, Mauniepagas (Mawnipwa), Mopagas (Mawpwa), Bghais (Bwes), and Pant-Bghais. When she allowed each tribe to put a banner on the building, the Karen ladies in these villages competed in weaving and embroidering the most beautiful flags. As these banners flew high, Saw Quala became excited with the idea of a national emblem or union standard for all Karen people. Mrs. Mason said, "Quala took up the subject with earnestness, and sent epistles to the churches. They chose a device for them, which was a Bible with a sword across it."[128]

This desire to be recognized as a nation was reported in the following article published in the New York World on August 8, 1860:

> In the Mariner's church, in Cherry street, last Sunday evening, a national banner was presented by one of the largest Bible societies in America, to the most interesting and hopeful nation in all Asia, the Karens. This strange, wild people are being rapidly Christianized, and they have sent to America for a national flag to commemorate their exodus out of heathenism! The most curious and exhilarating request that we have ever heard of from a nation.[129]

Evidently, this was the first time the Karen national identity was recognized by the western world. As a scholar in 1983 said, "A communal Karen imagination of a nation has been in the making since 1830, and it is not merely a foreign creation. The Karen had indeed been active participants in the making of their own history."[130]

Indeed, the education introduced by the missionaries had an inexorable effect on the Karen people. It transformed Saw Quala from a simple country Karen boy into a capable leader, whose intelligent mind and skills were highly praised. Francis Mason pointed out that just as the history of the Tavoy mission had been the history of Saw Quala, so the Toungoo mission was his history also. From its foundation, Saw Quala was its moving spirit.[131] Mason, the missionary, was not alone in applauding Saw Quala's wisdom and contributions. The British governor, Major Arthur Phayre, offered him a government position with a salary that was five times the mission salary. Saw Quala refused the offer and said, "I will not mix up God's work with government work. There are others to do this, employ them."[132]

Higher Education for the Karen People

The events outlined previously testify to the progress of the Karen people through the zeal of the American missionaries and the self-supporting spirit of the Karen. As some of the Karens became capable of leadership roles, missionaries began to assign them to areas where they were required. However, the Karens wanted to uplift their educational level and open schools teaching English (in addition to their native Karen). They pleaded for higher education to conduct their work effectively like their missionary colleagues. The missionaries in the Karen field, who had witnessed the success of the schools and churches along with the consistent support of the Karen people, wanted to make it happen. An opportunity became imminent when the Karen churches began to work collectively with the American missionaries in Burma at the time the Baptist Mission Board in America changed its policy on education.

The 1853 ABMU policy, including the limitation of boarding schools and the ban on teaching English, had caused the resignation of five missionaries in the Karen mission field in Burma. That changed when the Karen Christian schools and educational institutions in Bassein and Rangoon started to thrive. The ABMU began to make efforts for the reunification of the Karen churches that had left the ABMU along with their missionary leaders. Attempts were made to reunite those who separated with those Baptist Christians whose missionaries had remained with the ABMU.

Mr. Justus Vinton passed away in 1858 before reunification was attempted. His son, J. Brainerd Vinton, continued his father's work among the Karens in Rangoon alongside his mother, Calista. In 1861, Rev. Brayton, Rev. Harris, and Rev. Rose were reappointed by the ABMU. Rev. Beecher did not return but took part in the promotion of good relationships between the Karens of Bassein and Rangoon and other Christians.

In October 1865, the missionaries and seventy national leaders met for a week in Rangoon to form the Burma Baptist Missionary Convention, which had been in planning since 1864. Rev. Beecher, Rev. Luther, and Rev. J. Brainerd Vinton of the Free Baptist Mission joined the meeting and participated eagerly in working out the details of the constitution. Consequently, the first annual meeting of the convention was held in 1866 at the Baptist Headquarters in Rangoon with the attendance of

360 people. Cephas Bennett of the mission press was elected as the first president. The four vice presidents were Rev. J. S Beecher, Saya U En, and two Karen pastors, Thra Quala and Thra Po Kway.[133]

Following the convention meeting in Rangoon, the delegates returned home and reported to their churches and associations. In 1870, the Karen churches in Bassein and Rangoon joined the convention.[134] The formation of the Burma Baptist Convention made possible the establishment of a Christian college that had been long pleaded for by the Karen Christians.

PROPOSAL FOR A HIGHER INSTITUTE OF LEARNING FOR THE KAREN PEOPLE OF BURMA

It is appropriate to cite the words of Judson College graduate and Karen scholar Professor Tun Aung Chain, who said, "The origins of Judson College go back to a proposal of the American Baptist missionaries working among the Karens."[135] At a meeting held in December 1869, the missionaries in the Karen field drew a proposal for higher education. The proposal was sent to the American Baptist Missionary Union with the title a "Proposal for a Higher Institution of Learning for the Karens of Burma."

> To the friends of Karen education, We, the undersigned Karen missionaries, feel that fidelity to our Master will no longer allow us to visit without meeting a special effort to start a General Institution, where the children of our native Christians can get a good education without being obliged to go to Roman Catholic schools for it. For years past our hearts have pained to see the work on our hands suffering severely for the want of such an Institution. What we want is,
>
> 1. That at least one Institution should be in Burma for general education among the Karen; that from however low a point the Institution may depart and however small may be the beginning, the Institution and instruction should annually go forward until there is here in Burma secure by what may properly be called a liberal education for the Karens.
> 2. That the Institution should be provided with suitable teachers, buildings and means of giving effective instruction, etc. and that suitable persons who wish to do so shall be allowed to pursue their studies through the medium of the English language.
> 3. It is our earnest wish that this work should be done indirectly in connection with the Karen Theological Seminary by the American Baptist Missionary Union, But—
> 4. Should they not desire to engage at once in such a work it should be until otherwise decided under the direction and advice of a Com-

mittee appointed for that purpose, or in such a way by the donors and supporters of the Institution.

5. It is our wish and united request that Dr. Binney, with such assistance as he may select, should present and push this subject among the friends of the Karen Mission to some immediate practical result.

All the missionaries in the Karen mission field signed the document, including J. Wade, J. G. Binney, D. L. Brayton, N. Harris, D. A. Smith, C. H. Carpenter, I. D. Colburn, J. F. Morris, and A. Bunker on the date, January 1, 1870.[136]

At the fifty-seventh annual meeting of the Missionary Union in Chicago in 1871, this resolution was adopted:

> That the Union approve the establishment of a school among the Karens in which the higher branches of education will be presented; and that the Board be requested to instruct the Executive Committee to take measure for raising the sum of $100,000 by special contribution within the present year for the foundation of such an institution, of which not more than one half shall be expended for buildings and apparatus and that provision is to be made for its current expenses beyond the income of the permanent funds by annual appropriations.[137]

Consequently, the committee, which was selected to establish the college, presented the following report, which was adopted:

> We recognize the value of liberal education both in itself and a source of power to pious young men of the Karen race, and indeed, to the sons of Christian parents generally. We also feel the importance of giving them this education ourselves instead of having to seek it in school sustained by men of different religious faith. And therefore, we propose the adoption of the following resolution by the Executive Committee;
>
> 1. That as soon as suitable teachers can be secured a school for liberal studies to be commenced in Rangoon to be called Rangoon Baptist College.
> 2. The pious young men and the sons of pious parents among the Karens, be encouraged by the missionaries, at their discretion, to pursue courses of study in the school embracing, when it is thought best, the English language.
> 3. That the young men or their friends be required to bear a reasonable part of these expenses of their education in this school.

4. That the premises of Mr. Brayton be used for the present to accommodate this school. At a subsequent meeting the subject of the location of the College was deferred till further information should be received. At the same time Rev Dr. Binney was appointed President of the Institution.

The committee also authorized a subscription of a limited amount for the nucleus of an endowment for the college. The secretary was likewise instructed to secure a suitable man, a layman, if possible, to assume the principal charge of instruction as a professor.[138] When all was set, the school opened in 1872. The report of the *Missionary Magazine* in September stated, "The Karen College in Rangoon opened May 28th with 17 pupils, promising young men."[139]

Rangoon Baptist College was designed exclusively for the Karen people by the American missionaries who deeply cared for the Karens. The college was first started on property bought from Mr. Bennett, which was located across a street from the Karen Theological Seminary, which was established in Moulmein and transferred to Rangoon in 1853. With a small beginning of only seventeen young men as students in the first year, the number increased to forty-eight, including three girls in the second year. From its opening in 1872 until 1882, it remained a secondary school in the British system with only three classes: the fifth, sixth, and seventh standards.[140]

In 1874, Rev. Chapin Howard Carpenter succeeded Dr. J. G. Binney as principal. He recommended that the college become a Karen institution and move to Bassein, where there was a larger Karen population. But the Burma Baptist Convention, itself multi-ethnic, insisted that the college should serve all groups cooperating in the convention and that Rangoon was the best place in which to serve the youth of the nation. When his proposal was rejected, Rev. Carpenter resigned in 1876, considering that he could not serve the Karens effectively in Rangoon. He was replaced by Dr. John Packer, who struggled for twelve years until 1887 to advance the institution into something more than a low-grade school.

In 1882, at the end of a ten-year period, the University of Calcutta recognized that the standard of the college was high enough to prepare candidates for its matriculation examination, which was the first step in the academic growth and recognition of Rangoon Baptist College.[141] In 1887, Mr. E. B. Roach from Shurtleff Academy was appointed president, but due to his absence in 1890, he was succeeded by Mr. David C. Gilmore, who arrived that year to teach. That year, a few non-Christian students misbehaved, and the Karen Christians became unhappy with the institution and weakened their support causing a decrease in attendance. But Gilmore soon learned the Karen language and was better equipped to regain their confidence and support. As a result, the number of Karen students once again increased. During that period, there was renewed agitation to make the institution an exclusively Karen institution.[142]

In 1892, Dr. Josiah N. Cushing succeeded Mr. Roach, who decided to devote his whole time to the mission press. Dr. Cushing, who first arrived in Burma in 1867 as a missionary among the Shan, had used his literary skills to translate the Bible into Shan. He also compiled a Shan grammar and dictionary. His close relationship with the managing body of the Missionary Union strengthened the college staff, as he was able to convince the board that an adequate staff would attract a larger student body. Looking forward to the preparation of teachers for the increasing number of local schools, the Burma Education Department urged the mission to open schools for teacher training. Mr. Gilmore was appointed to supervise the establishment of two such schools in connection with the Baptist college.[143]

Also in 1892, Rangoon Baptist College Church was organized, and Mr. David Gilmore was ordained to become the first pastor. Since the opening of First Arts classes would involve the teaching of Pali, and there was no one who could do so, Rev. Gilmore had to take up Pali. Gilmore began the tradition of a pastorate that not only provided spiritual care but also backed it with intellectual accomplishment.

Under Dr. Cushing's vigorous leadership, the college faculty was strengthened. With the improved staff in 1892, Calcutta University recognized the Rangoon Baptist College to be a First Arts college and authorized it to prepare students for examinations, which would take place after the first two years of distinctly college instruction. The subjects taught were English, history, mathematics, Pali language, chemistry, physics, and logic. There were also daily Bible classes though not in preparation for university examinations. Rev. Gilmore, besides teaching Pali, prepared and published the *Sunday School Lesson Paper* in S'gaw Karen.[144]

For twenty years, since its first initial instruction with 17 students, Rangoon Baptist College had been growing and living up to its original aspirations. In 1893, attendance doubled when the normal schools for teacher training and their affiliated practicing schools opened. The following year, when the freshman and sophomore classes were initiated, there was another increase of 50 percent. Enrollment rose to 438 when these classes took their first Calcutta examinations. Between 1890 and

1900, the student body increased from 113 to 567 in all departments.[145] To accommodate the increased student population, the college acquired the land and buildings of the Karen Theological Seminary, which had moved to Insein.

In 1909, Rangoon Baptist College became a full-fledged degree institution and received approval to add junior and senior courses. The first bachelor of arts (BA) classes started, and the first honors work in philosophy was undertaken. The first candidate for honors work was a Karen student named Saw San Ba of Bassein. About this Karen student, Dr. Wallace St. John wrote, "This ambitious young Karen, on finishing his honors course, set out for America and entered a post graduate theological seminary. A professor of that seminary volunteered the statement that Saw San Ba was the best prepared student entering the class."[146] Upon returning to Burma, Saw San Ba was selected to teach theology in the Karen Theological Seminary at Insein. Subsequently, his own high school in Bassein, which was then recognized as the best equipped of all the Karen schools with more than one thousand students enrolled, invited him to be its principal. In 1930, he accepted the position and worked there until the invading Japanese killed him in bombing the city of Bassein in 1941.[147] Saw San Ba is also remembered for composing the lyrics for the Karen national anthem in 1938.

FROM BAPTIST COLLEGE TO JUDSON COLLEGE

Although it became clear that the college was for all ethnic groups, the Karen Christians provided important support for the school. During Dr. Packer's time, his staff consisted of his wife Frances Pattison Packer, Miss Emma Chase, and two Karens, Thra Ya Bah and Thra Pa Ka Tu, both of whom were educated in America. Enrollment figures indicate that Karens were the dominant ethnicity attending the college. In 1877, 106 students were enrolled, among whom 76 were Karens, with 26 Burmans, 2 Indians, and 2 Anglo-Burman.[148] Eventually, more non-Karens and non-Christians came to the college. During the 1929–1930 academic year, 110 Burman, 88 Karen, 24 Anglo-Indian, 16 Chinese, and 16 others passed the matriculation exams.[149]

In 1919, the name was changed from the Rangoon Baptist College to Judson College. Professor of philosophy Dr. St. John of Judson College claimed that changing the name was "suggesting the intellectual relation of the institution to the first western scholar who made a large contribution to Burma's welfare. Through Adoniram Judson's dictionaries and his *Grammar of the Burmese Language*, he contributed vastly to Burmese intellectuality."[150]

Following the name change from Rangoon Baptist College to Judson College, the College Church also became Judson Chapel. By that time, the College Church's mission concerns had widened. Five Sunday schools were conducted by faculty and students for children who were not connected with Baptist schools. The church also contributed to the support of Saya Myat Min, a college alumnus who became a mission worker in the Shan states. The college also provided a home for the Rangoon Baptist City Mission.[151]

In 1920, Judson College withdrew its affiliation with the University of Calcutta and joined Rangoon College in the establishment of the University of Rangoon. Student enrollment increased sharply in the new Judson College. When bachelor of arts classes began in 1909, 27 students were enrolled in the college. When bachelor of science classes were added in 1917, enrollment increased to 125. But the real increase came in the early 1920s:

1921–1922 136
1922–1923 195
1923–1924 262
1924–1925 308
1925–1926 337

This increasing number of students created problems with accommodations. The challenge was addressed by moving to a new campus near Inya (then Victoria) Lake.

Before Judson College moved to its new fifty-four-acre site on the university estate, American Baptists conducted the Judson Fund Drive from 1927 to 1930, just before the onset of the Great Depression. John D. Rockefeller Jr. contributed generously so that the new plant was completed in 1934, despite the Depression. The government paid half the cost of the buildings, excluding the chapel and pastor's residence. This arrangement was made with the understanding that if the government should ever need to take over the Judson buildings, it could do so by paying compensation to the amount of the Baptist investment, or half of the buildings' value at the time of the takeover.[152] In 1935, the college facilities accommodated some 320 full-time students. The faculty numbered thirty-six lecturers with approximately one-third American, one-third Indian, and the balance being Burmans, Anglo-Burmans, and Karens.[153]

The enrollment suggested that Christian Karens continued to form a large portion of the student body. In 1937, 108 of 197 self-identifying

Christian students were Karen. Seventy-five Buddhists, 48 Hindus, and 14 Muslims also attended. In 1938, there were 105 Christian Karen students out of 210 total Christians enrolled (105 Karens, 78 Indians, 31 Anglo-Burmans, 7 Chinese, 2 Mons, 4 Shans, and 1 Armenian).[154]

In 1941, the college became a government college.[155] The primary goal of Judson College, which was to enrich the backward Karen ethnic group, was achieved and evidenced by the number of graduates who became teachers and leaders of communities in different parts of Burma. In addition to academic successes, the Karen athletes' outstanding skills became prominent through their training at Judson. Professor John F. Cady said that in 1937, Judson's performance in the intra-university meet of December 21 was much improved over the previous year and that "my best Karen runner again won six events."[156]

One unexpected consequence was the influence of Karen females on the establishment of schools for girls. Such Karen Christian women as Kittie Po Thein (S'gaw Karen) and Eleanor San Tay (Pwo Karen) served as headmistresses of schools following the heritage of Ann Judson. These schools for girls were open to all groups. When families understood their daughters were safe under the supervision of these female educators, Burmese and Shan parents sent their daughters to these schools. For the Karens, however, coeducation became an accepted system. Of more than twenty-three thousand students in Karen Baptist schools, well over one-third were girls, while about half of the teachers were women.[157]

Several Karen students graduated from Judson College and assumed high positions in government service, while others joined the mission field. By the middle of the twentieth century, in addition to serving in schools and mission fields, many Karen graduates held positions such as township officers, lawyers, medical doctors, and even as parliamentary members in the British administration. In 1932, when the Burma Legislative Council came into existence, Judson College's treasurer, Saw Mya Pon, was elected to be a member of the legislature by the Karen constituency. His success was acknowledged as an outstanding contribution "to the Christian community and Judson College."[158] Other Karens who attended Judson College and obtained high political positions in the British administration include Saw San Baw (member of British government legislative council in 1932); Saw Johnson D. Po Min (parliamentary member in 1937); and Mahn Ba Khin (1937). Additionally, Mahn Win Maung, the third president of independent Burma in 1957, was also a Judson College graduate.

The End of an Era: Judson's Legacy (1872–1965)

Following World War II, Judson College resumed operation by the Burmese government in 1950. Separate colleges were discontinued, and the University of Rangoon assumed responsibility for all teaching. The government took over most of the previous college campus and buildings. Only Judson Chapel and the pastor's residence, which had received no government financial grant, were left to the Baptists. The government paid compensation as previously agreed. These funds, together with a large gift from Dr. Wallace St. John, were used to erect a Student Christian Center building across Prome Road from the chapel. A Karen, Mr. William Lay, was appointed as the director of student activities. A Burman, Rev. U Ba Hmyin, became the pastor at the Judson Chapel and continued Christian worship on the university campus. Part of the compensation funds was used to establish an extensive student aid program (known as Judson Aid) for Baptist students to attend the University of Rangoon, as well as Baptist seminaries and Bible schools.[159]

The original school complex that started in 1872 as the Baptist College (which became Judson College in 1920) continued to exist as an Anglo-vernacular high school called United Christian High School until 1964. This campus worked together with twenty-two other Baptist high schools run by various Baptist language groups, all self-supporting and with national leadership. Some of these schools continuously existed from the days of Adoniram Judson, while others were a century old, and a few were developed later, particularly in the frontier areas. All these Christian schools ceased to exist, along with other private schools in Burma, when the military took control of the nation and made it a socialist country after 1965.

With the political changes in Burma, the Christian college in Burma came to an end. However, many Judsonians carried on the Christian educational legacy. The institution that was initially intended only for the Karens had set no boundary for uplifting the intellectual culture of all the people in Burma.

The American Baptist Convention announcement from 1929 that began the opening of this chapter, "We have a complete education system in Burma," was no exaggeration but rather a simple statement testifying to the accomplishments of zealous American Baptist missionaries in the field of education. Sir San C. Po, a member of Burma's legislative council and the most prominent Karen leader of that time, received his early education from the Karen Christian school in Bassein. He eventually obtained his degree in medicine from Albany Medical College in the

United States in 1893 and proudly claimed, "The Burmese youth, and the young people of other races, have sought and are seeking admission to the Karen schools."[160] Christian education, initiated by the Judsons and developed by other American missionaries, transformed the Karen people from a shy, backward status to advanced leadership roles in society beyond the Christian evangelical hemisphere.

Notes

1. Committee on Survey of the Northern Baptist Convention, *Second Survey of the Fields and Work of the Northern Baptist Convention*, Presented in Denver, Colorado, June 17, 1929 (New York: Northern Baptist Convention Board of Missionary Cooperation, 1929), 145.

2. *Annual Report on the Administration of the Province of British Burma for the Year 1875–1876*, paragraph 417.

3. James D. Knowles, *Memoir of Mrs. Ann H. Judson, Late Missionary to Burmah*, 4th ed. (London: Lincoln and Edmands, 1831), 72.

4. Ibid., 138.

5. John F. Cady, *A History of Modern Burma* (Ithaca, NY: Cornell University Press, 1960), 60. Various officials in higher levels of government frequently received their advanced training from the *pongyis* (monks). Literacy education for girls was provided under lay auspices, frequently within private families, but it was never as widespread as that provided for the boys.

6. Dana L. Robert, *American Women in Mission: A Social History of Their Thought and Practice* (Macon, GA: Mercer University Press, 1997), 14–16, 43–46.

7. Ibid., 48; also in *Christian History and Biography* 90 (Spring 2006), 3.

8. Emily Chubbock Judson [Fanny Forester], *Memoir of Sarah B. Judson, Member of the American Mission to Burmah* (New York: L. Colby and Company, 1848), v.

9. W. F. B. Laurie, *Our Burmese Wars and Relations with Burma*, 2nd ed. (London: W. H. Allen & Co., 1885), 56–57.

10. Walter Sadgun DeSai, *History of the British Residency in Burma, 1826–1840* (Rangoon: University of Rangoon Press, 1939), 36–39. The protection given to the robbers by the Burmese minister disrupted the peace and security of the people living in the British territory. Maingy sent his forces and attacked Martaban in 1829.

11. Ibid., 41.

12. Arabella Stuart Willson, *The Three Mrs. Judsons*, Missionary Series, ed. Gary W. Long (Springfield, MO: Particular Baptist Press, 1999), 150.

13. Ibid., 148.

14. Ibid., 151.

15. Ibid., 193.

16. Ibid., 288.

17. Maung Shwe Wa, *Burma Baptist Chronicle*, ed. Genevieve Sowards and Erville Sowards (Rangoon: Burma Baptist Convention, 1963), 116.

18. Willson, 293.

19. Ibid., 294.

20. Cady, *History of Modern Burma*, 81.

21. Willson, 296.

22. Judson, 118.

23. Maung Shwe Wa, 116.

24. R. R. Langham-Carter, *Old Moulmein (1875–1880)* (Moulmein: Moulmein Sun Press, 1947), 86.

25. Francis Wayland, *A Memoir of the Life and Labors of the Reverend Adoniram Judson, D.D.*, vols. 1 and 2 (Boston: Philips, Sampson and Company, 1853), 2:67.

26. Maung Shwe Wa, 119–21.

27. Ibid., 120–21.

28. Ibid., 121.

29. Ibid.

30. Randolph L. Howard, *Baptists in Burma* (Philadelphia: Judson Press, 1931), 40.

31. Ibid.

32. Ibid., 41.

33. Maung Shwe Wa, 122–23. The seminary was transferred to Rangoon in 1859. See Henry I. Marshall, *On the Threshold of the Century: An Historical Sketch of the Karen Mission, 1828–1928* (Rangoon: American Baptist Mission Press, 1929), 13.

34. Ibid., 123.

35. T. Thanbyah, *The Karens and Their Persecution, 1824–1854* (Rangoon: American Baptist Mission Press, 1904), 110.

36. Walter Newton Wyeth, *The Wades: Jonathan Wade, D.D., Deborah B. L. Wade, A Memorial* (Philadelphia: published by the author, 1891), 110–22.

37. Wayland, 2:14–15.

38. Ibid., 2:67.

39. Maung Shwe Wa, 316.

40. Thanbyah, *Karens and Their Persecutions*, 110.

41. Marshall, 13.

42. Daniel C. Eddy, *Heroines of the Church* (Boston: H. Wentworth, 1866), 157.

43. Wayland, 2:115.

44. Thanbyah, *Karens and Their Persecutions*, 113.

45. Maung Shwe Wa, 117.

46. Ibid.

47. Ibid., 328, When Rev. Vinton and his wife returned to America in 1848, he chose two Pwo Karens to assist him in revising the New Testament translated by Rev. Mason and published in 1842. These two were Mya Aye and Kong Lonk (Kon Luht). See P'doh Tha Bwa Oo Zan, *History of the Baptist Mission among the Karen in Burma* (Rangoon: Go Forward Press, 1961), 50, 52.

48. Maung Shwe Wa, 118.

49. Thanbyah, *Karens and Their Persecutions*, 112.

50. Maung Shwe Wa, 102–3.

51. Wayland, 2:43.

52. Maung Shwe Wa, 105–6.

53. Howard, 65; Marshall, 19.

54. Maung Shwe Wa, 106; also see Marshall, 19.

55. Howard, 62.

56. Ibid., 64.

57. Robert G. Torbet, *Venture of Faith: The Story of the American Baptist Foreign Mission Society and the Women's American Baptist Foreign Mission Society, 1814–1954* (Philadelphia: Judson Press, 1955), 70.

58. Maung Shwe Wa, 113.

59. *Annual Reports, American Baptist Foreign Mission Society, 1852*, 64–65.

60. Maung Shwe Wa, 113.

61. Cady, *History of Modern Burma*, 86–90.

62. Maung Shwe Wa, 135.

63. Ibid., 167.

64. Thanbyah, *Karens and Their Persecutions*, 98.

65. Vinton, 112.

66. Laurie, 144–45.

67. Chapin Howard Carpenter, *Self-Support, Illustrated in the History of the Bassein Karen Mission from 1840–1880* (Boston: The Franklin Press, 1883), 196.

68. Thanbyah, *Karens and Their Persecutions*, 63-64; eyewitness Klaw Meh was one of Abbott's students.

69. Howard, 61-62; see also Marshall, 19.

70. Thra Ba Tu, 29; the other three were Kan Gyi, Soo Kyi, and Shwe Mya.

71. Carpenter, 199; also Maung Shwe Wa, 168.

72. Howard, 66.

73. Ibid., 67.

74. Maung Shwe Wa, 170–71.

75. Carpenter, 202.

76. Maung Shwe Wa, 171.

77. Carpenter, 203.

78. *Annual Reports, American Baptist Foreign Mission Society, 1856*, 80.

79. Carpenter, 242.

80. Marshall, 21.

81. Carpenter, 279; Maung Shwe Wa, 176.

82. Marshall, 21.

83, Thra Ba Tu, 40–41.

84. Ibid., 43–44.

85. Maung Shwe Wa, 178.

86. Ibid., 179.

87. Ibid.

88. Ibid.
89. Thra Ba Tu, 55.
90. Ibid., 56.
91. Ibid., 58–59.
92. Ibid., 60.
93. Marshall, 23.
94. Maung Shwe Wa, 179.
95. Oo Zan, 50, 52.
96. T. Thanbyah, *Karen People and Development* (Rangoon: American Baptist Mission Press, 1906; republished by Global Karen Baptist Fellowship, 2010), 16.
97. Ibid., 14.
98. Thra Ba Tu, 59.
99. Ibid., 47.
100. Ibid.
101. Ibid., 49.
102. Thanbyah, *Karen People and Development*, 7.
103. Carpenter, 253.
104. Thra Ba Tu, 42.
105. Howard, 79.
106. Ibid., 81.
107. Ibid., 43.
108. Marshall, 22.
109. Lian Hong Sakhong, *Religion and Politics among the Chin People in Burma (1896–1949)* (Uppsala: Studia Missionalia, 2000), 217.
110. Marshall, 91.
111. Sakhong, 217–19.
112. Maung Shwe Wa, 414.
113. Ibid.
114. Marshall, 91–92.
115. Ibid., 74–75.
116. Calista V. Luther, *The Vintons and the Karens: Memorials of Rev. Justus H. Vinton and Calista H. Vinton* (Boston: W. G. Corthell, Mission Rooms, 1880), 100.
117. Maung Shwe Wa, 161; also see Luther, 101.
118. Luther, 105–10.
119. Marshall, 16–17.
120. Maung Shwe Wa, 164.
121. Maung Shwe Wa, 165; also Marshall, 17.
122. Marshall, 17.
123. Francis Mason, "Saw Quala, 'The Second Karen Convert,'" *Baptist Missionary Magazine* (1856), 385.
124. Maung Shwe Wa, 185.
125. Ibid., 189.
126. Donald Mackenzie Smeaton, *The Loyal Karens of Burma* (London: Kegan Paul, Trench & Co., 1887), 193; also in A. R. MacMahon, *The Karens of the Golden Chersonese* (London: Harrison, 1876), 175–76.
127. Ellen Huntly Bullard Mason, *Great Expectations Realized; or Civilizing Mountain Men* (Philadelphia: American Baptist Publication Society; New York: Blakeman & Mason; Chicago: Church, Goodman and Kenny.1862), 265.
128. Ibid., 332–33.
129. Ibid., 333.
130. Mikael Gravers, "The Karen: Making of a Nation," in *Asian Forms of the Nation*, ed. Stein Tonnesson and Hans Antlov (Richmond, Surrey, England: Curzon, Nordic Institutes of Asian Studies, 2000), 268. Cf. Ranajit Guha, *Subaltern Studies: Writings on South Asian History and Society*, vol. 2 (Oxford: Oxford University Press, 1983), 33.
131. Mason, "Saw Quala," 552.
132. Ibid., 555.
133. Maung Shwe Wa, 254–55.
134. Ibid., 255–56.
135. Tun Aung Chain, "The Early Church," *Judson Chapel Golden Jubilee* (Rangoon: Thamee Hnit Tha Press, 1983), 103.
136. *Baptist Missionary Magazine* (1871), 241.
137. Ibid. See also Wallace St. John, "Chronicle," in *Judson Chapel Golden Jubilee* (Rangoon: Thamee Hnit Tha Press, 1983), 130–31.

138. St. John, 131–32.

139. Ibid., 132.

140. Tun Aung Chain, 103.

141. Maung Shwe Wa, 215.

142. St. John, 134.

143. Ibid.

144. Ibid., 135.

145. Maung Shwe Wa, 237–38. The number of students in the college and the associated schools exceeded sixteen hundred in 1913.

146. St. John, 143.

147. Oo Zan, 120.

148. Maung Shwe Wa, 237–38.

149. St. John, 173.

150. Ibid., 156.

151. Ibid.

152. Ibid., 172.

153. John F. Cady, *Contacts with Burma, 1935–1949, A Personal Account* (Athens: Ohio University Southeast Asia Series 61, 1983), 4.

154. St. John, 180.

155. Ibid., 47.

156. Cady, *Contacts with Burma*, 18.

157. Ibid.

158. St. John, 173–74.

159. Ibid.

160. San C. Po, *Burma and the Karens* (London: Elliot Stock, 1928), 13.

4

Christian Karens and Buddhist Burmans under British Rule (1826–1940)

Now to us Karens God has given books and teachers, and now we too have schools and school-houses, all our own. Therefore, it is well if we rejoice with exceeding great joy; and now let us erect a National Banner, as other book nations have done. Let us erect it over our school-houses, and let us choose for our emblem, not a lion or any beast, but the weapon which God has given us by which to subdue our enemies—even the "WORD OF GOD, which is the SWORD OF THE SPIRIT."[1]

Christianity and the Seeds of Karen Nationalism

The opening passage is from a letter by Saw Quala, originally published in *The Star*, a monthly Karen-language paper. It was initially addressed to "all the churches in Tavoy, Maulmain, Rangoon, Bassein, Henthada, Kyoukyee, Shwagyn, Toungoo, Prome, Thayet."[2] But the letter was announced to the world when the *New York World* of August 8, 1860, reported, "This strange, wild people are being rapidly Christianized, and they have sent to America for a national flag to commemorate their exodus out of heathenism! The most curious and exhilarating request that we have ever heard of from a nation."[3] *The New York World* reported the entire ceremony detailing the "Letter of Quala, the Second Karen Apostle,"[4] the proposal, and the recognition of the Karen national identity plus a description of the flag.[5]

The commendation of the Karens as a "nation" in the *New York World* elevated the Karens' status from local to global recognition. It is appropriate to recall a statement of Mr. Edwin Rowlands: "Missions have 'made' the Karens,—called a 'nation' into being, giving them a place in the sun!"[6] Without doubt, the Karen national consciousness came through the churches and the education initiated by the American Baptist missionaries.

Through this manifestation of a nation with a national flag, the solidarity of Karendom was complete. Intentionally or not, Saw Quala sowed the first seed of Karen nationalism and made himself the first activist of the Karen nationalist movement. Saw Quala said in his letter that God has given the Karens books, teachers, schools, and that "now let us erect a National Banner."

The seeds of Karen nationalism that Rev. Saw Quala planted grew to fruition under the next generation of Karen leaders who received their education from the Karen Baptist Christian schools. As mentioned previously, before 1860 several Karens had studied in America.[7] Among these, T. Thanbyah from Rangoon was the first to graduate with a bachelor of arts degree in 1871, followed by Myat San Po Khway from Bassein and Ka Hser from Shwegyin in 1872.[8] By the end of 1875, an additional nine Karens graduated from American universities, including two medical doctors and one lawyer.[9] The first three Karen graduates from the United States joined in the work of the mission instead of taking government positions that were available to them at that time.

T. Thanbyah was born in Kangyidaung village, Bassein, in 1842. He first studied in the Kyuta village school, then at the Vinton School in Rangoon before continuing at the government high school. In 1865, he went to the United States for further studies and obtained a master of arts from Rochester University in 1871. He returned to Rochester University in 1874 to study theology, during which time he earned a second master's degree and was ordained as a pastor. On his return to Burma, Rev. Thanbyah served as a teacher at the Baptist College in Rangoon, Ko Tha Byu School in Bassein, and Vinton School in Rangoon. He was conferred an honorary doctor of divinity by Rochester University.[10] He authored twenty-five books in the Karen language[11]—one of the primary sources in writing this history.

Similarly, Myat San Po Kway studied first in Vinton School, and then Ko Tha Byu School, before he went to study at Colgate University in the United States. After he obtained his bachelor of arts degree, he studied theology at Crozer Theological Seminary and returned to Burma in 1874. He served as a teacher, first at Vinton School and then at Ko Tha Byu School for twenty years, after which he became a pastor in Bassein until his death. He was conferred an honorary doctor of divinity by Colgate University. Like Rev. T. Thanbyah, he also wrote many books and was one of three who started the *Dawkalu* newspaper, serving as editor for many years.

Ka Hser was the third Karen who graduated from schools in the United States. He obtained his bachelor of arts degree from Colgate

University in 1872, and after returning home, he served as a missionary in Shwegyin until his death.[12]

By the end of the nineteenth century, many Karens who received their education from the Karen Baptist Christian schools joined the ranks of the British government, with several moving up to become members of parliament. Among them was Dr. San C. Po, the first to be appointed to a seat in the Burma legislative council in 1916,[13] and who later became known as the father of the Karen nation. He was a product of Ko Tha Byu Baptist Christian School in Bassein, and from there his missionary teacher, Dr. Charles Nichols, sent him to the United States where he obtained his medical degree from Albany Medical College in 1893. He was given citizenship in the United States in 1886, but surrendered it after he returned to Burma.

When he returned to his native land he practiced medicine, but his concern for and involvement in Karen national affairs changed his career from a medical doctor to a political leader. He received the Delhi Durbar Medal in 1919, followed by even more awards from His Majesty, specifically the Commander of the British Empire (CBE, 1925–1926). In 1933, Dr. Po was given the title Knight Bachelor of the King Emperor, alias Sir, in recognition of his service to the British colonial government. After Burma was separated from India in 1937, and as the Senate and House of Representatives were established, he was nominated a senator and was made an honorary major of the 11th Burma Rifles. Like all other educated Christian Karens of his time, he was committed to his Christian faith. For that, he was elected at Ohngyaung in 1933 Layman Missionary in Charge at the Bassein-Myaungmya Karen Baptist Churches.[14]

Another outstanding Karen Christian leader from the same period was U San Baw, who received his early education from the Karen Tharrawaddy Baptist mission school, run by an American missionary, Sarah "Sally" Higby. Later, he attended the Baptist College in Rangoon (Judson College) and, after graduation, returned as a teacher and headmaster for twenty years. He also led evangelical work among the Tharrawaddy Karens while serving as the executive secretary of the Tharrawaddy Karen Association in the 1930s.[15] When U San Baw ran for the legislature, his opponent was a Buddhist lawyer with the slogan: "Fellow Buddhists, vote for one of your own race and religion. Don't vote for a Christian Karen." And yet, U San Baw won the election.[16] For his outstanding services, U San Baw received two awards from the British government: the Kaiser i Hind (KIH) in 1900 and the OBE in 1933.[17]

These Karen Christian leaders, and many others who received their education from Karen Baptist Christian schools, continued to enthuse the Karen nationalist aspiration that Rev. Saw Quala had prompted in 1860. As a result, the Karen nationalist movement gained momentum in the early twentieth century under British rule.

The First Karen National Association: KNA or Daw Kalu

Lower Burma came under British rule after 1852, and Christian Karen schools began to thrive under the Union Jack. This combination greatly contributed to the rise of a Karen national consciousness. Gatherings of Karen Christian churches at annual meetings and conventions allowed leaders to develop their ideas for building Karen national identity. Following in Rev. Saw Quala's footsteps, another pair of Karen Christian ordained pastors became exceptionally active in developing Karen solidarity, which would become their legacy for Karen nationalism. Rev. T. Thanbyah and Rev. Saw Tay formed in 1881 the first Karen national organization: Karen National Association (KNA) or Daw Kalu (meaning "the whole race" in the Karen language).

Upper Burma was still controlled by the Burmese king, while lower Burma was under the charge of the British viceroy stationed in India. In December 1880, Rev. T. Thanbyah and Rev. Saw Tay heard news of an impending visit by the British viceroy from India. They planned to meet the viceroy and propose to him the recognition of the Karens as a group of people, who then numbered around four hundred thousand. Just before the viceroy's arrival in Rangoon, they went to the office of the British governor, Major Poole. They asked permission for a choir of Karen students to gather and welcome the viceroy. Rev. T. Thanbyah authored a letter thanking the British government for the protection accorded to them under British rule of law and order.[18] On his arrival, the viceroy and his coach stopped in front of the Karen gathering and listened as the choir sang in his honor. When the Karen leaders presented their letter, the viceroy accepted it with a nod. The following day, Rev. T. Thanbyah was given an audience, which inspired him to organize the Karen National Association.

The KNA's original objectives were to unify the Karens of all different clans, Christians and non-Christians; to promote Karen identity, leadership, education, and literature, and to bring about the social and economic development of the Karens.[19] The newly formed KNA's executive members were T. Thanbyah (president); Rev. Saw Tay (vice president); U Shwe Maung Ohn (treasurer); Saw Loo Ni (secretary); Ko Ei Keh; Ko Tha Taw; Thra Shwe Nu; Thra Mya Meh; and U San Lone. After T. Thanbyah, the Karen leaders who served as president of the

KNA were Dr. Myat San Po Kway; Dr. Durmay Po Min; Dr. San C. Po; Saw Pah Dwai; Saw San Baw; and Saw Ba Maung.[20]

Noticeably, the KNA leaders were all S'gaw Karen Christians. Its executive members were ordained pastors, lay missionaries, or educators. In every Karen Christian community, the leader was the pastor, who was also the teacher and educator upholding the moral standard of the community. Trust in his leadership often made him responsible for selling the community's paddy, hiring oxen and coolies, executing estates, acting as judge in local disputes, and keeping records of rental contracts.[21] Karen leaders revered American missionaries for transforming their culture from illiterate to literate, uneducated to educated, and from rural to urban. Although KNA leaders were all Karen Christians, their goal was to bring about the social and economic advancement of all Karen peoples, regardless of religion and location. In the words of Donald Mackenzie Smeaton, acting chief commissioner of British India in 1896:

> A National Karen Association was founded as representative of all the clans, Christian and heathen, with the avowed object of keeping the nation together in the march of progress; of allowing all Karens, without distinction of belief, to meet on a common platform. . . . far from any separatist tendencies showing themselves, the enlightened Christian party—which is the party of progress—is daily evincing a keener desire to preserve the national unity and elevate the entire race.[22]

Unifying the Karens under the KNA umbrella, with its objectives to promote Karen identity and leadership, was instrumental in shaping the Karen political journey. The Karen nation-building process based on Christianity could be a simple political development under British rule. Or, like all other colonial subjects in other parts of the world who challenged colonial deposition, Karens could fight the British for the rights of self-determination and to build the Karen nation. On the contrary, regarding the British as their protector, Karens had no desire to oppose the British. They appreciated the security provided by the British military, plus the policy of the British government, which gave grants-in-aid to qualified private schools, thus allowing hundreds of Christian schools in the Karen areas.

Numerous records reveal Karens' deep appreciation for the British along with their teachers, the American missionaries. In the words of Sir San C. Po, "The Karens were not ashamed or afraid to proclaim to the world publicly or in private that . . . they owe what progress and advancement they have made, to the missionaries whom they affection-ately called their 'mother' under the protection of the British Govern-ment whom they rightly called their 'Father.'"[23]

General Smith Dun, the first commander-in-chief of independent Burma's armed forces until the Karen insurrection of 1949, also ex-pressed gratitude, saying the arrival of the missionaries and the Brit-ish for the Karens was "a fulfillment of their long-cherished hopes and expectations of the 'Young White Brothers' return to give them succor from oppression."[24] Visibly, the Karens were energized by their libera-tors' coming, the missionaries and the British, and there was almost no resistance to British rule.

If the British were liberators, who did the Karens consider as their oppressors? Who were they challenged to fight for their freedom? In the words of Sir Dr. San C. Po:

> The position of the Karens before the advent of the British was that of a subject race in true oriental fashion. They were treated as slaves, hence they made their homes on the mountain side or on tracts of land far away from the towns and larger villages occupied by the Burmans. High stockades surrounded those Karen villages, and sure death was the fate of all intruders.
>
> Many stories have been told of Burmese cruelty to the Karens, and the Karen retaliation, in which the latter figured more as sinners than saints. Love of independence is inherent in all hill tribes, and the Karens are no exception.[25]

How bad were the Burmans to their Karen neighbors? Or did the Ka-rens exaggerate their woes? For a fair and balanced assessment of the relationships, it is crucial to look back into the historical past before taking a run forward—the past far, far before the arrival of their so-called white brothers, the missionaries and the British.

Relations between the Karens and the Burmans Prior to British Occupation

The Karen scholar Saw Hanson Tadaw commented that not all the Karen groups had the same political history. Different Karen groups had different political experiences with the rulers of Burma, based on their geographical location and physical environment.[26] Prior to Brit-ish occupation, Burma experienced a series of political changes under different kingdoms built by the Mons, Burmans, Arakanese, and Shan.

Historians agree that the Mons established the first notable Buddhist kingdom in the Thaton area until king Anawratha of Bagan took over their empire in 1067.

The Bagan dynasty, the first Burmese kingdom, prospered from the eleventh to the thirteenth centuries. After the Bagan empire collapsed, Burma went through a series of wars under several different rulers. From the sixteenth century, the Burmese kingdom, with its capital in Toungoo, and the Mon kingdom, with its capital in Pegu, were fighting with each other until king Alaungpaya conquered and founded the Konbaung dynasty in the 1750s. A Burmese source claimed that there was a Karen kingdom, the Gwe, in the eighteenth century.[27] The British annexed the last Burmese kingdom, the Konbaung dynasty, in three stages of war: the first in 1824–1826, the second in 1852, and finally in 1884–1885 when its last king was dethroned.

Based on the political structure of the ruler, the Karen people living in different areas of Burma had different life experiences. Among the many different Karen tribes, the S'gaw, Pwo, and Bwe (or *Bghai*) were the most numerous. The first enumeration of all the Karens in British Burma, taken in 1911, showed a Karen population of 1,102,695, out of which 872,825 were S'gaw and Pwo.[28] It is believed that the Pwo were the first Karen settlers, who migrated from southern China and made their homes in areas where the first Mon kingdom was established.[29] The S'gaw Karen groups, who lived mostly on the plains of lower Burma, remained more or less under Burmese or Mon rule until the British seized Burma. The Bwe group, living within the isolated and difficult terrain of the Toungoo and Karenni hills and far from the old capitals of Burma,[30] not only defended themselves against outside invasion but also were aided by the difficult terrain to retreat safely after their raids into the Burman areas. On the other hand, the S'gaw and the Pwo groups living on the plains of lower Burma had to take refuge in the forests, which were physically not as effective a defense as the highlands and therefore were not able to avoid being subjected by their neighbors.[31] According to a report, more than 631,000 Karens lived in the districts of Amherst, Thaton, Bassein, Myaungmya, and Ma-ubin in 1930.[32]

During the period of the Mon kings, the Karens were considered the ruled and the Mon were the ruler. Hanson Tadaw opined that the absence of animosity between the Karens and the Mons gave the impression that Karens were not ill-treated or suppressed by Mon rulers.[33] A Karen history book written in Burmese further claimed that there was a Karen king who had good relations with the Mon kingdom and joined the Mons in fighting against the Burmese kings.[34]

Under the Burmese king's administrative system, residents of towns or villages were divided according to the service they had to undertake.[35] The Burmese kings assumed the title of "ruler of the Karens, and the Sgaw and Pwo were the subjects of the rulers."[36] During that period, the Karens never organized politically beyond the village level. Leadership in a Karen village was based on the person who asserted authority and leadership, which could be lost in a challenge or passed on at death to a son or nephew. In some cases, the village would be split due to the emergence of a contender, and each leader would take their followers away to build a new community.[37] The Karens were usually termed "slaves of the land," since they were assigned to till the fields and were not called up for military duty or to work in other public services. But in emergencies, the Karens were forced into hard labor, carrying food for soldiers, building roads, and working on various other construction projects.[38]

One scholar in the field of Burman people groups states, "The minority that suffered most in the hands of the Burmans and was afforded the least opportunity to intermarry and associate with them was the Karen."[39] The Karens were treated differently under various Burmese rulers. In 1632, when the Burmese king Thalun Min Tayagyi reorganized the administration of revenue, the five Karen districts were treated separately from the native Mon population of Hanthawaddy Pegu.[40] The Burmese court taxation system also treated the Karens as a separate category. The hill Karens, who worked the teak forests, had to pay a 10 percent tax, which was remitted after paying a 5 percent tax to the local officials. The Burmans taxed the hill Karens fifteen rupees per family per year, which meant per longhouse. The Karens who grew rice in the plains areas were taxed eighteen rupees per yoke of buffalo per year.[41]

It was claimed that the actual tax levied on the Karens was not high but was increased by the collection charges, which might amount to as much as 80 percent of the original assessment. An additional tax in kind such as wax, ivory, or other products, might be given to the king. It is estimated that the rate of assessment per head on the Karens was about double that of the more civilized Burmans and Talaings (Mons). Unlike the Burmans or Mons, Karens were not subjected to extraordinary contributions to the crown. Yet, it is obvious that the tax burden on the Karens was heavy.[42]

Under the Burmese kings, the Karens were the major food producers for the population living in Burma. Little or no cultivation was found by the earliest British envoys around the Burman and Mon settlements on the banks of the rivers, implying they depended entirely on the produce of Karens living in the interior locations.[43] Inhabitants of big villages and towns, such as Rangoon and Pegu, also relied heavily on Karen cultivation. Even in the late eighteenth century, Karens residing on the plains and near the Burman settlements were engaged in agriculture to supply food to their more "advanced" neighbors, the Burmese, the Thai, and the Mons.[44] An official's record of 1826 stated that the Karens "supply the markets with ivory, wax, honey, sesame oil, cardamoms, and other articles."[45]

In peacetime, the agricultural dependence on the Karens would not be so critical. But in times of civil strife and external war, most male Burmans were called up for military duties. Sometimes even Karens were called up for minor duties, making it difficult for them to fulfill their obligations of supplying food to the Burman population.[46] In addition, without any Karen official representative, Karens were unable to appeal their complaints directly to the Burmese kings. If local officers were oppressive, Karens could do nothing but find a new place to hide. They moved into the hills or remote areas of the plain and delta to avoid forced labor, high taxation, and other persecution. Naturally, the Karens felt they were victims of the oppressive Burmans. This sentiment would be intensified during the three Anglo-Burmese wars beginning in 1824.

British Annexation and the Growing Karen-Burman Conflict

The experience of persecution and slavery forced Karens to remain in remote areas in anticipation of any force that would help free them from their persecutors. Even before they met the American Christian missionaries, Karens supported the British troops during the first Anglo-Burmese war (1824–1826). In his record of that war, a British officer, Major Snodgrass, recorded the good services of the Karens in their campaign against the kingdom of Ava.[47] After the death of the Burmese General Maha Bandula in April 1825, Karens and Mons joined in active assistance to the British in supplying food, labor, and guide services before the British captured Rangoon.[48] The Yandabo treaty was crafted in 1826 with the aid of Adoniram Judson, bringing peace to the Karens living in the Arakan and Tenasserim areas, which came under British rule. But more hardship was experienced by those living in Pegu and other provinces, which were still under the Ava court's jurisdiction. Punishment of Karens for their collaboration with the British began when the British negotiator, John Crawford, withdrew from Rangoon. Burmese troops destroyed both the Mon and Karen villages, and the captives were either killed or carried away as slaves.[49]

Mass conversions to Christianity, which began in the 1830s, became another reason for the Burmans' growing hatred for the Karens. Under American Baptist missionary teachers' leadership, the Karens became so advanced they joined literate civilizations with schools and books. The Burmans attempted to hinder the Karens' progress by preventing them from visiting their missionary teachers. As late as 1851, the Burmese viceroy threatened to shoot any Karen who was able to read.[50] The Burmese authorities used force, which included torturing the Karens and burning their villages. Statements like "the first persecution waged fiercely; the converts were beaten, chained, fined, imprisoned, sold as slaves, tortured, and put to death" appeared in various records.[51] Eventually, the Karens came to believe that to be free from such torments and discrimination, they must be removed from the Burmese monarchy. Their only resort was to assist the British, who came to take over the territory.

Ironically, British policy until that period was not in favor of the Karens, who looked upon the British as their liberators. According to records, in 1844, the Karens in the delta made an ardent plea to the British commissioner in Moulmein for protection from the Burmese. Since Burma had been annexed to the Indian colony, the British office in Calcutta warned their agents in Tenasserim not to get involved in any plans for a Karen uprising against Burmese authority.[52]

The further the British advanced into the heartland of Burma, the greater the hostility grew between the Karens and the Burmans. During the second Anglo-Burmese war in 1852, the Karens assisted the British by launching attacks on Rangoon and capturing Shwedagon Pagoda. Burmese troops withdrew but made a full swing of retaliation against the Karens. They burned all Karen villages within fifty miles of Rangoon, seizing or destroying stocks of rice and killing men, women, and children in barbarous ways.[53] A serious refugee problem developed in Rangoon and Bassein, when large numbers of Karens flooded into the British-held areas for protection. The British officer in command, General Henry T. Godwin, initially refused to take responsibility for protecting these refugees without specific instructions from Calcutta.[54] Relief activities for Karens in the Kemmendine quarter of Rangoon and Bassein were initiated by American Baptist missionaries. Although they had only native arrows, spears, swords, and some limited supplies from the British army, the Karens, under the leadership of Dr. Justus Vinton in Rangoon and Dr. Charles Nichols in Bassein, helped suppress the anti-British forces.[55] The situation pushed the Karens to rely even more on the missionaries, who extended their leadership and protection in times of danger.

Between the second and third Anglo-Burmese wars, the Karens actively captured rebels and robbers for the British. Some of these rebels were former Burmese court officials (*wuns, myo-thu-gyis*) and Buddhist monks (*pongyis*). In May 1852, British troops, led by Captain Nibbett and Captain Brooking, had difficulty capturing a Burmese deputy, Myat Htoon, who had turned into a bandit chief. While he and his seven thousand male followers were roaming, killing, and burning in Danuphyu, Zaloon, and other villages, another bandit leader, Shway Ban, was also plundering and murdering in Rangoon and Dalla region. A Karen chieftain, Myat Za, came to British officers in Rangoon in November and asked assistance to repel Shway Ban. A British officer commended the action of this Karen chief as follows: "So collecting about seven hundred men of his tribe, he armed them after the fashion of the country, and soon captured upwards of thirty robbers, three of whom he executed on the spot, and sent in the rest to Rangoon. It is pleasant to record such energy on the part of a Karen chief."[56]

The third Anglo-Burmese war of 1884–1885 ended with the British occupation of the capital city Mandalay and the abdication of King Thibaw. The removal of their king infuriated the Burmans because it meant the loss of their national religion. Donald Mackenzie Smeaton, the British finance commissioner in lower Burma from 1879 to 1884, reported, "The Burman cannot conceive of a religion without a defender of the Faith—a king who appoints rulers of the Buddhist hierarchy. The extinction of the monarchy left the nation, according to the people's notions, without a religion."[57] He then admitted, "We have to govern a turbulent people inhabiting a vast territory of hills and plains, forests, jungle, and swamp, impassable to troops during more than half the year."[58]

The uprising against the British was more aggressive and extensive than the aftermath of the previous two wars. Dr. Maung Maung stated, "The Burmese armies had broken up and melted into the jungle where they formed bands of guerrillas and harassed the British troops."[59] The anti-British movements were led by former princes, court officials, and Buddhist monks. As in the past, Karen villages became battlegrounds, and under the leadership of their teachers, the Christian missionaries, they started to fight these insurgencies. In a letter dated May 15, 1886, American Baptist missionary J. (Justus) Vinton described the political turmoil that compelled the Karens to fight in defense of their homes and villages in the Toungoo area without receiving any support from the British.

> I have been driven to my wits' end to protect my villages. I have been dacoit-hunting literally all the time, and paying my own expenses.... I

have succeeded in protecting my villages. You may judge of the encouragement our Karens have received by the fact that three Karens have been arrested for murder, and two actually tried. Their only crime was that they had bravely defended themselves and villages when attacked. The cowardly and disloyal Burmese police have not pulled a trigger, but they do their best to discourage the only loyal and brave men in the province.[60]

According to Rev. Vinton, the rebels were mostly upcountry Burmans, except for one uprising by the Shans at Shwegyin. The leaders were Mayankhyoung and Kyouk-kalat pongyis (Buddhist monks). They attacked Shwegyin and defeated the British detachment under Major Robinson. In his letter, Rev. Vinton described how these rebels attacked the Karen Christian villages and how the Karens resisted these attacks with their archaic weapons and captured the leader of the rebels:

The Buddhist priests have headed everywhere, and actually fought themselves—a thing unprecedented in history. . . . They were at first far too strong to be attacked by the Karens in their head-quarters. The Karens, therefore, confined themselves to cutting off their foraging-parties. They had, of course, few guns, and the Government would give them none, . . .

The rebels burst like a torrent on our poor Christian villages. The fighting was hard everywhere. I can note but one case. The village of Tha-ay-kee was attacked on Sunday, while the people were all assembled at the service in the chapel.

The Karens had no arms, but still the dacoits dare not attack them in the chapel, but merely surrounded them, while a few looted the village. The moment the dacoit left, the whole village rushed out and picked up the few guns they had hidden in the bushes while they went to church, and pushed off in pursuit, picking up recruits from the neighboring villages.

They fell into an ambush, and their pastor and several of their party were shot dead. Though numbered three to one, the Karens rallied, and infuriated by the death of their pastor, they flew at the dacoits and dispersed them. . . . Finally, the whole rebellion was surrounded in the Kaw-me-kho valley, near the foot of the great range east of Toungoo.

The Karens had few guns in their hands, but mostly used spears, shields, and bows. . . . I got fifty smooth-bores from Mr. Bernard [the British commissioner]. . . . the guns were handed over to the Karens. In thirty-six hours they were on the field, and . . . the Mayankhyoung poongyee was taken.[61]

Other American missionaries living in Karen villages, like Dr. Vinton, rendered their leadership in fighting Burmans who attacked the villages. Dr. Bunker was the hero in the pursuit of the Mayankyoung pongyi in Toungoo.[62] About the same period, under the leadership of a British officer, a group of Karens helped crush another strong anti-British group led by the Minbu leader Oktama.[63]

Due to their courageous work in organizing troops and collecting arms from the British, many Karen villages eventually received protection. But from the Burman perspective, challenging Burmese court officials and killing Buddhist monks, in cooperation with the American missionaries, was an act of betrayal. The Karens deserved punishment for their unforgivable crime.

Yet, the British authority was reluctant to acknowledge the effectiveness of the Karen troops. Despite the Burmans' resentment toward the Karens for their participation in suppressing the anti-British troops, "Mr. Bernard [the British commissioner] thought the Karens cowards to be so easily frightened."[64] A British memorandum on July 8, 1886, clearly demonstrated the British reluctance to supply arms to the Karens and proposed increased stringency to enforce the Arms Act. In response, Dr. Vinton appealed to the British government emphasizing that the Burmese officials would use the memorandum to disarm and harass loyal Karens. He pleaded: "I respectfully submit that the universal loyalty of the Karens, heathen as well as Christian, has earned for them a special exemption by name from the operation of this memorandum."[65] Unfortunately, his petition was not heard. The frustration of Dr. Vinton at the end of the third Anglo-Burmese war was visible in his letter of August 24, 1886: "Karens are ordered all over the country to hand in their arms to Burmese officials."[66]

Evidently, making Karens one of the most favored people in Burma was not in the British political agenda. Smeaton witnessed the bravery and sacrifices of the Karen levies (locally recruited troops) under Dr. Vinton, Rev. Bunker, and Dr. Nichols and made the following report: "Dr. Vinton's feelings may have been embittered by the coldness of the authorities towards his people. . . . It is high time that the British people lent their ear to the plight of the Karens and redressed the wrong done to them by listlessness and neglect of our own government."[67]

Furthermore, Mr. Smeaton expressed the instrumental role of the Karens in the annexation and pacification of Burma by writing in his book that "had the Karens joined the insurrection, the Queen's Government would in all probability—for a time, at least—have ceased to exist; [and that the British] invading force would have been hemmed in by an armed people fired to fierce resistance by our reverse in the south."[68]

The Burmans lived peacefully and prospered for thirty years under British rule yet joined guerrilla warfare against British troops as they advanced north in 1884–1885. Smeaton validated that the Karens were "at heart true to the British Government; the Burmese are not."[69] He advised the British government to give the Karens "every facility for developing a national civilization and a national religion."[70] Smeaton was the first British high-level official to acknowledge the Karen loyalty to the British and wholeheartedly supported Karen nationalism.

Though lacking the British commissioner's support, under the leadership of their American missionaries, Karens continued to fight insurgents and robbers. For the Karens, backing the British in the pacification of Burma was protection for their communities. Following the leadership of the Christian missionaries and the British officials, however, alienated the Karens from the Buddhist Burmans.

The Karen Peoples' Privilege in the New British Province

In January 1886, the British declared Burma a province of India and eventually divided Burma into two parts: Ministerial Burma in the plains and the frontier, and the scheduled areas in the mountains. Ministerial Burma was governed directly by the British (Indian civil service officers), covering all of lower Burma and most of upper Burma, a territory largely inhabited by the majority Burmans. The scheduled areas were under Burma frontier service officers and excluded from British direct rule. The areas comprised the hilly regions inhabited by Shan, Kachin, Chin, Arakanese, Mons, and Karens.[71]

The rebel movement, however, was active in every district, so Indian troops and Indian police were brought in to help quell the rebellions. In March 1887, Commissioner Bernard retired, and Sir Charles Crosthwaite assumed the task of pacification.[72] After peace was restored, the first significant political change occurred in 1897 when a new law was enacted that elevated the chief executive officer from chief commissioner to lieutenant governor. Additionally, a nine-member legislative council was created of which four were officials and five were nominated non-officials.[73] Following the reorganization, the British government introduced a series of administrative and political changes.

Before any political reforms were developed, British authorities reorganized the armed forces by ethnic composition. Few Burmans enlisted, and the new units of the first army and police forces were almost exclusively from minority and alien segments of the population who were loyal to the crown. The new army followed the Indian pattern of organization, "and the military tradition was of close identification of the soldier with his tribe or community rather than with the nation at large."[74] During the third Anglo-Burmese war, some Karen units were raised by the missionaries and British officers, but they were not given adequate recognition. After Sir Charles Crosthwaite became the new commissioner of Burma in 1887, he acknowledged the Karens' loyal service and encouraged the recruitment of Karens into the new military. In his memoir, he stated, "The Karens in Lower Burma were loyal and generally staunch, especially, the Christian Karens." He added that the "American Baptist missionaries have done an inestimable service to the Karen race" and made the Karens "useful and orderly members of society" by teaching them "discipline and obedience." He went further in saying that "the Government of Burma owes a debt to the American Baptist Mission which should not be forgotten."[75]

During 1887–1888, a selected Karen levy of a hundred men was used effectively in upper Burma. Thereafter, Karens were recruited in large numbers into the newly formed military police and the army. By 1890, Karens made up three-quarters of the indigenous military forces. In recognition of their loyal service, the Karens were brought into the ranks of the military, the police, and the bureaucracy of the British colonial government.[76]

Meanwhile, the Karen National Association's leadership role and objectives took various forms according to the safety of its people. In addition to strictly following its main objectives, the KNA became involved in military activities. It recruited soldiers, procured arms and ammunition, and fought anti-British troops in Karen villages. The KNA's leadership in recruiting soldiers for the British did not stop with Burma's pacification. It went further and defended the British Empire during World War I. As the situation required, the government of India expanded the Indian Army, and four battalions of Burma Rifles were formed for general service. Non-commissioned officers were drawn from military police, and recruits came mostly straight from native villages. The record has it that "Karens provided the largest elements."[77]

In 1912, serving as the Bassein Municipal Commissioner, Dr. San C. Po was also an honorary recruiter of the Burma Rifles.[78] In his second book, compiled by his granddaughter, Dr. San C. Po described the story of two Karen soldiers from Bassein, one from Kozu village, and the other from Tatszin Kyung village, who were killed as they crossed the river Tigris in Mesopotamia.[79] In appreciation to the loyal service and in recognition of the Karen soldiers' bravery, a British official, A. G. Campagnac, made this note: "In Mesopotamia the Karen contingent did yeoman service, and the first man shot dead on that field was a Karen youth of Kozu. Loyalty to the British Raj is ingrained in their very constitution, and fidelity to the King-Emperor is a duty, sacred and religious."[80]

During World War I, the British policy that banned Burmans from its armed forces was altered, and the Burmans were recruited along with Karens and other minorities in Burma. Unfortunately, after the war, the number of Burma Rifle battalions was reduced to three. Recruitment of Burmese was terminated in 1925.[81] For Burmans, denial of an official role while minorities were drawn into the ranks of the military and police was an insult. One scholar opined, "By opening the armed forces to the minority peoples and barring them to the Burmese, it fostered racial antagonism and subverted the internal balance of power, rendering it unstable."[82] Indeed, it infuriated the Burmans to see their traditionally subordinate Karens in positions of military authority. This ill feeling toward the Karens developed during the 1920s and 1930s, as the British gave Karen leaders equal opportunity to actively participate and claim their national aspirations and political rights.

British Reforms and the Rise of Karen Political Leaders

Until the end of the nineteenth century, the Karen National Association was the only well-organized indigenous organization that was morphing from a cultural to a political organization. The social and economic growth of the Karens under British rule helped the KNA's objectives in bridging the gap between Christian and non-Christian Karens and between the Karen linguistic divisions. In addition, rapid educational progress under Christian missionaries that generated Karen nationalism and political awareness made the KNA leadership stronger and helped the KNA to become the most respected organization among the Karens. Considering the British as their liberators from the oppressive Burmese, it was unnecessary for the Karens to challenge British rule. Without any powerful Burmese nationalist party, the Karen anxiety over being subjected to majority Burman rule faded, and the Karen nationalist movement adopted a gradual process under KNA leadership.

According to one Burmese historian, the absence of a Burmese nationalist movement until around World War I yielded negative results. He reported, "People had lost heart and strong national leaders were not forthcoming," and the "British rule . . . was not manifestly oppressive."[83] The first Burman national organization, the Young Men's Buddhist Association (YMBA), in the pattern of the Christian YMCA, was formed in 1906 by a group of western-educated young men.[84] Its annual meetings opened with the British national anthem and with cheers and prayers including, "God save the King," although the YMBA later changed the lyrics to "Buddha save the King." Until 1917, the YMBA leaders made speeches of appreciation and gratitude to the British rulers such as, "We the delegates of YMBA in the districts are loyal subjects of the Majesties. We speak English and appreciate the western way of life. We consider it a privilege and an honor to serve our rulers."[85]

The YMBA founders were western-trained politicians who worked with the government through peaceful negotiation. Its initial aims were more cultural than political, like that of the KNA. Its early movements focused on the fostering of their Buddhist religion, endorsing education, and the social requirements of the people.[86] Although YMBA expressed the Burmese nationalist sentiment through the prism of the Buddhist religion, no extreme religious or nationalist activities challenged the British government. Remarkably, no serious clashes between the leaders of the KNA and the YMBA occurred in this period of peaceful coexistence.

Rev. Henry Marshall, a second-generation American missionary in Burma, claimed that by embracing traditional American Baptist principles of complete separation of church and state, missionaries in Burma took no part in controlling Karen nationalist leaders. Marshall ascertained that the future of the Karens lay "not as a separate people, living apart and seeking special advantages for themselves will they make the most progress; but, forgetting racial feelings as far as possible and throwing themselves into the life of the land in which they find themselves and adding their quota to the general good, they will not only raise themselves, but also the level of the common life which they must share with their neighbors."[87]

The focus of the KNA, the only well-organized indigenous organization in Burma at that period, was the promotion of Karen religious and educational interests. Community leaders made full efforts to keep peace and harmony. The Karens even opened the doors for non-Karen and non-Christian students to attend their college and schools, which were initially intended only for the Karens.

Burma was the largest province of British India under the governor general in New Delhi and was politically stable until World War I. The security brought by the new British administration encouraged rural and hill Karens to move into the plains and delta areas, living peacefully side by side with the Burmese. Nevertheless, some Karens still lived in fear of resubjugation and of Burman control. San C. Po observed that the Karens historically do not believe the Burmans and the customary Burmese view concerning the poor, inferior Karens.[88] Indeed, their suspicion was transformed into tense conflict when the Karen nationalist movement gained momentum, and KNA leaders started to challenge the Burman nationalists, as the British introduced a series of political reforms for Burma.

The clash began with the 1909 Morley-Minto reforms for India. As a province of India, these reforms also applied to Burma. For that purpose, the Burma lieutenant governor's legislative council was enlarged with special political representation for economic and political interests through the creation of special and restricted electorates. When the legislative council was expanded from seventeen to nineteen members in 1915, Dr. San C. Po became one of its new members, the first Karen in recorded history to achieve the highest political position under British rule.

The Karens and Burmans became increasingly divided in their reaction to the next set of reforms, specifically the Montagu-Chelmsford reforms. Edwin S. Montagu, secretary of state for India, issued a policy statement on August 20, 1917. It stated that the British government's policy was "that of the increasing association of Indians in every branch of the administration" and to develop "self-governing institutions, with a view to the progressive realization of responsible government in India as an integral part of the British Empire."[89] Representatives were invited to talk with Secretary Montagu and Viceroy Chelmsford in India, where the topic was to be more self-governing institutions. In December 1917, delegations were sent to Calcutta, India, from the YMBA, the KNA, and a few other organizations. The Karen delegation included Dr. San C. Po, Sydney Loo Ni, and Ya Ba (as advisor). In his memoirs, Dr. San C. Po recalled that they went to India "to discuss the Reform Scheme with the Rt. Hon. Edwin Montague, M.P. and the Viceroy Lord Chelmsford in Calcutta," with the following goal: "Our [Karen] aim was to have a share in whatever came to Burma, while there were two distinct groups among the Burmese delegates. . . . the younger members, including Mr. May Oung, wanted something like a complete Home Rule or a dominion status, while the older group, including U Ba Tu, U Thin and U Po Tha would be satisfied with a gradual granting of a Democratic Constitution for Burma."[90]

In records of his encounters with the British leaders, San C. Po said his impression of Mr. Montagu was that "he was ready to grant a great deal of democratic and constitutional rights to India and Burma and he took considerable pains to elicit the conditions and positions as they were and was trying to get a definite decision," and that "Lord Chelmsford was not too patient with the members."[91] After their return to Burma, Thra Yaba Hto Lo and Dr. San C. Po called a meeting and gave a presentation at Vinton Memorial Hall, where the Karens anxiously waited for the news. Later, the Karens sent the following memorial to the secretary of state:

> Looking at the progress made by the people of Burma in all points, we, the Karens of Burma, are sensible that the country is not yet in a fit state for self-government. Burma is inhabited by many different races, differing in states of civilization, differing in religion and social development; hence Burma will have still to undergo many years of strenuous training under British governance before this boon can be conferred on it with security and success. From what have transpired in the past when injustice and despotism reigned supreme, the Karens of Burma do not clamor and agitate for the fruition of questionable privileges and the ushering in of dubious political eras. The history of our province indicates that it is in the state of transition still and yet the benefits of free government are not quite fully appreciated.[92]

The Karens' reaction to the Montagu-Chelmsford reforms antagonized the Burmese nationalists, who proposed that Burma be separated from India and the foundation laid for a democratic government under British tutelage. The Montagu-Chelmsford report of April 1918 included the statement that "the problem of political evolution of Burma must be left for separate and future consideration."[93] This aroused suspicion that Burma would be denied any real development toward self-rule and made the Burmans feel that the British government favored the Karens. While the reform movement to create a separate administration for Burma was pending, numerous Burmese associations were formed that included more extreme Burmese nationalists who demanded self-rule.

In 1920, YMBA changed its name to the General Council of Burmese Association (GCBA) and claimed to represent all the peoples in Burma.[94] The GCBA leadership was less westernized, more radical, more closely aligned with, and more willing to collaborate with political-minded Buddhist monks. It was the time when the people of Burma, like those in other Asian nations, were inspired by Asian nationalism resulting from the Japanese victory over Russia in the Russo-Japanese War of 1904–1905. In addition, after World War I, Woodrow Wilson's idea of self–determination widely permeated the hearts of people in Burma, encouraging them to ramp up nationalistic movements. The independence of its former rival, the Buddhist Kingdom of Siam (Thailand), reminded the Burmans of their former glory.[95] The tide of Burmese nationalism was rising.

A series of reforms followed the Montagu-Chelmsford report. Along with that, the division between the Karens and the Burmans broadened. The nationalist goals and tactics of the two groups were turning in opposite directions. The first reform, known as Craddock's scheme of 1919–1920, started with Sir Reginald Craddock, who became the governor of Burma in 1919. He was authorized to formulate a tentative scheme to separate Burma from Indian British rule. Craddock, however, made proposals and administrative schemes that were not in favor of a separate state for Burma. Instead, he proposed that Burma as a country was not ripe for a general extension of the elective principle. Craddock's proposal pressured Burmese nationalists, who were in fear of being denied the benefits promised to India. The moderate political leaders of YMBA (now the GCBA) advocated acceptance of Craddock's scheme. Younger nationalists, however, led by U Ba Pe and U Thein Maung, refused to accept it. In July 1919, a delegation led by U Pu, representing the newly organized Burma Reform League, went to London in protest of Craddock's scheme.[96] The delegation returned home in December 1919 with an assurance from Secretary Montagu that Burman opinion would be consulted before any bill affecting Burma would be brought before Parliament.[97]

Meanwhile, in early 1920, Governor Craddock was called to India for discussions. By March, a final version of the proposed reform was settled. According to the Craddock scheme, a constitution on the Indian model could not be imposed on Burma, due to the conclusion that Burma's political development was a generation behind that of India.[98] Having received news that the revised Craddock report was sent to London, the YMBA sent a delegation of three to London, where they demanded Burma's separation from India under a dyarchy (co-rule) constitution.

Like YMBA leaders, KNA leaders also changed their position when the 1920 Craddock reforms were proposed. With the possibility of a dyarchy constitution being established, they began to believe that the Karens might get better treatment if Burma became a separate state. A Karen lawyer and KNA leader, Sydney Loo Nee, submitted a criticism of the Craddock reforms in which he mentioned that the Karens, as an indigenous race second in number only to the Burmans, "should not only precede the aliens in Burma but also progress and advance step by step along with the Burmans." He further stated that the Karens, who were strong believers in the doctrine of self-help, had served bravely in the army and proved their loyalty to the British government. The Karens' interests should be protected, and their identity maintained through separate electorates and special or communal seats.[99]

In December 1920, the British government agreed to extend the Montagu-Chelmsford reforms including the dyarchy form of government to Burma. By then, the YMBA was replaced by the GCBA, whose leaders were not in favor of the negotiation strategy of Western-oriented Burmese politicians. This new generation of Burmese nationalist leaders saw the reforms of the British as a partial measure that favored minorities. They organized a strike of university students in 1920, which was the most aggressive anti-British act undertaken to that date. By collaborating with Buddhist monks, GCBA gained Burmese Buddhist mass support, forming multiple political parties and movements ranging from peaceful to violent to revolutionary.

Amid rising political tension in Burma, the British government appointed a new committee of inquiry known as the Whyte Committee to investigate political reform proposals for Burma. The Whyte Committee implementation generated another political collision between the Karen and Burman leaders. Chaired by Sir Frederick Whyte, president of the Indian Legislative Assembly, the committee included two Burmans, an Indian, and a Karen, Dr. San C. Po. The committee consisted of two members of the Burma legislative council, Dr. San C. Po and U Myint; one Burman member of the governor's council of state, U Po Bye; an Indian member of the legislative assembly, P. P. Ginwala; the British editor of the *Rangoon Gazette*, Frank McCarty; and a senior British government official, R. E. V. Arbuthnot.[100] The committee was selected with the view of enlisting public confidence, but even before Whyte's arrival in August 1921, the GCBA organized a boycott of the committee. A historian claimed, "An important factor influencing the GCBA to boycott the committee hearings, it was revealed, was the inclusion of one Karen, an Indian, and an Anglo-Indian member on the committee."[101]

During the itinerant Whyte Committee hearings in November and December 1921, the members met with strong opposition organized by the GCBA in Mandalay, Rangoon, and Moulmein. The hostility in Wakema was so obvious that even the vendors in the market refused to sell their goods. Some strikers shouted abusive words and threw firecrackers and bricks into the steamer that carried committee members from hearing to hearing. In Moulmein, under the leadership of U Chit Hlaing, strikers created problems for the committee and even disturbed a prominent Karen leader who was going to give testimony before the committee.[102]

Unlike the Burmans, the Karens welcomed the Whyte Committee. As a member of the committee, Dr. San C. Po said, "The Karens, wherever possible, welcomed the Committee, giving concerts in their honor, and the elders had personal interviews with the chairman."[103] Musical entertainments were performed at Rangoon in Vinton Memorial Hall and at the Ko Tha Buh Memorial Hall in Bassein. In Toungoo, a white elephant show was prepared for the committee by the owner, Dr. Saw Durmay Po Min. He believed in "the Karen prophecy that when three 'whites' [the Whyte Committee, the white governor, and the white elephant] meet there will be peace and plenty, progress and prosperity, and an ideal Government will reign supreme."[104] Unfortunately, due to limited time, the governor could not make it to Taungoo for the white elephant show. However, he described the welcome concert in Rangoon in these words: "The members of the Committee, and a number of high officials were invited to a Welcome Concert by elders of the Karen Community of Rangoon, Insein and vicinity. The Vinton Memorial Hall was packed to overflowing with Karens. Even the doors and windows were so jammed with people that standing-room could not be found."[105]

Dr. San C. Po reported that he received great help from the Karen elders in serving as witnesses, eliciting the Karen case, and convincing the committee. Their representation revealed their deep-seated distrust of Burman rule. Sydney Loo Nee declared that, however much the leaders of the two groups might cultivate mutual respect by cooperative effort, the Burmese absorption of the Karens was outside the range of possibility. Karen clannishness alone could, and would, preserve the group, for they knew what to expect from the return of Burman rule. Real toleration or equality was negated in practice by the superior airs of the Burman people. He wanted British rule to continue and a Briton to administer Karen educational affairs.[106]

Another Karen representative, barrister-at-law Saw Pah Dwai, who graduated with a law degree from England, was asked "if he thought the Karens were still as much as oppressed by the Burmans as in the olden days." He answered, "The Karens are to-day ten times more oppressed and downtrodden than in former days."[107] In response to the proposal of Saw Pah Dwai, an Arakan leader, U Shwe Zan said that the Karens had advanced in education and would have no trouble in electing their representatives.[108] The Burmese leader, U May Oung, opined his view by declaring that Burmans were becoming aware of the need for a broad national effort, and their willing cooperation with Karens would bridge the ethnic gap if given a little more time. Separate representation, he argued, would keep the Karens and the Burmans forever apart.[109] He argued that the Karens in every respect are like the Burmese in their habits, ideas, and characteristics and that no separate constituency was necessary.

As a Whyte Committee member, San C. Po tried to give his explanation of the differences between the Karens and the Burmans. Mr. D. F. Chalmers, the former deputy commissioner of the border district of Thaton, had many years of close contact with the Karens. He went quite extreme and said, "The man who says Karen and Burman interests are identical is either blind, ignorant, or untruthful. . . . If I were a Karen, I would fight for proper communal representation; If I could not get it I would clear out for Siam."[110] The chief secretary, Mr. F. Lewisohn, and Sir Charles Morgan Webb were "decidedly in favor of communal representations for the Karens," basing their opinion on "extensive personal experience."[111]

A Whyte Committee member, Mr. S. A. Smyth, also the commissioner of the Irrawaddy division, asked whether a Karen might be elected from a predominantly Burman district like Hanthawaddy. The reply was no. San C. Po clarified the situation with these remarks: "It is obvious to all that no Karen candidate would ever be elected since no district in the province has a Karen population anywhere near as large as that of the Burmese."[112] Consequently, British members of the Whyte Committee were convinced by the evidence that a Karen's chance at being elected in any district was extremely thin if communal representation were not established.

On the Whyte Committee's recommendation, the British parliament brought Burma within the scope of the India Act. Burma became a full governor's province under the dyarchy or dual government on January 1, 1923.[113] Dyarchy allowed Burma a substantial amount of democracy and opportunity for politicians to learn parliamentary practice. Under the new constitution, fifty-eight of the elected members of the legislative council were chosen in general constituencies. Fifteen were elected communally (eight Indians, five Karens, one Anglo-Indian, and one British), while the remaining seven represented various business groups and the university.[114] In the first election of 1922, fewer than one in fourteen of eligible voters participated in balloting, but Karen Christians participated actively. In two general constituencies, Tavoy and Tharrawaddy districts, the Karen candidates won election.[115] The success of the two elected members was due to the absence of Burmese candidates, who were preoccupied with boycotting the election.[116]

Most Burmans were unhappy with the new dyarchy government because Burma was still under British India. By this time, GCBA leaders split into three main groups, but they all opposed the dyarchy constitution and demanded self-rule or home rule. Another section, the 21 Party led by U Ba Pe, sheared off to contest the elections, while the GCBA decided to boycott the elections.[117] The term *wunthanu* or "nationalism" became popular with some who resorted to a revolutionary movement represented by the village *athins* (societies). The village *wunthanu athins* (nationalist societies), active in the Burmese non-cooperation movement of 1921–1922, developed *Bu athins* (no societies). By 1927, as many as 303 athins of various types were declared unlawful due to their violent activities. Among these athins' leaders were many pongyis, since many of these athins were connected with the General Council of *Sangha Sametgyis* (Coalition of Pongyi Associations), which was formed in 1921.[118]

Dr. Moscotti stated, "Buddhism, as a major facet of the national identity of the Burmese, became intimately entwined with the popular concept of nationalism," and that it brought "the villagers into the nationalist movement." The political pongyis who "embodied the old respect for tradition and the new demand for self-determination" became "the agent in spreading the nationalist doctrine to the villagers."[119] Consequently, the pongyis became most instrumental in the development of the noncooperation movement among the local athins. U Ottama, U Wizera, and U Wizaya were the prominent political pongyis of the 1920s. U Ottama was the leader in the agitation for home rule. He was arrested and imprisoned several times. He became a threat to the government when his thirty thousand followers attended the General Council of Burmese Association (GCBA) conference in May 1924, with an anti-tax resolution proposal. U Wizaya, a prince-pretender (the *Setkya Min*), emerged as a public voice when political leaders challenged British rule under the dyarchy system. U Wizera's death in 1929, resulting from a hunger strike of more than 166 days, stimulated popular unrest. He became Burma's pongyi martyr second only to U Ottama.[120] The religious aspect of the Burmese nationalist movement was in great momentum with the support of the dominant Buddhist population.

While the Burmese nationalist movement became increasingly aggressive, KNA leaders took a new turn lifting Karen nationalism to a higher stage. The Karen leaders, who were initially happy with five seats among the communal representatives and two seats from the general constituencies in the dyarchy system, changed their view after a few years. They felt that, with an overpowering Burman majority in the legislative council, communal seats and special electorates would not affirm Karen nationalist aspirations. A rapid decline in the number of the Karen-speaking populations in the delta area made the Karens feel that their culture and national identity were in danger. The idea of an independent Karen state seemed to become a necessity for many Karen leaders. And the preservation and promotion of the Karen tradition and culture became every Karen's responsibility.

During 1924 to 1927, Dr. Saw Durmay Po Min conducted one of the most remarkable efforts in promoting Karen national identity on the global level. He missed his opportunity to perform his white elephant show for Sir Frederick Whyte. Born in 1877, in a village near Than-daung township in the Taungoo district, he received his early education from the American Baptist Mission school and later went to Calcutta, where he earned his diploma in traditional medicine. Like all other KNA members, his nationalist ambition was to make Karens globally recognized through his elephant exhibitions. At his own expense, he traveled to London and then to America, showing the uniqueness of the Karen people through his elephant exhibitions. During the Wembley Exhibition in London, Dr. Saw D. Po Min sent two elephants, one black and one white, with his Karen *mahout* (trainer or keeper) to enhance the exhibition's attractiveness. His exhibition with the white elephant was successful in making the Karen people better known to the western world. During his London stay, he found his name mentioned in an article that stated that "the Burmese method" of catching elephants was unique and humane and that the result was good. Immediately after he saw the article, he published a response in the *London Observer* that clarified he was a Karen, not a Burman, and that indigenous elephant catchers were Karen, not Burman. In addition, he assisted Mr. Smeaton in writing *The Loyal Karen of Burma*. It was unsurprising the book emphasized the loyal service of the Karens and highly recommended the creation of a separate Karen state.[121]

Using his political prominence as a member of the government legislative council, Dr. San C. Po put in an all-out effort and drew up a design for a future Karen nation. In addition to appealing for Karen rights in the government's official meetings, he wrote the proposal to have the Karens recognized as a distinct national group in Burma. His book, *Burma and the Karens*, published in 1928, described in detail how the Karen character and culture differed from the Burman. Dr. San C. Po made several arguments describing why the Karens could not expect fair treatment from the hands of the Burmans. He wrote about his deep concern for the Karen schools, due to complaints that district councils were neglecting Karen schools. He also exposed intimidation suffered at the hands of the Burman wunthanu athins, who attempted to enforce non-payment of taxes.[122] Additionally, he described several hostile incidents that occurred due to acts of discrimination and coercion by Burmese officials. Dr. Po gave an example of a Buddhist Burmese township officer going to a Karen church during Sunday worship service and ordering worshippers to carry his luggage to his residence. Dr. Po summarized, "co-operation is impossible when there exists a form of oppression which has created much ill feeling."[123]

From the opening page of his book, Dr. San C Po made it clear that his purpose was to present and explain to the reading public and "to those who are in authority, the condition of the Karens . . . and their aspiration as a nation second in importance of the indigenous races of the province in Burma."[124] His vision for a separate Karen state is clearly stated:

> It is their [Karens] desire to have a country of their own, where they may progress as a race and find the contentment they seek. It is this contentment which gives a man or a nation that satisfaction and goodwill and creates that patriotic feeling so essential to the well-being of the nation. Self-respect in a nation begets respect from other nations and races. What a grand thing the achievement of their ambition will be for the Karens, and who shall have praises and blessing will be showered upon those who shall have made it possible. The Karens will then be in a position to show sincere respect to other races, especially to the Burmese, with whom they have been at variance, and in turn the Burmese will find them worthy of respect and esteem.[125]

Referring to the Karens' loyal services to the British crown, he questioned, "Will Government or its officials redeem past neglect by lending an ear to a national request? If Government is convinced that the Karens are deserving of a fair trial, have they not the courage of their convictions before it is too late to do the Karens a good turn, and in turn benefit from the co-operation of a loyal people of proven worth?"[126] Given the population ratio of seven Burmans to one Karen, he claimed that Karens should have an entire division in the seven divisions of Burma province and that Tenasserim division should be the one since its residents are mostly Karens.[127] If the appeal for the "Karen nation" was "not given their legitimate aspiration in a proper direction, as inspired by its feeling of patriotism and loyalty to the government," Dr. San C. Po warned, "it is greatly to be feared that a new group or generation of Karen extremists or obstructionists will arise."[128]

According to Dr. Po, the Karens wished to work "with and under the direct supervision of the British" in a section of the country. Citing the British nation formed by England, Scotland, Ireland, and Wales as a model, San C. Po suggested that Burma could be organized with four principal groups in the country, the Burmans, the Karens, the Arakanese, and the Shans. Each nation has its own country. Envisioning an independent "Karen Country," San C. Po exclaimed, "how inspiring it sounds!"[129]

The February 1929 arrival of the Indian Statutory Commission, known as the Simon Commission and led by Sir John Simon, provided a venue for the Karens to present the case that Dr. San C. Po projected in his book. The commission was appointed in London on November 26, 1927. It was charged to study the working of the reforms and recommend further steps in India's progress toward self-government.[130] Prior to the commission's arrival, the newly elected council nominated from its own membership a Burmese committee of seven men: three Burmans and four representatives of minorities, a Karen (Mahn Shwe Ba) and three Indians, to sit with the British commission.[131] The Burmese leaders who favored separation cooperated, but those who opposed separation organized a boycott of the commission. Most active in the boycott movement was the Sangha Sametgyis GCBA.[132] During this period, many Burmese leaders also changed their position from separation to anti-separation from India.

The KNA represented some ten Karen groups residing in the Irrawaddy delta and Sittang Valley extending from below Prome on the west to Toungoo on the east. In their memorandum, the Karens proposed that Karen seats allotted to the council be included in a single Karen voting constituency covering all of Burma. They also proposed that a similar proportional allotment be made for local representation on a district-wide basis. The Karens asked explicitly for a fair share of the district school funds and for their own school inspectors. The KNA opposed special representation on the council for commercial groups and the university. They also requested that more polling places be set up and that guarantees be provided against the impersonation of voters and against improper counting of votes.[133]

As representatives of the Karen elders, Sydney Loo Nee (S'gaw) and Mahn Shwe Ba (Pwo), presented a statement emphasizing Karen loyalty to the British raj and their concern to preserve their separate Karen nationality. They proposed that eleven new Karen electorates be added to their five under the existing dyarchy council and that 16 percent of public service appointments be reserved for Karens. One major concern was for the preservation of Christian Karen schools.[134] In constitutional reform terms, the KNA wished to move cautiously toward the gradual development of self-governing institutions. The KNA admitted dominion rule "might be bloody rule, but blood often purifies rules, it at least simplifies them."[135]

Karen representatives at the meeting with the Simon Commission did not raise the question of a Karen independent state, probably because the Karen leaders found that it was not the right moment. There were a series of upheavals from demonstrations to armed rebellion movements during the hearings. The leaders, however, were effective in unifying the Karen people of different clans and faith. In 1929, KNA and Saw Durmay Po Min's Society of Righteousness (*Brahamsoe*) from the Taungoo Karens joined together for a Karen conference. During that conference, the KNA president, Saw Pah Dwai, and the Society of Righteousness president, Saw D. Po Min, took turns as chairperson of the meeting, after which they declared the following memorandum:

1. An independent Karen state to be established in one of the seven divisions of the Burma province as proposed in San C. Po's book, *Burma and the Karen*,

2. To send a Karen delegation to London and appeal for Tenasserim Division as the Karen independent state.[136]

The peaceful legal approach of western-trained Karen nationalists was not an urgent matter for the British government because of the political upheaval instigated by the Burmese national liberation movements during 1930 and 1931. The pongyi-led party, through its executive Hundred Committee, instigated the complete boycott of the Simon Commission and organized hostile demonstrations in Rangoon and Mandalay. These leaders advocated for non-separation from India and for cooperation with the National Congress movement in India. Mohandas Gandhi's visit during the commission's hearing in March 1929 further encouraged aggression. The death of U Wizera in prison in 1929 created another mass crusade joined by the entire Buddhist population.[137]

The Saya San peasants' rebellion was another of the strongest and most violent movements, which demonstrated the Buddhist influence and anti-British sentiment during this period. The revolt was led by a former monk, Saya San, who was also a district leader of the GCBA. Saya San organized associations to resist the collection of the capitation tax. The organizers under him were political pongyis who worked through the local wunthanu athins. Saya San's anti-tax campaign was joined by unhappy peasants who suffered from a dramatic decline in paddy prices in 1930. Following a date and time selected by learned Burmese astrologers, on October 28, 1930, Saya San was proclaimed quite secretly to be the *Thupannaka Galon Raja*. The *galon* was a mythical bird, which could destroy the *naga* (snake) foreigner. The white umbrella, an ancient Brahman symbol of divine kingship, was raised over the new raja's head. After the new king was crowned, his five queens, his followers, and Galon army members were tattooed and provided with amulets to protect them from machine-gun bullets.[138] The revolt began in December 1930 from his base in the Tharrawaddy division in Pago Yoma and spread to other districts as far as Mandalay in upper Burma. The British government brought in 3,640 additional Indian army troops from central India to suppress the rebellion. In April 1932, the resistance groups were finally broken.[139]

When the rebellion started, Saya San, a former Buddhist monk supported by the extreme nationalist Buddhist monks and the Burmese population, declared that all Christian Karens should be eliminated. Following his instruction, many Karen villages were attacked and burned by his Galon army in Tharrawaddy. Rev. Saw San Baw, pastor and president of the KNA of Tharrawaddy district, recruited volunteers and fought the Galon army. He was assisted by other Karen pastors, including Thra Po Nyunt, Thra Po Kyaw, Thra Shwe Thee, Thra Kyaw Bu, and Thra Maung Kyin, who were later awarded a gun by the British government for recruiting the highest number of volunteers. With nearly six hundred volunteers and guns from the British government, Rev. San Baw helped quell part of the Saya San rebellion, for which he received the OBE.[140] The key role played by the armed Karen irregulars in offensive operations against the rebellion, plus the Karens' involvement in the capture of Saya San and his followers, produced a thorn in the cultivation of good relations between the Burmans and the Karens.

Amidst the political turmoil, some British officials joined the Karens in advocating for the creation of a separate Karen state in the British Burma province. Perhaps the proposal came from Dr. San C. Po, a highly respected Karen leader who was a member of the legislative council, or perhaps the British appreciated the Christian Karens, who shared their faith and constantly helped in crushing the rebellions. When considering Dr. San C. Po's proposal for the Tenasserim division as the Karen nation, British authorities were cautious because the Karens constituted a minority element in most Tenasserim districts.

According to the 1931 India Census, Karens made up almost all the population of the sparsely populated Salween district and a bare majority of 52 percent in the Thaton district. In the other districts of Tenasserim, Karens made 6.9 percent in Tavoy district; 11.8 percent in Mergui; 20.5 percent in Toungoo district; and 20.7 percent in Amherst.[141] In addition, the Karen population of various groups resided in areas encompassing Ministerial Burma and the scheduled areas, the Karenni states, and the southwest Shan states. The spread of the Karen population and its diverse ethnicities made it complicated to gain a consensus in the government to allocate a separate state to the Karens. Additionally, the British feared fanning the flames of the growing momentum for Burmese nationalism if they satisfied the Karen nationalist aspiration.

The question of whether Burma should be separated from India, which was initiated by the Montagu-Chelmsford reforms, opened the door for Karen leadership in Burma's politics. Given equal opportunity with Burmese politicians, Karen leaders presented their political views in Burma, Calcutta, and London, attacking the separation of Burma from India and working against the Burmese nationalist leaders. Later, when it became obvious that the dyarchy system would be established, the KNA's leaders began their demand for communal seats. As a result, the Karens were granted five seats in the council and two seats in the senate. Envisioning a Karen separate state in a separate Burma, the Karens cooperated with the Simon Commission hearings in 1929, while the Burmese extreme nationalists boycotted the hearings and advocated for continued association with India. The Karens insisted on communal representation in the council for each of the sixteen districts of lower Burma, reasoning that Karens could not expect fair treatment from Burman officials. The Burmans considered this an insult. The new constitution for Burma under the Government Act of 1935, however, extended privileges to the Karens and elevated the political positions of many Karen leaders.

The Government Act of 1935: Road to the Karen New Year Celebration

In 1930, the Simon Commission finally published its report with several recommendations for the new Burma governmental establishment. Among the changes was the separation of Burma from India.[142] Consequently, conferences were held to implement recommendations, including the discussion of a constitution for a separated Burma. The first India

Round Table Conference, which met in London from November 12, 1930, to January 19, 1931, lacked Karen representation. The next Burma Round Table Conference convened in November 1931 with thirty-three representatives: nine members of Parliament, twelve Burmans, and two representatives each from minority groups—Indians, Karens, Shans, Chinese, Anglo-Indians, and the British.[143]

Two Karen delegates, Sydney Loo Nee and Mahn Shwe Ba, strongly advocated separation from India, under a system of full self-government and not inferior to India's constitution.[144] The Karen delegates demanded three things: the creation of a federation of five different groups in Burma comprising states of Burmans, Karens, Shans, Kachins, and Chins to be welded together into a "solid nation"; a separate Karen army regiment; and a provision that would prohibit discrimination on ethnic or religious grounds. Sydney Loo Nee also insisted on communal representation in the council for each of the sixteen districts of lower Burma. He made the same proposal in the hearings of the Simon Commission. Opposing the Karen delegate's proposal, U Ba Pe, a separationist Burman representative, argued that the Karens were not a distinct ethnic group and that the viewpoint of the majority of the Karens was the same as that of the Burmans.[145]

Also attending the conference were the anti-separationist Burmese headed by the GCBA, U Chit Hlaing and Tharawaddy U Pu. They refused to participate after they felt that the discussion did not meet Burma's aspiration for immediate and full responsible government with dominion status. Despite the turbulent sessions of the Round Table Conference, the delegates generally agreed on the framework for the constitution that would place upon a legislature the responsibility for the government of the colony. Consequently, the British government announced a detailed policy statement in January 1932 that Burma would have a separate unitary government consisting of a bicameral legislature and a governor assisted by ministers with limited powers.[146]

In 1932, a general election was held to determine the people of Burma's feelings. Acting as an indigenous element of Burma's population, the KNA supported the termination of Burma's ties with India and the efforts to secure a bond with the majority nationalist sentiment in lower Burma. After the election, a Christian Karen, Saw Pe Tha, was elected deputy president of the legislative council.[147] Unlike most other Karen leaders who received their education through the American missionaries, Saw Pe Tha came from a wealthy family and studied law in London at his own expense, after obtaining his bachelor's degree (BA, bar-at-law) from Rangoon College. Although a native of Bassein, he represented the Myaungmya constituency in running during the election.[148] In other constituencies, anti-separationists won in 1932. However, when the legislature met, they did not make any explicit decision, and it was left to the government to decide on separation from India and to draft the new constitution.[149]

After five years of debates between the British government and Burmese nationalist leaders, Burma's new constitution was approved on May 30, 1935. The government of Burma Proper (excluding the hill areas) relied upon a cabinet led by a premier and responsible to Parliament. The "excluded areas" (the Shan states, Karenni, the Salween district, and the remaining hill areas) were set aside from ministerial Burma and remained under separate forms of administration.[150]

Under the 1935 act, the first and only election took place in 1936, and Dr. Ba Maw of the Sinyetha Wunthanu Party became the first prime minister of Burma. The new constitution embodied the Government Act of Burma of 1935, which came into force on April 1, 1937, granting the full introduction of a responsible cabinet government. The new constitution set up two chambers of Parliament, a House of Representatives of 132 members, and the Senate of 36 members. Of the 36 Senate seats, half were to be nominated by the governor and the remainder by the House of Representatives on proportional representation. In the House of Representatives, 92 seats were filled on a non-communal territorial constituency basis, while the rest were reserved as follows: 12 Karens; 8 Indians; 2 Anglo-Burmese; 3 Europeans; 11 commerce and industry representatives; 1 representative from Rangoon University; 2 Indian labor representatives; and 1 non-Indian labor representative.[151] The 12 Karens in the House of Representatives were Sydney Loo Nee, Saw Pe Tha, Mahn Kan Aye, U Po Myin, Mahn Htun Khin, Mahn Ba Khin, Mahn Shwe Nyunt, Saw Mya Sein, Saw Po Chit, U Hla Pe, Saw Pah Dwai, and Saw Johnson D. Po Min. In addition, Dr. San C. Po, Saw San Baw, and Mahn Shwe Ba obtained senate seats.[152] When Premier Dr. Ba Maw formed a coalition cabinet, Saw Pe Tha became the minister of agriculture and forests, the first Karen minister in Burma's first government under the new 1935 act.[153]

The Government of Burma Act of 1935 made two major contributions to broadening democratic self-government. First, it discarded the dyarchy system, and second, it added thirty-three new general constituents to the House of Representatives, including an increase in the number of Karens from five to twelve.[154] The Government Act of 1935 granted the Karens unprecedented privileges and strengthened Karen political leadership in Burmese politics. Holding a block of twelve

Karen seats in the House of Representatives in the new administration invigorated the Karens to enhance their nation-building process. The growing nationalistic movements of the Burmans, indicated by the Saya San rebellion, the student strike of 1936, and the formation of the Thakin organization, warned the British of the urgency in their activism.

Karen leaders gained political experience and confidence from their confrontations with the opposition Burmese leaders and government in the legislative council. They moved swiftly to make the Karens an important group receiving equal status as other ethnic groups in Burma. Through discussions, it was decided that a bill would be introduced for the recognition of a Karen New Year's Day. Since all bills were to be first submitted to the House of Representatives, responsibility was given to Saw Johnson D. Po Min, who was one of the twelve Karen members of the House.[155]

To implement the project, Saw J. D. Po Min met with learned Karen elders from his Toungoo constituencies to determine two facts: "How many years have the Karen people had?" and "What is the appropriate Karen New Year Day?" Three dates were suggested for the Karen New Year Day: January 1, July 13 (Judson's arrival date), and the first and second day of the Karen month Thalay.[156] After discussion, the task was given to Thra Molo, who did the research and reported that the Karen New Year should be the first and second day of the month Thalay in the Karen calendar.[157]

Regarding the Karen year, Thra Molo recommended 739 BCE as the year that Karens arrived in Burma. That calculation was based on words of the ancient elders transmitted through oral history in accordance with the historical facts that the Karens were the earliest group of people to settle in various parts of mainland Southeast Asia, spreading from areas that today comprise Burma, Thailand, and Cambodia. It was like that of the Karen historian Saw Aung Hla's migration theory discussed earlier in chapter two of this book. The calendar was to be set by adding 739 BCE, representing the arrival of the Karens in Burma to 1937 CE, which was the year Karen received political recognition (739 BCE + 1937 CE = 2,676).[158]

The KNA approved Thra Molo's proposal as the Karen New Year Bill (Bill #26 of 1937) and dated August 2, 1937. It was signed by Saw Johnson D. Po Min and submitted to the House of Representatives with the short title, "The Karen's New Year Day Recognition Act of 1937."[159] The definition for the "Karens," according to the bill, "means all races." The bill included "clans or tribes forming part and parcel of

the Karen people of Burma in spite of their castes, creeds and religions."
It continued:

"The Karen's New Year Day" means exactly the same as the New Year
Days of other races, people, or nations, which being the first days of
another prosperous year. The Karen New Year Day falls on the first and
second day of the month of THALAY, according to Karen calendar year,
corresponding to the first waxing moon of the month of Pyatho of the
Burmese Calendar month. It is in this month of THALAY (beginning from
the first waxing moon of Pyatho) that the Karen begin to build new
bamboo houses, renew or replace old things, etc. (noticeable in the Hilly
districts) for the New Year. These days are recognized by all the Karens
everywhere. Many religious festivities, such as offering to Nats, etc. by
the heathen Karens; offerings to Phongyis and going to Kyaungs or Pagodas for worship by the Buddhist Karens, etc. and thanksgiving prayer
services, etc. by the Christian Karens, and Karens are organized on a big
scale by all classes of Karens according to their religious beliefs. In fact,
the Days being the greatest gala days annals of Karens' history. . . .

The Karens only want ancient customs, etc., to be respected in as
much as they have respected others. For this sole purpose, this Bill is
introduced and sincerely hopes for enthusiastic support from their
Burmese members and sons of the soil and brothers of the same land.[160]

When the House met on August 23, 1937, Saw J. D. Po Min proposed the bill, and it was seconded by U Po Hmyin (representatives of
Amherst Karen constituencies). After discussion, the council chair, U
Chit Hlaing, ruled that "the Karen New Year Day Recognition Bill,
1937, be granted. The motion carried."[161] Since the House meeting record showed as "presented" rather than "passed," the Karen leaders in
the Senate, Saw San Baw and Dr. San C. Po, took that matter to Saw
Pe Tha, who was a minister in Premier Dr. Ba Maw's cabinet, to decree
the bill. Using the cabinet executive power, the cabinet approved the
bill and forwarded it to Governor Archibald Douglas Cockrane's office.
Just before the end of 1937, the Karen New Year Bill was passed. The
Karen New Year Day became an official national holiday by Section 25
of the Negotiable Instrument Act.[162]

Since the law was passed only in December 1937, there was not
enough time to organize a mass celebration of the first Karen New Year
Day, which fell on January 1, 1938 (Thalay 1, 2677, Karen calendar).
Nevertheless, Sydney Loo Nee delivered a speech on national radio in
commemoration of the first Karen national holiday.[163] Following the

Karen calendar, the next Karen New Year, Thalay 1, 2678, was celebrated on December 21, 1938, and a greeting letter was read:

> We are emerging from isolation into the stream of national affairs. Our conviction is that our two million Karens have a significant part to play in Burma's destiny.
>
> We owe our existence as a people not to organization or any political arrangements, but to certain distinctive qualities that have been given us. Our traits include simplicity, a love of music, honesty, steadiness and a sense of God. . . .
>
> We are at a crisis. For us the choice lies between protection through isolation, or adventure through active participation in the life of Burma. United ourselves, we could help to make Burma a nation. We recognized that as leaders we must be fully committed to our country free from fear, personal ambition, racial and religious prejudices.
>
> Today we recall our heritage, our ancient poets and prophets and our tradition of Ywa (God). We believe every individual, every home, every village has a place in the new advance. Progressive in thinking, constructive in planning, and courageous in living, we can share responsibility with other communities for the making of Burma a united people.
>
> Are we ready on this New Year's Day to put the best traditions of our people at the service of this whole country?[164]

During this period, Karen leaders also selected the Karen national flag and national anthem. The then KNA president and senator, Rev. Saw San Baw, organized a contest for the Karen national flag and asked the Karen community to design and submit their work. More than one hundred sample flags were submitted, and after a thorough evaluation, the flag designed by Mahn Ba Kin was finally chosen—the same flag which is in use today.[165] The lyrics of the Karen national anthem were written by Rev. San Ba, a Judson College graduate, and music was composed by Saw Tha Aye Gyi.[166] The anthem is played by musical bands and sung by audiences attending the Karen New Year celebration each year. Since it is printed in the S'gaw Karen hymnal,[167] all S'gaw Karen Christians can always sing the song. The influence of Baptist Christians is obvious in the Karen national anthem.

Following the emergence of the Karen New Year Day, one record claims that Senator Rev. Saw San Baw proposed the government allocate a Karen National Day as a national holiday for Burma. The government became concerned that, if the proposal was granted, it might further provoke Karens to demand more ethnic rights and creation of an independent "Karen Free State or Republic" in the eastern hills, which Karen leaders had been proposing since 1928. The proposal was withdrawn.[168]

The recognition of Karen New Year Day was, as stated in the greeting letter of the five Karen leaders, "the historic day" for the Karens and "the first officially recognized national holiday" that allowed the Karen people to stand abreast with other groups in the family of nations. Without the unwavering nationalist spirit, solid judicial wisdom, and strenuous efforts of KNA Christian leaders, it was impossible for the Karens to contest their former despot Burmans or to challenge the British rulers. While climbing the political ladder through the platform of the Karen nationalist movement, these Christian leaders shaped the character of the Karens from an apolitical to a political people. The political journey of the Karens would continue to be long and difficult as they pursued their struggle for their national aspiration of building the Karen nation.

Notes

1. Ellen Huntly Bullard Mason, *Great Expectations Realized; or Civilizing Mountain Men* (Philadelphia: American Baptist Publication Society; New York: Blakeman & Mason; Chicago: Church, Goodman and Kenny, 1862), 335.

2. Ibid., 333.

3. Ibid.

4. Ibid.

5. Ibid., 337.

6. San C. Po, *Burma and the Karens* (London: Elliot Stock, 1928), 38.

7. *Baptist Missionary Magazine* (February 1871), 62.

8. T. Thanbyah, *Karen People and Development* (Rangoon: American Baptist Mission Press, 1906; republished by Global Karen Baptist Fellowship, 2010), 49.

9. Ibid., 52.

10. Ibid.

11. Maung Sin Kyeh, *Bamarpyi Chit Kayin Amyo Tha Kaung Hsaung Myar* (Bangkok: *Pyitaungsu Kayin Amyotha Apweh Choke*, 2003), 25.

12. U Htun Aung Chain's collection. He is a former professor of history, Rangoon University, and a grandson of Saw Shwe Chain, one of the Karens who studied in the United States in the late nineteenth century.

13. Great Britain, House of Commons, *Sessional Papers*, vol. 30 for 1920 (cmd. 746), 5-6, cited in John F. Cady, *A History of Modern Burma* (Ithaca, NY: Cornell University Press, 1960), 141.

14. Thyra Po, *Sir San C. Po, C.B.E., M.D., A Karen Pioneer* (Yangon: Privately published, 2008), 125, 98. While he was studying in New York, he made the Fifth Avenue Baptist Church his home church, where the Rockefeller family was in charge of the Sunday school. San C. Po was a member of John D. Rockefeller's Sunday school class.

15. Maung Sin Kyeh, 54–57.

16. Randolph L. Howard, *Baptists in Burma* (Philadelphia: Judson Press, 1931), 108–9.

17. P'doh Tha Bwa Oo Zan, *History of the Baptist Mission among the Karen in Burma* (Rangoon: Go Forward Press, 1961), 197–99 (KIH award for his outstanding performance as a school administrator; OBE award for recruiting volunteers for the government in Tharrawaddy during the Saya San rebellion in 1930–1932).

18. Thanbyah, 63.

19. Ibid. The KNA came into existence in 1881, before any major national associations in Asia were formed. Even the legendary Indian National Congress, with similar objectives for the Indian people, was formed in 1885, four years after the KNA was formed. The first Burmese national association, Young Men's Buddhist Association (YMBA), was formed twenty-five years later in 1906.

20. Maung Sin Kyeh, 44, 56; Pu S'Kaw Ler Taw, *Ka Nyaw Ta Ber Hser Tar Si Soh Teh Soh* (KNU publication, 1992), 118.

21. Donald Mackenzie Smeaton, *The Loyal Karens of Burma* (London: Kegan Paul, Trench & Co., 1887), 220-27; also Cady, *History of Modern Burma*, 138.

22. Smeaton, 201.

23. San C. Po, 58.

24. General Smith Dun, first commander-in-chief of Independent Burma's Armed Forces, *Memoirs of the Four-Foot Colonel*, Data Paper number 113 (Ithaca, NY: Cornell University Southeast Asia Program, Department of Asia Studies, 1980), 65.

25. San C. Po, 1–2.

26. Saw Hanson Tadaw, *The Karens of Burma: A Study in Human Geography* (London: University of London, 1961), 18.

27. U Pyin Nyar, *Kayin Yarzawin* (Rangoon: Zwe Sar Bay, 1929), 142. According to this author, the Gwe Karen king named Gonar Ain Thuryin Saw ruled the area east of Irrawaddy.

28. *The Census of India*, 1911, vol. 9 (Rangoon: Government Printing, 1912), 275.

29. John F. Cady, "The Karens," in *Annotated Bibliography of Burma*, ed. Frank N. Traeger (New Haven, CT: Human Relations Area Files, 1956), 826–28.

30. Henry I. Marshall, *The Karen People of Burma: A Study in Anthropology and Ethnology* (Columbus: The Ohio State University Press, 1922), 8.

31. Tadaw, 18–19.

32. India Statutory Commission, Vol. 11: *Memorandum Submitted by the Government of Burma to the Indian Statutory Commission* (London: His Majesty's Stationery Office, 1930), 10.

33. Ibid., 19.

34. U Pyin Nyar, 142.

35. J. S. Furnivall, *An Introduction to the Political Economy of Burma* (Rangoon: Burma Book Club, 1938), 37, 47.

36. *History of Hanthawaddy*, Burmese manuscript, India Office Library Catalogue, No. 3505.

37. Marshall, *Karen People of Burma*, 129.

38. John James Snodgrass, *Narrative of the Burmese War* (London: John Murray, 1827), 21, 141.

39. Josef Silverstein, *Burmese Politics: The Dilemma of National Unity* (New Brunswick, NJ: Rutgers University Press, 1980), 15.

40. J. S. Furnivall and W. S. Morrison, *Insein District Gazetteer*, vol. A (Rangoon: Government Press, 1914), 107.

41. Horace Hayman Wilson, *Documents Illustrative of the Burmese War with an Introductory Sketch of Events of the War and an Appendix* (Calcutta: Government Gazette Press, 1827), xiv.

42. John Crawfurd, *Journal of an Embassy from the Governor-General of India to the Court of Ava in the year 1827* (London: Henry Colburn, 1829), 421–23.

43. Dr. F. Buchanan, *Journal of Progress and observations during the continuance of the deputation from Bengal to Ava in 1795 in the dominion of the Barmah Monarch* (IOR: MSS Eur. C. 13), 37.

44. Ibid.; also in Snodgrass, 141.

45. Tenasserim (Burma) Office of the Commissioner, E. A. Blundell to Sec. to the Sudden Board of Ft. William, December 9, 1839, *Selected Correspondence of Letters issued from and received in the Office of the Commissioner Tenasserim Division for the Years 1825–26 to 1842–1843* (Rangoon: Superintendent, Government Printing and Stationery, 1929), 186.

46. Buchanan, 37.

47. Snodgrass, 141; see also Furnivall and Morrison, 30.

48. Cady, *History of Modern Burma*, 73–75.

49. Ibid.

50. Henry I. Marshall, *Burma Pamphlets No. 8: The Karens of Burma* (New York: Longmans, Green & Co., 1945), 32.

51. H. R. Winston, *Four Years in Upper Burma* (London: C. H. Kelly, 1892), 97.

52. India Office Archives, India Secret Proceedings, vol. 114 (1844), no. 165, October 18, 1844.

53. Furnivall and Morrison, 30.

54. India Office Archives, India Secret Proceedings, vol. 180 (1852), reported by H. Godwin, May, June 9 and 22, and August 23, 1852.

55. Calista V. Luther, *The Vintons and the Karens: Memorials of Rev. Justus H. Vinton and Calista H. Vinton* (Boston: W. G. Corthell, Mission Rooms, 1880), 89–106.

56. W. F. B. Laurie, *Our Burmese Wars and Relations with Burma*, 2nd ed. (London: W. H. Allen & Co., 1885), 259–60.

57. Smeaton, 4.

58. Ibid.

59. Maung Maung, *Burma in the Family of Nations* (Amsterdam: Djambatan, 1958), 69.

60. Smeaton, 12-13. This and several letters of Rev. Vinton were quoted in Smeaton's book.

61. Ibid., 13–16.
62. Ibid., 54.
63. Charles Crosthwaite, *The Pacification of Burma* (London: Edward Arnold, 1912). 51.
64. Smeaton, 37.
65. Ibid., 30.
66. Ibid., 48.
67. Ibid., 61.
68. Ibid., 1.
69. Ibid., 237.
70. Ibid.
71. Angelene Naw, *Aung San and the Struggle for Burmese Independence* (Chiang Mai: Silkworm Books, 2001), 194.
72. Cady, *History of Modern Burma*, 134.
73. Silverstein, 27.
74. Hugh Tinker, *The Union of Burma: A Study of the First Years of Independence* (London: Oxford University Press, 1957), 315; Silverstein, 34.
75. Crosthwaite, 51.
76. J. S. Furnivall, *Colonial Policy and Practice: A Comparative Study of Burma and Netherlands India* (New York: Macmillan; Cambridge: Cambridge University Press, 1948), 178-84. See also Indian Office Archives, Home Department (Upper Burma) series, vol. 2303 (1888), 163.
77. Tinker, 23.
78. Thyra Po, 124.
79. Ibid., 154.
80. San C. Po, 38.
81. Reasons given for discontinuance of Burmese recruitment are stated in *Report of the Statutory Commission*, xi, 23. See Tinker, 314; Silverstein, 34; Godfrey E. Harvey, *British Rule in Burma, 1824–1942* (London: Faber & Faber, 1946), 40–42. In regards to British policy Harvey wrote, "History shows that the Burmese were not unfit; and the failure to recruit them may be one of the causes underlying the increase in crime, for instincts which can be sublimated in the army must find an outlet."
82. J. S. Furnivall, *The Governance of Modern Burma* (New York: Institute of Pacific Relations, 1958), 22.
83. Maung Maung, 82.
84. Cady, *History of Modern Burma*, 179-80. U May Aung graduated from Cambridge University and later became a justice of the high court and a member of the governor's executive council. U Khin was knighted by the British king. Others included U Ba Pe, Sir Maung Gyee, U Ba Dun, U Ba Yin, U Sein Hla, and U San Ba Ba.
85. Maung Maung, 83.
86. Ibid.
87. Marshall, *Karen People of Burma*, 314.
88. San C. Po, 27.
89. Great Britain, House of Commons, *Parliamentary Debates*, fifth series, vol. 97 (1917) col. 1695–1696. See Albert D. Moscotti, *British Policy and the Natioinalist Movement in Burma, 1931–1937* (Honolulu: University of Hawaii Press, 1974), 24.
90. Thyra Po, 121.
91. Ibid., 122.
92. San C. Po, 66; Thyra Po, 123 (Karen Memorial presented in 1917 to Lord Chelmsford and the Right Hon. Edwin S. Montagu, M.P.).
93. PP, C, vol. 8 for 1918 (cmd. 9109), p. 162, para. 198. See Cady, *History of Modern Burma*, 200-201; Moscotti, 60-61.
94. Cady, *History of Modern Burma*, 192.
95. Moscotti, 23.
96. Ibid., 21, 22.
97. Cady, *History of Modern Burma*, 208.
98. Ibid.
99. Silverstein, 45; Great Britain, Government of India Act, 1919, appendix N, 82.
100. Cady, *History of Modern Burma*, 224.
101. Ibid., 223.
102. San C. Po, 6–8.
103. Ibid., 7–8.
104. Ibid., 8.
105. Ibid., 74.
106. Great Britain, Burma Reforms Committee, Record of Evidence, 3 vols. (London, 1922), 1:227-37 (hereafter cited as BRCE); Cady, *History of Modern Burma*, 229.

107. San C. Po, 8.

108. Ibid., 9.

109. BRCE, 1:276; 2:99, 131; 3:52-53, 64; Cady, *History of Modern Burma*, 228.

110. BRCE, 2:197-205; Cady, *History of Modern Burma*, 229.

111. San C. Po, 9.

112. Ibid.

113. *Burma, Report on the Administration of Burma for 1922–1923*, ix (hereafter cited as RAB).

114. Cady, *History of Modern Burma*, 242–43.

115. American Baptist Foreign Mission Society, *Annual Report for 1923*, 97-98 (hereafter cited as ABFMS).

116. San C. Po, 70.

117. Tinker, 3.

118. Moscotti, 40.

119. Ibid., 39.

120. Cady, *History of Modern Burma*, 260–61.

121. San C. Po, 48–49.

122. Ibid., 70–76.

123. Ibid., 12–13.

124. Ibid., 1928, v.

125. Ibid.

126. Ibid., 78–79.

127. Ibid.

128. Ibid., 80.

129. Ibid., 81.

130. Maung Maung, 86.

131. Cady, *History of Modern Burma*, 283. U Aung Thwin was the chairman of the Burma Committee.

132. Moscotti, 55.

133. Cady, *History of Modern Burma*, 293.

134. Report of the India Statutory Commission, Vol. 11: *Memorandum Submitted by the Government of Burma to the Indian Statutory Commission* (London: His Majesty's Stationery Office, 1930), 359-466.

135. Ibid., Vol. 17: *Memorandum Submitted by the Government of Burma to the Indian Statutory Commission* (London: His Majesty's Stationery Office, 1930), 418-424; Moscotti, 228.

136. Ibid. (both sources)

137. RAB, xi, cited in Cady, *History of Modern Burma*, 281.

138. Cady, *History of Modern Burma*, 311.

139. Ibid., 316.

140. Oo Zan, 198–99.

141. Census Commissioner, *Census of India*, 1931, vol. ix, part 1, 192-93, 212-13; see Cady, *History of Modern Burma*, 371.

142. Great Britain, *Report of the Indian Statutory Commission*, ii, 187-91; see Tinker, 4.

143. *Burma Round Table Conference Proceedings* (London: His Majesty's Stationery Office, 1932); Cady, *History of Modern Burma*, 328.

144. *Burma Round Table Conference Proceedings*, 60.

145. *Burma Round Table Conference Proceedings*, 60, 74; Cady, *History of Modern Burma*, 333.

146. Moscotti, 92–94.

147. Cady, *History of Modern Burma*, 372.

148. Maung Sin Kyeh, 58–59.

149. Maung Maung, 87.

150. Tinker, 4.

151. Ibid., 4-5.

152. Maung Sin Kyeh, 56.

153. Cady, *History of Modern Burma*, 386.

154. Ibid., 351–52.

155. Thra Kalaw Lah, Thramu Naw Mya Aye, and Thra Ku Kuh, comps., *Karen New Year* (Publication of Karen New Year Celebration Committee, 2019), 12.

156. Maung Sin Kyeh, *Kayin Bawa Dalay* (Rangoon: Miba Myitta, 1967), 135. Judson's arrival day was not accepted in order to unify all non-Christian Karens.

157. Thra Kalaw Lah, Thramu Mya Aye, and Thra Ku Kuh, *Karen New Year*. 12. His main resources were from the books written by professors of Asian history Gordon Hannington Luce and Godfrey E. Harvey, and Burmese scholar U Po Kyar's *History of Burma*.

158. Thra Kalaw Lah, Thramu Naw Mya Aye, and Thra Ku Kuh, *Karen New Year*, 12. Aung Hla, 61-80.

159. Thra Kalaw Lah, Thramu Mya Aye, and Thra Ku Kuh, *Karen New Year*, 27; see Bill #26 online.

160. Ibid.

161. Excerpt from the *Burma Legislative Proceedings of the first House of Representatives*, vol. 2, no. 5, second session, fifth meeting, Monday, 23 August 1937, 326–27.

162. Thra Kalaw Lah, Thramu Naw Mya Aye, and Thra Ku Kuh, *Karen New Year*, 44.

163. Ibid., 13.

164. Ibid., 27.

165. Cultural Committee of CE 2000 for Christ, comp., *Ka Na Kee Katoh Kanyaw Ta-hset-ta-la Ahlit Heet Khgar* (*Culture Handbook*) (Yangon: Karen Baptist Convention, 1996), 238. Mahn Ba Khin was the first Pwo Karen who became the general secretary of the KNA. He served as the principal of the Pwo Karen Seminary before he became a member of the House of Representatives in the 1937 British administration. In 1945, he became one of British Governor Dorman Smith's Executive Council members.

166. *100 Year History of the Karen Convention 1913–2013* (Yangon: Karen Baptist Convention, 2013), 183.

167. *Lit Tha We Ka Sa Ywa* (*Karen Hymnbook*) (Yangon: Karen Baptist Convention, 1867, 1972, 2018), no. 519.

168. Thra Tha Hto, "Karen Calendar," in Thra Kalaw Lah, Thramu Naw Mya Aye, and Thra Ku Kuh, comps., *Karen New Year* (Publication of Karen New Year Celebration Committee, 2019). 49–50.

5
Karen National Challenges during World War II

The loyal attitude of the Karens has been reported to me by my officers. Loyalty through so long a time in your difficult and dangerous circumstances is worthy of the highest praise. I know many of you have borne arms in defence of your country and will bear them again to ensure final victory. —(Signed) C. J. E. Auchinleck, Commander-in-Chief, India Command. November 17, 1943[1]

The Burma Nationalists' Collaboration with the Japanese

When World War II started in Europe on September 1, 1939, British Burma was struggling with a series of serious political problems instigated by young nationalists who called themselves *thakins* (meaning "master" in Burmese). Many future young national leaders joined the Dobama Asi-Ayon (DAA), including Aung San and U Nu.[2] Under DAA leadership, the Revolution of 1300 (named after the Burmese year 1300) united workers, students, and peasants, making it the most important rebellion in the history of the nationalist movement in British Burma. It led to Prime Minister Dr. Baw Maw's forced resignation in February 1939. U Pu became head of the new administration.[3]

When the governor of Burma, Sir Walter Booth Gravely, declared that Burma was at war with Germany on October 24, 1939,[4] U Pu argued in the House that his countrymen should support Britain.[5] But Dr. Ba Maw and his Sinyetha party urged people to wage war against the British. Meanwhile, Aung San became the new general secretary of the DAA and made all-out efforts to unite the many different political organizations. Accordingly, on November 18, 1939, the People's Revolutionary Party (PRP) formed as a branch of the DAA, and the leaders began to discuss plans for procuring weapons for an armed uprising against the British.[6] A successful alliance was formed between DAA and the Sinyetha Party, creating a new political organization, Freedom Bloc, with Aung San as secretary and Dr. Ba Maw as *Arnarshin* (dictator). The Freedom Bloc's policy was combative opposition to Burma's participation in the war against Germany. In April 1940, the DAA claimed itself as the "Democratic front of all the people of Burma" and declared a manifesto urging all the youth of Burma, plus all socialists and nationalists, to unite with the DAA in an anti-imperialist struggle.[7]

When the British government started arresting the leaders of the anti-British movement, Aung San went underground. The PRP smuggled Aung San and Hla Myaing to China to seek Chinese aid. While they were wandering about without any contact with the Chinese, a Japanese army officer sent by Colonel Kiyoshi Tanaka, senior staff officer of the Japanese Army Command in Taiwan, contacted them.[8] The Japanese had already started their covert operations in Burma as early as 1935. The Japanese spread propaganda, using the slogan "Asia for the Asians." As the most advanced Asian nation, Japan intended to eliminate western domination in Asia, a stance which attracted many Burmese nationalists. In 1940, a DAA leader, Thakin Ba Sein, met with one of the agents and gave a draft of "A Secret Plan for Burma Independence" to a Japanese agent and asked for Japanese aid. The Japanese consulate in Burma contacted Dr. Ba Maw, who decided to accept the Japanese support for an armed revolution against the British. Before the confirmation of the assistance, the British discovered the plan and arrested Ba Maw.[9] It was through these earlier collaborations that the Japanese found Aung San and Hla Myaing in China.

They arrived in Japan in November 1940 and discussed a plan for Burma's independence. On February 1, 1949, the *Minami Kikan* (Minami Intelligence Organization) was established.[10] A series of meetings followed between the Minami Kikan and members of PRP Thakins, drawing up plans for the invasion of Burma. Consequently, from February to July 1941, thirty young Burmans, known as the Thirty Comrades, were smuggled out of Burma and sent to Hainan Island for military training. After training, the Burma Independence Army (BIA) was formed with Burmese expatriates in Thailand in December 1941. Colonel Suzuki was made a general and commander-in-chief, Captain Kawashima was second in command, and Aung San became a major general and third.[11]

Four days after the attack on Pearl Harbor, on December 11, 1941, the first invading Japanese forces began their Burmese campaign.[12] Along with the Japanese invading armies, the BIA entered Tenasserim. By the end of January 1942, the entire Tenasserim division, including its strategic ports and airfields in Mergui, Tavoy, and Moulmein, came under Japanese control. Mass evacuations to India began just after Rangoon suffered its first two air raids on December 23 and 25, 1941.

Early in 1942, about 150 American Baptist missionaries evacuated to the US, India, and China. Some remained in the northern Kachin and Chin areas until early 1943 when all missionaries were compelled to evacuate. Among the last to go were missionary doctor Gordon Seagrave, who led the mobile hospital until the last minute, and Brayton C. Case, who gathered "Vegetables for Victory" to help feed Chinese armies to the east. While sheltering in Assam and China, many missionaries served in the medical corps, trained troops for jungle warfare, or volunteered as chaplains to Burmese troops in India.[13]

When Rangoon fell on March 8, 1942, the BIA's strength had swollen to ten thousand men.[14] As the advance drove on, more volunteers enlisted in the BIA. Within a few months, the number rose to thirty thousand.[15] Trained and armed by the Japanese, the BIA facilitated Japan's war effort in Burma, not only in attacking the British forces but also in organizing an underground movement.

In April 1942, just over two weeks after the fall of Rangoon, the Japanese commander of the BIA, Colonel Suzuki, established the Burma *Baho* (central) government, with Thakin Tun Ok as its chief administrator. This Baho government lasted only about two months, but it is marked as one of the most tragic and darkest moments in the Karen people's history. Because of mismanagement, many BIA members committed vicious slaughters and savage mayhem in heavily Karen-populated areas in Salween district and the Irrawaddy delta region. The most notorious occurred in May 1942 in Myaungmya, which later turned into a communal war. According to an official report, in the Myaungmya district alone, more than eighteen hundred Karens, including Christian priests and pastors, were killed. Four hundred Karen villages were destroyed.[16] The barbaric atrocities of the BIA caused relations between Karens and Burmans to deteriorate to such an extent as to make the breach almost irreconcilable.

The Karen People's Plight under Early Japanese Occupation (1942–1943)

> There was not a day in which we did not receive news of great friction between the Burmese and the Karens, and the Japanese taking part with some of the Burmese section, and great slaughter, killing and raping of people.[17]

In January 1946, British governor Sir Reginald Dorman-Smith wrote this statement in a report to Lord Pethick-Lawrence, the secretary of state for India and Burma, concerning the Karen areas during the Japanese occupation. The Karens became the first victims of the Japanese and BIA forces since their villages were located on the path of the Japanese forces entering Burma. The BIA began to exploit their authority when the Japanese army moved northward, leaving the administration of lower Burma absolutely in BIA hands. Viewing the Karens as pro-British, the BIA restricted Karen movements. Tensions rose when the BIA required that Karens, who had served under the British army and were returned home at the end of March 1942, surrender their weapons. After the BIA collected the Karens' guns, the looting, robbing, raping, and killing of the Karen people began. The retaliation led to a communal war that engendered more suffering and no justice for the Karens.

THE KARENS IN THE SALWEEN DISTRICT

Located on the early Japanese military campaign zone path, the Karens in the Salween district encountered brutality first. The clashes between the BIA soldiers and Karens started when the BIA arrived in the Papun area on March 21, 1942. Two BIA officials, Boh Nya Na and Bo Htun Hla, announced that they were taking over the administration in Papun and demanded that arms be surrendered to them. When villagers brought only a few ancient, rusty shotguns, BIA officers arrested Karen leaders. Tensions escalated when Boh Nya Na was killed in an ambush. On April 4, Bo Htun Hla lined up seventeen Karen elders who had been locked up by BIA soldiers and mowed them down with automatic weapons on the hill behind the police station. Bo Htun Hla himself killed with a bayonet two Karens who initially survived the machine-gunning. Among those killed were three teachers, an ex-policeman, a forest ranger, an agricultural supervisor, and several prominent elders of Papun.[18]

This massacre triggered a state of open war between the Burmese and the Karens in Salween district. On April 25, 1942, Karen volunteers under Saw Darlington decided to attack Papun and drive the BIA out. They requested help from Major Hugh Paul Seagrim,[19] a British officer stationed in Pyagawpu village, who sent down two hundred Karen levies. They held a meeting in the Roman Catholic mission compound, where a French priest from Aquitaine stayed to protect the Karens and their villages. These Karens attacked the BIA and rescued some Karens, Indians, and Shans who were in the Papun jail. In retaliation, the BIA gathered all the Karens who remained in Papun and put them in the deputy commissioner's compound with machine guns trained on them. Almost every day, the BIA went around Papun, burning down nearby Karen villages. By May 1942, all the Papun residents deserted the town and fled into the forest.[20]

In a report to Dr. Ba Maw, who became the head of the new administration under the Japanese in August 1942, the incident in Papun was summarized as follows:

> To appreciate the real trouble in Papun District, one has to go back with regret to those so-called B.I.A. days. The B.I.A. burned many Karen villages, resulting in many homeless. They took their properties, gold and silver, even daily utensils. They murdered many Karen including seventeen leading citizens and elders. Lastly, and most important of all, they took away many of the Karen women-folk, and twenty young girls were taken to Papun as prostitutes in line for the B.I.A. soldiers. The B.I.A were then in charge of one Boh Tun Hla and he is said to be solely responsible for all these happening.[21]

The Karens in Shwegyin, another town located to the west of Papun, encountered similar abuse. On hearing the news of the coming Japanese, the Karens fled into the mountains, hiding in the remote forest. When the BIA arrived, they arrested all the remaining Karen men and women in Shwegyin. All the women, both old and young, were raped. Thirteen Karen men were slaughtered after being subjected to beatings, slapping, kicking, and other brutal torture.[22]

THE KARENS IN THE DELTA

Unlike Karens in Salween district, Karens in Bassein, the chief town of the delta, escaped BIA torment under Dr. San C. Po's good leadership. Before the British Commission evacuated on March 2, 1942, San C. Po, then seventy-two years old, was asked to temporarily take charge of the administration in Bassein. At the end of March, the BIA arrived, and its commander, Bo Win, sent a note demanding, "San C. Po, if you don't surrender all your arms and ammunition by four this evening, we shall take military action."[23] Some Karen leaders voiced support for attacking the BIA, but San C. Po tried to negotiate with Bo Win. After some discussion, the BIA and Karens reached an agreement to co-operate in keeping order. Due to his political experience and diplomatic skills, the BIA administration in Bassein continued without much violence.[24]

Unfortunately, BIA brutality reached a chaotic high in Myaungmya in the delta. The Karens suffered utter savagery and massacres. On March 1, 1942, a self-appointed committee of three young Burmans took over the administration after the British officials evacuated. They released more than a thousand criminals from jail saying they could not take responsibility for these prisoners. Immediately, these criminals started looting houses and property belonging to the Karens, Chinese, and Indians.[25]

On March 5, an advance detachment of the BIA arrived, consisting of about twenty-five Burmans armed with *dahs* (long, knife-like swords). They were led by a Buddhist monk, also carrying a dah and a double-barreled shotgun. The following day, the BIA's main body arrived, led by Bo Aung, also a Thakin, and his second-in-command, Bo Myint. As true in Papun in Salween district, they were undisciplined and started looting. They confiscated money from government servants and insisted that all notes be stamped. They did not permit individuals to keep more than two hundred rupees. The BIA also tried to recover all arms in the district and killed ex-soldiers who had served in the British army, all of whom were Karens. In front of BIA headquarters, two Karens were bayoneted in public, and their bodies hacked into small pieces.[26]

Initially, Karen leaders in Myaungmya tried their best to maintain peace by following BIA demands. When the first Japanese troops led by Lieutenant Colonel Ijima arrived in Myaungmya, two Karen leaders, Saw Pe Tha, a former judge and prewar cabinet minister in the Burma government, and Saw Dar Peh Lu greeted them cordially and demonstrated their sincere cooperation.[27]

As advised by Saw Pe Tha, the Karens started surrendering their arms to the BIA. Within a few days, however, well-armed gangs attacked and looted Karen villages. Since the BIA was the only armed group in the area, the Karens felt that the BIA was behind this robbery and looting. In addition, the active leadership of a dah-wielding Buddhist monk among the BIA created more suspicion and threatened the security of the Karen Christian community. The Karens decided to defend themselves by not surrendering their remaining weapons. If necessary, the Karens were ready to strike back with equal violence. Fueling the heat were the criminals who had been released from the jails so they could join in the prevailing disorder. From the end of March, this chaotic political situation led to a brutal full-scale communal gang war in the Myaungmya district and spread to adjoining Karen areas in Bassein, Henzada, and Pyapon.[28]

Lieutenant Colonel Ijima was killed in one of the attacks. In retaliation for his close friend's death, Japanese commander Colonel Suzuki gave orders to exterminate two large Karen villages, Kanazogon and Thayagon, although they had no part in Ijima's death. The BIA surrounded the villages at night and set fire to one end. As the villagers ran in panic from the other end, BIA troops waiting in ambush cut down everyone—men, women, and children—within reach of their swords in traditional Japanese fashion. Only a few escaped. All the wounded were left to die in the flames.[29]

The savage brutality intensified the Karens' resentment toward the Burmans, and open war developed between the Karens and the Burmans in the delta area. BIA forces occupied Myaungmya, where both Burmese and Karens came under police regulations. The Karen community lived as virtual hostages in Burmese hands. The Karens who did not surrender their arms to the BIA began to make plans to attack Myaungmya to rescue the Karens there. The initial movement was led by a Buddhist Karen, Mahn Shwe Tun Gya, later known as "the Tiger of the Delta," who formed large bands for the protection of the villages.[30] In May 1942, he contacted Saw San Po Thin, a Christian Karen who served in the British army, and formed a Karen association called *Taw-mei-pa* in Bassein.[31] San Po Thin agreed to join Shwe Tun Gya in his plan to attack the BIA in Myaungmya. On May 23, San Po Thin and two hundred followers, armed with twelve shotguns, five rifles, spears, crossbows, and staves, left for Myaungmya. At the village headman's home, the two leaders with their lieutenants discussed their war plan to attack the BIA. The meeting opened with prayers by the Karen pastor, who cited a verse from Philippians: "I can do all things through Christ who strengthened [sic] me."[32]

Without consulting with other Karen leaders, San Po Thin initiated a secret military rescue plan to free Saw Pe Tha and the rest of his Karen community by attacking Myaungmya with three Karen columns. As Professor Cady described, Saw San Po Thin was "possessed of more valor than discretion."[33] His secret plan was leaked to the BIA prior to the attack, due to his misjudgment of human character. He sent a secret message to Saw Pe Tha by a Burmese courier, who took the message first to BIA authorities. After noting its content, the BIA told him to deliver it to Saw Pe Tha and bring back the reply before taking it to Saw San Po Thin. Saw Pe Tha replied that his efforts to restore communal peace had failed, and he would leave San Po Thin to act as he thought best.[34]

Erroneously assuming the reply as Saw Pe Tha being part of the conspiracy, the BIA and Thakin leaders prepared for his arrest while strategizing for their counterattack. Meanwhile, more cautious Karen leaders, including Dr. San C. Po, succeeded in persuading two of the proposed attacking columns to abandon the planned rescue attempt.[35] Unsurprisingly, the attack failed from the start, when the one and only Karen unit fought the well-prepared, fully armed, and equipped BIA on May 26, the fixed date of the attack.

Subsequently, a horrendous punishment followed for the Karen community in Myaungmya. The BIA opened fire on the Roman Catholic mission compound. They massacred 152 men, women, and children, most of whom were Karen, Anglo-Burman, and Anglo-Indian refugees. The Burmans burned down the clergy house and the church, killing Father Blasius, the Karen priest in charge, who was sick in the house, along with his two helpers. They also burned down the orphanage after killing two Karen priests (Father Pascal and Father Gaspar), two lay sisters, and dozens of children. Most of the girls were cut down inside the mission compound and on the road outside. A six-month-old baby was among the children killed.[36]

Another Thakin-led mob went to the other Karen quarter, Shwe Dah-gone, on the other side of the town. They killed another fifty-two Karens including men, women, and children.[37] Among those killed were Saw Pe Tha, his English wife, and three children; a Karen police officer and his pregnant wife, who had just begun her labor. The Thakin, who held a grudge against Saw Pe Tha for refusing him a favor when Saw Pe Tha was a government judicial minister, led the massacre. They surrounded the house, broke in, and slaughtered him and his entire family, except for a young son who miraculously escaped. Then, they burned the entire house down. For several weeks after May 26, batches of Karen hostages were shot daily. Those Karens in Myaungmya who escaped these two massacres were put in the town prison. A few days later, forty-seven Karen men were taken out and bayoneted to death.[38] A Thakin eyewitness described how Karens were tortured: "I saw a row of Karens kept standing on shaky logs with their raised arms tied to a beam high above their heads. It was a slow and excruciating form of torture the BIA had learnt from the Japanese. Those men had been kept like that for hours without food, drink, or respite of any kind. No one seemed to know how long the torture would continue."[39]

Sharing Christian faith with the British rulers was a primary reason the Karens were regarded as the Buddhist Burmans' enemy. Thus, they became the targets of the BIA Thakins. They arrested the Karen pastors and tortured them before killing them. In Myaungmya district alone, twenty-four Karen village churches were burned down and destroyed.[40] My maternal great-grandfather, Rev. Po Nyo, was the pastor of the church in Kalauktheik village, one of the twenty-four destroyed during this period.[41]

Arguably, the Christian Karens' suffering in Thaton, Tenasserim district was equally painful as in Myaungmya. After the Japanese occupied Tenasserim, their army marched northward and left the BIA in control of the area. The BIA used their newly found power to persecute Christians. They arrested a Baptist Karen pastor, Rev. Sein Ko, and three other church leaders. They killed them after torturing them with various cruel techniques including skin peeling, slicingof body parts, nakedness in public, and starvation. The BIA closed Christian churches, ordered people to not hold worship services, placed materials about Buddhism inside churches, and made Christian pastors cook meals (*Hsun*) for Buddhist monks.[42] In addition, the BIA went into villages, looting, robbing, killing, and destroying properties, including churches, just as they did in the delta area.

Later in a report to the British government, leaders of the KNA gave this abridged account of the Karens' suffering during the Japanese occupation:

> While Burma was under the Military Administration of the Burma Independence Army . . . they branded the Karens as rebels, and persecuted and tortured them in all possible ways and in certain districts resorted to wholesale massacre, not even leaving babies, and set the Karen village on fire in this way, more than 1800 Karens were slaughtered, and their wives and daughters before being massacred, were subjected to immoral degradation in the presence of their husbands and fathers. . . . Their Mission centers were looted and set on fire. . . . Many died the death of Christian martyrs under horrible conditions. At that time, no influential Burmese leaders raised his hands and called a halt to such a senseless massacre.[43]

Some high-ranking members of the BIA Thakin leadership admitted that the more hot-headed among the ranks were responsible for the situation. One such leader claimed, "the young local *thakins* who were then on the way to power started the terrorism," and that "most of the incidents were provoked by their atrocities."[44] U Nu, the first prime minister of independent Burma, highlighted BIA responsibility for the ferociousness and admitted, "during the war, some bad Burmans, with the Japanese behind them, took advantage of their position to harm the Karens. That was how the Karen-Burman conflict originated."[45]

Reconciliation Attempts between the Karens and the Burmans

Recognizing excessive abuse of power within the BIA, the Japanese restructured both the military and civil administration in Burma. On June 7, 1942, a Burma Executive Administration with Dr. Ba Maw as its head officially replaced Thakin Tun Ok's Burma Baho government. On July 24, the whole BIA was disbanded, and in its place, the Burma Defense Army (BDA) was installed on August 26, 1942. A year later, on August 1, 1943, the Japanese declared Burma an independent state, which was recognized by all the Axis powers. In September, the Japanese changed Aung San's BDA to Burma National Army (BNA). Dr. Ba Maw, as the head of the new state, assumed the title of *Naing gan daw adipati* or *generalissimo*. Ba Maw formed his cabinet with sixteen ministers, without any Christian Karens.[46] On August 13, 1943, Japanese Tokyo Radio reported that the Karen-Burma strife had ended.[47]

After the Myaungmya incident, in their effort to protect the Karen community, the old KNA leaders and some young Karens met in Rangoon on June 23, 1943. There, they formed the Karen Central Advisory Board (KCAB).[48] These leaders, Dr. San C. Po, Mahn Ba Khin, Saw Tha Din, Mahn James Tun Aung, Saw Ba U Gyi,[49] Dr. Po D. Lone, Dr. Dwe, Saw San Po Thin, and Mahn Shwe Tun Kyar toured the Karen delta area, talking in favor of peace. The Karen community listened to their words. Also involved were Mahn Saw Bu from Myaungmya,[50] Thra Tha Hto from Kyunpyaw, Paul Aye Nyein from Myaugmya, Saw Po Ku from Papun, and Saw Sein Kho and Saw San Shwe from Toungoo.[51]

Meanwhile, BIA's disbanding dissatisfied the soldiers and young Burmese nationalists. Further, the public was unhappy with Japanese abuses. With growing suspicion of the so-called Burmese independence, Aung San and his colleagues began to plan anti-Japanese movements. Fathoming that the Karens had secret contact with the British in India, some Burmese leaders started to seek Karen cooperation. Subsequently, San Po Thin, through the arrangement of Thakin Than Tun, met Aung San. Reconciliation between the Karen leaders and the Burmese leaders began to develop in late 1943.

San Po Thin and his *Taw-mei-pa* Association joined other Karens in making contacts with the British for an anti-Japanese movement in late 1942. In early 1943, he met with Thakin Than Tun, who was the minister for commodities and transport in Dr. Ba Maw's government in Rangoon. Than Tun told San Po Thin that he was not happy with the "independence" Burma was given by the Japanese. He arranged for San Po Thin to meet Aung San for further discussions on cooperation. When San Po Thin met Aung San in November 1943, he advised Aung San to recruit Saw Hanson Kyar Doe, an ex-British army officer and a Karen who had been trained at Sandhurst. The next day, San Po Thin visited Saw Hanson Kyar Doe to persuade him to join the BDA. Saw Hanson Kyar Doe was not willing to join, considering no Karen would ever be given a colonel's position in the Burmese army. He told San Po Thin he would join if Aung San made him a lieutenant colonel in the BDA. Unexpectedly, in September 1943, the government gazette announced that Saw Kyar Doe was appointed a colonel, and San Po Thin was appointed a captain in the BDA.[52]

The progress of Karen-Burman reconciliation was so important for the resistance against the Japanese that Aung San continued to seek San Po Thin's advice to win the Karens' confidence. As advised, Aung San invited Dr. San C. Po, Saw Ba U Gyi, Mahn Shwe Tun Gya, and other Karen leaders to meet him in Rangoon. Several Thakin leaders joined that meeting, and Thakin Than Tun initiated reconciliation with the Karen leaders. Thakin Tun apologized for thakin misconduct during the Myaungmya incidents. Both parties then agreed to put aside ill feelings and strive for unity to fight the common enemy, the Japanese.[53]

In September 1944, Aung San and Bo Let Ya followed Saw Kyar Doe, San Po Thin, and other Karen leaders touring the delta areas. During this tour, Aung San offered his apologies for his men's misdeeds. The apology touched the hearts of many Karen people. Aung San's appointment of BNA Captain Saw San Po Thin as a military musical band leader was effective in winning delta Karen Christian support. The delta Karens were accustomed to singing choirs and used musical instruments in their church services. The reconciliation seemed to proceed so well that Thakin Nu, who went to a Karen village in Myaungmya in late 1944, claimed, "The people greeted us like long lost cousins."[54]

By the end of 1944, Aung San, Than Tun, and other Burmese leaders met for a secret discussion at the War Office with Saw Kyar Doe, Saw Johnson Kangyi, Saw Ba U Gyi, and other prominent Karen leaders. They all agreed to work together in the resistance movement.[55] Except for Mahn Shwe Tun Kyar, all Karens involved in the reconciliation efforts were Christians. Observing the role of Christian Karens in the unification of Burma, the prime minister in 1943, Dr. Ba Maw, who initially worked only with the Buddhist Karen National Association (BKNA),[56] added two Christian Karen leaders, U Hla Pe and San C. Po, to his cabinet.[57]

Despite the apparent reconciliation, sour memories of tragic incidents were imprinted so deeply on the minds of many Karens living through the period that the resentment for the Burmans never went away. After forty years, in 1985, famed journalist Martin Smith met the KNA leader Saw Tha Din, who told him candidly, "How could anyone expect the Karen people to trust the Burman after what happened during the war—the murder and slaughter of so many people and the robbing of so many Karen villages? After all this, how could anyone seriously expect us to trust any Burman government in Rangoon?"[58]

Allied Military Campaigns and the Karen Connection

The wealth of World War II events in Burma built a repository for scholars and writers of different interests to generate numerous volumes about Burma of that period. In almost all these books, each author presented the role of the Karen people in various arrays. In his renowned book, *Burma: The Longest War (1941–1945)*, Louis Allen detailed World War II military campaigns and claimed that "a great variety of races and motivations was involved: British, Japanese, Chinese, American, Indian, Gurkha, East and West African, Burmese, Karen, Kachin."[59] Ian Morrison, who chronicled Major Seagrim's fascinating adventures and heroic death in the war, described the delta massacre as "one of violence, and crime, of heroism, brutality and secret intrigue, of the clash and inter-relationship of men of four races, British, Japanese, Burmese and Karen."[60]

Without paying attention to other Karens' involvements in World War II, the Myaungmya incident alone testified that being Christians and serving in the British military cost Karens their lives. A governmental official report dated December 15, 1942, and addressed to the prime minister, Dr. Ba Maw, made a clear statement that "loyalty of the Karens towards the British" was a major cause of tragic episodes.[61]

The Karens' military service and loyalty to the Allied cause of liberation from the world of fascism in World War II was only a sequel to their long tradition of serving in the British military service since the first Anglo-Burmese war in 1824. Soon after their annexation, the British acknowledged that Karens were as good at soldiering as the Gurkhas of Nepal. Because of their valuable service, Karens were recruited in the Burma Military Police, the Burma Sappers and Miners, the Burma Mechanical Transport, and the Burma Rifles fighting for the British in World War I. The Karens participated in suppressing all movements against the British government, in actions that their leaders proudly recorded: "the Chin Hills rising, the Shwebo rising, the San Pe rising, the crime waves of 1925–1927, and the Burma Rebellion of 1930–32, in which not only Karens of the Regular Services, but also Leaders, Elders, and the Karen irregulars played prominent parts."[62]

At the beginning of World War II, while the majority Burmans were taking advantage of the war as an opportunity to fight the British for independence, the Karens demonstrated their loyalty to the Union Jack.

General Smith Dun's statement is true that "the character of the Karens is such that death is preferred to betrayal."[63] Not only the Karen soldiers but also the whole Karen community, including Christian pastors and priests, were involved in fighting the Japanese alongside the Allied forces to the end of the war. The Karens have the right to claim, "In this Great World War II, the Karens occupy no second place in Burma both in numbers, integrity and daring achievement."[64]

THE BURMA RIFLES AND THE KARENS

Professor Hugh Tinker, who compiled and published British government documents and official correspondences of World War II in Burma, wrote, "When the British forces retreated through the border hills into India the only men from Burma to accompany them were Karen soldiers of the 2nd Burma Rifles."[65] It appeared as a testimony to Karen soldiers' loyalty. However, one can further question, "Why the 2nd Burma Rifles?" The answer is simple, but one must travel back to the past.

The Burma Rifles were one of the British military forces in which the Karens could serve. Up until 1935, it was composed of three battalions: the 1st, the 2nd, and the 3rd. In each battalion, there were two companies of Karens, one of Chins, and one of Kachins. The officers were either British officers who had a short assignment in England after being newly graduated from Sandhurst; or British officers from the Indian Army, serving in Burma; or educated Burmans, Karens, Chins, and Kachins who had been awarded King's Commissions.[66]

In 1937, the 4th Battalion of the Burma Rifles was established with the same original composition. After war broke out in Europe, two more battalions were formed, which included one company of Burmans. The 7th Burma Rifles was formed with a battalion of military police, mainly composed of Gurkhas and Kumaonis. A battalion of the Burma Frontier Force, composed of two companies each of Sikhs and Punjabi Muslims, was formed into the 8th Battalion. The 9th was the reinforcement battalion based at Meiktila, and the 10th was a training battalion in Maymyo. Due to the wartime emergency, the next four, the 11th, 12th, 13th, and 14th, all territorial battalions, were urgently recruited for service inside Burma.[67] In 1939, there were 472 Burmans compared with 3,197 Karens, Chins, and Kachins in the Burma Defense Force.[68]

When Japan declared war, the 2nd Burma Rifles were at Mergui in south Tenasserim, commanded by Lieutenant Colonel D. C. H. O'Callaghan. After the Japanese cut across the Kara isthmus to Tavoy, the 2nd Burma Rifles evacuated by sea to Rangoon.[69] They were then ordered to go to Moulmein to join the command of the 17th Indian Division but were halted at Kyaikto. Then in March 1942, they were assigned to go to Papun, a town only twenty miles from the Thai border. The plan was to block any attempted Japanese crossing of the Thai-Burma border at Dagwin. Two companies of the battalion, one by mule and another by motor transport, moved to Papun. One company was stationed on the frontier near Dagwin with another stationed further south to contest any northward push by the Japanese. The final two were kept in reserve in Papun and stationed temporarily in the police lines.[70]

As the Japanese advanced further into Burma, the 2nd Battalion Burma Rifles were ordered to withdraw west to Shwegyin. Rear headquarters with seventeen elephants set off first. Immediately after arriving at Shwegyin, they encountered an attack by the BIA under a Japanese officer. The battle was over after thirteen of the enemy, including the Japanese officer, were killed.[71] Meanwhile, the 2nd Burma Rifles' main body withdrew to Toungoo and Kyaukkyi. On their way, about March 10, carrying all their stores on ninety-three elephants, they passed through Pyagawpu, a Karen village northwest of Papun. During this period, about twenty Karens of the 2nd Burma Rifles, who suffered from malaria and fever, were left in Pyagawpu. A Catholic priest, Father Loizot, was the last European to evacuate through this village.[72]

At the time the Japanese reached the east bank of the Irrawaddy, the 2nd Burma Rifles had withdrawn to Allanmyo on the Irrawaddy north of Prome, crossing the river at Thayetmyo. In the long retreat, soldiers marched from Pakokku, Gangaw, Kalemyo, Tamu, and Palel into India. When the 2nd battalion reached Imphal in India, there were between four hundred and six hundred men, mostly Karens. As with most of the other battalions, Burma Rifles had already been discharged east of Chindwin, and only about eight hundred men of the Burma Rifles reached Imphal. They were given the choice either to stay with the British forces or return home with full pay, ten days' ration, a rifle, and fifty rounds. More than half volunteered to stay and fight. Evidently, most of them were Karens.[73] It is claimed that the total number of Karens following the British in India was two thousand.[74] If so, the remaining Karens (around five hundred) in the 2nd Burma Rifles would constitute 25 percent of the Karen population in India during the war.

The 2nd Burma Rifles was the only battalion that stayed in India where they received training. They were eventually reorganized by Lieutenant Colonel O'Callaghan into ten platoons of forty men each designed for reconnaissance. After joining Major General Orde Charles Wingate's troops and fighting through the first expedition, Wingate said the Karens were the finest body of troops he ever had. After Wingate's special force was dispersed, the 2nd Battalion was reformed in March 1945, on an ordinary infantry basis, one-third Karen, one-third Kachin, and one third Chin. By then, there were eight Karen officers with commissions from the King plus three Chins and one Kachin.[75]

THE KAREN LEVIES, MAJOR HUGH PAUL SEAGRIM AND FORCE 136

Because of their military service and loyalty at the time of the British evacuation to India, the Karens in the 2nd Burma Rifles secured due recognition. In addition, the valuable contributions and sacrifices of many other Karens during the war were equally, or more, outstanding as described below:

> There are no less than one Lieut. Colonel, seven Majors, over twelve Captains, fifteen Lieutenants, and more than sixty VCOs [Viceroy's Commissioned Officers] of the Burma Rifles, in addition to hundreds of Karens in the ranks. There are also over one hundred young Karens holding the status of British Other Ranks in the BAF [Burma Auxiliary Force], and the BIC [Burma Intelligence Corps], add to this the young Karens of the Burma Army Signals and the GPT [General Purpose Transport], the Burma Navy and the Burma Hospital Company. These are the young men who neither hesitated nor looked back in a struggle for Freedom and Justice. Then again the world-renowned Wingate expeditions, which paved the way for the successful re-occupation of Burma, and which consisted mainly of picked young Karens who gladly sacrificed their noble lives in the Valley of Death for the King and Country. Last but never the least our Karen Levies, numbering well over ten thousand who are no fair weather friends to the Allies.[76]

The important role of the Karen levies in World War II is fundamentally associated with Force 136's underground movements. Force 136 was the Southeast Asia branch of Special Operations Executive (SOE). The British Ministry of Economic Warfare established SOE in Southeast Asia, with the primary function to contact local resistance forces, assess their potential, and provide arms, if they determined that an armed uprising would help the returning British. Through this information network, the British exile government, headed by Governor Sir Reginald Dorman-Smith in India's summer capital of Simla and Lord Louis Mountbatten, the Supreme Allied Commander (SAC) of the Southeast Asian Command (SEAC), in Kandy, Ceylon, received valuable news about the anti-Japanese preparations in Burma.

The Burma Section of Force 136 commander, from 1943 until the end of the war, was John Ritchie Gardiner, who had connections with Burmese political groups since the prewar period. Force 136 contacted anti-Japanese groups inside Burma and stimulated resistance movements. Through their activities, the anti-Japanese units inside Burma began to coordinate with Allied forces in 1944, leading to successful military campaigns to reoccupy Burma.

Force 136 worked with two divisions in Burma, with Burmans on the west bank of the Sittang River and Karens on the east bank, from which Karen levies contributed much intelligence throughout the war. The first encounter was in early 1942 when Karen soldiers of 2nd Burma Rifles and about 150 levies tried to stop the Japanese army and their BIA auxiliaries from coming up the road from Toungoo into the Shan state. In this fierce fight, after which two British officers received awards for their brave service, a Karen officer, the second in command of the company, was captured and beheaded by the Japanese.[77] Another more important engagement was in 1945, when the Japanese marched down the road to Toungoo from the Shan states.[78] In fact, the Karens suffered most during the war period in 1943–1944, when the Japanese sent punitive expeditions in search of Major Seagrim, the British intelligence officer who organized Karen levies and initiated the link with anti-Japanese groups inside Burma for Force 136.

Major Hugh Paul Seagrim was one of the British agents who stayed behind when the British evacuated from Burma. In December 1941, Noel Steven, assistant superintendent in the Burma Frontier Service, had the job of raising guerrilla levies from the hill tribes in Burma. He recruited Seagrim, then attached to the 12th Battalion, to defend the Mingaladon airfield near Rangoon. Having been among the Karens prior to the war, Seagrim proposed to raise levies in the Karen hill area. At the 17th Division headquarters in Moulmein, it was agreed at a conference with General Smyth that Seagrim should organize a force of Karens in Papun, the capital of Salween district, and about twenty miles from the Burma-Thai border. On January 20, 1942, Seagrim, accompanied by Lieutenant Ronald Heath of the Oriental Mission, drove to Papun with some ammunition collected for him by Noel Steven. There, he organized a force of Karens, with the help of George Chettle, a Burma police officer, who prepared his contingent of fifty-five armed police and two hundred civil police for the attack through the border.[79]

Since Papun was on a motor road easily reached by the Japanese and the BIA, Seagrim moved to a village, Pyagawpu, which is inaccessible except by mountain tracks. Pyagawpu is a Karen village with a small church and a police station deep in the forest northwest of Papun.[80] Ta Roe, a well-to-do elephant owner, provided Seagrim accommodations, and from Pyagawpu, he organized and trained the Karen levies. Within a week, he received eight hundred applications to join the levies, but due to a weapons shortage, many Karens were sent back after their names were registered.

Seagrim's organization consisted of three lieutenants: Saw Willie Saw, a former forest ranger; Saw Darlington, a former teacher at a Wesleyan mission school and an ex-military policeman; and Saw Digay, a timber contractor. Saw Willie Saw had nine sections, Saw Darlington had twenty sections, and Saw Digay had eighteen sections. Each section was composed of eleven men with the section commanders serving in the Burma Rifles. The levy sections were assigned to protect their village from robbers, to help soldiers who had been cut off, and, most importantly, to carry out their primary task and report intelligence to Seagrim by fast runner.[81]

Despite success in recruiting the levies, Seagrim was short of arms and ammunition to equip them. In search of weapons, he sent Ta Roe to the Mawchi mine where the northern Karen levies operated under the command of Noel Boyt. Noel Steven sent Boyt, timber manager for Steel Brothers, and H. C. Smith of Burma Forest Service, to organize levies on the Toungoo-Mawchi road.[82] Although Boyt and Smith were civilians, under their leadership the northern Karen levies effectively fought the Japanese in this strategic location, which was one of the main routes into the Shan states by way of Mawchi, Loikaw, and Taungyi. Morrison wrote, "In 1942, Karens performed a valuable service delaying the Japanese going *up* it. In 1945, they were to perform an even more valuable service delaying the Japanese coming *down* it."[83]

Though he received some ammunition from Boyt, Seagrim was short of other necessities, including money, medical supplies, and communication with the outside world. In April 1942, Seagrim traveled north searching for an army headquarters with the main purpose of obtaining a wireless receiver and transmitter. Seagrim set out to Mawchi with his Karens (Subardar Ba Din, Halvidar Saw Charlie, Havildar Tha U, Lance-Naik Ah Din), eight other riflemen of the 2nd Battalion, two Kachin stragglers from the 4th Battalion, and seven Gurkha stragglers, not knowing that Mawchi was already occupied by the Japanese. After a few days, Seagrim stopped his search when almost all the team members, including Seagrim himself, came down with malaria.[84]

Seagrim was a committed Christian, and he always carried his two Bibles with him. On April 27, somewhere near Taunggyi, Seagrim decided to send back two of his team members, Ba Din and Po Gay, to Pyagawpu to manage the levies. Seagrim gave one of his two Bibles to Ba Din and told him, "Only God can help us now." He also wrote a certificate addressed to army headquarters stating:

> This is to certify that I have today released from service Sub. Ba Din, 2nd Bn, Burma Rifles and No. 7979 Rfn. Po Gay, 3rd Bn. Burma Rifles. I am sending them back to volunteer H.Q., Pyagawpu (near Papun), where they will remain and work with the volunteers as long as the volunteers remain in operation. . . .
> I wish to state that these two men have shown great loyalty and have followed me for many miles in my search for A.H.Q.
> They are NOT deserters, . . . and I have on my own responsibility told them that their service with the volunteers will count as Military Service.[85]

During his stay in the north, several Karen Christian pastors looked after Seagrim, supplying food and providing guides from village to village. In recognition of their support, Seagrim wrote several certificates including one dated April 20, 1942, for a Karen pastor, Thra Shwe Lay:

> This is to certify that Thra Shwe Laye has assisted the British Government during the period February–April 1942. . . . He has persuaded the Karens of the Mawchi area to remain loyal to the British.
> This man, by remaining loyal, has endangered his life. Being a Karen leader, the Japanese have offered a big reward for his capture. He could run away but is afraid that if he did so other Karens would suffer at the hands of the Japanese. He therefore prefers to remain with his people and accept the consequences.[86]

Two other pastors, who became very close to Seagrim and played a prominent part in recruiting the northern Karen levies, were Thra May Sha of Mawtudo village and Thra Kyaw Lay of Ubo village. Both were graduates of the Karen Baptist Seminary in Insein.[87]

Seagrim came to know these two pastors in late May 1942, when he arrived at Mawtudo after he and his guide, a Karen officer of northern Karen levies, Lieutenant Ba Thein, were ambushed by Shan bandits. Seagrim alone escaped and reached Mawtuda.[88] For the next four months, the two pastors hid him in a small hut near the village. Thra May Sha visited him with some trusted Karens several times a week and supplied him with food. They brought him the latest news of the BIA, the Japanese, and the course of the war. In this camp at Mawtudo, Seagrim had three Karens and two Kachins living with him. Every evening, they had prayers round the fire, and Seagrim read a passage from the Bible in English, explained it to the Karen boys in Burmese, and said the Lord's Prayer. With Thra May Sha and Thra Kyaw Lay, Seagrim discussed religious themes, sometimes giving them Bible passages and asking them to think about them.[89]

When Seagrim organized his underground movement, Thra May Sha took the responsibility for keeping him supplied with food, while Thra Kyaw Lay worked as the outside contact and chief gatherer of news. In June 1942, Seagrim sent Thra Kyaw Lay to Pyagawpu, giving him a bag of messages to send to India, with instructions that whenever a British plane flew over Pyagawpu the letters KV (Karen Volunteers) were to be laid out in strips of white cloth on an open patch of ground. The bag was to be attached to a cord hanging above the ground, in hope that if the British plane flew over and saw the bag, it might try to hook the cord with the bag attached. Unfortunately, no British plane appeared during his three-month stay at Pyagawpu. Thra Kyaw Lay had to return to Seagrim's headquarters at Mawtudo.[90]

In December 1942, at Seagrim's request, his friend Ta Roe from Pyagawpu sent two of his elephants for him to move back to Pyagawpu. On his way, he met with an Anglican Karen priest, Francis Ah Mya, who shared information that the bishop in Rangoon, Rev. George West, was interested in the British movement. On December 5, he arrived at Chawido, a small village near Pyagawpu. Since it was unsafe for Seagrim, Ta Roe made the villagers build a hut for Seagrim in a dense forest a few miles east of Chawido and sent food supplies, rice, salt, oil, and vegetables. However, after a month, Seagrim moved into Pyagawpu, in Ta Roe's old house, where he previously stayed. Amid the Japanese threat, Seagrim attended the church and sometimes preached. He told Ta Roe that, after the war, he wanted to become a missionary and work among the Karens.[91] During his stay here, he met Father Calmon, a Roman Catholic priest, who was later arrested and tortured by the Japanese in Papun.

Ta Roe and the Karens took many risks to protect Seagrim from the Japanese. On February 25, 1943, at his village in Chawido, a young Karen came on foot from a village midway between Papun and Pyagawpu with a message that the Japanese were on their way and would arrive at Pyagawpu that morning. To save Seagrim, Ta Roe immediately rode his elephant to Pyagawpu, where he made a quick arrangement and sent Seagrim back to his original hiding place east of Chawido.[92]

Just half an hour after Seagrim left, about seventy Japanese soldiers arrived at Pyagawpu. The lieutenant in charge ordered his men to search the village and ask questions if they found British officers or soldiers. The Japanese ordered Ta Roe and two elders to follow them to Papun. Before he left, Ta Roe whispered to a Karen elder whom he trusted to move Seagrim to another place in the mountains northwest of Pyagawpu. Seagrim moved to a small place in the forest near a village called Payasedo, about twenty-three miles west of Pyagawpu.[93]

Surprisingly, Ta Roe and his team were allowed to return after the Japanese officer gave them a lecture that they must cooperate with Maung Shwe, the new district commander of the Salween district, a Burman. On his return, Ta Roe received a letter from Seagrim asking for supplies. Without hesitation, Ta Roe loaded rice and other supplies on one of his elephants and sent them to Seagrim's hiding place. Ta Roe continued to supply food and other needs of Seagrim during the months he stayed there.[94]

In early 1943, an ex-officer of the 11th battalion Burma Rifles, Saw Po Hla from Myaungmya in the delta, joined Seagrim. Po Hla was a graduate of Rangoon University and, after working for the Irrawaddy Flotilla Company, joined the Burma Rifles in January 1941. He was commissioned shortly after and became quartermaster of the battalion until it was disbanded in 1942. He went back to his hometown but had to flee from one place to another as the Japanese *Kempeitai* tried to arrest him. Finally, through the contact of a Karen levy in Kyaukkyi, Po Hla came to Seagrim's headquarters in Payasedo.[95]

Seagrim made Po Hla his liaison officer who traveled about the hills, carrying messages of encouragement from Seagrim to the levies and collecting news. Meanwhile, Dr. Ba Maw's government took some Karen leaders' advice and appointed Karen officers in the Karen-populated areas. As such, Saw Tommer became the district commander of Salween district in place of Maung Shwe. Another Karen, Arthur Ta Bi, was made the Papun township officer. On hearing of the appointment of the Karen official in Papun, Seagrim sent Po Hla to Papun to convey his personal greetings, along with the assurance that they could count on the levies' full backing in maintaining peace and order. After delivering the message, Po Hla toured the levy section headquarters in the south and told them that, on Seagrim's orders, they were to give every support to Saw Tommer and Arthur Ta Bi.[96] Subsequently, Seagrim had regular contacts with Saw Tommer and Arthur Ta Bi, exchanging information about Japanese movements. Later in October 1943, Arthur Ta Bi informed Seagrim about the details of a big Japanese airfield at Chiang

Mai. Later, the Allies raided that airfield. He also reported the location of a big Japanese workshop on the Burma-Thai railway and some petrol dumps on the Toungoo-Thandaung road.[97]

Meanwhile, Force 136 planned a special operation in the Karen hills. They chose the location with the assumption that Seagrim was safe with the Karens who were loyal to the British, but the geographical location was the main reason for their choice. It was a good strategic base for operations against the main Japanese north-south line of communication from Rangoon to Mandalay, against their east-west line of communication from Rangoon to Moulmein to Bangkok, and operations in Thailand.[98]

In late 1942, general headquarters in Delhi approved a four-stage plan. The first stage was to drop a Karen officer, Second Lieutenant Ba Gyaw, with three other Karen parachutists, very lightly equipped without a wireless transmitter, into the Karen hills. On landing, Ba Gyaw was to explore and investigate if it was safe for a transmitter. If so, the rest of their communications kit would be dropped. The second stage would follow a few nights after Ba Gyaw's team was dropped. A Lockheed Hudson aircraft was to fly over the same dropping zone. If certain prearranged signals were seen from the ground, the transmitter and kits would be dropped. The third stage was for Ba Gyaw to communicate if it was safe to drop a British Force 136 officer, Major James Nimmo, with a team of Karen wireless operators. The fourth and final stage was to drop Captain McCrindle if Major Nimmo landed successfully and considered it safe for another officer to join him. Once the dropping finished, the remaining task was to establish three operational centers in the Karen hills, each under a British officer with a transmitter. Seagrim was to be the overall commander in the central area, with Nimmo's headquarters north of the Mawchi road and McCrindle in the south around Kadaingti.[99]

The first stage of the operation was successful when Second Lieutenant Ba Gyaw and three other Karens, Pa Ah, Thet Wa, and Tun Shwe, parachuted on February 18, 1943.[100] To distract Japanese attention on that day, a bombing was staged on Toungoo. The stage two plan could not continue due to the weather. Attempts were made on each full moon night between February and October 1943, without success. Finally, on the night of October 12, Major Nimmo and four Karens, Tun Lin, He Be, Saw Sunny, and Saw Pe, parachuted into the jungle with wireless equipment.[101] Nimmo found both Ba Gyaw and Seagrim in two days delivering to Seagrim his needed wireless transmitter. Choosing the young Karen parachutist, Thet Wah, as his wireless operator, Seagrim was able to establish communication with headquarters in India on October 15, 1943.[102]

Prior to Major Nimmo's arrival in September 1943, Seagrim sent Po Hla down into Rangoon to collect information and communicate with the Karen leaders in the city. In Rangoon, he met Saw San Po Thin and Saw Hanson Kyar Doe, who were officers in a Karen battalion of Aung San's BDA. San Po Thin had been Po Hla's music teacher in Bassein prior to World War II. They crossed paths again in 1940 while training in Mandalay. The two told Po Hla that anti-Japanese sentiment was strong among the Burmese and that BDA leaders were already preparing to revolt against the Japanese.[103]

The information Po Hla collected and brought back to Seagrim was transmitted to the military headquarters in India. Po Hla's information was extremely useful for Allied military operations. In addition to BDA movements, he reported to Seagrim the details of useful targets, Japanese unit identifications, troop movements, and other general conditions, such as food, clothing, prices, and communications in Rangoon. The details of all the big Japanese workshops in Insein led to a highly successful Allied bombing raid in early December. Furthermore, at Po Hla's suggestion, Seagrim advised India Command not to bomb the New Law Court in Rangoon, one of the Kempeitai headquarters, because many captured British and American pilots were imprisoned there.[104]

The fourth and last stage of Force 136 special operation in the Karen hills was accomplished on December 9, 1943, when Captain McCrindle parachuted in with more wireless equipment and four Karens.[105] Just a few days after McCrindle landed, Seagrim called a meeting at his camp where he introduced Nimmo and McCrindle to sixty Karens who worked with him closely, including pastors and schoolmasters from Chawido, Pyagawpu, and the villages around Salween district. The meeting began with a short worship service in Karen conducted by the pastor of Pyagawpu. After Bible reading and some prayers, they sang a hymn and the Karen national anthem. Saw Po Hla and three of the parachutists sang the hymn "Rock of Ages" in English. They finished with the Lord's Prayer.[106]

When the service was over, Seagrim offered his welcome message in Burmese and read a letter brought by McCrindle from Karens who followed the British to India in 1942 and were still there. The letter said, "We know that you Karens in Burma are undergoing much suffering. But we always remember you in our prayers and we ask you to remember us in your prayers."[107] Seagrim showed certificates that were received from India, some signed by General Auchinleck, commander-in-chief for India, and some by Lieutenant General Pownall, chief of staff to Admiral Mountbatten (Lord Mountbatten). All praised the Karens for their loyalty and thanked them for what they had done.[108]

The next day, Nimmo traveled north to establish a command center in Karen country north of Mawchi road. Along with him, he took a wireless set and three Karen parachutists, Aaron, Tun Lin, and He Be.[109] Until January 6, 1944, Nimmo stayed with Francis Ah Mya, the Anglican Karen priest who had previously met Seagrim. His assistant, Tun Lin, went further north to contact Thra May Sha, the Mawtudo village pastor. As they previously did for Seagrim, Thra May Sha and Thra Kyaw Lay built huts for Nimmo in the forest. On January 10, Nimmo arrived in Mawtudo and started to work immediately at their new camp. In his team, Nimmo had his four parachutists; Ji Bu, the elephant driver; Saw Myin, a wireless operator; Saw Media, who was a theological student at Insein Baptist Seminary; and two old Burma Riflemen. He established contact with several Karen timber contractors, whom he had known before the war, and other officials in the northern Karen levies. Nimmo built an efficient intelligence organization and started to send useful information to India about targets in Toungoo, as well as Japanese movements and unit identifications.[110]

Meanwhile, Saw Tommer, Karen district commander in Papun, informed Seagrim of three Karen agents from India parachuting south of Salween in late December 1943. These three Karens belonged to another group engaged in special operations without the knowledge of Seagrim. The problem was one of them had landed on a tall clump of bamboo and the other two had to get him down with the help of nearby villagers. In his message to Seagrim, Saw Tommer warned that information could reach the Japanese, since the area was on the outskirts of the Karen country, and there, people intermingled with the Burmans.[111] The news did reach the Japanese because, in the middle of January 1944, the search for Seagrim intensified. Considering Seagrim's situation, Ta Roe arranged to move the camp to the mountainous area near the village of Komupwado about ten miles southwest of Pyagawpu.

A few days later, Ta Roe received a message from one of the levies from Kyaukkyi. The Japanese were holding Po Hla's family. If Po Hla did not surrender, the Japanese threatened that the family would be punished. Seagrim and McCrindle discussed and considered different options, but in the end, Seagrim was most concerned for the safety of Po Hla's family. He told Po Hla to surrender with a good story to deceive the Japanese. Po Hla's story was that he was the spoiled son of rich parents, but his parents did not give him enough money, so he went out trading medicines in the Karen hills. Po Hla would say that he met Seagrim in 1942 but never again since. On his way back home, in a village near Mawchi, Po Hla met Nimmo and his team. Upon learning of Po Hla's plan to surrender, some followers wanted to kill Po Hla. But Nimmo warned them that, even if they killed Po Hla, the Japanese suspicion would not go away, and the punishment would be more severe on his relatives.[112]

In late January 1944, Po Hla surrendered to Warrant-Officer Nakayama in Nyaunglaybin and was then transferred to Rangoon. The Japanese accepted his story, and the commander of the Kempeitai in Rangoon invited him for dinner and asked him to help the Japanese obtain the cooperation of the Karens. Eventually, Po Hla was able to send a letter, telling Seagrim what happened.[113]

Meanwhile, by mid-January, the Japanese Kempeitai received news of Seagrim's organization and the parachutists. Subsequently, they began a widespread campaign of arrest and torture in the Karen hills. A detachment under Captain Motoichi Inoue started to use Kempeitai methods of usual Japanese brutality in Kyaukkyi. While they put on cinema shows for the townsfolk, they arrested and tortured several Karens including an ex-soldier of the Burma Rifles who was Seagrim's levy commander, Maung Wah. He was interrogated about Seagrim, the Karen parachutists, and levies. With hands tied behind his back, Maung Wah was strung to a beam with his feet off the ground, and the Japanese lashed him back and front with bamboo poles. After three days, the Japanese told him that he must go up the hills and return within one week with full details of Seagrim, including a map of his camp and sentry posts. If he did not come back with the information, they would act against his family. Maung Wah had no choice. He went to Seagrim in the new camp at Komupwado and told him everything. The appearance of Maung Wah with the red swelling on the wrists and the bruises on his whole body moved Seagrim, who sadly said, "This is the price which you Karens are paying for your loyalty."[114]

Seagrim instructed Maung Wah to report about him to the Japanese. However, before Maung Wah's return, the Japanese found Seagrim's location and the secret place of the levy weapons through their punitive use of torture, killing, beating, and burning of Karen villages. Segarim, Nimmo, and McCrindle had to run from one hiding camp to another. Of the three wireless transmitters, Seagrim gave one to Karen officer Ba Gyaw and Thet Wah, the operator, with the instruction that they should go north and hide. If anything happened to him, Nimmo, or McCrindle, they were to signal the British in India. He and Nimmo each had one wireless transmitter, but in a few days, Seagrim informed India that he was going off the air.[115]

Toward the end of January, the Japanese expanded their methods of torture in the villages, although they knew that most of these Karen villagers knew little about Seagrim. When a few levies could not stand the torture, the Japanese discovered the new location of Seagrim and McCrindle. On February 13, 1944, Captain Inoue and his Kempeitai detachment and a company of infantry under the command of Captain Yamaguchi arrived in Pyagawpu, making the church their headquarters and arresting Ta Roe, Po Hla, and several elders.

By using their usual methods of torture, they soon obtained information about Seagrim's new location. On February 14, they reached Seagrim's camp that was about a mile away from Komupwado on the side of a ravine amid groves of bamboo. It was a dark place, where the sun seldom penetrated through the overhanging branches of the trees. The fight took about a half-hour. All escaped except McCrindle. This British officer of Force 136 was in Karen dress when he was shot and killed in the deep Karen jungle.[116] The Japanese did not get Seagrim, but they found Seagrim's Bible. The following day, on February 15, Japanese troops under the command of Captain Morino, Kempeitai chief at Toungoo, attacked and killed Major Nimmo in his camp in the forest near Mawtudo.[117]

Hidden by loyal Karens near Mewado village, Seagrim escaped for nearly a month after the death of Nimmo and McCrindle. Two Karens, a young parachutist, Pa Ah, and Ba Gyaw, an ex-soldier of the Burma Rifles, were with him. Pa Ah contacted the headman of Mewado, and they agreed to conceal Seagrim and supply food.[118] Unfortunately, the capture of the two British officers' equipment furnished the Japanese with all the information they required about Major Seagrim and his activities. In their efforts to locate him, the Japanese arrested at least 270 people, including elders and headmen, many of whom were tortured and killed in the most brutal fashion. In addition to the most common forms of torture including beating, clubbing, and slapping, the Japanese Kempeitai's method of torture included cigarette burns, electric shocks that applied the terminals to the most sensitive parts of the body, and hanging people upside-down from a beam in the ceiling for hours. Even under such pressure, the Karens continued to assist and hide Major Seagrim.

In March 1944, Captain Inoue came to Mewado village and threatened the headman who concealed Seagrim. Unless Seagrim's exact location was revealed, Inoue would burn the whole village to the ground. All the villagers—men, women, and children—would be arrested. Major Seagrim could not cause this violence to be imposed on his beloved Karens, so he decided to surrender. He and his two loyal Karens, Pa Ah and Ba Gyaw, surrendered to Captain Inoue, who was stationed in Mewado village. They were taken to Papun on March 14 and sent to Rangoon on March 16, 1944.[119]

In Rangoon, Seagrim was taken to the New Law Courts and put in the Kempeitai cells. On September 2, Major Shunji Koga came to the cell with four Japanese officers and two interpreters. The death sentence was passed on Major Seagrim and seven of his Karens: Lieutenant Ba Gyaw, Saw He Be, Saw Tun Lin, Saw Sunny, Saw Pe, Saw Peter, and Saw Ah Din. On hearing the sentence, Major Seagrim, still wearing Karen dress as he did in the villages, pleaded that the Karens be excused since the war was between the Japanese and the British. He explained the Karens were just following his orders. He alone should be sentenced to death. His attempts to save the Karens were to no avail. Not long after, with their hands tied behind their backs, they were driven to the Japanese execution ground at Kemmedine cemetery.[120]

Other Karen followers of Seagrim, Saw Po Hla, Saw Ta Roe, Saw Digay, Thra May Sha, Thra Kyaw Lay, Saw Rubert, Saw Henry, Saw Po Myin, Saw Tha Say, and Saw Yay, were sentenced to eight years of rigorous imprisonment. Later, some of them escaped to participate in special operations fighting the Japanese troops in 1945.[121]

Seagrim's heroic death at age forty-three was a sad story. However, his labor produced great results after his death. Seagrim's network and his Karen levies opened the channel for Force 136 to coordinate anti-Japanese activities inside Burma with the Allied forces. By 1945, twelve thousand Karen levies fought in the legendary military campaign dubbed Operation Character, a decisive battle in defeating the Japanese forces in Burma.

THE KAREN PEOPLE AND OPERATION CHARACTER

In 1944, Lord Mountbatten was drawing an operation plan Dracula to recapture Rangoon using a joint seaborne and airborne exercise. He supported Force 136, since he agreed with the belief of its commander, Colin Mackenzie, that "a strengthened guerrilla movement in Burma would greatly assist his own operation behind the enemy line."[122] Until the end of 1944, neither British Prime Minister Winston Churchill nor Major General C. F. Pearce, the chief of Civil Affairs Service (CAS [B]) in India, was in favor of his plan. Believing that they could win without air and navy support, the top army commanders, including Lieutenant General Sir Oliver Leese and General William Slim, had opposed the Dracula plan.[123]

The Allied invasion of Burma began in December 1944 under General Slim, governor general of Australia. Slim's 14th Army, consisting of seven divisions and two armored brigades, advanced into Burma from India. By March 4, 1945, they reoccupied Meiktila. General Slim wanted to finish his operation before the monsoon started and set the goal to reach Rangoon before May 15.[124] Encountering aggressive Japanese resistance in Meiktila, General Slim reconsidered the role of Dracula and eventually consented to Mountbatten's amphibious-*cum*-airborne assault into Rangoon.[125]

Mountbatten wrote, "I considered it vital that the Toungoo airfields should be in our possession by 25 April, if efficient air support was to be given to DRACULA."[126] Indeed, Toungoo was one of the two places on the north-south axis where the Japanese troops were positioned to fight a fierce battle. Toungoo was more dangerous due to its location, 166 miles north of Rangoon and at the junction of the road leading into the Shan states via Mawchi, Loikaw, and Taunggyi. It was imperative to seize Toungoo before the Japanese reinforcement troops from the Shan states arrived. Three Japanese divisions were in the Shan states. If the Japanese could bring even one division down the road to Toungoo in time to make a stand there, General Slim's 14th Army might find itself in a very difficult position and might not reach Rangoon on schedule. Therefore, it became urgent to delay the movement of Japanese reinforcements from the Shan states to Toungoo.[127] As Louis Allen stated, "It was at this point that Force 136 and the armed Karens played a crucial role."[128]

Force 136 officers were sent ahead of the 14th Army's advance into the Karen hills with the understanding that operations in the Karen country should be closely tied with the regular military operations. The special operation began with Major R. G. Turrall of the Intelligence Corps, the first to jump into the Karen hills. On February 20, 1944, he parachuted near Pyagawpu. Three days later, Lieutenant Colonel F. H. Peacock landed with two Dakota airplanes full of British, Burmese, and Karen parachutists. Peacock's second in command was Saw Butler, a Karen officer, who was a school headmaster in Toungoo before the war. He also served two years with the northern Kachin levies and won the Military Cross for exemplary gallantry. Within a week of arrival, Peacock armed 250 mobile and 350 static levies. A month later, another headquarters was set up north of the Mawchi road under the command of Lieutenant Colonel J. C. Tulloch. Many Padaung people, akin to the Karens from the Loikaw and Karenni areas, served under his command. One Karen who dropped with Tulloch was Kan Choke, a subedar-major holding the honorary rank of lieutenant, who had served twenty-eight years in the Burma Rifles as a regular soldier.[129]

Operation Character was divided into four areas: Walrus, Otter, Hyena, and Mongoose. Tulloch commanded the Walrus area north of Mawchi road between Bawleke and Loikaw. Otter, commanded by Peacock, was responsible for both sides of Mawchi road from the foothills near Toungoo to Bawleke. Hyena, commanded first by Turrall and then by Lieutenant Colonel H. W. Howell, operated around Pyagawpu. Mongoose, the last area to be formed, was operated by Lieutenant Colonel R. A. Critchley, M.C., a regular soldier who served in Abyssinia with Wingate.[130]

Operation Character's scale was enormous. More than eighty British officers and thirty British non-commissioned officers (NCOs), mostly wireless operators, parachuted in, as did probably twice that number of Karens. More than twelve thousand Karens joined Operation Character to fight the Japanese troops. The main function of the British officers and NCOs was to train, plan, and lead the Karens into their first actions and show them how to do it. One officer wrote:

> The Karens are not militarily aggressive and do not love war for its own sake. On the whole the villagers in my area were timid and given to panic when first taken into action. But once successful under competent officers, once shown how easy it was for well-armed parties to ambush the Japanese, their fighting spirit rose high. They produced their own leaders and displayed initiative and a spirit of attack. They took rapidly to explosives and used them a lot without accident to themselves.[131]

By April 1945, the troops were ready for Operation Character. Tulloch's Walrus and Peacock's Otter divisions sat across the Mawchi road, awaiting orders from General Slim, whose army had taken Pyinmana, sixty-nine miles north of Toungoo. Soon they received orders from General Slim, indicating that April 13 was the moment for Operation Character.[132] As the Japanese 15th Division came down the tracks and roads, they were ambushed by the Karen levies, "bridges were blown ahead of them, their foraging part[ies] were massacred, their sentries stalked, their staff car shot up."[133] By the time they reached Mawchi, the Japanese troops were too exhausted to fight the levies, who were prepared to stage a pitched battle with them. The Karen levies could hold the

Japanese troops for more than a week by blocking and demolishing roads and attacking them. Without reinforcements, on April 22, Toungoo fell quickly into the hands of General Slim's 14th Army. It turned out as Mountbatten had planned because Allied aircraft had bombed Toungoo the previous day.[134]

Subsequently, the story of Operation Character in World War II and the Karen people is summarized as follows: "Operation Character exceeded all expectations. Apart from the delay imposed on the 15th Japanese Division which, it might be argued, had a decisive bearing on the Burma campaign, the Karen levies that summer of 1945 killed at least 12,500 Japanese and indirectly were responsible for the deaths of thousands more, through air attacks directed by levy officers."[135] Without Karens' participation, the war might have turned in a different direction. Karen people performed with honor in Operation Character, and the history of Allied military campaigns of World War II in Burma will identify the Karen people with valor.

The Karen individuals who were involved in this operation took pride in being acknowledged for their work, although it was incomparable to the price they paid. Probably, they treasured more having association with the name Seagrim, who they addressed as *Poo Taw Kaw*, meaning "grandfather longlegs." They remembered him climbing up and down the hills, wearing Karen dress, eating the Karen-made food that no other Europeans would dare, and sleeping on the ground without shelter in the jungle. Above all, the Karens were inspired by his Christian faith, the major common factor connecting him and the Karens. They knew the Americans were pastors or teachers, but they had never encountered an Englishmen, especially an army officer like Seagrim, talking about Christianity, reading the Bible with them, and encouraging them to find their strength through prayer. Saw Po Hla, Seagrim's liaison officer, who was arrested and put in jail along with Seagrim, remembered Seagrim's last Christmas celebration in 1943 with the Karens. Seagrim asked Saw Po Hla to translate the message to his followers and the levy commanders. The message appears as Saw Po Hla remembered it:

> Today is Christmas Day, the day when the greatest hero the world has known was born. We Christians celebrate this day because we are His followers. If I speak to you Karens today of 'bravery', you cannot fail to associate this word with those who fought and died in this war. We Christians are soldiers of the Cross, soldiers who are commanded by our heroic leader to be brave in destroying evils.

The Cross is the badge worn by every true Christian. It distinguishes him from others. The Cross, as Christ wants us to understand it, signifies suffering. We Christians, His true followers, must suffer if we are to free our fellow-men from the evils of this world. If we wonder why we must suffer, let us remember that Jesus Christ, who was without sin, was nailed to a cross and suffered the most shameful death which could come to any man. How then can we, who profess to be His followers, who wear a Cross as our badge, expect to be free from suffering? By the way in which he faces suffering does a true Christian show his quality.[136]

A few days before Seagrim's execution, a British officer died from dysentery in the cell. Seagrim was asked to perform a short service for him. Another British officer who witnessed the occasion said that Seagrim included a prayer for his Japanese captors in the words of Christ, "Lord, forgive them, for they know not what they do."[137]

True to his Christian faith, Seagrim met his death bravely, and so did his seven Karen comrades. Apart from the Christian faith that tied them, the heroic death of Seagrim and his Karen comrades portrayed the story of faith and loyalty in human relationships, as recorded in the three awards Seagrim received. The first honor, awarded in 1942, is called the Most Excellent Order of the British Empire (MBE) and began with, "It was to this officer's faith in Karen[s] that the formation of the Karen Levies was largely due."[138] Later in the Distinguished Service Order (DSO) award, the introduction states: "This officer had remained 380 miles within enemy-held territory ever since its occupation by the Japanese forces in April 1942. During this period he has sustained the loyalty of the local inhabitants of a very wide area and thereby has provided the foundation of a pro-British force whenever occupying forces arrive in that area."[139]

The last award, the George Cross, was recorded posthumously in the government gazette on September 12, 1946. It explicitly pronounced Seagrim's Christian faith as the key to the Karens' loyalty and endurance. Unfolding Seagrim's last few days in the cell, it claimed: "He made every effort to comfort his men and sustain their courage by his Christian example, and the degree to which he had inspired them may be realized from the fact that they all expressed their willingness to die with him."[140]

All the words and actions inevitably affirmed the role of Christianity in binding the ties between Seagrim and the Karens. Besides, their sacrifices produced the great legacy of the Karen levies, when many thousands of additional Karens followed their paths and joined the war, enduring the suffering and facing death fearlessly. Indeed, the Christian faith bonded two different groups of people, one from the west and the other from the east, and changed the course of the war in history.

Notes

1. Hugh Tinker, *The Union of Burma: A Study of the First Years of Independence* (London: Oxford University Press, 1957), 456.

2. Aung San, "Burma's Challenge," in *The Political Legacy of Aung San*, ed. Josef Silverstein, Southeast Asia Program series, no. 11 (Ithaca, NY: Cornell University Press, 1993), 41. Aung San said that he joined the DAA because it was "the only militant and intensely nationalist political party" at that time.

3. John F. Cady, *A History of Modern Burma* (Ithaca, NY: Cornell University Press, 1960), 393–402.

4. IOR: L/R/5/207, Burmese Press Abstract, No. 43 of 1939, 274.

5. Maurice Collis, *Last and First in Burma (1941–1948)* (London: Faber and Faber, 1956), 22.

6. Ibid., 58. Also Thutaythana Ye Baw, *Ye Baw Thone Kyeik Hnint Ba Ma lut lat ye Tat Ma Taw Sit Kyaung Myar* (*The Thirty Comrades and the Military Campaign Routes of the Burma Independence Army*) (Rangoon: Ye Baw Yargyaw, 1975), 15.

7. Surendra Prasad Singh, *Growth of Nationalism in Burma, 1900–1942* (Calcutta: Firma KLM Private Ltd., 1980), 124.

8. Angelene Naw, *Aung San and the Struggle for Burmese Independence* (Chiang Mai: Silkworm Books, 2001), 58–66.

9. Ba Maw, *Breakthrough in Burma: Memoirs of a Revolution, 1936–1946* (New Haven, CT: Yale University Press, 1968), 49, 62–63.

10. Sugii Mitsuru, *Minami Kikan Gaishi* (*An Unofficial History of the Minami Organization*) (Rangoon: n.d.), 8–9.

11. Aung San, 47; U Ba Than, *The Roots of the Revolution: A Brief History of the Defence Services of the Union of Burma and the Ideals for Which They Stand* (Rangoon: Director of Information, 1962), 20.

12. Ba Maw, 145.

13. Elsie Northrup Chaney with Jeannie Lockerbie, *In Judson's Footsteps* (Philadelphia: Association of Baptists for World Evangelism Publishing, 2001), 153–68.

14. Ba Than, 25–26.

15. Tinker, 8.

16. Hugh Tinker, Andrew Griffin, and S. R. Ashton, *Burma: The Struggle for Independence, 1944–1948: Compilation of Documents from Official and Private Sources*, vol. 1 (London: Her Majesty's Stationery Office, 1983), 494.

17. Ibid., 1:635. It was the information he received from Dr. San C. Po.

18. Ian Morrison, *Grandfather Longlegs: The Life and Gallant Death of Major H. P. Seagrim, G.C., D.S.O., H.P.* (London: Faber and Faber, 1947), 69–70.

19. Ibid., 222. Seagrim was the British officer who formed the Karen levies and remained 380 miles within enemy-held territory since its occupation by Japanese forces in April 1942.

20. Ibid., 71.

21. Ibid., 92.

22. Ibid., 164.

23. Ibid., 184.

24. Ibid., 183–85.

25. Ibid., 186.

26. Ibid., 187.

27. Thra Ba Tu, 94.

28. Ba Maw, 187–88.

29. Ibid., 189.

30. Morrison, 188. He was not a Christian, but the Christian Karens followed his leadership in fighting the Japanese. His last name, Gya, means "Tiger."

31. Ibid., 190–91.

32. Ibid., 188.

33. Cady, 443.

34. Ba Maw, 190.

35. Cady, 443.

36. Morrison, 188–89.

37. Burma Intelligence Bureau, *Burma during the Japanese Occupation*, October 1, 1943, 23–28.

38. Ba Maw, 190–91.

39. Ibid., 191.

40. Ba Tu, 98.

41. Ibid., 94.

42. Pu S'Kaw Ler Taw, *Ka Nyaw Ta Ber Hser Tar Si Soh Teh Soh* (KNU publication, 1992), 164–65.

43. IOR: M/4/3023, The Humble Memorial of the Karens of Burma to His Britannic Majesty's Secretary of State for Burma (see online); Tinker, Griffin, and Ashton, 1: 492–97.

44. Ibid.

45. *Nation*, January 6, 1954.

46. Tinker, 10-11.

47. Burma Intelligence Bureau, 25–26.

48. Pu Gee Doh, *Mahn Ba Zan Hnint Kayin Taw Hlan Yay* (*Mah Ba Zan and Karen Revolution*) (KNU publication, 1993), 125.

49. Maung Sin Kyeh, *Bamapyi Chit Kayin Amyotha Kaung Saung Myar* (Bangkok: Pyitaungsu Kayin Amyotha Apwee Choke, 2003), 88-105. Saw Ba U Gyi was born in 1905 in a village near Bassein. He came from a well-to-do Christian family and received his early education from American Baptist Mission schools and later obtained his law degree in England. Karen people commemorate August 12, the day he was killed, as Martyr's Day.

50. Ibid., 131–33. Mahn Saw Bu was a S'gaw Karen who donated his land to establish a Karen seminary in Myaunmya. He was also vice president of the KNU before the 1949 insurrection.

51. Maung Maung, *Burma and General Ne Win* (Mumbai: Asia Publishing House, 1969), 139.

52. Morrison, 197–99. The term BDA was used in many official records although it was changed to BNA.

53. Tetkatho Sein Tin, *Saw San Po Thin Attopatti* (*The Biography of Saw San Po Thin*) (Rangoon, Chin Dwin, 1974), 236–40.

54. U Nu, *Burma under the Japanese*, ed. and trans. with introduction by J. S. Furnivall (London: Macmillan; New York: St. Martin's Press, 1954), 105.

55. Naw, *Aung San*, 107.

56. The BKNA was formed when the KNA and the Loyal Karen Association joined to work together in 1929. Saw Pe Tha was its president. U Pinnawuntha and Saw Ba Than Shwe were executive members. Maung Sin Kyeh, 61–69.

57. U Hla Pe was a Pa'O Karen.

58. Martin Smith, *Burma: Insurgency and the Politics of Ethnicity* (New York: St. Martin's Press, 1999), 62, his interview with Saw Tha Din on December 23, 1985.

59. Louis Allen, *Burma: The Longest War, 1941–1945* (London: Phoenix Press, 2000), xvii.

60. Morrison, 183.

61. Tinker, Griffin, and Ashton, 1:635.

62. Ibid., 1:493.

63. Smith Dun, *Memoirs of the Four-Foot Colonel*, Data Paper number 113 (Ithaca, NY: Cornell University Southeast Asia Program, Department of Asia Studies, 1980), 67.

64. Tinker, Griffin, and Ashton, 1:635.

65. Ibid., 1:xx (Tinker's introduction).

66. Morrison, 31.

67. Ibid., 212.

68. D. G. E. Hall, *Burma* (London: Hutchinson's University Library, 1950), 167.

69. Morrison, 212.

70. Ibid., 212–13.

71. Ibid., 213.

72. Ibid., 52.

73. Ibid., 213.

74. Ler Taw, 190.

75. Morrison, 213–14.

76. Tinker, Griffin, and Ashton, 1:493.

77. Dun, 114.

78. Morrison, 158.

79. Ibid., 36–37.

80. Ibid., 52.

81. Ibid., 53.

82. Ibid., 54–55.

83. Ibid., 55.

84. Ibid., 58.

85. Ibid., 60.

86. Ibid., 59.

87. Ibid., 74.

88. Ibid., 59.

89. Ibid., 74–78.

90. Ibid., 79.

91. Ibid., 80.

92. Ibid., 86.

93. Ibid., 87–88.

94. Ibid., 88.

95. Ibid., 95.

96. Ibid., 96.

97. Ibid., 111.

98. Ibid., 101–2.

99. Ibid., 101–2. Both Nimmo and McCrindle joined Force 136 because, like Seagrim, Steven recruited them in the prewar years.

100. Ibid., 104, 150.

101. Ibid., 108, 133.

102. Ibid., 108–9.

103. Ibid., 200. Aung San's contact with Force 136 was Thakin Thein Pe. See Naw, *Aung San*, 110-11.

104. Ibid., 113.

105. Ibid., 116.

106. Ibid., 117.

107. Ibid.

108. Ibid., 117–18.

109. Ibid., 118.

110. Ibid., 133–34.

111. Ibid., 123.

112. Ibid., 125–26.

113. Ibid., 127.

114. Ibid., 127–28.

115. Ibid., 129.

116. Ibid., 131.

117. Ibid., 133.

118. Ibid., 136.

119. Ibid., 139.

120. Ibid., 154–55.

121. Ibid., 155.

122. Admiral Louis Mountbatten, *Report to the Combined Chiefs of Staff by the Supreme Allied Commander, Southeast Asia, 1943–1944*, as quoted in Maung Maung, 142.

123. Allen, 460.

124. Collis, 232–33.

125. William Slim, *Defeat into Victory: Battling Japan in Burma and India, 1942–1945* (London: Cassells and Company, 1956), 481.

126. Allen, 472.

127. Morrison, 158.

128. Allen, 472.

129. Morrison, 158–60.

130. Ibid., 160–61.

131. Ibid., 161.

132. Allen, 472–73.

133. S. Woodburn Kirby, *War against Japan: The Official History of the Second World War*, vol. 4: *The Reconquest of Burma* (London: Her Majesty's Stationery Office, 1957–1969), 249–50.

134. Allen, 472.

135. Morrison, 164.

136. Ibid., 119.

137. Ibid., 151.

138. Ibid., 221.

139. Ibid.

140. Ibid.

6

The Karen Political Journey (1945–1947)

> That this Mass Meeting of the Liberated Karens of Burma considered and unanimously resolved to ask the British Government and the Conference of the United Nations of the world to (a) Extend the Excluded Area in Schedule II of the 1935 Act in Tenasserim Division mentioned in the last paragraph of the White Paper, to include the remainder of the Tenasserim Division and Nyaunglebin Sub-Division of Pegu District in Pegu Division, and to add to it later adjacent Karen Areas in Thailand, and designate the whole as the United Frontier Karen States to be administered by the Karen directly under a Governor.[1]

World War II paused the movement for a separate Karen state, which started in 1928 under the leadership of the Karen National Association (KNA). Immediately after the war, the younger generation of Karen nationalists joined the KNA leaders and rejuvenated that mission. Even before the Japanese surrender, these Karen nationalists organized the first mass meeting from June 30 to July 5, 1945. At that meeting, a resolution signed by five Karen leaders, two old KNA leaders, Saw Tha Din and Mahn Ba Khin, and three other nationalists, Saw Mya Thein, Saw Ba U Gyi, and Saw Johnson Khan Gyi (Judson College faculty), was passed. On September 26, the resolution, entitled "The Humble Memorial of the Karens of Burma," was forwarded to His Britannic Majesty's secretary of state for Burma. After a series of letters and telegrams between Karen political leaders and British rulers, it became known as the Karen Memorial. With the expectation that Burma would stay within the British Commonwealth after its independence, the Karens repeatedly requested a separate Karen state under the guidance of a British governor. During the postwar years, one of the most disputed dialogues among the political leaders of Burma centered on the Karen Memorial, in which the above-quoted territorial Karen demands lasted the longest.

Return of British Civil Administration and the White Paper Policy

Long before Rangoon's recapture from the Japanese, the British government discussed and prepared a future policy for postwar Burma. On May 17, 1945, the secretary of state of the House of Commons issued a document entitled "Burma: Statement of Policy by His Majesty's Government."[2] Known as the White Paper, it proposed a return to the old status quo established under the 1935 Burma Act. Accordingly, the British civil government would keep Burma under the direct rule of the governor for a period of three years, after which elections would be held. The governor would set up an executive council, and during the interim period, a general election would be held. Then, the elected representatives would be tasked to draw up a new constitution. This constitution would form the foundation on which Burma would be granted dominion status that would allow for self-government within the British Commonwealth. Once all came into place, the people of Burma would be free to establish a republic as they wished. Regarding the scheduled areas, which were not under direct control of Ministerial Burma, the White Paper stated that it should remain separate "until such time as their inhabitants signify their desire for some suitable form of amalgamation with Burma proper."[3]

Under this policy framework, Governor Reginald Dorman-Smith prepared to return to Burma from Simla, India, where he resided during the war. The Imperial British Army recaptured Burma in May 1945, and its Civil Affairs Service (Burma) (CAS B) was filling the rank-and-file jobs with ex-civil servants and businesspeople who formerly resided in Burma. The British presumed that the Burmese population, who were grateful for deliverance from the Japanese, would welcome their return in great joy. This greatly flawed perspective was discovered when Governor Dorman-Smith returned to implement the White Paper policy in Burma.

The British press observed the Burma political situation and commented on the White Paper policy. *The Times* representative in Burma, Ian Morrison, wrote to the foreign news editor of the *Times* on June 1, 1945, that only a "brief unofficial summary" of the White Paper was available in Burma. It was unfortunate that, after the fall of Rangoon, no senior member of the Burma government visited Rangoon to study what conditions were.[4] Morrison also noted that "the AFO [AFPFL] is almost the only political force to be reckoned with in the coming months."[5]

Indeed, under the leadership of Aung San, Than Tun, Thakin Mya, and U Nu, the Anti-Fascist Organization (AFO),[6] later known as the Anti-Fascist People's Freedom League (AFPFL), developed into a powerful political organization before the British restored the civil administration led by Governor Dorman-Smith. Representatives from every indigenous political group in Burma, including the Karens, joined the AFPFL. In the Conference of Burma Leaders official minutes, taken at a meeting held on June 4, 1945, at the headquarters of the AFPFL in Rangoon, the names of two Karen leaders, Saw Ba U Gyi and Saw Ba Maung, were included on the list of the twelve leaders.[7] Resolution number one in this meeting stated, "The final objective of the People's Freedom League, as it has been hitherto, is the attainment of the right of self-determination for Burma."[8]

Through his contact with Force 136,[9] Than Tun had already sent this statement policy of the AFPFL on May 25 to Lord Louis Mountbatten, the head of the military administration in Burma. As Supreme Allied Commander (SAC) of the Southeast Asian Command (SEAC), Mountbatten acted from his military perspective. He believed that, unless some solution was acceptable to Aung San and his AFPFL, he might have to fight a civil war against some ten thousand Burmese troops. Mountbatten's major concern was to prevent civil disturbances in Burma, which might derail his upcoming military campaign to reoccupy Malaya and Singapore. Mountbatten's plan was to get Aung San's BNA under control, hoping to disarm and disband redundant units and restore law and order for the speedy resumption of civil government under Governor Dorman-Smith.[10]

The Anti-Fascist People's Freedom League (AFPFL) and the Karen Nationalists

The initial contact between Lord Mountbatten and AFPFL occurred because of the work of Force 136 and the Karens. Major Seagrim's Karen liaison officer, Saw Po Hla, learned from San Po Thin and Saw Kyar Doe in Rangoon in October 1943 that the BNA was preparing for an uprising against the Japanese. The report of Force 136 confirmed, "Initial contacts with the Burmese, and in particular, the BDA [BNA], were made from the Karen Levies in December 1943."[11] Although other factors may have influenced Lord Mountbatten's decision to incorporate Aung San's BNA into the Allied force, it was through this early connection with the Karen levies that Force 136 endorsed the BNA to Lord Mountbatten. Without that Karen connection, Aung San's BNA would not have had the opportunity to develop into a powerful political entity known as the AFPFL. In the words of Professor Cady, "The story of the formation of the A.F.P.F.L. can be put together only in a fragmentary way. One of the first overt steps, apparently taken in late 1943, was the reconciliation achieved by Thakins Aung San and Than Tun with the minority anti-Japanese group among the delta Karens. This group was led by Saw San Po Thin, who also harbored Allied agents parachuted in by plane."[12] Aung San's effort to reconcile with the Karens, which began with San Po Thin, allowed Aung San to earn the Karens' trust and opened the door for his BNA to join the Allied forces in the anti-Japanese movement.

As previously revealed, through San Po Thin's persuasion, Hanson Kyar Doe accepted a position in the BNA, which Aung San offered him. Many Karens willingly joined the BNA Karen battalions since the leader was Hanson Kyar Doe, an ex-British army officer, who was very well respected by the Karens. Mahn Win Maung,[13] Saw Tun Sein, Saw San Gyi, and Saw Yaw Han joined the BNA and were highly recognized for their service in fighting the Japanese with the Allied forces.[14] In late 1944, Thakin Thein Pe Myint, a leader of the AFO and Communist Party of Burma (CPB), wrote, "Among the minorities, the Karens are the strongest anti-Japanese force. Two Karen battalions are being formed by BDA [BNA] with the special purpose of associating the Karens in the Anti-Japanese uprising. . . . if correctly approached, every Karen village can become a fortress of resistance against the Japanese."[15]

On August 7, 1944, the first AFO meeting was held with Than Tun, Thakin Soe, and Thakin Ba Hein. They decided to send six BNA members to India for military training. A Karen, Mahn Win Maung, was one of the six AFPFL sent to India.[16] The Karens in the BNA became the founders of the Karen Youth Association (KYA) and collaborated with the AFPFL after World War II.

Indeed, the AFPFL became the strongest political force in 1945. When the league organized a conference of Burma political leaders on August 16–17, 1945, many political, religious, and business organizations, including the Karen Central Organization (KCO),[17] joined the conference.[18] At the AFPFL mass meeting on August 19 in *Nay Thu Yein* theater hall, nearly six thousand attendees endorsed the AFPFL resolutions, including its goal to declare the freedom of all people to determine their own destinies, with emphasis on Burma's demands for full sovereignty.[19]

After the Japanese surrender in August 1945, Aung San was appointed the Deputy Inspector General (DIG) of the Burma Army with the rank of brigadier general, and his BNA became the Patriot Burmese Force (PBF).[20] On September 5, 1945, at Kandy in Ceylon, Aung San, Than Tun, and Mountbatten signed the disposal of the PBF, on the condition that PBF could stay until the civil government took over the military administration.[21]

The Origins of the Karen Memorial

Many Karen leaders joined the AFPFL with the assumption that they shared the same goal in fighting fascist Japan. Both the old KNA leaders, Saw Ba Maung and Mahn Ba Khin, and young Karen nationalist leaders, Saw Ba U Gyi and Thra Tha Hto, became members of the AFPFL supreme council and executive council.[22] However, the AFPFL's demand for full sovereignty made the Karens uncomfortable, and they began to feel that their vision for independence differed from that of the AFPFL. As early as June 4, 1945, after the Conference of Burma Leaders of the AFPFL, Dorman-Smith made a report: "The Karen leader, Saw Ba U Gyi, who was to have accompanied Than Tun and Aung San, backed out of coming aboard at the last moment as he was not satisfied that the attitude which these two were going to adopt was consistent with the loyalty which the Karen people bear towards His Majesty the king."[23]

Again, on August 15, 1945, another report said:

> In discussion with Sydney Loo-Nee and Saw Ba U Gyi, elder and younger leaders respectively of the Karen community, the apprehension of the Karens towards Dominion Status have clearly emerged. Quite obviously, they fear that under a Burmese government they will receive the dirty end of the stick. . . .
>
> Both Loo-Nee and Ba U Gyi left me in no doubt that the Karens intended to ask for a parcel of the country (part of Tenasserim Division was mentioned) where they would propose to constitute a "Karennistan". It appears the intention would be to seek the inclusion of this territory inside the Scheduled Areas, whereby it would come under the direct control of the Governor. . . . [24]

These reports were true. The Karens, who were educated through the Christian faith and achieved high political and military positions under British rule, had more confidence in the British and preferred dominion status. The KNA leaders, who had diligently worked to obtain the "Karen Country," were especially alarmed by the White Paper policy that declared the "full self-government within the Commonwealth" for Ministerial Burma, but "the Scheduled Areas (the Shan States and the other hill areas), would remain subject to a special regime under the Governor."[25] The areas claimed for the Karen state since 1928 included all the Karen inhabited areas from Tenasserim division (which was part of the governor's Ministerial Burma to Part I and Part II of the scheduled areas), the Karenni states, and the southwest Shan states.

The old KNA leaders started to revive the task they dropped due to World War II. By then, many old members had passed away. Those surviving leaders, such as Sir San C. Po, Sydney Loo Nee, and Mahn Ba Khin, tried to revitalize the movement with more energetic young Karen leaders. Under their guidance, old and young Karen leaders from all the Karen liberated areas organized a mass meeting from June 30 to July 5, 1945, at Ahlone Karen quarters in Rangoon. During this meeting, KNA leaders proposed reviving the Karen Central Advisory Board (KCAB), which formed in 1943 after the 1942 Myaunmya incident. Accordingly, Saw Ba U Gyi, Thra Tha Hto, and Mahn Ba Khaing were elected as KCAB board members before an official Karen organization (the Karen Central Organization or KCO) could be officially established.[26]

The most significant action in this Karen mass meeting was the passing of a resolution later known as the Karen Memorial. This resolution was declared in July and was sent to the secretary of state for Burma on September 26, 1945, with the title "The Humble Memorial of the Karens of Burma,"[27] and it was signed by the following Karen leaders: Saw Tha Din, president of the KNA; Mahn Ba Kin, general secretary of the KNA; Saw Mya Thein, ex-member of the House of Representatives; Saw Johnson Kan Gyi, lecturer, Judson College; and Saw Ba U Gyi, vice president, Karen Social and Service Club. These were the executive members of the Karen Central Organization.

As quoted in the opening of this chapter, the memorial asked the British government and the United Nations to give serious consideration of their resolution:

> to (a) Extend the Excluded Area in Schedule II of the 1935 Act in Tenasserim Division mentioned in the last paragraph of the White Paper, to include the remainder of the Tenasserim Division and Nyaunglebin Sub-Division of Pegu District in Pegu Division, and to add to it later adjacent Karen Areas in Thailand, and designate the whole as the United Frontier Karen States to be administered by the Karen directly under a Governor.[28]

They stated in the resolution that only Karen leaders from the liberated Karen areas were at the meeting. The Karens from the Tenasserim could not attend since the Japanese still occupied the entire country east of the Sittang River at the time. Apparently, the Karens had to wait for the return of the British civil administration to continue their fight for their national home for which they had been striving since 1928.

Governor Dorman-Smith and the Karen Nationalists' Demands (1945–1946)

The military administration in Burma ended when Governor Dorman-Smith returned to Burma on October 16, 1945, and restored the civil administration. On the day of his arrival on board *Cleopatra*, two Karen leaders, Sydney Loo Nee and Ba U Gyi, were among other dignitaries, political leaders, and military personnel who welcomed him at Rangoon port. On October 19, Dorman-Smith met with AFPFL representatives and other political parties to discuss nominations to his new executive council. Among the eleven candidates that the AFPFL submitted to the governor were two Karen leaders, Mahn Ba Khin and Saw Ba U Gyi.[29] However, his negotiations with the AFPFL failed. Governor Dorman-Smith formed his executive council with six former political leaders of Burma and two Europeans, Sir Raibeart MacDougall and Sir John Wise. Subsequently, Dorman-Smith included three AFPFL members in his executive council, one of whom was the old KNA leader, Mahn Ba Khin.[30] In December 1945, the governor formed the Governor's Advisory Council with thirty-four members, including five Karen lawyers, Thra Shwe Ba, Saw Ba Lon, Sydney Loo Nee, Saw Ba Thein, and Saw Mya Thein.[31]

From Old to New Karen National Organizations

To deliberate plans for the Karens in the new administration, the Karen Central Advisory Board held a mass meeting from October 1–3, 1945, at No. 2 U Loo Nee Road in Rangoon. The resolutions on the first day meeting included

> (2) That the five advisers to the Military Administration, and two representatives of the Karen Youth Association be co-opted members of the Karen Central Organization . . .

> (8) Resolved that this meeting urges the Governor to appoint three Karen Representatives as his Councilors.

(9) This meeting elected the following gentlemen to be Councilors to the Governor of Burma as Representatives of the Karens: (*i*) Sir San C. Po, (*ii*) Mahn Ba Kin, (*iii*) Saw Ba U Gyi. . . .

(11) This meeting elected the following gentlemen as members of the Executive Committee: (i) Saw Tha Din (Chairman and Treasurer), (ii) Saw Ba U Gyi (Asst. Treasurer), (iii) Mahn Ba Kin (Secretary), (iv) Thra Tha Hto (Joint Secretary), (v) Saw Mya Thein, (vi) Mahn Ba Khine (Khaing). . . .

(12) Resolved that the name of the Karen Central Advisory Board be henceforth known as the Karen Central Organization and it shall consist of the Executive Committee, two representatives from each District, and two from the Karen Youth Association. And the office of the Executive Committee shall also be the office-bearers of the Karen Central Organization.

(13) Resolved that this meeting urges the Governor to have Karen representatives in the Public Service Commission.[32]

Certainly, resolution 12 officially confirmed the KCO as the leading Karen political organization after World War II, taking over the mission responsibilities of the KNA, with U Tha Din as its first president.

On the meeting's second day, the KYA had arranged a gala dinner for all Karen representatives from different Karen districts. The long list of the Karen representatives included Thra Baldwin, D. C. U Ba Htun, Sydney Loo Nee, Saw Johnson D. Po Min, U Htun Aung (bar-at-law), Pa'O Hla Pe, Major Lionel Po, Saw Mya Thein, U Pya Gyi, Saw Thar Aye, Saw Po Lay Tay, Saw Cushing Htwe, U Sein Maung, Thra Hto Ku, U Saw Thu (Myaungmya), Saw Po Maung (bar-at-law), and the KCO members. By invitation, the AFPFL leaders Aung San and Than Tun attended, delivering messages and well wishes at the gala dinner.[33]

To gain public attention, the KCO leaders, Saw Tha Din, Mahn Ba Khin, Saw Ba U Gyi, and Thra Tha Hto, presented their case in the *Bama Khit* newspaper. They explained that the Karens needed a Karen state with their own administration to develop their culture and language and to protect their social, political, and economic rights nationwide. They added that Karens were willing to live peacefully with all Burmans who desired the development of the Karens.[34]

The Buddhist Karen National Association (BKNA),[35] founded in 1929 by Saw Pe Tha, U Panawuntha, and Saw Ba Than Shwe, shared the same goals as the KCO and renewed their activities to secure a separate Karen state. Since Saw Pe Tha was killed in the 1942 Myaungmya incident, one of its original founders, Sayadaw U Panawuntha, became the president. In addition, two other Buddhist monks, U Nareinda and U Kumara, were executive members of the BKNA. Other leaders were Saw Myat Thein (vice president and member of KCO), U Gyi Bay (secretary), Mahn Kan Aye (treasurer), Saw Ba Than Shwe, and Saw Ba Lon.[36] Since its executive members were Buddhist monks and Buddhist Karen leaders, its followers were largely Buddhists.

Sharing the same goal to secure a separate Karen state, members of the KYA joined the KCO as a branch of the KCO, but they also felt it was necessary to improve relations between the Karens and Burmans.[37] They were ex-BNA members and strong supporters of the AFPFL movements. Its first executive council members were Major Saw Tun Sein (president), Saw Kyaw Sein (secretary), Saw Myint Thein (assistant secretary), and Saw Oliver (member). But Major Tun Sein returned to the army, and the KCO leaders appointed Saw Ba U Gyi and Saw Tha Hto to fill in his post. Both declined this opportunity. After the Karen meeting in October 1945, the KYA decided to withdraw from the KCO.[38] Subsequently, on December 14, 1945, the Karen Youth Organization (KYO) was established as an independent organization, with Mahn Ba Khaing as president and Mahn Win Maung, who had returned from India in late October, as vice president. Saw Kyaw Sein and Saw Myint Thein continued to serve as secretary and assistant secretary. A Karen woman, Naw Mercy Gyi, served as treasurer.[39] She thus became the first female involved in the Karen nationalist leadership.

The Karen Memorial: Recurring Issues

While younger Karen leaders were trying on their part, Sir San C. Po, from his retirement home in Bassein, continued to make all-out efforts to get the governor's attention for the Karen state. On December 19, 1945, Dorman-Smith received a letter from San C. Po, stating that the Karens had been loyal to the British for an entire century. He wrote that the Karens "by religious and national traditions" had given their best and their lives to the British cause. He affirmed that the Karens would "never grudge our Burmese friends" the "freedom and independence" for which they had repeatedly clamored. Referring to his book *Burma and the Karen*, chapter 12, "A Nation's Desire," Sir San C. Po requested again, as he did before, to include the Tenasserim division as part of the Karen country. He explained that Karens wanted to live peacefully with all the people of Burma with his "plan of Federal Union; USB will be the United States of Burma."[40] Sir San C. Po's letter expressed the Karen willingness to have peaceful cooperation with the Burmans as well as their desire for a Karen state, where Karens could have their own administration to preserve their Christian faith, culture, and language.

Through his longtime political experience, Sir San C. Po noticed fragmentation among the Karens, and with the intention of Karen unification, he advised the KCO to organize a meeting. Accordingly, the KCO, BKNA, and KYO leaders met on January 8, 1946, and agreed to resubmit the Karen Memorial, which had been sent to the secretary of Burma in September 1945.[41] This time, it was sent to Governor Dorman-Smith with a new date of January 16, 1946, but signed by the same leaders. The governor's private secretary, T. L. Hughes, replied to the KCO on January 17 that the Memorial was receiving attention.[42]

Some assumed that the KCO had to resubmit the Karen Memorial of September 26, 1945, to the governor because it was addressed only to the secretary of Burma, and the matter was not brought to the attention of the governor for his action. Governor Dorman-Smith had indeed received a copy of the Karen Memorial and, "officially, the Governor had not taken cognizance of the Memorial."[43] His indifferent reaction to the Karen Memorial seemed to be due to these comments by Sir Herbert Dunkley: "The resolution is absurd. How can the Secretary of State for Burma, or the whole British Government for that matter, decide to include part of Thailand in a new Karen state. . . . Under Section 155 of the Government of Burma Act, new areas cannot be transferred to the Second Schedule from Ministerial Burma. It will require an Act of Parliament to do this."[44]

In fact, on October 22, 1945, Hughes wrote to the president of the KCO: "I am desired to acknowledge the representation from the Karen Central Organization addressed to the Secretary of State for Burma and to say that representations of this nature should in the first case be addressed to His Excellency the Governor of Burma. The Memorial is returned."[45]

For unexplained reasons, the KCO did not receive the reply until one month later, on November 21, 1945. The matter was discussed again at a meeting held on January 8, 1946. Accordingly, attaching a copy of the Memorial dated September 26, 1945, the KCO chairman wrote, "With reference to your letter No. 1Q1/GS45, dated 21st November, I have the honour to re-submit the Memorial enclosed herewith." The next day, Hughes replied, "I have the honour to acknowledge receipt of your letter dated 16th January 1946 forwarding a Memorial from the Karens of Burma to His Excellency and to say that the Memorial is receiving attention." In consequence, the Memorial was henceforth referred to as the Karen Memorial of 16th January 1946, although no such document existed.[46] Since then, the governor's office referred to it as the "Karen Memorial of 16 January 1946."

Compelled by repeated Karen appeals, on January 31, 1946, Dorman-Smith wrote his long report of "the Karen problem" to Lord Pethick-Lawrence, secretary of state for Burma, with the introduction that "the suggestion of a 'Karenistan' is not by any means a new one." He explained that Sir San C. Po had asked for "the Karen Country," with the Tenasserim division in 1928, but as shown in the latest Memorial, the Karens also asked for certain areas across the border in Thailand. Governor Dorman-Smith remarked that "no effort has been made to advocate 'separation' of the Delta and Pegu Yoma Karen 'islands', nor has there been any proposal to transfer population from these areas to a separated Karen area." He further stated, "It seems obvious to me that something radical must be done to resolve this unhappy problem," and gave the following four suggestions:

> i. To put the Karen Part I and Part II Areas under the Frontier Areas Administration and refuse to consider inclusion of any other Areas or to make special provision for Karen elsewhere;
>
> ii. To include under the Frontier Areas Administration certain contiguous Ministerial Areas in Tenasserim where Karens predominate, in addition to the Karen Part I and Part II Areas, and to make special administrative arrangement in Karen "islands" in Ministerial Burma to give the Karens the social and economic opportunities they want;
>
> iii. To include the whole of the Tenasserim Division under the Frontier Area Administration as an Area in which the administrative would be only Karen or Talaing;
>
> iv. To declare the Tenasserim Division, the Karen Hill Areas in Part I and Part II and, by agreement with the UNO, the Karen Areas in Siam [Thailand], as an independent Karen State.[47]

Dorman-Smith's following explanations signified that he had a dilemma when dealing with the Karens' request for a Karen state:

> 10. Whatever alternative we follow we must anticipate strong opposition from many Burmese quarters if we attempt in any way further to dismember Burma. Already there is much criticism of our policy towards the Frontier Areas on the ground that we are deliberately following a "divide and rule" policy. . . . Many Burmese seem willfully determined to ignore the existence of any minority problems in spite of all evidence. . . .

12. Whichever way we look, the difficulties are numerous and formidable. The Karens have contrived to retain their nationhood through centuries of Burmese oppression and I feel we must recognize that this is an indestructible feature of the Karen character. . . . that the more we attempt to denationalize and Burmanise the Karens the more we shall embitter them. With an Area of their own which they could look upon as a Karen homeland it is probable that tension among the Karens and the Burmese throughout Burma would lessen at once. It is argued that the Burmese have no greater claim to dominance over the Karens than we have to dominance over the Burmese. The case is precisely similar— the Burmese conquered the Karens and we conquered the Burmese. If, therefore, modern internationalism demands that we give the conquered Burmese their freedom, by the same token the Burmans must grant the conquered Karens their freedom.

13. . . . the fact is that we have as yet given this problem very little attention and until I have considered it fully with my Counsellors and advisers and leading Burmans and Karens I cannot suggest a concrete line of action. This letter represents my tentative examination of some of the facts we know.[48]

Dorman-Smith's letter revealed that no action was taken in consideration of the Karen Memorial. At least two people at the governor's office took a serious interest in this matter: the governor's private secretary, T. L. Hughes, and the additional secretary at that time, H. N. C. Stevenson. Serving as the director of the frontier areas for many years, Stevenson had fought with Chin levies and respected the heroic war record of the Chins, Kachins, and Karens. Through his initiative, the Karen Memorial, hitherto neglected, was brought to the governor's executive council. In fact, Stevenson was responsible for the move laying out the claims of the Karens and advocating for the Karen Memorial.

On February 2, Hughes and Stevenson prepared and submitted a memorandum to the governor with an introduction that the Karens "have presented a Memorial to His Excellency containing the following demands":[49]

i.   To extend the Scheduled Areas to include

   (a) the whole Tenasserim Division and Nyaunglebin Sub-Division of the Pegu Division

   (b) the area across the Thailand border between the Salween River and ChiangMai, the Mesodh area; between the Thoungyin

River and Rahenge Hills and the old Prathuwun State called Kyaukkhong.

ii. To call the Karen sections of the Scheduled Areas "United Frontier Karen States".

iii. To retain the Scheduled Areas under the Governor.

iv. His Excellency to form his own Advisory Board for the Karen Areas.

v. The administration of the Karen Areas to be by a specially selected administrative staff of Karens or, if Karens are not available, only those selected by the Karen Advisory Board.

vi. The Scheduled Areas remain under this specially selected administrative staff until such time as the people are willing to accept some forms of incorporation into Burma proper.

Also included in the memorandum:

Against these demands, in respect of the Karens, the existing tentative proposals of the Government are that:

(a) The Part I and Part II Karen Areas be included, together with the Karenni States, in a Karen District under the Frontier Areas Administration;

(b) The Plains Karen Areas are administered as at present, with perhaps, if later governments see fit, some re-alignment of constituency boundaries.

The memorandum additionally proposed that the governor call a conference and discuss with his executive councilors what could be done to meet the Karen desires in a manner acceptable to both the Burmese and Karens. The proposed conference was to include "leaders of all important Burmese parties and representatives of the various Karen Areas, including Karenni," with twelve representatives of each side and an independent chairman. After reading the memorandum on February 11, the governor ordered consideration by the executive council.[50] As a result, "Memorial to His Excellency from Karen Leaders" appeared as Minute 6 of the 16th Executive Council Meeting held on February 20. The minute directed that "the Karen Leaders should be invited to discuss their views with Burmese Leaders." With the agreement that no publicity be given to the meeting, Home Member Sir Paw Tun was assigned to organize the meeting. However, he took no action to implement the decision of the minute.[51]

Despite these efforts, the Karen Memorial was overshadowed by the AFPFL's mounting political movements during this period. The All-Burma Congress of AFPFL was held January 17-25, 1946, in the Shwedagon Pagoda precincts. It had thirteen hundred delegates with a public attendance of more than one hundred thousand. It became the largest political gathering of the time. One major resolution claimed, "The demand of the people of Burma is National Self-Determination. It means complete independence from the imperialist rule of British monopolist-capitalism."[52]

Obviously, the Karen leaders, who had been striving for a Karen state within the Commonwealth for decades, found the AFPFL's demand for "complete independence" unacceptable. They acted aggressively, demanding meetings with the leaders of the AFPFL and Governor Dorman-Smith during the month of February. To display Karen unity for the common cause, all the Karen leaders of the KCO, BKNA, and KYO held a meeting February 4-6, 1946, and unanimously passed four resolutions:[53]

1. To have Karen representative in the Public Service Commission
2. The administration of the Karen Areas to be by a specially selected administrative staff of Karens.
3. All the Karens of age 18 to have the right to vote
4. To create a Karen State for the safety and development of the Karen people

A Karen State Standing Committee was also formed for the implementation of the above resolutions. A few days later, on February 12, this committee held a meeting and decided to send a delegation of four leaders, Saw Tha Din, Saw Sydney Loo Nee, Saw Po Chit, and Saw Ba U Gyi, to London to demand the Karen state.[54]

The Karen leaders understood that it was essential for them to negotiate with the AFPFL in pursuing their goal for the Karen state. Accordingly, on February 13, at KCO headquarters, Karen representatives met with AFPFL leaders to discuss the future of the proposed Karen state. Representing the KCO at this meeting were Saw Po Chit, Saw Tha Din, Sydney Loo Nee, Mahn Ba Khaing, Ba U Gyi, and Thra Tha Hto. During that meeting, Saw Po Chit explained that the main Karen desire was to have a separate Karen state. They requested that the AFPFL not object to the Karens' proposal for such. Aung San expressed his desire to have peaceful relationships between the Burmans and Karens. He said that the AFPFL had written a letter to the governor to include two Karen representatives in the governor's executive council. He affirmed that those who opposed the proposal for the two Karen representatives in the governor's council were from the governor's executive council, not the AFPFL.[55]

Records indicate that the opposition from the governor's executive council was Home Member Sir Paw Tun. He did not take his assigned action from the executive council meeting, held on February 20, 1946, in connection with the Karen Memorial.[56] Dorman-Smith sent a letter to the Burma secretary of state dated January 25, which said, "I am also considering fitting in another Karen who might take over the Judicial which at present is under Home. Paw Tun does not altogether see eye to eye with me over this, as he thinks Karens are adequately represented now."[57]

In another letter dated February 6, 1946, Dorman-Smith wrote:

> Karens are at present represented in my Executive and Legislative Councils by one Executive Councillor and four Legislative Councillors. Compared strictly arithmetically with representation in the old House of Representatives, a total of five seats may be deemed adequate. But I am anxious to give them an additional Executive Councillorship for two reasons:
>
> (i) It will tend to unite all Karen organizations,
> (ii) As a community they have deserved more than well of us.[58]

Both letters indicated that the governor was in favor of the Karens' proposal. However, he did not take prompt action, as in the same letter he stated, "Some of my Executive Councillors do not see eye to eye with me on this proposal and I will have to proceed cautiously."[59]

While awaiting a response, the Karens again held a mass meeting at Toungoo from April 25-27, 1946. On April 25, the mass unanimously endorsed a resolution. It was the same resolution of the mass meeting held at Rangoon on June 30, 1945, which was the original September 1945 Karen Memorial, with supplementary clauses signed by Saw Johnson D. Po Min for the governor's attention:

> The Karens are unanimous in their desire to be separated from the Burmans. This sentiment was fully realised by Mr. Amery in his statements in the House of Common on the 1st June 1945. . . .
>
> . . . Our ambition and aspiration are to be a Member of this great Commonwealth of Nations. We do not deem ourselves inferior to the

Burmans in any sphere of life and can never stand any measure to merge us with them. We are distinct from them in every way—dress, language, culture, custom and especially moral character.... Future bloodshed which the advocates of merging wanted to prevent can never be prevented unless the Karens and the Burmans are given distinct separated territories.

... The Burmans had sold their birthright to the Japanese. The Karens stood loyally by the British. In Europe, it is found that such traitors were punished and friends rewarded. The opposite happened in Burma in spite of the assurance of Mr. Amery that we deserved "a double claim" on the consideration of the British Government....

... In spite of all the efforts of the Governor of Burma for Burma's good name, the natural propensity of the Burmans for thieving and cheating again published in the SEAC, dated the 10th April 1946.... The word "Burmese" generally means all the races of Burma including the Karens. How can the Karens who naturally loathe thieving and cheating, therefore, associate to such a people and agree to any attempt to merge themselves with the Burmans? That is one of the chief reasons why the Karens want to be separated from Burma and the Burmans.

The concluding statement said, "The Karens, therefore, strongly urge the British Government to have the moral courage to declare definite policy towards the Karens with regards to a separate Karen State with a form of Government not lower than that to be given to Burma."[60]

Despite repeated submissions of the Karen Memorial of September 1945 or January 1946, the Karens received no clear answer. Later in 1947, Governor Hubert Rance admitted that "the Karens have never had an official reply to their memorial other than the original acknowledgement," and that "the matter appears to have stopped."[61]

Meanwhile, the political strength of Aung San and his AFPFL increased after Aung San formed the People's Volunteer Organization (PVO) with most of its members being ex-BNA. By the end of February 1946, PVO men were appointed in thirty-two districts, wearing uniforms and training with arms. They were organized in classical military patterns, taking the order from their commander, Aung San.[62] Backed by the PVO military, Aung San's AFPFL posed a real threat to the British administration. Seeing the overwhelming support for the AFPFL, some of the old Burmese politicians who were members of Governor Dorman-Smith's executive council advised the governor to negotiate with Aung San. By April 1946, Aung San and the AFPFL had gained mass support, though Dorman-Smith and his executive council acted as the legitimate government. To prevent an open revolt, Dorman-Smith met Aung San and invited him to join the executive council. On June 11, 1946, Dorman-Smith left Burma after receiving Prime Minister Clement Attlee's May 18 telegram that said, "I should be glad therefore if you could arrange to return to report on the situation."[63]

Backed by his PVO, which now numbered around ten thousand armed men, Aung San could demonstrate his military strength and demand complete independence. With continued mass support, Aung San and his AFPFL were ready to challenge the new governor who would replace Dorman-Smith. As in the past, the separate Karen state proposal during the postwar period under Governor Dorman-Smith was overshadowed by the Burmese liberation movement. The Karens had to continue their fight for their long-overdue nationalist goal, "the separated Karen State."

The Karen Goodwill Mission of 1946

Before the new governor arrived, Sir Henry Knight served as the acting governor from June 11 to August 31, 1946.[64] He dealt with various political issues raised by the minorities, the communists, and especially the AFPFL demands. Secretary Stevenson, who apparently sympathized with the Karens, did not hesitate to bring the Karen case to the acting governor's attention. On June 15, Stevenson sent the Karen resolution adopted on April 25 at the Toungoo Karen mass meeting to Sir Henry Knight, with a long comment including, "I have come to the regrettable conclusion that the present Karen quiescence means simply that they refuse to quarrel with us. But when we go, if go we do, the war for the Karen State will start. For this reason I think we ought to tackle the Karen problem seriously—make a thorough check of census figures, ask the Karens to provide a detailed plan of how they propose to administer the Karen Area. . . . "[65] On July 1, Stevenson forwarded to the governor's secretary another KCO letter inquiring about steps the government had taken regarding the Karen demand for the Karen state.[66]

Upon request, Sir Henry Knight met with Karen leaders, including Mahn Ba Khin, Sydney Loo Nee, Saw Tha Din, Saw Po Chit, Saw Sein Tin, and Thra Tha Hto, on July 13, 1946. As before, the Karen leaders requested the creation of Karen areas, comprised of the Tenasserim division and Nyaunglebin subdivision of the Pegu district, to be within the frontier areas administration and under the control of the governor. They also requested that a Karen goodwill mission be allowed to go to London.[67] Sir Henry Knight, in his report, said, "The mission would of course take the opportunity of stating the Karen attitude towards future political developments in Burma, in particular their own demand for Karenistan."[68]

Throughout this period, Stevenson made all-out efforts to support the Karen aspirations. In the following letter dated August 4, 1946, Stevenson attempted to convince Sir Henry Knight to take prompt action to the Karens' request:

1. The other Part II Constituency Areas upon which an early decision is necessary are those comprising the Karen Hill areas of the Toungoo, Thaton and Amherst Districts.

2. Resolutions at Karen meetings since liberation have constantly reiterated the demand for the transfer of these areas to Part I, and the Karen leaders have recently petitioned HE the Governor to effect the transfer immediately, that is to say, before the preparation of the electoral rolls.

3. . . .

4. . . .

5. In my view these part II Karen Areas should be transferred to Part I. . . . The transfer should be made without prejudice to the Karen claims for other parts of Tenasserim Division, which will obviously take some months if not years of negotiation to settle.

6. The immediate transfer of these Karen Part II Areas might well, indeed, go a long way towards reducing Karen apprehensions about the motives underlying HMG's hitherto complete neglect of their claims, and thus make easier an amicable agreement over the larger and much more formidable request for transfer of the whole of Tenasserim into the Frontier Areas.

He further suggested that "it would be most unwise to allow this matter to drift up to the time of the elections, for the very good reason that, if we have by then taken no steps to settle at least the patently justifiable Karen claims, election heat might well develop into something much more dangerous."[69]

Meanwhile, the Karen goodwill mission, led by four London-educated Karen lawyers, Sydney Loo Nee, Saw Tha Din, Saw Po Chit, and Saw Ba U Gyi, was on its way to London. Except for Ba U Gyi, the three left Rangoon on July 26, 1946, in the *SS Carthage* and arrived in London on August 25.[70] Ba U Gyi came later and returned early due to his appointment in Aung San's new executive council. During their four-month stay in London, August to December 1946, the Karen delegation made contacts in England and Scotland, including unofficial conferences with Lord Pethick-Lawrence and other members of the Labour government.[71]

They presented their case through a published booklet entitled *The Case for the Karens*, with information like the Karen Memorial that was previously sent to the London office. It traced the Karen origins, pointing out they were the first settlers in their present location in lower Burma and in parts of Siam. Given the long history of Karen mistreatment at Burman hands and the latest 1942 incidents, it mentioned the alleged extermination of the Karen ethnic group. They remained strictly loyal to the British throughout World War II and rendered every possible assistance for the successful defeat of the Japanese. The booklet also pointed out the Karen desire to be given a state with a seaboard and to continue their existence within the Commonwealth. The delegation presented two alternative requests to London:

1. That a special act of Parliament establish from Burma territory a Karen State equipped with a liberal constitution, operating under British protection, and having a seaboard or

2. That the same Karen State be permitted to join a Federation of Frontier Area States separate from Burma and enjoining dominion status within the Commonwealth.

The delegation received good press coverage, but Mr. Attlee had already decided to send the new governor for Burma to negotiate with Burman nationalists.[72] The goodwill mission received a respectful hearing and some sympathy in Conservative political circles but no official agreement. Mr. L. B. Walsh Atkins of the Burma Office met with the delegation and made a note that the goodwill mission had asked for a separate state, based on the Tenasserim division with a separate governor, and that they envisaged a federation with Burma.[73]

Recently, an author opined that the Karen goodwill mission came back to Burma "empty handed and betrayed."[74] Conversely, Sir Gilbert Laithwaite, then deputy undersecretary of state for Burma, commented in February 1947 that "the good-will mission, though it came to London in terms only as a mission of good-will, had every opportunity, had it so desired, to make its political ambitions known. Whether from good manners or not, it took no steps to do so and no coherent scheme representing Karen ambitions emerged during their stay in this country."[75]

Professor Tinker observed that the Karen leaders had "formulated their claim in an elaborate petition and they did not understand that the politics of petition were now out of date, replaced by the politics of demand." He further wrote, "The Karen Mission to England had relied upon British goodwill to realize their wishes; they did not understand that polite receptions at the Burma Office meant absolutely nothing. The Karen war record was not forgotten in Britain but it carried little weight beside the pressures being exerted by AFPFL, based on the threat of force."[76]

It was unclear if the Karen goodwill mission failed due to their meekness or overreliance on British goodwill. However, a general strike led by Aung San's AFPFL and backed by his PVO military force presented a major challenge to the new governor, Sir Hubert Rance, who arrived in Burma in September 1946. The situation threatened to paralyze the British administration, and Governor Rance conceded to the demands of the AFPFL. A new executive council was formed on September 28, composed of six AFPFL members, all in major posts, with Aung San as Governor Rance's counselor for defense and external affairs as well as deputy chairman of the council.[77] Two Karen leaders, Ba U Gyi and Mahn Ba Khaing, became the minister for information and minister for industry and labor respectively, in this new executive council.[78] The Burma political situation changed in favor of the AFPFL before the Karen goodwill mission returned home in December 1946.

Aung San-Attlee Agreement and the Dilemma of the Karen People

After joining the government council, Aung San intensified his demand for Burma's independence. On September 29, he spoke at an anti-White Paper demonstration under AFPFL auspices. His call for unity and strength to support the full freedom of Burma received unprecedented backing. After a series of discussions, the British government invited Aung San to London for final negotiations. In January 1947, the Burma delegation, led by Aung San, traveled to London to press for assurance that Burma shall "be given her freedom" by January 31, 1948.[79]

On January 27, 1947, Prime Minister Attlee and General Aung San signed an agreement on behalf of the United Kingdom and Burma respectively, which became known as the Aung San-Attlee Agreement. The agreement's main features included guarantees that a constituent assembly would be elected in April; that the executive council of the governor would function as an interim government along the lines of the dominion government in India; that certain matters which had previously been formally reserved for the governor would in the future be brought before the executive council; and that the Burma Army would come under the control of the interim government.[80] Regarding the frontier areas, it was agreed to achieve early unification of the frontier areas and Ministerial Burma with the free consent of the inhabitants of those areas and in the meantime

(a) There shall be free intercourse between the people of the Frontier Areas and the people of Ministerial Burma without hindrance.

(b) The leaders and representatives of the peoples of the Frontier Areas shall be asked either at the Panglong Conference to be held at the beginning of next month or at a special Conference to be convened for the purpose, to express their views upon the form of association with the Government of Burma which they consider acceptable during the transition period. . . .

(c) After the Panglong meeting, or the special conference, His Majesty's Government and the Government of Burma will agree upon the best method of advancing their common aims in accordance with the expressed views of the peoples of the Frontier Areas.

(d) A Committee of Enquiry shall be set up forthwith as to the best method of associating the Frontier peoples with the working out of the new Constitution for Burma. . . . Such Committee shall be asked to report to the Government of Burma and His Majesty's Government before the summoning of the Constituent Assembly.[81]

The agreement in connection with the frontier areas created dire concern among the Karen leaders. For them, their long-overdue dream of building a Karen state that included the frontier areas seemed endangered.

Sadly, Sir San C. Po, principal leader of the Karen nationalists, who initiated the inclusion of the Tenasserim division in the movement for the Karen state, passed away on July 17, 1946. Without their prime mentor, KCO leaders were compelled to react to the challenges of the changing political atmosphere. Unsurprisingly, they were prompt in action. KCO leaders called a meeting for January 17, 1947, and they passed a resolution thanking the Burmese delegation for raising the

Karen questions. However, they added, "no decision concerning Karen will be accepted as a matter of course by the Karen people in the absence of their representatives."[82]

The End of KCO and the Birth of the Karen National Union (KNU)

Realizing the dire need for pan-Karen cooperation, the KCO called a Karen Congress for February 5-7, 1947, in Rangoon, where seven hundred representatives participated.[83] The meeting's first day focused on Karen unification. As a result, the KCO and KYO agreed to merge and formed the Karen National Union (KNU). San Po Thin was elected as president, Ba U Gyi (minister for information) as vice president, and Thra Tha Hto as secretary of the newly formed KNU. The KYO leaders Mahn Ba Khaing (minister for industry and labor), Mahn Win Maung, Saw Sein Tin, and Saw Kyaw Sein joined as the executive members.

However, during the next day's meeting, the issue of whether to accept the Aung San-Attlee Agreement and participate in the Constituent Assembly election divided Karen leaders. San Po Thin and other KNU leaders considered that they should not participate. On the other hand, the KYO leaders, Mahn Ba Khaing, Mahn Win Maung, and Saw Kyaw Sein, who were ex-BDA members, argued that they should participate in the election. Consequently, they left the KNU, reinstating the previous KYO.[84] Despite disagreement and division, the meeting resolution was sent to the British prime minister by telegram on February 8. Signed by its secretary, Thra Tha Hto, the KNU declared:

> The Karen Congress . . . emphatically protests against Aung San-Attlee agreement affecting Karen interest, particularly:
> 1. Inadequate Karen quota in the proposed Constituent Assembly.
> 2. Undefined number of Karen seats in the Interim Legislature.
> 3. Non-observance of settled practice in respect of Karen fighting forces.
> 4. Failure to give cognizance to the claim of Karens for a separate state and
> 5. Failure to consult Karen opinion.
> 6. Congress decides non-participation unless modifications are made to the entire satisfaction of Karens by the 3rd March.[85]

The chief demands, as revealed above, were for an increased number of Karen seats in the assembly and for a separate Karen state. Sir David Monteath, the permanent undersecretary of state for Burma and

India, and Sir Gilbert Laithwaite, the deputy undersecretary of state for Burma, studied the issues and exchanged notes from February 13 to 15. They further reviewed the old Karen Memorial of September 1945 in their efforts to assess the Karen demands.

Sir Gilbert Laithwaite commented that the Karen problem was "far from simple," since most Karens lived in the plains with many residing in the delta, and they could not intervene from London. Concerning the Karen quota in the Constituent Assembly, his view was, "The Karens, with 24 seats in the Constituent Assembly and two seats in the Executive Council (if they keep those) are in excellent position to bring pressure to bear on behalf of the Karen Community in an Assembly which AFPFL clearly were not too sure will contain an overwhelming AFPFL majority, and it is in that Assembly that they must make their case."[86]

He also stated the more complicated fact he found from Burmese political circles that "there was no desire on the part of Buddhist Karens for any separation" and "the separatist tendency, or the desire for any form of separate state, is for practical purposes confined to the relatively small element of educated Christian Karens."[87] Such statements suggested the important role of religion in the Karen nationalist movement.

Sir David Monteath remarked that "the Karens have deserved well of the British not only in the 1939–1945 war, but before, and it should be a matter of conscience to see that they are not 'let down.' This applies to the Plains Karens and to the Hillmen."[88] Despite these serious discussions, Lord Pethick-Lawrence wrote to Governor Hubert Rance on February 17 that the Karen representation in the Constituent Assembly would proceed as stated in the Aung San-Attlee Agreement, and the Karens could obtain a separate Karen state through their representation in the Constituent Assembly. He added, "We cannot allow our decisions to be governed by the Karen threat of non-participation."[89] Obviously, the Burma Office in London had no intention to intervene in the Karen affairs that would, one way or another, upset the Aung San-Attlee Agreement.

The Panglong Conference and Uncertainty about Affairs Related to the Karen People

Following the Aung San-Attlee Agreement paragraph 8 guidelines, a committee of enquiry was set up with Lord Arthur Bottomley, British undersecretary of state for dominion affairs, as chair. Their task was to find the best method of involving the frontier peoples in working out Burma's new constitution. After Lord Bottomley arrived in Burma on

February 7, 1947, he discussed the frontier area matters with members of the executive council at a meeting held at the Government House in Rangoon. The members of the executive council in that meeting were Aung San, Tin Tut, Thakin Mya, and two Karens, Saw Ba U Gyi and Mahn Ba Khaing. When Lord Bottomley asked how he could help, Aung San suggested that he should make it clear to frontier representatives at Panglong that His Majesty's government desired unification of the frontier areas and Ministerial Burma. The meeting, which solely focused on the questions of the method of interim association between the frontier areas and Ministerial Burma, was obviously not in the interest of Saw Ba U Gyi and Mahn Ba Khaing. Since becoming the KCO leader, Ba U Gyi, particularly, had repeated the demand for a separate Karen state with the frontier areas. Unsurprisingly, the meeting records state "the two Karen members said not a single word throughout the discussion."[90]

The Panglong Conference met in the Shan state, February 7-12, 1947, with the objective of hearing the frontier peoples' wishes and determining whether the frontier areas would like to cooperate in a new Union of Burma. On February 9, Lord Bottomley met with representatives of the Shan states, the Kachin hills, and the Chin hills. They discussed the rights and responsibilities in the future Union of Burma. Understanding that the participation of frontier area people in the Constituent Assembly was essential in building the new Union of Burma, the Burman leaders tried to create good relationships with the non-Burmese groups, who hitherto claimed that they preferred to continue under British control. Aung San even offered Shan leaders an opportunity to write their own terms of cooperation and pledged continued financial assistance from Burmese revenues. The Shan and Kachin negotiated the right to secede from the Union of Burma after ten years if they were not satisfied with their political status.[91] Four Karen delegates went to Panglong, but on their arrival, they found that arrangements had been made for the Shan leaders (Sawbwas) to sign the agreement, so they took no further active part in the proceeding.[92]

After the conference, on February 14, 1947, Lord Bottomley wrote in his report to Lord Pethick-Lawrence that the "Whole of Karen problem ... is exceedingly delicate and outside the scope of my mission." He concluded the "decisive fact as to these and other (small) groups not represented at Panglong is that the 1935 Act and therefore the power of the Governor and ultimately of His Majesty's Government to protect their interests remains unaltered."[93]

As Lord Bottomley stated, unlike the Karen situation, other minority affairs were simple, since the territories of Shan, Kachin, and Chin were almost entirely within the frontier areas-part I, separated from Ministerial Burma. On the other hand, the territories that the Karens had been seeking for a separate Karen state were under three separate administrative systems. One was the Karenni state, home of the Red Karens, which had never been under British administration and was nominally sovereign under British suzerainty. The inhabitants of the Salween district were almost entirely Karens and were under the frontier areas administration. The delta region, where the Karens formed the population's majority, was under Ministerial Burma. Most Karen nationalist leaders were born and raised in the delta since Bassein, one of the major Burmese seaports, was the birthplace of the Karen Christian educational movement. For both cultural and economic reasons, it was crucial that this delta region be included in the Karen state.

Apparently, Karen demands for a Karen state within three different zones of administration became a complicated issue to resolve for successive British authorities. During this period, like Stevenson, the commissioner of Tenasserim division, D. B. Petch, took an interest in Karen affairs. He studied the Karen demands. Just before signing the Aung San-Attlee Agreement, he submitted his sympathetic view of settling the Karen case. He proposed "autonomy in cultural and domestic affairs should be given to the Tenasserim division, to which Salween district, the Karenni and a reasonable part of Toungoo district would later be joined."[94] Apparently, Petch's proposal received no attention before or after the Panglong Conference.

The Panglong Conference promised frontier peoples wide-ranging political freedom in association with independent Burma. For further action, the Panglong Agreement recommended that a representative of the hill peoples, selected by the governor on the recommendation of representatives of the Supreme Council of the United Hill Peoples (SCUHP), should be appointed a councilor to the governor to deal with the frontier areas. The said councilor would be assisted by two deputy councilors representing ethnic groups of which he was not a member in carrying out their joint responsibility for the three areas.[95]

Accordingly, the Frontier Areas Committee of Enquiry (FACE) was formed on February 21, 1947, with nine persons, four from Ministerial Burma and four from the frontier areas, with Mr. Rees-William appointed as chair.[96] The four members representing Ministerial Burma in the FACE were composed of a very strong Burman contingent headed by U Tin Tut, together with U Nu, U Khin Maung Gale, and U Myint Thein. Among these leaders, only Tin Tut favored accepting Commonwealth membership. Rees-William discovered that U Nu and U Khin Maung

Gale were prepared for some kind of association but not membership in a British Commonwealth.[97] The four members representing the frontier areas were Sao Sam Htun (Shan), Hsinwa Nawng (Kachin), Vum Ko Hau (Chin), and the KNU council member Saw Sankey, a Karen who was an ex-Force 136 captain and the schoolmaster of Salween district.

The committee made an eleven-day preliminary tour extending southward from Myitkyina in the Kachin hills to Loikaw in Karenni state. Then from March 19 to 26, the committee held hearings in Rangoon and from March 27 to April 21 in Maymyo. After all the hearings, the FACE submitted the report on April 24, signed by the nine members.[98] The report concluded that frontier witnesses wanted to participate in the work of the Constituent Assembly. It recommended that 45 frontier representatives should join the 210 elected members from Ministerial Burma. The 45 seats were divided as follows: Federated Shan States including Kokang and Mongpai 26, Kachin Hills 7, Chin Hills with Arakan Hill Tracts 6, Karenni 2, Salween District 2, Somra Tract 1, Homalin Subdivision 1.

When the FACE started to work, representative witnesses from the Karens in Salween district expressed their view that they did not wish to unite with Burma. However, in early April, another small group of Karens in Papun in Salween district, headed by Saw Lu Lu, gave evidence that the Karens in the Salween area were in favor of participation in the Burma constitution.[99] Accordingly, the FACE reported that there was a "desire for incorporation in Ministerial Burma as an ordinary district" and recommended the inclusion of the Salween district in Burma as an ordinary district. In reality, the Salween district Karens were largely in favor of the KNU perspective, desiring a separate Karen state with full internal autonomy. On May 6, Saw Ba U Gyi wrote to the government of Burma that Saw Lu Lu and his companions were not the representatives of the Papun area. He enclosed two letters from the Salween district Karen leaders as evidence. One letter was from ex-Force 136 officer Marshall Shwin, who was president of the Shwegyin Karen Association. The other letter, signed by four Karens who were ex-Force 136, Saw De Gay, Saw T. San Twa, Saw Baw, and Saw Aku, claimed that the evidence Saw Lu Lu gave to the FACE was not true, and he had done an injustice to the Karens' cause and aspirations.[100]

The committee further suggested, "Eastern Toungoo, Kyain, Myawaddi and Thaton Part II Area should be included in Ministerial Burma and should have full constituency and other rights, but negotiations to this end should take place in the Constituent Assembly."[101] Regarding the Karenni state, the report recommended, "The chiefs or administrators of the three states may be asked to consult the wishes of their peoples and to nominate jointly the representatives for the Constituent Assembly."[102]

With the signing of the Panglong Agreement on February 12, 1947, all frontier area major ethnic leaders except the Karens committed to a permanent union with Ministerial Burma. Indeed, the Panglong Conference was a great success for the Burmans, as it was the foundation the Union of Burma with people from the frontier areas. However, for the Karens, the Panglong Agreement diminished the Karen Memorial and ushered in more challenges in the struggle for the Karen separate state which Sir San C. Po had originally envisioned to be in "the Federation Union; the United State of Burma."[103]

Notes

1. IOR: M/4/3023, The Humble Memorial of the Karens of Burma to His Britannic Majesty's Secretary of State for Burma; Hugh Tinker, Andrew Griffin, and S. R. Ashton, *Burma: The Struggle for Independence, 1944–1948: Compilation of Documents from Official and Private Sources*, vol. 1 (London: Her Majesty's Stationery Office, 1983), document 286, 1:492–97. See the memorial online.

2. Tinker, Griffin, and Ashton, 1:262–64, Statement Given by the Secretary of State for Burma in the House of Commons, 17 May 1945. The name referred to the government white paper.

3. Ibid.

4. Tinker, Griffin, and Ashton, 1:288, Ian Morrison to Ralph Deakin, Foreign News Editor of the *Times*.

5. *The Times*, 1, "Nationalism in Burma," May 31, 1945; 2, "Ambitious Program of Self Help," June 1, 1945; Tinker, Griffin, and Ashton, 1:288.

6. Ba Than, *The Roots of the Revolution: A Brief History of the Defence Services of the Union of Burma and the Ideals for Which They Stand* (Rangoon: Director of Information, 1962), 49, Aung San's proposal to create the Anti-Fascist Organization in the secret meetings in August and September 1944; Angelene Naw, *Aung San and the Struggle for Burmese Independence* (Chiang Mai: Silkworm Books, 2001), 109.

7. IOR: M/3/1735, General Secretary, AFPFL to the Secretary of State for Burma (through HA Force 136); see also in Tinker, Griffin, and Ashton, 1:316.

8. IOR: R/8/20, Thakin Than Tun, General Secretary, AFPFL to Lord Louis Mountbatten (through HQ Force 136), in Tinker, Griffin, and Ashton, 1:290.

9. It was through Thakin Thein Pe Myint's connection with Force 136 in 1944 that Than Tun had access to Mountbatten.

10. Naw, *Aung San*, 126.

11. PRO: WO/203/53, Lieutenant Colonel Cumming, Group "A," Force 136, to Brigadier, General Staff (Operation) ALFSEA; Tinker, Griffin, and Ashton, 1:136.

12. John F. Cady, *A History of Modern Burma* (Ithaca, NY: Cornell University Press, 1960), 479.

13. Mahn Win Maung parachuted along with other British officers in Taungoo division, Htantabin township on March 28, 1945.

14. *Tatmadaw Thamaing* (*History of the Armed Forces*), vol. 1 (Rangoon: Myawaddy Press, 1996), 251; Thutaythana Ye Baw, *Ye Baw Thone Kyeik Hnint Ba Ma lut lat ye Tat Ma Taw Sit Kyaung Myar* (*The Thirty Comrades and the Military Campaign Routes of the Burma Independence Army*) (Rangoon: Ye Baw Yargyaw, 1975), 269.

15. IOR: M/4/2601, Note by Thakin Thein Pe Myint, Burma Patriotic Front (AFO) and the Communist Party of Burma; Tinker, Griffin, and Ashton, 1:109.

16. Pu S'Kaw Ler Taw, *Ka Nyaw Ta Ber Hser Tar Si Soh Teh Soh* (KNU publication, n.d.), 181.

17. They were then the members of the Karen Central Advisory Board, which was to become the Karen Central Organization in October 1945. See Maung Sin Kyeh, *Bamapyi Chit Kayin Amyotha Kaung Hsaung Myar* (Bangkok: Pyidaungsu Kayin Amyotha Apweh Choke, 2003), 68.

18. PRO: WO 203/5240, Leaders' Conference, 16–18 August 1945: Report by Thakin Than Tun; Tinker, Griffin, and Ashton, 1:238, 298–99.

19. PRO: WO 203/5240, Leaders' Conference, 16–18, August 1945: Report by Thakin Than Tun; Tinker, Griffin, and Ashton, 1:238, 396–401.

20. IOR: M/4/1320, Rear Headquarters, Supreme Allied Commander, South East Asia, SAC (Misc.) 13th meeting, 23 June 1945; Tinker, Griffin, and Ashton, 1:342–45.

21. Tinker, Griffin, and Ashton, 1:433–34.

22. Ibid., 1:316, 370.

23. IOR: L/PO/9/10, Sir Reginald Dorman-Smith to L. S. Amrey, Rangoon Meeting; Tinker, Griffin, and Ashton, 1:347.

24. IOR: M/3/1676, T. L. Hughes (Governor's Representative with twelve Army) to H. N. C. Stevenson (Governor's Secretary), dated 15 August 1945; Tinker, Griffin, and Ashton, 1:398.

25. Tinker, Griffin, and Ashton, 1:262-64, Statement Given by the Secretary of State for Burma in the House of Commons, 17 May 1945.

26. Maung Sin Kyeh, 68.

27. IOR: M/4/3023, The Humble Memorial of the Karens of Burma to His Britannic Majesty's Secretary of State for Burma; Tinker, Griffin, and Ashton, 1:492–97.

28. Ibid.

29. Ibid., 1:523.

30. Ibid., 1:l, li; also see plate 4, facing 1:545, photo of executive council appointed by Sir Reginald Dorman-Smith, November 1945.

31. Loo Htu U Hla, *Thadin-sarmyar Pyaw-pya-thaw Sit Pyee-sa Bamar-Pyi*, vol. 1 (Rangoon: Gyi Bwa Yay Press, 1969), 168.

32. PRO: FO 643/66 (51/GSO/47Pt 1), Minutes of a Mass Meeting of the Karen Central Organization held for three days, 1-3 October 1945, at No. 2 U Loo Nee Street, Kemmendine, Rangoon; Tinker, Griffin, and Ashton, 1:499.

33. *New Light of Burma* (newspaper), October 16, 1945; also in Lu Htu U Hla, 1:139–40

34. Maung Sin Kyeh, 70–71.

35. Ibid., 61.

36. Ibid., 69.

37. IOR: M/4/2422, Governor of Burma to Secretary of State for Burma, telegram; Tinker, Griffin, and Ashton, 1:642.

38. Maung Sin Kyeh, 70.

39. Pu Gee Doh, *Mahn Ba Zan Hnint Kayin Taw Hlan Yay* (*Mah Ba Zan and Karen Revolution*) (KNU publication, 1993), 126.

40. PRO: FO 643/66 (51/GSO/47 Pt I), Sir San C. Po to Sir Reginald Dorman-Smith; Tinker, Griffin, and Ashton, 1:573–74.

41. Maung Sin Kyeh, 71.

42. PRO: FO 643/66 (51/GSO)/47 Pt. I), Chairman, Karen Central Organization to Governor's Secretary; Tinker, Griffin, and Ashton, 1:592.

43. PRO: FO 643/66 (51/GSO/47 Pt I) Sir Herbert Dunkley to Sir Reginald Dorman-Smith; Tinker, Griffin, and Ashton, 1:516.

44. Ibid.

45. Ibid.

46. Tinker, Griffin, and Ashton, 1:592, Chairman, Karen Central Organization to the Governor's Secretary.

47. IOR: M/4/3023, Sir Reginald Dorman-Smith to Lord Pethick-Lawrence; Tinker, Griffin, and Ashton, 1:634–36.

48. Tinker, Griffin, and Ashton, 1:637.

49. PRO: FO 643/39 (9G10 II), Memorandum by H. N. C. Stevenson and T. L. Hughes, Karen Memorial; Tinker, Griffin, and Ashton, 1:650–53. Stevenson drafted the memorandum and made Hughes sign it before it was submitted to the governor. PRO: FO 643/66: 51/GSO/47 PI; Tinker, Griffin, and Ashton, 1:650.

50. Ibid.

51. IOR: M/4/2553, Executive Council, 16th Meeting, Minute 6; Tinker, Griffin, and Ashton, 1:655.

52. IOR: L. PO/9/15, Report by Thakin Than Tun on AFPFL Congress, 17–23 January 1946; Tinker, Griffin, and Ashton, 1:374.

53. Maung Sin Kyeh, 72.

54. Ibid.

55. Ibid.

56. IOR: M/4/2553, Executive Council, 16th Meeting, Minute 6; Tinker, Griffin, and Ashton, 1:655.

57. Tinker, Griffin, and Ashton, 1:626, Governor of Burma to Secretary of State for Burma, Rangoon, 25 January 1946.

58. Tinker, Griffin, and Ashton, 1:642, Governor of Burma to Secretary of State for Burma, 6 February 1946.

59. Ibid.

60. Tinker, Griffin, and Ashton, 1:740-42, Resolution adopted by Mass Meeting of the Karens, 25-27 April 1946.

61. IOR: M/4/3023, Sir Hubert Rance to Lord Pethick-Lawrence, 7 March 1947; Tinker, Griffin, and Ashton, 2:453.

62. Naw, *Aung San*, 149.

63. Tinker, Griffin, and Ashton, 1:797.

64. Ibid., 1:844, Home Department, General Branch (520) dated 18 June 1946; also *The Burma Gazette*, 22 June 1946.

65. PRO: FO 643/66 (51/GSO/47 Pt I), Observation by H. N. C. Stevenson on Karen Resolution, adopted 25 April 1946; Tinker, Griffin, and Ashton, 1:850.

66. PRO: FO 643/66 (51/GSO/47 Pt II), Chairman, Karen Central Organization to H. N. C. Stevenson; Tinker, Griffin, and Ashton, 1:859.

67. IOR: M/4/3023, P. G. E. Nash to Sir Gilbert Laithwaite, Rangoon, 12 August 1946; Tinker, Griffin, and Ashton, 1:949.

68. PRO: FO 643/56 (1Q1/GS46 Pt II), Governor of Burma to Secretary of State for Burma Rangoon, 17 July 1946, 12:40 hours (telegram); Tinker, Griffin, and Ashton, 1:898-99.

69. IOR: M/4/2807, Director, Frontier Areas Administration to Governor; Tinker, Griffin, and Ashton, 1:929.

70. Smith Dun, *Memoirs of the Four-Foot Colonel*, Data Paper number 113 (Ithaca, NY: Cornell University Southeast Asia Program, Department of Asia Studies, 1980), 80.

71. Cady, *History of Modern Burma*, 553.

72. Ibid.; also in *The Times*, August 4 and December 6, 1946.

73. Hugh Tinker, Andrew Griffin, and S. R. Ashton, *Burma: The Struggle for Independence, 1944–1948: Compilation of Documents from Official and Private Sources*, vol. 2 (London: Her Majesty's Stationery Office, 1984), 2:254–55.

74. Benedict Rogers, *Burma: A Nation at the Crossroads* (London: Rider Books. 2012), 53.

75. IOR: M/4/3023, Karen Claims: Note by L. B. Walsh Atkins, Burma Office, 13 February 1947; Tinker, Griffin, and Ashton, 2:407.

76. Tinker, Griffin, and Ashton, 2:xxvi. Tinker wrote in his introduction that the Karen leaders asked for a separate state, based on the Tenasserim division, with a separate governor. They envisaged a federation with Burma.

77. *The Burman*, 27 September 1946, 1.

78. Tinker, Griffin, and Ashton, 2:xlv. Saw Ba U Gyi was sworn in on 23 October 1946 but resigned after boycotting the election on 9 April 1947. Mahn Ba Khaing was sworn in on 28 September 1946.

79. Tinker, Griffin, and Ashton, 2:257, Memorandum by the Secretary of State for Burma.

80. Tinker, Griffin, and Ashton, 2:378–82, Conclusion reached in the Conversations between His Majesty's Government and the Delegation from the Executive Council of the Governor of Burma, January 1947. Cmd. 7029.

81. Ibid.

82. Tinker, Griffin, and Ashton, 2:279, circulated under Burma Conversations: United Kingdom Papers B.U.K. (47) 24, 21 January 1947.

83. Tinker, Griffin, and Ashton, 2:417.

84. Maung Sin Kyeh, 90–91.

85. Tinker, Griffin, and Ashton, 2:407, Text of telegram to Prime Minister from Karen Congress dated 8th February.

86. IOR: M/4/3023, Karen Claims: Note by Sir Gilbert Laithwaite, 13 February; Tinker, Griffin, and Ashton, 2:408.

87. Ibid.

88. Tinker, Griffin, and Ashton, 2:408, Note by Sir David Monteath, 15 February.

89. Tinker, Griffin, and Ashton, 2:416, Lord Pethick-Lawrence to Sir Hubert Rance.

90. IOR: M/4/2805, Record of Meeting on Frontier Areas, 7 February 1947; Tinker, Griffin, and Ashton, 2:397.

91. IOR: M/4/2811, Note by John Leyden on the Panglong Conference; Tinker, Griffin, and Ashton, 2:423–30.

92. PRO: FO 643/66 (51/GS/80/47), Note of a meeting of a Karen Deputation with the Governor on Tuesday 25th February 1947; Tinker, Griffin, and Ashton, 2:438.

93. IOR: M/4/3025, Telegram, Rangoon, 14 February 1947, Arthur Bottomley to Lord Pethick-Lawrence; Tinker, Griffin, and Ashton, 2:412.

94. PRO: FO 643/66(51)GSO/47 Pt II), Study of Karen demands by D. B. Petch (Extract), Rangoon, 31 December 1946; Tinker, Griffin, and Ashton, 2:217.

95. Tinker, Griffin, and Ashton, 2:404-5, 423-30.

96. Ibid., 2:417, 490.

97. Ibid., 2:482, D. R. Rees-William to Lord Pethick-Lawrence.

98. Tinker, Griffin and Ashton, 2:483–90, Report of the Frontier Areas Committee of Enquiry: Chapter III. 24 April 1947.

99. Tinker, Griffin, and Ashton, 2:512, President of the Karen National Union to the Government of Burma, 6 May 1947.

100. Ibid.

101. Tinker, Griffin, and Ashton, 2:483–90, Report of the Frontier Areas Committee of Enquiry: Chapter III.

102. Ibid.

103. PRO: FO 643/66(51/GSO/47 Pt I), Sir San C. Po to Sir Reginald Dorman-Smith, December 19, 1945; Tinker, Griffin, and Ashton, 1:573.

7

The Political Battles of the Karen People (1947–1949)

> As a race, we Karens have always been law-abiding, peace loving and unprovocative, and we are proud of this very quality inherent in our nature. Let us, therefore, in our constitutional fight for a separate Karen State, live up to this noble ideal and desist from acts which are likely to lead to communal tension or clash.
>
> Executive Committee KNU, July 25, 1948
> No. 5, U Loo Nee Street, Lower Kemmendine, Rangoon[1]

The above opening statement was included in the Karen National Union's announcement under the headline "An Appeal to the Karens." It testified to the KNU's peaceful approach in their attempt to achieve their separate Karen nation. That lasted until late 1948. Even when the whole of Burma seemed out of control due to communist and other rebellions, the KNU helped restore peace, following the command of General Smith Dun, the Karen commander of the Burma Army. The Karen leaders promised Prime Minister U Nu to seek a separate state only by peaceful democratic means. Sadly, a series of challenges pushed the Karens to arms by 1949.

The Karen Congress of February 1947 and Its Unanswered Demands

While the rest of the hill peoples came to terms with the Burmans at the Panglong Conference and the follow-up work of the Frontier Areas Committee of Enquiry (FACE) was in progress, the Karen National Union continued its struggle for their Karen state. On February 17, five days after the Panglong Conference conclusion, the KNU sent a follow-up letter to the prime minister, restating the protest against the Aung San-Attlee Agreement with a more detailed explanation. The major issues that the Karen Congress objected to in the Aung San-Attlee Agreement were the Constituent Assembly (paragraph I), Interim Legislature (paragraph 3), Defense (paragraph 7), Frontier Areas (paragraph 8), and Other Matters (paragraph 10). The first objection was the proposal to elect to the Constituent Assembly two representatives instead of one from each constituency.[2]

The Karens believed that, out of 210 members to be returned to the Constituent Assembly, only 24 Karen representatives would be able to give full weight to their views in the assembly, which would draw up a constitution for a new Burma. With that reasoning, the Karens asked for more representatives based on the latest Karen population in all Karen-inhabited areas. The reason for the second objection was like the first one; hence, the Karens demanded more than 20 seats in the Legislative Council. The third objection was about the proposal to place forthwith all Burmese forces under the control of the government of Burma. The Karens asked for the right of "exclusiveness," which they enjoyed in prior years when they were in the fighting forces of Burma.

The objection to the issue of the frontier areas was the most important matter for the Karens since it was directly related to the Karen state for which the Karens had been working for decades. The areas that Karens repeatedly wanted to include in the Karen state were partly in the frontier areas. Again, added in the letter was that the Karens "could not possibly participate in the preliminary steps leading up to the creation of a Constitution-making Body, unless and until the revised White Paper of 1947 is modified to meet the legitimate aspiration of the Karens by the 3rd of March 1947."[3]

The relentless Karen nationalist movements during this period negated the allegation that the Karens were not aggressive in their demands for a separate Karen state. Just a few days after sending the letter on February 17, the Karen National Union, Karen Youth Organization (KYO), and Buddhist Karen National Association (BKNA) worked together and held a meeting on February 22, 1947. Again, they sent the following letter to the British government:[4]

> 1. (a) That the Forthcoming Elections to the Constituent assembly the Karen seat be given each of the Constituencies in the Districts noted below:
> Insein North and South Constituencies
> Tharrawaddy North, South, West and Central Constituencies
> Pegu North, South and Central Constituencies
> Hanthawaddy North, South and East Constituencies
> Pyapon North and South Constituencies
> Tavoy Town and rural Constituencies

Mergui One Constituency

(b) That 25% of the total seats in the Governor's Executive Council in the Interim Government be allotted to the Karens.

2. That in order to ensure the viewpoints of the Karens being given full weight in that Legislative Council to be set up after the elections to the Constituent Assembly are completed, 25% of the total seats in the Interim Legislature be allotted to the Karens.

3. That the right of "exclusiveness" at the present enjoyed by the Karens serving in the Armed Forces, be continued.

4. That the question of the creation of a Karen State, with seaboard, in the United Burma be accepted in principle.

5. That in the future administration of the country real and definite steps be effectively taken by the Government to have the Karens fully represented in all services on the basis of population.

6. That immediately following the setting up of the Constituent Assembly a true census of the population of Burma to be taken with as little delay as possible.

San Po Thin Sankey
Chairman, Council of Action Secretary, Council of Action

In connection with these demands, the Karen leaders were granted two meetings, one with Governor Hubert Rance on February 25 and the other with Aung San's executive council on February 28, 1947. Saw Tha Din, San Po Thin, Mahn James Tun Aung, U Hla Pe, and Thra Tha Hto attended the first one with Governor Rance. Saw Tha Din reiterated that, if the points made by the Karen Congress of February 5-7 were not conceded, the Karens did not consider themselves secure and would keep aloof from the elections. He also said the Part II Karen areas were anxious to remain outside Ministerial Burma. Mahn James Tun Aung and San Po Thin spoke of the situation in Myaungmya and Bassein, and their concern for ethnic and communal outbreaks, due to arms collections and the Burmese chanting slogans against the Karen Rifles.[5]

At the meeting with Aung San and the members of the executive council on February 28, 1947, the representatives of the KNU, KYO, and BKNA discussed the demands listed in their letter of February 22. Members of the Council of Action (KNU) called a meeting on March 1 where the chairman, San Po Thin, explained in brief the results of their interview with the members of the executive council. He opined that, although the reply given by the executive councilors was not entirely satisfactory, it would be mutually beneficial to the Karens and the Burmese if the former worked in cooperation with the latter in their struggle for attaining independence. Unhappy with the result, a member remarked, "Boycott the coming election."[6] However, Mahn Ba Khaing, then minister for industry and labor, claimed that his KYO should contest seats at the forthcoming election. The chairman told the members not to decide immediately. He and the secretary, Thra Tha Hto, would meet the Honorable Aung San again in pursuance of the demands.

On March 2, San Po Thin brought Aung San to the headquarters of the KNU, where Aung San explained to the Karen elders and the members of the KNU that he was not able to accept the principle of a Karen state in United Burma. He advised the KNU to work together with the Burmans. He also assured them that the Karens would be included on every selection board and in the public services commission and that he would try his best to safeguard the interests of the Karens. Mahn Ba Zan of Maubin, U Pe, Saw Belly of Insein, and Thra Tha Hto requested Aung San accept the principle of a Karen state by giving various reasons, among which was the right of self-determination by minorities. Aung San told the Karens that he was not empowered to accede to the Karen demands. San Po Thin, then president of the KNU, said that Karens could not depend upon the Europeans for help. Therefore, they had no choice but to work with the Burmans. His personal choice was that "he would not ask for the creation of a Karen State and would work in harmony with the Hon'ble U Aung San."[7]

In explaining his decision, San Po Thin said that he had sought advice from a certain European who told him that Europeans could do nothing for the Karens. It was not clear from whom San Po Thin received his information. Presumably, it came from someone who found H. N. C. Stevenson's letter to the governor's secretary, P. G. E. Nash, dated February 15. In it, Stevenson pleaded with Nash to warn the Karens that "nothing is being done and nothing can be done by London," and therefore, "The future of the Karens lies wholly in the hands of the Karen themselves, and if they wish to make any representations they must make them to the Constituent Assembly." He insisted that "it is necessary that it should be made abundantly clear to them," and went further by adding that "If [Governor Rance] does not feel that anything can be stated by Government House to the Karens officially, perhaps you [Nash] could mention the matter unofficially to Saw Ba U Gyi on my behalf."[8] Ba U Gyi seemed to be uninformed of the warning and chose a different direction.

The KNU executive members gathered that same evening at the house of ex-minister Mahn Ba Khin and discussed further action. Since they received no reply from Prime Minister Attlee in connection with the modification of the Aung San-Attlee Agreement, some suggested that Ba U Gyi should resign and that the Karens should boycott the coming general election. Ba U Gyi assured KNU members that he would abide by the decisions of the Karens. The members decided that the KNU Council of Action should meet on March 3 at 6:00 pm for further discussion and final decision.[9]

Finally, on March 3, 1947, the KNU general secretary received an official letter from Aung San beginning with an introduction: "I am directed to refer to your letter of the 22nd February 1947 addressed to the Hon'ble Deputy Chairman of the Governor's Executive Council." The letter detailed the result of the meeting held on February 28, explaining the reasons why the demands were turned down.[10] Concerning the question of a separate Karen state, raised in Resolution 4, the letter said, "I am to say that this is the question which can only be decided by Constituent Assembly." Apparently, most of the reasons were to wait for the coming election for the Constituent Assembly. The Karen leaders were disappointed with the refusal, particularly their demand that "the creation of a Karen State, with a seaboard, in the United Burma be accepted in principle."

However, Aung San seemed sincere in his promise in regard to Karen resolution 3, to which he stated, "In regards to Resolution 3. . . . The martial qualities of the Karens are well known to the Hon'ble Members and they rely on the services of the Karens making the future Burma Army a highly efficient and contended force."[11]

Later in May 1947, Aung San nominated a Karen, Colonel Smith Dun, as deputy general officer commanding (GOC) to the Burma Army, with the presumption that in due course, Smith Dun would succeed the British GOC, General Thomas.[12] That appointment did lead the way for General Smith Dun to become the army and police's commander-in-chief when Burma gained independence. Smith Dun had a long service record in the British Army, having joined the Burma Rifles while a teenager with his friend Henson Kyar Doe. He received the Sword of Honor from the Indian Military Academy, and his outstanding record in the 17th Indian Division (the Black Cats) during World War II impressed Aung San. Smith Dun was the obvious choice to lead the Burma Army in the future Union of Burma. Born into a Karen Christian family with his basic education from American Baptist Mission's Pwo Karen School in Bassein, Smith was a very committed Christian.[13] It was the main reason that his tenure as commander-in-chief in the new Union of Burma was short-lived.

The General Elections of 1947 and the Split between
KNU and KYO

On March 3, from 6:00 to 10:00 pm, the KNU leaders held a meeting with San Po Thin as chairman and Thra Tha Hto as secretary. Thra Tha Hto recalled the resolutions passed at the February Congress and reiterated the fact that, if no reply was received from England's prime minister by March 3, 1947, Ba U Gyi (minister for information) was to resign from the governor's executive council. A heated debate ensued as some members began to argue that, without a reply by that date, they had no option except to reaffirm their decision at the Congress to boycott the forthcoming general election.[14]

Chairman San Po Thin and Saw Kyaw Sein opposed boycotting the elections reasoning that there would be trouble between Karens and Burmans, and the Karens would suffer as there would be no members in the Constituent Assembly to safeguard the interests of the Karens. They tried to persuade the members to allow Ba U Gyi to remain in his present post and safeguard the interests of the Karens. Most members were unwilling to accept San Po Thin and Saw Kyaw Sein's reasons. They challenged the chair to call for a decision on whether they should participate in the coming election and whether Ba U Gyi be asked to resign, since the prime minister of England had ignored their request. Realizing that he would be defeated if votes were taken, San Po Thin asked members to accept his resignation as president of the KNU and left the meeting. Saw Kyaw Sein followed him.[15]

The rest of the KNU leaders decided to stay. The meeting continued under the chairmanship of Mahn Ba Khin, former minister in Governor Dorman-Smith's executive council. They unanimously decided to reaffirm the resolutions passed at the Congress that they should not participate in the coming general elections and that they should ask Ba U Gyi to resign.[16]

On March 4, 1947, Ba U Gyi tendered his resignation. Governor Rance met with him on the next day, hoping to persuade him to stay. Ba U Gyi responded that he would have to consult with the Karen elders. The governor followed up on the same evening by sending a letter to Ba U Gyi saying that he declined to accept his resignation. Ba U Gyi told the governor that he would see if it were possible to have a discussion with the Karen elders to reconsider their decision, but he also pointed out that many of the elders had left Rangoon.[17] Without Ba U Gyi's participation in the election, Governor Rance could no longer withhold his resignation. Finally on April 9, Governor Rance announced the resignation of Ba U Gyi and substituted San Po Thin as a member of the Constituent Assembly.[18] While the requests to reconsider the KNU boycott were in process in early March, Aung San had proposed San Po Thin as the substitute for Ba U Gyi in the forthcoming election, and San Po Thin had already accepted the offer.[19]

A determining factor in the KNU decision to boycott was the lack of answer to the February 8 telegram the Karen Congress sent to the prime minister. That long-awaited reply finally came on March 7, urging the KNU that "any representations regarding the proposed separate Karen State and other matters should properly be made in the Constituent Assembly." The letter also asked the Karens to reconsider the recent decision to boycott the elections and refrain from participation in the Constituent Assembly. Upon receiving the letter, Thra Tha Hto, then KNU secretary, replied on March 12 that it was too late to reconsider the decisions of the KNU. Almost all the members of the KNU action committee were already out to the rural Karen districts organizing necessary actions regarding the non-participation resolution. He also suggested that, unless the election dates could be postponed to the month of November as usual (previous elections in 1932 and 1936 were held during November and December), there was no time to reconsider the decision.[20]

By this time, in all areas where Karens were concentrated, there was a Karen association. One of these was the Shwegyin Karen Association in Salween district, which was under the administration of the frontier areas. On March 10, 1947, an ex-Force 136 officer, Marshall Shwin, president of the Shwegyin Karen Association, wrote a letter to Governor Rance with the title "Hill Karens wish to be under the direct control of the Governor." It explained that 95 percent of the Karens in that area were still illiterate and at least 90 percent did not understand Burmese. He suggested that they had not forgotten the atrocities and rapes committed at Papun by their Burmese neighbors in April and May 1942, and that the Burmese encouraged hateful measures of religious intolerance, high-handedness, and barbarism. Therefore, "instinct of self-preservation has urged them to cling to the British even in the event that Burma Proper secedes from the British Commonwealth of Nations." Recalling their wartime exploits with Force 136, they reiterated some of the promises then given to them by Lord Mountbatten and General Auchinleck. One challenging statement that predicted the future problem was: "Under the circumstances the Karens in this Area firmly claim that their right of self-determination be recognized by the concession of a separate Colony for the Karens. If the British fail to honor this great responsibility of theirs the Karen should not be blamed if they think of other alternatives to achieve their legitimate objectives."[21]

Predictably, the response to this group was not different from the one that the KNU received. The letter from the governor's additional secretary, R. W. D. Fowler, dated March 31, stated that the governor insisted they take their case to the Constituent Assembly, as he had urged the leaders of the KNU, and that the Karen community take the opportunity afforded by the Constituent Assembly for reaching an agreement with the Burmese regarding Karen affairs. Also included in the letter was a note that the governor "regrets the recent decision to boycott the election and to refrain from participation in the Constituent Assembly taken by certain Karens," and wished for the reconsideration of those decisions.[22]

Following the Aung San-Attlee Agreement, elections were held in April to fill the Constituent Assembly of 255 members with 210 communal seats from Ministerial Burma and 45 non-communal seats from frontier areas. Out of the 210 seats, 4 were given to 2 Anglo-Burman constituencies and 24 to the 12 Karen constituencies. Of the remaining 182 seats, 91 went to general constituencies, comprising 77 rural constituencies (154 seats) and 14 urban (28 seats).[23]

The cleavage of opinion among the KNU regarding boycotting the election culminated in the resignation of its president, San Po Thin, and six out of sixteen members of the executive committee of the union.[24] Soon after that, leaders of the KNU and other affiliated Karen organizations toured Karen areas, urging the Karen public not to vote in the general election. The KYO leaders resigned from the KNU and prepared to contest in the elections, asking the Karen people to vote for them. In Bassein, thousands of people attended the debates between the KNU leaders, Ba U Gyi and James Tun Aung, and KYO leaders, San Po Thin and Mahn Win Maung.[25] The very low number of voter registrations in the Bassein and Toungoo constituencies suggested that the KNU campaign "not to vote" was quite successful. In Toungoo, where Johnson D. Po Min was standing for the KYO, only 7.7 percent of the electorate voted[26] and in Bassein only 5,750 voted out of more than 14,000.[27]

Since the elections in the twelve Karen communal constituencies took place against a boycott by the KNU, there were nominal contests only in three constituencies and no contest in nine where the Karen Youth Organization candidates were given a walkover.[28] Accordingly, nineteen of the twenty-four Karen seats fell uncontested to the KYO representatives, and the rest went to independent Karen candidates.[29] As recommended by the Frontier Areas Committee of Enquiry, the Karens received five seats: two from Salween, two from Karenni, and one from Mongpai.[30] When the elections were held in the Salween district, Saw Lu Lu and his supporters, who recommended staying in Ministerial Burma, suffered a severe defeat, and their opponents, Saw Were (We Re) Gyaw and T. Po Ku won the Salween district.[31]

In the Karenni states, U Bee Tu Ree and Saw Thein were selected as Karenni representatives. But later in June, they decided not to participate in the deliberations of the Constituent Assembly. They claimed that the Karenni state was an independent country with full sovereign rights, and "when Burma achieved its independence, Karenni will be prepared to enter *a treaty of alliance* with her, or with whatever party is in power at that time."[32]

Aung San's AFPFL won 176 out of the 182 seats in 91 general constituencies.[33] Adding the AFPFL-backed KYO members, AFPFL won 204 out of 255 seats in the Constituent Assembly.[34] After the elections, the Constituent Assembly met to draft an agreement or treaty to regulate the transfer of power. This draft agreement would be submitted to Parliament simultaneously with the legislation required to endorse a new constitution if Burma remained within the Commonwealth or to approve the surrender of sovereignty if it went out.[35] However, since the election results from upcountry were not available until the third week of April, the Constituent Assembly had to wait until June 1947 to convene its first meeting.

Efforts for Reunification of the Karen People

On April 13, 1947, the *Sunday Statesman* newspaper in London published Aung San's exclusive interview with the Rangoon correspondent of the *Daily Mail*, stating that there was "no chance" of Burma remaining within the British Empire, adding, "personally, I would like the closest relation with Britain, but not a British Dominion."[36] It became clear that, once the Constituent Assembly met to draft the constitution for Burma, the AFPFL-dominated Constituent Assembly would press for a Burma outside of the British Commonwealth.

The situation was a threat to KNU leaders, who had been striving for a separate and fully autonomous Karen state within the Commonwealth. They moved swiftly by calling an emergency Karen Congress on April 23 and 24 and passed several resolutions:[37]

1. To take as a national concern the cause of any Karen individual or any Karen organization harmed in their political struggle for Karen living-space and self-determination.

2. To urge the Government to appoint a priest or a religious instructor for Karen Buddhist soldiers for each Karen fighting unit.

3. To not recognize those Karen members who have been returned to the Constituent Assembly as being real representatives of the Karens.

4. To place on record a deep sense of gratitude to those Karens who did not participate in the general elections.

5. To empower the Executive Committee of the Karen National Union to draw up the future policy and to issue necessary instructions for guidance of the Karen masses in their fight for the right of self-determination and to contact leaders of other minorities with a view to forming a "minority united front."[38]

Apparently, resolution 2 of this Karen Congress made it clear that unlike its original KNA founded in 1881 whose members were essentially Christians, this time KNU membership consisted of all Karens, including Karen Buddhists.

During the congress, Saw Ba U Gyi was congratulated on his resignation from the governor's executive council. He was elected KNU president in place of Saw San Po Thin. However, realizing that unity among the Karens was imperative, KNU leaders reconsidered their policy and abandoned resolution 3 of the Karen Congress, and reunited with KYO leaders who contested in the elections and were elected to membership in the Constituent Assembly. Accordingly, KNU leaders called a Karen conference in June inviting all Karen leaders.

The first day of the Karen Joint Executive Meeting, June 4, 1947, was held under the chairmanship of Saw Ba U Gyi with the members of the KYO and the BKNA at KNU headquarters. The united group unanimously agreed to press for a separate Karen state. This decision was followed by a lengthy discussion on the demarcation of the proposed Karen state. Saw Ba U Gyi and Saw Hunter Thar Hmwe of the KNU suggested that the Tenasserim division and the delta areas should be included in the Karen state. Saw Mya Thein of the BKNA expressed the view that if the Karen community could prove that their population in lower Burma was more than that of Burmans, he saw no reasons why lower Burma should not be made "Karenistan." Mahn Win Maung, a member of the Constituent Assembly, said he would recommend to the Constituent Assembly the establishment of a separate Karen autonomous state with a constitution better than proposed in the draft constitution.[39]

The Joint Executive Committee of the KNU, KYO, and BKNA continued on June 5, under Saw Ba U Gyi's chairmanship. Mahn Win Maung informed the chairman that, with the exception of the Honorable Mahn Ba Khaing and his few supporters, the Karen members of the Constituent Assembly would support demands for a separate Karen state, and it was agreed to press for its establishment.[40] Johnson D. Po Min, another Karen representative in the Constituent Assembly, wrote to Governor Rance that he would propose a motion in the Constituent Assembly providing for a separate Karen state in Toungoo and the Pyinmana hill tracts.[41]

The Birth of the Karen National Defence Organization (KNDO)

The KNU conference held in April 1947 laid the foundation for the formation of the Karen National Defence Organization (KNDO). Following resolution 5, which proposed the "minority united front," Ba U Gyi mobilized Karens in July who had military training and experience during World War II and formed the KNDO. Mahn Ba Zan became the first commander with Saw Hunter Thar Hmwe and Saw Sankey as military strategists and S'gaw Maw Lay as commanding officer for training.[42] Twenty more officers were also recruited for twenty Karen districts to take charge of the military units set up in their villages. More than ten thousand Karens joined the KNDO, without counting the Karens who were already serving in other infantry, navy, air force, and signal army units.[43]

The KNDO's sole purpose, according to Saw Bellay, a retired Karen customs officer, was to defend and safeguard the lives and properties of Karens in general against lawless elements and criminal acts. The Karens had suffered at the hands of the Japanese and the Burma Independence Army during World War II. The formation of the KNDO was considered "essential for the future welfare of the Karens as conditions prevailing in the country were never too peaceful; that was the aim and purpose for which the KNDO was formed."[44]

Though formally inaugurated in July 1947 as the Karen National Defence Organization, arms training had already begun in many Karen villages in the delta. As the Red Flag Communists and the People's Volunteer Organization (PVO) continued their violence, the KNU sent instructions to district party organizations to set up their own local defense militias.[45] These local Karen defense units acted on their own to protect Karen interests in various regions of lower Burma with limited arms and ammunition. On June 6, 1947, members of the district organization of the Karen Youth League discussed the advisability of asking the government

i. To issue firearms to members of the Karen Defence Organization.
ii. To recruit members of the Karen Defence Organization to the Burma Armed Police Striking Force on a fifty-fifty basis, and
iii. To appoint Karen high officials in the districts where Karen population is large.

KYO president Mahn Ba Khaing opposed the issue of arms to the Karen Defence Organization on the grounds that other organizations like the Red Guards and Galon Tat would make similar demands for their own firearms. He preferred to arm the village defense units, but the majority of members did not agree. Eventually, proposals 2 and 3 carried unanimously. A subcommittee was formed with Mahn Win Maung, Saw Kyaw Sein, Saw Myint Thein, Saw Bi, and Boh Tun Tin to implement the above decisions.[46]

The Karen local defense units protected their communities well. When a communist-bandit seizure threatened Moulmein city in July 1947, Karen defense units occupied the city quietly without bloodshed. Two months later, they withdrew voluntarily under conditions of a general amnesty. Also, through an understanding with the Karen commander of the Burma Army, General Smith Dun, local KNDO units took responsibility for protecting certain Karen areas. In addition, due to the communist threat, the Karen units were authorized to guard the Twante Canal leading from the Rangoon port to the main Irrawaddy channel.[47]

For a year or so, the KNDO remained inactive, with the organization more or less on paper with some skeleton branches all over the Karen areas. Burma gained its independence in 1948. A few months later the communist uprising began throughout Burma. That reawakened and activated the KNDO. It was only in 1948 that the KNDO was organized on proper lines as a defense organization.[48] But once the KNU organized its own paramilitary KNDO to parallel the Burman PVO, tensions between the AFPFL and KNU intensified.

Salween District Karen Movement

During 1947, the Karens from the Salween district became more united under the leadership of Marshall Shwin, an ex-officer of Force 136, who also was the Shwegyin Karen Association president. On June 16,

Marshall Shwin wrote to the prime minister (via Governor Rance), articulating reasons why the Karens in the Salween district refused to be brought within Ministerial Burma. He attached a copy of the resolution passed by the Salween Karen Association on May 23, 1947. Marshall Shwin first explained that the meeting was especially called because of the pro-Burmese evidence given by Saw Lulu before the Rees-William Committee. Endorsed by 1,441 Karens, the resolution pointed out the population of the area was exclusively Karen, with no Shans and no Burmans, and that they had no knowledge of the Burmese language. In addition, the Karens in these areas would never forgive and forget the murders of the Karen elders and the rape of women by the Burmese soldiers in Papun in 1942. Because of these reasons, they refused to identify themselves as members of Burma proper and refused to allow Ministerial Burma to extend its administrative jurisdiction over their area.[49]

After receiving the resolution, W. J. B. Ledwidge noted on June 23 that "Saw Lulu was defeated by the KNU candidate at the by-election of 17 June and the Salween people have now given their representative a clear mandate against incorporation in Ministerial Burma."[50] The governor's additional secretary, J. P. Gibson, reported to the Burma Office:

> His Excellency's view is that autonomy within a federated Burma would be acceptable to the majority of the Karens in the Salween District. Most of the Karen members of the Assembly appear to be in favor of an autonomous Karen State embracing Karenni, the Salween District and the Karen Part II areas of the Toungoo, Thaton and Amherst Districts. His Excellency feels that it is now quite clear for the Karen members of the Constituent Assembly to press for their proposal to be incorporated in the draft constitution.[51]

Despite the seeming unity among the Karens, the KYO emergency meeting on June 30 at the residence of Saw Kyaw Sein revealed unresolved issues among the KYO leaders. In his opening speech to a hundred representatives attending the meeting, Mahn Ba Khaing pointed out the inadvisability of establishing a separate Karen state under a British governor and suggested that the state should join federated Burma. He further said that the KYO had been working in cooperation with the AFPFL on equal footing and not as a subordinate organization. In conclusion, he warned that the Karen community should not fall prey to evil influences which might be working to create communal clashes to the detriment of Burma's independence. He urged cooperation among all the indigenous groups of the country. However, resolutions were passed demanding a Karen state comprised of Pyinmana, Toungoo, Thaton hill tracts, and Salween district; the granting of all minority rights to the Karens of other places; and the formation of a Karen Affairs Council with full powers to deal with the affairs of the Karen state and the interests of the Karens.

A proposal for a KYO and AFPFL amalgamation was discussed at great length, but the matter was postponed until the next annual congress to be held in October 1947. Discussions were raised against the proposal to make Buddhism a state religion under the constitution of free Burma. KYO members in the Constituent Assembly promised that they would oppose that proposal if brought forward at the Constituent Assembly.[52]

The Karens revealed the strength of their unity when the following comments of Rees-William, chairman of the FACE, were published in the *Sunday Times* in London, on June 22, 1947:

> The Chins are so divided . . . and it is difficult for them to affect any cohesion among themselves. The Karens are equally at variance politically: the Animist Karens have no interest in the Constitutional issue, the Buddhist Karens are inclined to side with the Burmans, while the Christian Karens who are about 25 percent of the whole, and the educated ones at that are divided among themselves into two groups, one of which supports Aung San and the other is against him.[53]

The Karens challenged Rees-William by issuing a press release via Reuter's news service on June 25 under the title "Karen Unity." It began with the introduction, "We, the Karens of Burma, strongly resent the gross misinterpretation of our case by Lieutenant Colonel David Rees-William" and continued:

> how far short of Col. Rees-William in his conclusion of this body of our kinsmen who dwell in the hinterland of the Toungoo mountains and the Salween districts down to the mountainous backbone of the Tenasserim to Victoria Point, one has only to meet these men of Otter, Mongoos, Hyena, and Walrus of Force 136 fame and Seagrim's levies. These are the "animist Karens" referred to as not being interested in issues affecting their future status. . . .
>
> He again writes, "the Buddhist Karens are inclined to side with the Burmans." If this were only partly true, we would not feel so anxious for the future. . . . The majority members of the Karen National Union are Karen Buddhists.

. . . that no matter whether a Karen lives in the mountain or in the plains, whether Animist, Buddhist, Christian or otherwise, whether from whatsoever tribe, S'gaw, or Pwo, White, Red or Black Karen—A KAREN IS A KAREN; one in blood brotherhood; one in sentiment; one in adversity and one mass of a Karen nationhood. . . .

People of Britain, we solemnly assert to you that we stand today, a strong united people. . . . We have stood by your darkest hours and if you choose to let us stand alone, we will, for we can. We take pride in our unity and kinship and do not bend the knee or bow the head in adversity.[54]

In response, Governor Rance reported on June 29 to the Earl of Listowel, the new secretary of state for Burma, that "the Karens are now virtually united in their demand for an autonomous state embracing the Salween and Thaton district and the Karen Hill Tracts of the Yamethin, Toungoo and Amherst districts."[55] On July 1, 1947, Governor Rance wrote again, "With increasing unity and solidarity among the Karens on the separate State issue, the AFPFL must now be prepared to concede a substantial part of the Karen demand."

Certainly, the KYO leaders, members of the Constituent Assembly, and the KNU remained outside of the assembly. They united to fight for their separate Karen state. They unanimously agreed that if the Burmans were given the choice to be a separate sovereign state outside or inside the British Commonwealth, the Karens should have the same right to choose whether to join Burma and to be within or without the British Empire.

Constitution for the Union of Burma and the Karen State

After elections were held for the Constituent Assembly, it was time to write the new constitution. As previously agreed, the Constituent Assembly had to create two houses in the legislature with the Chamber of Nationalities made up of ethnic representatives from each state and from central Burma. In addition, it was to establish four ethnic-based states: the Karen, Karenni, Kachin, and Shan states. On May 23 and June 16, 1947, the resolution moving Burma to be a sovereign independent republic to be known as the Union of Burma was passed unanimously by the Constituent Assembly.[56]

A constitution drafting committee was set up to draft the constitution of a sovereign and independent Union of Burma. Before completing the work, Aung San and his executive council members were assassinated on July 19, 1947, while holding a meeting in the secretariat. Governor Rance took immediate action and invited U Nu to become the prime minister and form the government.[57] Since Mahn Ba Khaing was also killed, U Nu replaced Mahn Win Maung in his cabinet. As constitutional events proceeded under U Nu's premiership, an agreement was reached on frontier areas with the Shans and Kachins but not with the Karens.

Referring to the documents of that time's events, historian Hugh Tinker commented that the Karen affairs remained uncertain mainly because of their own inability to agree whether they wanted a limited state (incorporating Salween district, and perhaps certain contiguous areas and possibly Karenni) or whether they wanted a special "Karen Affairs Council" to protect their interests in the Burmese majority district.[58] It seems necessary to study the whole situation of that time, to consider whether Tinker's justification is fair.

After Mahn Win Maung became minister, he and twenty KYO leaders devoted their energies to establishing a Karen Affairs Council, as proposed at the meeting on June 30, 1947. Their tentative proposal was that the Karen Affairs Council should be composed of six members, including a president, and the latter should be a member of the government of Burma cabinet, of which Prime Minister U Nu was in favor.[59]

By contrast, Karen leaders from Toungoo, Bassein, Salween district, and Mongpai preferred a Karen state, not a Karen Affairs Council. On August 14, 1947, the following letter was signed by six Karen members of the Constituent Assembly: Saw Johnson D. Po Min (Toungoo), Saw Win Tin (Toungoo), Tai Julius Ba Han (Mongpai), Saw T. Po Ku (Salween district), Saw T. We Re Gyaw (Salween district), and Saw Maung Daught (Bassein), and sent to the prime minister:

> We the undersigned have given a serious study of your proposal in respect of the power and function of the Karen Affairs Council and we desire to make the following new proposals.
>
> (i) The Salween District, Thaton Hill Tracts, Toungoo Hill Tracts, and Pyinmana Hill Tracts, shall form a Karen State to be known as Kaw-Thu-Lay and shall constitute one of the Federal units of the Union of Burma.
>
> (ii) This Karen State shall enjoy full autonomous status.
>
> From the above new proposal it will be apparent that the question of the constitution of the Karen Affairs Council no longer arises for the Karen State now envisaged.

> If this proposal is not acceptable by you and your colleagues we feel
> that no useful purpose will be served by our continuing as members of
> the Constituent Assembly.[60]

The next day, the Burmese political leaders gave the following counterproposal:

(i) The Karenni States, the Salween District and such adjacent areas
occupied by Karens as may be determined by a special Commission shall, if the majority of the residents of each area and of the
Karens living in the plains of Burma desire, form a constituent unit
of the Union of Burma with the same status as that of the Shan
State.

(ii) In default of such agreement and until such agreement is reached
the Salween District and such adjacent areas occupied by Karens
as may be determined by a special Commission shall be a special
region to be known as Kaw-Thu-Lay.[61]

Failing their demands, the six Karen leaders wrote to the president of the
Constituent Assembly that they would withdraw from the assembly.[62]

In his report to the London office dated August 15, Governor Rance
detailed the result of the deliberations in the Constituent Assembly:

> No agreement has been reached with Karen leaders. Some want a Karen
> State. Some want an Affairs Council with personal jurisdiction over all
> Karen. Some want both.
>
> The Assembly were unable to find a formula to which all would agree.
> The Burmese are not prepared to let Karens have a State if Karenni and
> Salween District and certain other Hill Tracts agree to form one and if
> Karens in Burma proper also wish it.[63]

Regarding the Burmese attitude toward the Karen demands, the governor's secretary, Mr. McGuire, reported his discussion about Karen affairs with Justice U Chan Htoon, legal advisor to the AFPFL, as follows:

> According to him, the present position appears to be that no one objects to a Karen State which would include the Salween District, Karenni
> and adjacent Hill Areas. But on the one hand the extreme Karens want
> a completely autonomous state straightaway and consisting mostly of
> these areas, while on the other hand the Karens of the Plains are disturbed lest their interests are forgotten. Plains Karens in fact say that

the Karen State will hardly help them at all, as it will concern itself only with the Hill Karens who are very much in the minority on the Karen population basis–Chan Htoon puts the figures at 1/3rd for the suggested Karen State as against 2/3rd for the Karens remaining in Burma. This fear of the Plain Karens is one of the chief reasons for the demand of a Karen Affairs Council which would have personal jurisdiction over Karens anywhere in Burma. . . .

Chan Htoon considers it most unlikely that the Burmese will agree to have both a Karen State and a Karen Affairs Council. The Burmese feel that even though a Karen State may not be able to speak for the Plain Karens the Constitution itself protects the rights of minorities also the Karens should be fairly well represented in the new Parliament and will probably have a Minister in the Cabinet. The Burmese feel this is sufficient.[64]

On July 18, Prime Minister U Nu told the governor that they had been as generous as possible to the Karens. He said that he offered a Karen state, almost on the same terms as the Shans, or a Karen Affairs Council, but not both. Like U Chan Htoon, U Nu said that the Plain Karens favored the latter, while the Hill Karens favored the former with the extremist section demanding a fully autonomous state immediately. U Nu worried over the legal position regarding Salween district and the fact that the two representatives from the district had withdrawn from the assembly. As the governor advised, U Nu asked Saw Ba U Gyi and other KNU leaders for a general discussion regarding Karen affairs.[65]

Since receiving Governor Rance's report that the Constituent Assembly "were not able to find a formula to which all would agree" in regard to the future of the Karens, the Burma secretary of state, the Earl of Listowel, sought ways to resolve the issue. Burma's deputy undersecretary of state, Sir Gilbert Laithwaite, analyzed the Karen position in a meticulous manner and prepared a proposal that all would come to agree. Secretary of State Earl of Listowel sent the draft proposal to Governor Rance on August 19, in which he mentioned the following:

My own view for what it is worth is that the right solution is:

(a) A Karen State on the same basis as the proposed Shan State which should include the Karenni States, Mongpai, Salween district, and the Toungoo and Thaton Part II areas and possibly the Pyinmana corner;

(b) A Cultural Council for the Plain Karens which might be a matter of arrangement and which need not necessarily find its place in the written constitution;

(c) A single Minister for the Karen State without prejudice to the possibility of the Cabinet containing a second Karen.[66]

Having determined to resolve the Karen affairs as his major agenda, the Burma secretary of state requested Governor Rance to arrange a meeting for him and the Karen leaders when he visited Burma August 27 to September 14, 1947. Before leaving London on August 23, he wrote to British Prime Minister Attlee that he proposed to give any help he could, in consultation with Governor Rance, U Nu, and the Karen leaders, to achieve a friendly settlement of the Karen problem.[67]

Fully equipped with knowledge of Karen issues, Sir Laithwaite accompanied the secretary of state on his trip to Burma. His notes to the secretary of state included:

> It seemed unlikely that the Burmans would yield and concede a Karen Affairs council with executive responsibilities in addition to a Karen State as defined.
>
> If that is so, it was a question of trying
>
> (a) to get the Hill and Plains Karens together, and so
>
> (b) of persuading the latter to drop their demand for a KAC to deal with all Karens inside and outside the Karen State . . .
>
> (c) possibly of gilding the pill (or building a bridge) by setting up, in addition to the Karen State as in para i(ii)[68] above, if the Burmans could be persuaded to agree, an emasculated Council to cover both the Hills and Plains, to be advisory in respect of cultural and educational matters to the Karen Minister in the case of the Karen State and to the appropriate Burmese Minister in respect of Burma proper.[69]

Laithwaite prepared for the secretary of state to meet the following Karen leaders.

1. Mahn Win Maung, the Karen Minister of Industry and Labor, who favored a Karen Affairs Council;
2. Saw Ba U Gyi, the ex-Karen minister, who favored a Karen state;
3. Representatives of the Karenni, and Shan state of Mongpai;

4. Saw We Re Gyaw and T. Po Ku, representatives of the Salween district and strongly in favor of a Karen state;
5. Johnson D. Po Min, Karen representative from Toungoo, who claimed for an immediate autonomous state.

Sir Laithwaite recorded the meeting with Mahn Win Maung, which lasted for an hour. According to him, Mahn Win Maung said that he was wholly in favor of a Karen state and ready to drop a Karen National Council so soon as the Karenni came in. He also said that a Karen state could not, however, be set up for at least eighteen months after the transfer of power, and that must be quite clearly understood. His reasons were that it was necessary to conduct a census; and he wanted to see how things were going. He agreed that the constitution contained no provision for any eighteen-month interval. Mahn Win Maung discussed that the interests of the Plains Karens were very important. He admitted, on the other hand, that the Plains were fully safeguarded by the minority provision of the constitution, that there was no risk of the Plains Karens falling below the qualifying figure of 10 percent and that they might indeed be raised above it still further as a result of a census. He thought, in the event of decentralization, areas such as Henzada and Bassein with Karen predominance would be still more strongly placed. Thakin Nu had assured him that there would be at least a second Karen minister by convention, in addition to the Karen state minister. As for the Karenni, he said that it was just too bad if it were to have to suffer, but that would be its own fault. He was not greatly moved by its position.[70]

On September 7, the secretary of state sent the following outline of the proposals that Sir Laithwaite prepared. He and Governor Rance agreed to offer the Karens

1. A Karen State, to include the following areas:
   The Karenni States
   The Mongpai State
   The Salween District
   The Part II areas of Thaton and Toungoo
   The Pyinmana Karen Hill Tracts
2. The process of demarcation to be taken in hand at once with a view to its being pushed through before the transfer of power, and if possible, by, say, 1st December.
3. The new State to come into being with effect from the date of the Transfer of power.

4. The State to be of the same status as the Shan State under the constitution, except that like the Kachin State, it would not have a right of
   secession in view of the territorial contribution which Burma proper
   will have made to its establishment.

5. The redraft of S. 191 of the Constitution so as to eliminate the words,
   "adjacent areas" possibly on the following lines:
   (i) The following areas, viz:
       (a) The Salween District
       (b) The Karenni States
       (c) The Shan State of Mongpai
       (d) So much of the hill areas of the Thaton and Toungoo Districts
           included in Part II of the Second Schedule to the Government of
           Burma Act, 1935, as have been determined and demarcated by
           the Special Commission appointed for the purpose,
       Shall form a constituent unit of the Union of Burma to be known as the
       Karen State.
   (ii) This Karen State shall have the same status as the Shan States
        except that, as in the case of the Kachin State, the provisions of
        Chapter X of this Constitution shall not apply to it.[71]

This letter from Burma's secretary of state to Prime Minister U Nu
was read at the eighth Special Meeting of the Council of Ministers held
on September 7, where they discussed the future of "A Karen Separate
State." At the meeting, U Chan Htoon, constitutional advisor, read the
text of the actual offer made to the Karens aloud, before provisions
relating to the Karens in the draft constitution were adopted by the
Constituent Assembly. U Chan Htoon was authorized to furnish the
secretary of state with a copy of the text he read.[72]

In his reply to the secretary of state, U Nu pointed out that no part of
the Pyinmana subdivision was in a Part II scheduled area but was an ordinary ministerial area in Burma. Because of that, a proposal to include
any small portion of the Pyinmana hill areas in the Karen state would
require scrutiny. The delimitation of that boundary portion of the Karen state would have to be subjected to carefully thought-out instruction. The secretary of state replied that he fully agreed to his points.[73]

On September 8, 1947, the secretary of state met with Karen leaders Mahn Win Maung, Saw Myint Thein, Saw Norton Bwa, Saw Kyaw
Sein, Saw Ba U Gyi, Saw Johnson D. Po Min, Saw We Re Gyaw, Saw T.
Po Ku, Saw Di Gay, Thra Tha Hto, Ko Bee Tu Re, and Dr. Dwe. In his
speech, he said his sole anxiety was to act as an intermediary in smooth-
ing out any possible differences, either between members of the Karen

community or between the Karens and the government of Burma. He also stated that final decisions in these matters must be for the Karens themselves. He expressed disappointment in not finding a basis of an agreement after all sincerely held discussions. He pointed out that Karen leaders were divided in their views, without hope to reconcile. Due to that, the matters should remain as they were when he reached Rangoon. Then he explained,

> In other words, if the draft constitution now before the Constituent Assembly is finally approved by that body, the principle of a Karen State will be accepted and it will be open to the Karens. In the meantime, the Karen Affairs Council described in the Constitution will function, and its operation, and the special protection which it is designed to provide, will extend to all Karens, whether in the hills or in the plains. Salween will also form a special region, to be included in the Karen area to be known as Kawthulay.[74]

In conclusion, he said, "In parting from you today, Gentlemen, I would like to add how much the good wishes and the affection of the people of the United Kingdom, who have for so long been associated with the Karens and who, during the war, received such valuable help from them, will go with you and how sincere are our hopes that the future will hold happiness and prosperity for them."[75]

Despite the unsettled Karen issues, the Constituent Assembly drafted and adopted a constitution. As Tinker claimed, "Because the AFPFL commanded an unchallengeable position in the Assembly there was little or no dispute over its passage."[76] According to the constitution enacted on September 24, 1947, the territories previously governed by His Britannic Majesty, through the governor of Burma and the Karenni states, were transferred to the Union of Burma, a sovereign independent republic. Part III of the constitution, entitled "The Karen State," started as follows:

Section 180

1. The following areas, viz. (a) the Karenni State, (b) the Salween District, and (c) such adjacent areas occupied by the Karens as may be determined by a Special Commission to be appointed by the President shall, if the majority of the people of these area and of the Karens living in Burma outside these areas so desire, form a

constituent unit of the Union of Burma to be known as the Karen State, which shall thereupon have the same status as the Shan State.

2. The procedure for ascertaining the desire of the majority in each of the cases mentioned in the last preceding subsection shall be such as may be prescribed by the law of the union.

Section 181.

Until the Karen State is constituted under the last preceding section, the Salween District, and such adjacent areas occupied by the Karens as may be determined by a Special Commission to be appointed by the President, shall be a Special Region to be known as "Kaw-Thu-Lay," subject to the following provision:

1. All the members of the Chamber of Deputies representing Karens shall constitute the Karen Affairs Council. They shall co-opt not more than five members of the Chamber of National representing Karens.

2. A Member of the Union Government to be known as "the Minister for Karen Affairs" shall be appointed by the President on the nomination of the Prime Minister, acting in consultation with the Karen Affairs Council, from amongst the members of the Parliament representing Karens.[77]

Pending the prospective Karen state's formation, the three chiefs of the Karenni states, and if the population of Mongpai should approve, its chief would also represent their territories in the Chamber of Nationalities. The Karenni minister and a state council, including all Karenni members of parliament, would constitute the government of that area.[78]

In brief, the constitution established three autonomous states, Shan, Kachins, and Karenni, and a special division for the Chins. The Karen state question was left for a special commission to determine. Meanwhile, the Salween Karens obtained a special region termed Kaw-Thu-Lay.[79] With the passing of the constitution, the London office prepared for the transfer of power. In October 1947, Prime Minister U Nu went to London and signed the treaty, known as the Nu-Attlee Treaty, consisting of fifteen articles. Following that, the Union of Burma came into existence on January 4, 1948, as a "sovereign independent Republic outside the British Commonwealth of Nations."[80]

Negotiations with the Government of the Union of Burma

The Karen state called Kaw-Thu-Lay, consisting mainly of the backward Salween district and adjacent Karen-majority areas, was not acceptable to the Karen National Union leaders. Unhappy with constitutional provisions for the Karens, the KNU held a two-day mass meeting on October 3 and 4, 1947, in the Karen School at Moulmein, Daingwunkwin quarters. More than seven hunded Karen representatives from all over Burma participated. They made seven resolutions, including the reactivation and reinforcement of the Karen National Defence Organization, which initially was one of the KNU's resolutions from the April 1947 meeting. They also agreed that the formation of the Karen state was to be delivered to the United Nations.[81] The other two most important resolutions made at that conference were

1. That this Karen Conference does not accept the constitution of the Union of Burma Government hitherto made because the said constitution does not include the granting of a state to the Karen to satisfy their aspiration.

2. To request an independent sovereign Karen State of the following areas:
   (a) Tenasserim division, including Toungoo district
   (b) Irrawaddy Division
   (c) Insein District
   (d) Hanthawaddy District and
   (e) Nyaunglebin sub-district.[82]

The conference concluded with the loud cheering of the following four slogans:

1. Give the Karen State immediately;
2. We do not want civil war (which means we want peace);
3. We do not want communal strife (racial conflict);
4. Show immediately—for the Karen one *kyat* and the Burmese one *kyat* (*kyat* is Burmese currency—an analogy for equality).[83]

When the KNU representatives returned to their towns and villages, they passed the information about the resolutions. The Karen masses embraced the news with great appreciation. Some Karens became so optimistic as to say that the British were broad-minded because they returned Burma to the Burmans, and on the same analogy, the Karens were sure to get their state from the Burmans.[84]

On January 5, a day after the celebration of the independence of Burma, the KNU made an announcement, including the fact that the Karen people of Burma are not a "tribe" of Burma but a Karen "Nation."[85] The term "Karen Nation" appeared again in the letter the KNU sent to Prime Minister U Nu on February 3, 1948, which included the following:[86]

1. That the constitution of the Union of Burma does not cater for an independent Karen State;

2. Therefore, to request from the Government of the Union of Burma an Independent Karen State to include the following areas:
   (a) Tenasserim division including Toungoo district
   (b) Irrawaddy division
   (c) Hanthawaddy division
   (d) Insein district
   (e) Nyaunglebin sub-district

In accordance with the two resolutions the President and Secretary of the KNU on behalf of the Karen nation are herewith forwarding an application to request a Karen State. The granting of a Karen State being a deserving case, a reply in the affirmative would be expected within a month after sympathetic considerations have been made by your Government.

Signed: Saw Tha Hto
Saw Ba U Gyi Secretary, K.N.U.
President, K.N. U., No. 5, U Loo Nee Street, Rangoon

Encouraged by the Karen mass enthusiasm supporting the resolutions, KNU leaders staged a demonstration to show the wishes and unity of the Karen people. On February 11, 1948, a demonstration with hundreds of thousands of Karen participants was carried out at all big Karen centers, with people shouting the four slogans of the Moulmein conference along the march. Among the four, "For the Karen one *kyat* and for the Burman one *kyat*" became the most popular catchphrase in the Karen nationalist movement. The huge number of Karens participating in the demonstrations convinced the KNU leaders, Saw Ba U Gyi, Thra Tha Hto, Mahn James Tun Aung, and Saw Tha Din, that the Karen masses were behind them and wanted them to redouble their efforts for the cause.[87]

On the other side, the Karen Affairs Council was formed with twenty-four KYO leaders. Saw Norton Bwa was nominated as its president. On March 1, 1948, Saw San Po Thin became the minister for Karen affairs.[88] He and the KYO leaders declared that it was unfair for the KNU to claim all the areas mentioned above. They said if the Karens must have a state, they should claim only the Karenni state, Salween district, and adjacent areas to be known as Kaw-Thu-Lay.[89] From March 1 to 4, 1948, representatives of the KYO and Saw San Po Thin, the Karen Affairs minister, met Prime Minister U Nu and expressed their views. They said they did not agree with the KNU demands, nor did they want a separate state. They wished to remain in the union under the existing constitution.[90] As General Smith Dun remarked, "The KYO leaders were really put in a very awkward position for not supporting the demand for the Karen State."[91] Dun opined that the Karen states envisaged by the KNU and KYO were in absolute contrast because the KNU was asking for the best part of Burma while KYO was asking for the worst part of Burma.[92]

On March 4, KYO representatives from all three divisions (Irrawaddy, Tenasserim, and Pegu) and government representatives in parliament held a meeting. It was decided at that meeting that the Karens unanimously agreed to ask for only Kaw-Thu-Lay as a Karen state. They agreed to form a committee to enquire and decide such matters as boundary demarcation and other issues concerning Kaw-Thu-Lay. The committee was to consist of four Burmans from the government side and four Karens from the Karen Affairs department, with the secretary to be a Burman from the Home Ministry. The four Karens were Saw Norton Bwa, Saw Pha Hti, Saw Ba Yin, and Saw Donation. Saw Norton Bwa was to be president, and the work was to be completed in four months.[93]

On the other side, the KNU held its annual meeting in Rangoon on March 3 and discussed future strategy for achievement of the Karen state. Upon the invitation of Prime Minister U Nu, KNU leaders Saw Ba U Gyi, Saw Tha Hto, Mahn James Tun Aung, Saw Tha Din, Saw Bu, and Saw Bellay met with U Nu and his AFPFL ministers.[94] During the meeting, Saw Ba U Gyi asked U Nu about the government attitude toward the Karen state. U Nu replied that it had already been laid down in the constitution in paragraphs 180 and 181, and the government had no power to act beyond that. If the KNU wished to have more than that, it was up to them to get into the parliament and change or amend the two paragraphs in accordance with paragraphs 207, 208, 209, and 210 of the constitution. He said, "Although the Karens ask only 'rupee for rupee' for the Karens and Burmese, it seems that the Karens are already getting half a rupee more." To which Saw Ba U Gyi replied, "Yes, I have heard that so many times before, but in actual fact the Karens have not yet received one anna."[95]

After discussions with KNU leaders, U Nu again met with KYO representatives from the Irrawaddy, Tenasserim, and Pegu divisions. Together with Saw San Po Thin, the Karen Affairs minister, U Nu made the following statement:

> It had come to the notice of the government of the Union of Burma that it was the intention of the KNU to run a parallel Government when they became strong enough by rousing the Karens with propaganda and demonstrations etc. It had also been learnt from the district officials that the Karens not only refused to surrender their unauthorized arms but were secretly trying to increase them by illegal purchases. This had been confirmed by the two Karen Ministers, Saw San Po Thin and Mahn Win Maung. . . . The demands of the KNU were not only unfair but an impossibility and were only the wishes of raw and uneducated people which would only result in splitting the Burmese and the Karens. To use the armed force was easier said than done. It was alright for the leaders to incite the followers to do so but it only meant death and destruction to villagers in the districts. Supposing the Karens had taken up arms, do you think the Burmese would take it lying down? And give their necks like sheep? Certainly not. If they could not return two bits for one they would at least return one.[96]

The speech made headlines. The subject of the Karen state became public talk all around the country. When the Burmese press elaborated on the news with their own comments and interpretations, the general public experienced alarm and fear concerning communal clashes.

The Karen People Save Burma from Burmans' Insurgencies

The Karen state issue was not an immediate danger to the newly independent Burma. Prime Minister U Nu was, in fact, facing other more crucial political issues with his own AFPFL Party and other dissident groups resorting to armed rebellion. The AFPFL Party consisted of the Burma Socialist Party and the Communist Party of Burma (CPB), but they began to divide during the negotiations with the British. Tension brewed even within the CPB itself. By 1946, Thakin Soe split from the party and led his Red Flag Communist Party into rebellion against the British and the "rightists" of the AFPFL. Political division intensified following Aung San's death, and his People's Voluntary Organization deteriorated in discipline. At the beginning of 1948, the ten thousand-plus members of the PVO split into pro-government and anti-government factions. Anti-government members became involved in criminal activities such as looting, robbing, and burning villages in lower Burma. When the government asked these PVO to hand in their arms, they refused. Some joined the communist rebellion. Adding the terrorist activities of the Mujahid Muslims in the far north of Arakan, the situation was beyond government control.

The worst threat came from Than Tun's White Flag Communists (CPB), who accused the AFPFL of being British imperialist tools. Than Tun was the prime AFPFL organizer, but his break with U Nu was over the terms of the Nu-Attlee Treaty. Initially, he continued to collaborate, but after attending the Indian Communist Party congress in February 1948, Than Tun returned to Burma with his colleague, Goshal, and two Yugoslav communists, declaring it was necessary to overthrow the AFPFL and set up a genuine people's government.[97]

The imminent coup made U Nu order the arrest of communist leaders on March 25, but the PVO intervened, pressing the government to come to terms with the communists. The negotiation failed. On March 27, Than Tun called for an armed uprising. The government issued orders for the communists' arrest, but Than Tun and his lieutenants went underground with some twenty-five thousand armed supporters. Throughout April, they seized police stations, occupied small towns and villages, looted rice, and sabotaged communications.[98] The PVO rebels extended their control from Bassein and Maubin in the south to as far upriver as Prome. Their movement reached the Hanthawaddy and Pegu districts north of Rangoon. The mutiny of two out of five fully equipped Burma Rifle battalions of the new Burma Army added to the threat of the communists and the PVOs.[99]

Before continuing, it is necessary to pause and explain how the new Burma Army was established, and why there was a mutiny. As discussed before, in September 1945, Lord Mountbatten and Aung San started to negotiate for the creation of a future Burman military. A series of meetings between Mountbatten and Aung San, together with other representatives of the Patriot Burmese Force (PBF, formerly BNA or Burmese National Army) and the AFPFL, were held to negotiate the disbandment of the PBF and the final creation of the Burmese wing of the regular Burmese Army. The agreement, later known as the Kandy Agreement, was reached on September 7, 1945, and signed by Mountbatten, Aung San, and Than Tun.[100] Aung San had the opportunity to nominate two deputy inspector generals. He selected Colonel Let Yar and a Karen, Colonel Saw Kyar Doe. Additionally, Aung San wrote in his letter that he had decided to leave the army.[101] As a result, Colonel Let Yar had to lead the defense agreement negotiations following the Aung San-Attlee agreement of January 1947. He signed the Britain-Burma Defense Agreement (also known as the Let Yar-Freeman Agreement), which provided for British military access to Burma and for the establishment of a British Services Mission (BSM). The BSM played an advisory role in the Burma military, which included vetting all arms purchased by the Burma Army.[102] At independence in 1948, Bo Let Yar became defense minister. British advisors appointed General Smith Dun as chief of staff of the army and Lieutenant Colonel Saw Shi Sho as chief of the air force.[103]

The new Burma Army in 1948 consisted of six Burma Rifles (1st to 6th Rifles), three Karen Rifles (1st to 3rd), two Kachin Rifles, two Chin Rifles, one Chin Battalion, and the No. 4 Burma Regiment of Gurkha soldiers. The commanding officers of the 1st, 3rd, 4th, 5th, and 6th Burma Rifles were former Patriot Burmese Force (PBF) officers and members of the Thirty Comrades, who trained in Japan and led the first BIA troops into Burma with the Japanese army in 1942. The rank and file were filled with Burmans only. However, the 2nd Burma Rifles was formed with a majority of Karen and non-Burman nationalities with a Christian Karen commanding officer, Lieutenant Colonel Saw Moo Di.[104]

The Karen infantrymen who served with the British before and during World War II were allocated only three battalions in the new Burma Army. However, Brigadier Chit Khin, a Karen, was appointed to command the 1st infantry brigade group. The quartermaster general, who controlled three-quarters of the military's budget, was a Karen. Another Karen, Lieutenant Colonel Saw Calvin Ogh, was the head of the Burma Regimental Center. Karen officers and Karens at other ranks commanded most of the support services, including the staff, supply and ammunition depots, artillery, and signal corps.[105] Karens had a predominant role in the new Burma military considering the fact that the number of ethnicities serving in the Burma British Army in 1945 consisted of 234 British, 7 Chin, 3 Kachins, 3 Burmans, and 33 Karens.

Noticeably, the following Christian Karens held staff and command positions as of 1948:

- Chief of Staff, Burma Army: Lieutenant General Smith Dun
- Vice-Chief of Staff, Burma Army: Brigadier Saw Kyar Doe
- Quartermaster General: Lieutenant Colonel Saw Donny
- Chief of the Air Force: Lieutenant Colonel Saw Shi Sho
- No.1 Infantry Division, Meiktila Brigade: Brigadier Saw Chit Khin
- Commanding Officer, 1st Battalion, Karen Rifles, Toungoo: Lieutenant Colonel Saw Min Maung
- Commanding Officer, 2nd Battalion, Karen Rifles, Prome: Lieutenant Col Saw Mya Maung
- Commanding Officer, 3rd Battalion, Karen Rifles, Mandalay, Pakokku: Lieutenant Colonel Saw Di Htoo
- Head of Army Training Depot, Maymyo: Lieutenant Colonel Saw Leder
- Head of Burma Artillery: Lieutenant Colonel Saw Aung Sein
- Head of the Burma Regimental Center: Lieutenant Colonel Saw Calvin Ogh
- Commanding Officer, 2nd Battalion, Burma Rifles, Naunglaybin: Lieutenant Colonel Saw Moo Di
- Head of Burma Signal Training Squadron, Maymyo: Major Saw Tun Sein

Like its political AFPFL government, the Burma Army was divided between the leftists and the rightists. Most of the former Japanese-trained Burma Defence Army (BDA) were leftists who felt that they were shut out of positions of authority in the army, state, and other privileges. They were concerned when they found that the new Burma Army that Aung San had established was filled with "the rightists" who had close ties with the British. Even one of their own, Defence Minister Bo Let Yar, was alleged a British loyalist. They accused the BSM of playing favoritism to the Karens for perquisites, promotion, and positions of authority in the reorganized Burma Army. These former PBF leaders in the Burma Army resented serving under Karen military leaders. Colonel Chit Myaing of the 3rd Burma Rifles complained that the British officers throughout the early postwar era substituted a policy of "Karenization of the Burma Army" for the "Burmanization" that had been agreed at Kandy.[106]

On June 16, the 6th Burma Rifles stationed in Pegu mutinied, and some of its members went over to the communists. On July 28, about 60 percent of the PVO went underground and resorted to arms. Two weeks later, two more ex-PBF battalions, the 1st Burma Rifles with headquarters at Thayetmyo and the 3rd Burma Rifles stationed in Mingaladon, mutinied. These commanders demanded posts or positions in the cabinet. When they were denied, the 1st battalion and the 3rd battalion jointly planned to march to Rangoon and take over the government. Their rendezvous was at Wanetchaung north of Rangoon. The 1st battalion marched down from Thayetmyo, but on August 9, they encountered an attack by the Karen Union Military Police Force (KUMP) stationed at Tharrawaddy. The 1st battalion was scattered, and many were injured. The 3rd battalion, which set out to link up with the shaken 1st battalion, was attacked by the Burma Air Force on August 10. The army mutineers abandoned their plan for government takeover but seized Thayetmyo and Prome.[107]

Units of the Burma Union Military Police (UMP), largely recruited from the PBF and PVO, also went underground, taking arms and cash valued at 119 lakhs (1 lakh = 100,000 kyats) from the government treasuries. Out of 311 police stations, 88 fell into rebel hands. Trains and river steamers almost ceased running outside of Rangoon. Martial law was enforced in some districts.[108] Prime Minister U Nu relied on the support of the minorities and especially upon the 6 battalions of Karen and Kachin Rifles.[109] These troops recaptured Prome, Thayetmyo, and the Pyinmana area for the government. The commander of the Burma Air Force who stopped the mutineers of the 3rd Burma Rifles was a Karen.

The regular Army, commanded by General Smith Dun, a Karen, and consisting now of mainly non-Burman Karen, Kachin, and Chin regiments, was able to prevent the mutinous Mingaladon and Thayetmyo battalions from joining hands for a march on Rangoon, a move which might have been fatal.[110]

Prime Minister U Nu relied on the KNDO, formed in July 1947, for the protection of Karens in various regions of lower Burma. Interestingly, U Nu admitted that it was inevitable that the Karens should form the KNDO, "because the times were unsettled and the Communists as well as the PVO had also armed their troops."[111]

Prior to independence in July 1947, the KNDO occupied Moulmein to protect the city from a communist-bandit seizure, without shedding blood. Two months later, they withdrew voluntarily after reaching an understanding with General Smith Dun that local KNDO units could continue to protect the Twante Canal leading from the Rangoon port to the main Irrawaddy channel.[112]

The government's helplessness, caused by the Burmese Army mutinies and the communists, led U Nu to invite KNU leaders and the KNDO military to protect Rangoon. The KNDO genuinely and successfully rendered their services. The former PBF leaders in the army did not consider the Communist Party as a real threat. Rather, the Karens were perceived as the real threat to the future Burma sovereignty. Burmese-language newspapers frequently reported on the Karen separatist movement with rumors that the Karens and other indigenous groups were conspiring with foreign allies to bring down the AFPFL government.

Distrust grew and clashes began between the Karens and the Burmans. Some local branches of KNDO became restless, wishing to resort to arms. Rumors circulated of the threatened outbreak of the Karen-Burmese riots in Labutta. In response, U Nu requested Ba U Gyi accompany him on a reconciliation tour in Labutta. A week-long tour started on June 22 consisting of two Karens, Saw Tha Din and James Tun Aung; a Kachin, Sima Duwa Sinwa Nawng; and a Chin, U Vam Thu Maung. The group visited and toured Maubin, Myaungmya, Labutta, and Bassein.[113] Ba U Gyi claimed, "During the tour, with mutual understanding and confidence, a close relationship was established between us and we became firm friends."[114]

Following the trip, on July 25, 1948,[115] the KNU executive committee wrote "An Appeal to Karens," as quoted in the opening paragraph of this chapter: "As a race, we Karens have always been law-abiding, peace loving and unprovocative, and we are proud of this very quality inherent in our nature. Let us, therefore, in our constitutional fight for a separate Karen State, live up to this noble ideal and desist from acts which are likely to lead to communal tension or clash."[116]

The Karen leaders expected that this was a demonstration of goodwill, of not taking advantage of government weakness during the communist rebellion. They hoped the KNU's efforts for reconciliation would convince the new government and the Burmese people of the genuine desire of the Karens for goodwill and peace. Instead, many Burmans interpreted the demonstration of Karen loyalty to duty as a sign of danger. Beginning in May 1948, the AFPFL government made conciliatory offers to communist rebels as part of its formal "Left Unity" proposal. Consequently, discussions among former PBF officers still in the army as well as AFPFL politicians offered amnesty to communist rebels and proffered the possibility of political power-sharing. Many Burmese deserters were taken back into the fold of the army.

The KNDO became restless and initiated anti-government movements. There were conflicts between the Karen and Burmese military units. On August 14, the Karen Union Military Police took Twante, followed by Thaton on August 31 and Moulmein on September 1. These operations were launched without bloodshed under the leadership of Saw San Key. Law and order were maintained after the occupations.[117] Temporary Karen mutinies occurred in the southern Shan states. Civil war also flared in Karenni, where KNU agents influenced the Karenni leaders to join the movement for the proposed Karen state.[118]

To restore peace, on August 25, Prime Minister U Nu traveled with General Smith Dun and Colonel Aung Gyi to Twante and negotiated with the KNU and KNDO leaders. Consequently, in October, Moulmein was handed back to the government representatives, and dissident Karen Union Military Police were persuaded to return to duty by the deputy chief of staff, Brigadier Saw Kyar Doe.[119] Regarding this settlement, General Smith Dun wrote:

> At this point great credit and honour should have been the lot of Karen leaders when they responded to the pleading of the Burmese Government to return Moulmein with the promise that the question of Karen State would be given first priority. The British press also gave prominence to the forming of the Karen State Committee in October 1948 under the able leadership of Chief Justice of Burma Sir Ba U, B.L. [bar-at-law]. Under their elders' instruction the Karen Armed Forces reluctantly handed over Moulmein. Saw Ba U Gyi took the word of the Prime Minister Thakin Nu that the Karen case would receive constitutional consideration.[120]

Even before the return of Moulmein, Saw Ba U Gyi and the KNU leaders tried to stop the criminal actions of the KNDO local units. At the KNU emergency meeting held in Bassein on September 17 and 18, Saw Ba U Gyi condemned the lawless movements, warning that Karen-Burma clashes could jeopardize the efforts for the formation of a Karen state and Burma's sovereignty. Therefore, one of the meeting's resolutions was that serious action was to be taken against those who committed crimes in the name of KNDO. Another significant meeting development was that KNU leaders unanimously agreed to form an alliance with the United Mon National Association (UMNA) for mutual defense and the formation of the Karen state. Saw Ba U Gyi claimed Mon and Karens, traditionally brothers and sisters, have always had the highest regard for each other and firmly believe that their destinies are identical and fates linked.[121]

In return for the KNDO's cooperation and to avoid further political deterioration, on October 9, 1948, the government set up a twenty-eight-member Regional Autonomy Commission. This commission was headed by Chief Justice Sir Ba U and consisted of six Karens, six Mons, five Arakanese, seven Burmans, and four from the other frontier areas. The commission's assignment was to explore the possibility of satisfying the "legitimate aspirations of the Mons, Karens, and Arakanese nationals." The six Karen representatives, including Saw Ba U Gyi, Saw Tha Din, and Mahn James Tun Aung, were to work for the materialization of the Karen state.[122] According to U Nu, the KNU's demands were: (1) a Karen state, (2) the right to secede from the union at will, and (3) incorporation into the Karen state the areas of the Pegu, Tenasserim, and Irrawaddy divisions. Of the three demands, U Nu said that he agreed to the first one, but he adamantly opposed the second. For the third, his cabinet had already determined to abide by the recommendation of the Boundary Commission.[123]

Brigadier Saw Ralph Hodgson, who served in the Karen National Liberation Army for fifty years, was probably correct in saying, "U Nu could speak very sweetly but you never knew if they were straight or crooked words."[124] During that time, U Nu showed sympathy for the Karen cause and kept cordial relations with Saw Ba U Gyi, but he also made plans to minimize Karen leadership. On September 9, U Nu ordered the reorganization of the AFPFL's special police reserves into the Burmese territorial forces (*Sitwundan* in Burmese), and placed Colonel Aung Gyi inside the Karen-dominated war office to take charge of these levies. Originally, the formation of special police reserves, or the Union Military Police (UMP), began in the wake of Aung San's assassination. When U Kyaw Nyein became Home Minister in August 1947, his socialist groups, together with other non-communist leaders of the AFPFL and leaders of the Burma Rifles units (General Ne Win, Colonel Aung Gyi, Colonel Maung Maung, and Bo Khin Maung Gale), discussed creating a paramilitary force to be a "single military force very loyal to the Government." Immediately after the communist rebellion in March 1948, the Special Police Reserves were established in the form of defense forces. To have full control, it was placed under U Kyaw Nyein, the Home Minister, outside the chain of command of the Karen commander-in-chief General Smith Dun. On October 1, 1948, U Nu transferred the Sitwundans to the war office, under General Ne Win. Colonel Aung Gyi was assigned the role of inspector general of police.[125] By that arrangement, the Karen commander-in-chief General Smith Dun had no authority over these Sitwundans.

The Sitwundan irregular forces were intended to strengthen the former PBF (the pro-AFPFL wing of the army) by increasing the numbers of troops who would remain loyal to the AFPFL government rather than Karen army leadership.[126] Even Defense Minister Bo Let Yar was unhappy with the arrangement of the Sitwundan and predicted, "There will be a civil war of a large scale between the socialists and anti-socialists if it [the Sitwundan scheme] is not checked in time."[127]

For many Karens, the creation of a new armed force and the Burmese government's acceleration of disarming irregular Karen armed forces brought back memories of the Myaungmya incident in 1942. In early September, the British embassy in Rangoon received news from Karen officials that local AFPFL officials demanded that many of the Karen villages in the Irrawaddy delta surrender any weapons they had, "with the object of reissue to Socialist levies."[128] Suspicion increased when the Karen regulars were dispersed throughout Burma away from their home areas. As a result, more Karens deserted the army and joined the KNDO. Simultaneously, friction grew between the Karen regulars and the new Sitwundan army. The combination of civil war due to communist uprisings and the divisions among the political and military leaders intensified confusion and chaos. To an extent, no room remained for the Karens in peaceful negotiation.

From Peaceful Negotiation to Armed Rebellion

In his effort to keep good relationships with the AFPFL government, Saw Ba U Gyi arranged two gala dinners in October, one at the Karen national club on Mission Road in Ahlone and another at his residence in Insein. Prime Minister U Nu and other Shan, Kachin, Karenni, and Mon national leaders joined the dinners. Saw Ba U Gyi's speech at the KNU meeting held on October 9 signified his statesmanship and his vision for a law-abiding Karen nation:

> We have been misunderstood by our demand for a separate Karen State. Some people misinterpret it as a manifestation of our desire to return to servitude under the British.
>
> We are not so foolish. We know them better than others and that is the reason why we steer clear of them. We further assure you that in our endeavor for the fulfillment of our aspirations for a separate State, we

will never adopt any unfair means. We will use only what is lawful. There are also many things of which our fellow Karens should be reminded. . . .

And so, let me remind you that, if you desire to have a separate State of your own, you must try to deserve it. A separate State is not for thieves and dacoits. Bear this fact firmly in your mind.[129]

The real menace, Ba U Gyi said, was the bad people, and to aver that the good people would have to unite among themselves for action he pledged, "We the members of the KNU will do whatever is in our capacity."[130]

When Insein and Rangoon were endangered due to communist insurgents and many police stations fell into their hands, the police and military found it hard to cope with the situation. Prime Minister U Nu asked for Saw Ba U Gyi's help. Saw Bellay, a retired Karen customs officer who lived in Insein, described the situation as follows:

Having come to some understanding with Prime Minister Thakin Nu, Saw Ba U Gyi did his best, and tried to influence the KNDO to help the Government especially in the Insein and Twante areas, and for the KNDO so employed to come directly under the command of General Smith Dun who was then the Supreme Commander. The KNDO in Insein were allotted areas like Hlegu, Taukkyan and Hlawga for defence and garrisoning duties. This arrangement enabled the regular forces to strike at the Communists. The KNDO, who were thus employed, with whatever arms they possessed, were allowed to move freely in the Insein district with their arms within their area of duty. In Twante the same arrangement was made. In the case of Twante arms and ammunition were even supplied to them after they wrested the town from the Communist hands with their own resources.[131]

The passing of the Twante Canal, on the doorsteps of Rangoon, into the KNDO's hands made the KNDO under Commander Mahn Zan more powerful. Some KNDO officers were frustrated by the slow negotiation process for the separate Karen state and were prepared for armed revolt.

During the time that tension began to increase between the Karens and Burmans in Rangoon, some Karens contacted their old allies in Special Operations Executive (SOE), Force 136. Some of the former SOE Force 136 officers who fought with the Karens in World War II were willing to support the KNDO. The key person was Lieutenant Colonel Cromarty Tulloch, who had led one of the three main groups during

SOE's wartime Operation Character. From Calcutta, he organized air-drops of supplies to the Karens flown out from Thailand and India and promised renewed assistance with training. His main go-between was Alexander Campbell, another ex-SOE officer, who had fought alongside the Karens. He was posted to Rangoon as a journalist for London's *Daily Mail*. The scheme to revive the SOE assistance was funded in part by Frank Owen, who ran Mountbatten's SEAC command newspaper during the war. By then, he was editor of the *Daily Mail*, a leading Conservative newspaper. Some funds from the newspaper were diverted to the Karen cause.[132] The Burmese government also received intelligence reports that some KNDO leaders were receiving aid from overseas to start an armed uprising.

Tulloch provided smuggled arms and training to help the KNDO. Having knowledge that all international mails were opened and read routinely, he used an airline steward named Rowland Symons as a courier to send his messages to Campbell in Rangoon. That courier sold out the information to the Burmese ambassador in Karachi and continued to work for the Burmese undercover, passing further information. Tulloch's plan began to unravel when the government discovered two recent arms shipments from Brisbane financed by smuggled gemstones.[133] On September 18, 1948, Campbell was arrested and expelled from Burma for complicity in provoking the Karen rebellion.[134] Tulloch and Campbell's movement had minimal supporters in England, but the Burmans viewed it as Karen intention to overthrow the AFPFL government. Unsurprisingly, U Nu expanded the irregular Sitwundans and kept them outside the command of the Karen General Smith Dun. The Karens, especially the KNDO, became more restless when they heard that Colonel Aung Gyi and other socialists had supplied Sitwundan units with as many as 480,000 rounds of .303 ammunition, as well as other weapons and supplies, in December.[135] Sitwundan units began recruiting Burmans living near Karen neighborhoods, causing alarm among the Karens. Their fear became a reality when the Sitwundan began to commit crimes in many Karen areas. Yet Karen infantry units and Karen officers in the army under the command of General Smith Dun continued to fight communist insurgents on behalf of the government of the Union of Burma.

Due to the uncertain political situation, the activities of the commission led by Chief Justice U Ba U started in October but moved very slowly and failed to visit important centers. In addition, some of the visits were, like in Tavoy, followed by anti-Karen demonstrations sponsored by the AFPFL. Before the commission could present its recommendations on November 13, 1948, the KNU, in association with two Mon nationalist groups, presented the government with a formal demand for an independent Karen-Mon state. The areas they asked for included the entire Tenasserim and Irrawaddy divisions plus all thirteen adjoining lower Burma districts, leaving only the capital city of Rangoon.[136]

This declaration was predicated on the dubious affirmation that the Karens of the area were not a minority but a large and compact population. The 1931 census had indicated that they were a majority in only two of the thirteen districts (Salween and Thaton) and constituted, together with the Mons, a bare 60 percent in a third district (Amherst).[137] The Karens challenged the accuracy of the essentially linguistic census of 1931 on the ground that many Burmese-speaking Karens in the delta area had been charted as Burmans.[138]

U Nu, who claimed to sympathize with the Karens, reacted to the demand by stating, "I am cent per cent [sic] in disagreement with the present creation of separate states [for Mons, Karens, and Arakan]."[139] In early December 1948, Sir Ba U's committee agreed in principle that the Karens should have their own state but within the Union of Burma.[140] That was not what the KNU leaders had negotiated for.

On the other hand, other Karen leaders acted on their own to obtain their goals. Saw Sankey and KNDO commander Mahn Ba Zan tried to persuade the Kachins to enter into an alliance. Two Karens boasted that they could seize Rangoon within a week.[141] A Kachin Parliament member, Sama Duwa Sinwa Nawng, passed the information to U Nu, who ordered an increase in the security forces of the Sitwundans.[142] Initially, U Nu's government authorized Sitwundan units to be raised in eighteen districts, six of which were KNDO strongholds and ten of which contained communist PVO or army deserter guerrillas. As KNDO and Karen army loyalties to the Union government became increasingly suspect, U Nu and Aung Gyi expedited its expansion to twenty-six battalions with the possible further expansion to fifty-two. By 1949, there were thirteen thousand Sitwundan levies in twenty-six battalions throughout Burma.[143] Most of the recruits came from the followers of the socialists and pro-government PVOs. Soon after they were given arms and official recognition, these Sitwundans were out of government control.

Viewing the Sitwundans as an unofficial private Socialist Party army, the Karen population became more frightened. The Karen leaders met in Bassein and "resolved that the KNU shall accept responsibility for safeguarding lives and property . . . in Karen majority areas."[144] Due to widespread civil disturbances, the government became weak and powerless to intervene. The civil war was in full blast with Burmans versus Burmans. Amid countrywide anarchy conditions, there was a widespread campaign of disarming Karen villages.

The Karens were not prepared for war, but the horrid massacre in the beautiful large Karen village of Palaw in the Tenasserim triggered war. Palaw was in the area between Tavoy and Mergui with its fine church and its own middle school. Government-armed Burmese auxiliary military police, accompanied by a long-standing Karen officer, entered the village and presented the government's request for elders to hand over all arms. Assurances were given and supported by the Karen officer. This happened on December 24, 1948—Christmas Eve. The Karen elders conceded, and arms were handed over in the interest of peace and understanding. The Burmese military police were invited to attend the carol celebration of the night and partake of the usual Christmas Eve refreshments. They did attend. The village assembled in the church before midnight to bring in Christmas with bells and worship. The carol parties had met in the church after their rounds of singing through the village. Immediately after the worship service began, the Burmese UMP surrounded and threw grenades in the church. Those who did not die in the church were mown down by automatic fire as they fled.[145] More than eighty Christian worshippers were killed on the spot.[146] Other Sitwundan and socialist levies attacked other churches in Karen villages, burning houses and schools and killing villagers. It was estimated that three hundred Karen lives were lost because of these atrocities.[147]

The horrid Palaw massacre enraged the Karens to retaliate. The Burmese Prime Minister, U Nu, flew down to the scene of the tragedy with Karen elders. Conversely, on his return to Rangoon, he announced the incident was "a mistake on the part of the police." This added insult to injury. Saw Ba U Gyi, at risk of losing his leadership with his people, still pleaded for patience and forbearance in his broadcast over Rangoon radio.[148] Ironically, in churches throughout the land, Karen pastors were following a lectionary guide and taking their text from Exodus and the lesson of Moses in Egypt. They preached on the lawfulness of leading their nation out of the hands of the unbelievers.[149]

Throughout January, more atrocities continued. The bombardment of a village in Taikkyi township, some forty miles north of Rangoon, by auxiliary military police was led by former PVO cabinet minister Bo Sein Hman. The raid destroyed twenty houses and killed maore than 150 Karens, with 30 being deliberately executed.[150] The KNDO retaliated and seized the armory at Insein and the treasury at Maubin. In return, Ne Win's regiment, the 4th Burma Rifles, burned the American Baptist

Mission school at Maubin.[151] All over the delta, the night sky turned red as villages burned. The government looked on, seemingly helpless in the face of these outbreaks, and tacitly accepted the claims of both the KNDO and PVO that they were working for the government.[152]

Tempers heated further when the Burmese press propagated public opinion against the Karens by publishing rumors about "Karen provocation." Only the *Nation* attempted to steer a non-partisan course. The climax was reached on January 31 in Rangoon, the capital city. The Karen elders in Ahlone Karen quarter were ordered to surrender all illegal arms. Regular Chin troops searched peacefully in daytime, but at midnight, Burmese troops surrounded the Karen quarter and bombarded the villagers with mortar and machine guns. Over two hours, Burmese troops slaughtered unarmed women and children. By daylight, a large portion of this Karen quarter was turned to ashes. Survivors were herded into so-called refugee camps behind barbed wire.[153]

A series of incidents took place at the Karen quarters at Thamaing, another Rangoon suburb. About 7:00 am on January 31, a young Karen serviceman was returning to work at Mingaladon after he spent the night at his village with his people. A Burmese soldier patrolling the Thamaing area shouted to him from across the main road not to leave the place. As the young man proceeded to get into the bus, the patrolman fired three shots as the bus moved away. These shots were immediately followed by a full blast of mortar, machine gun, and rifle fire from the Burmese government troops stationed just three hundred yards away.[154]

Just after this incident, enraged Karens raided Mingaladon Air Force Armory, carrying off arms and ammunition. In response, the government outlawed the KNDO. The anti-Karen policy of the Burmese government at that time was obvious to subsequent scholars: "The best evidence of . . . anti-Karen focus of the AFPFL came when the government outlawed the KNDO only four days after its adherents declared full-scale rebellion. By contrast, the CPB, which began its rebellion in March 1948, was not declared illegal until 1953."[155]

On February 1, 1949, U Nu removed Karen army, navy, and air force commanders and replaced General Smith Dun with General Ne Win as chief of staff. Within a week, General Ne Win was named "Supreme Commander of all Defence Forces and Police Forces."[156] Some Karens in the army joined the rebellion, but the rest were confined in the armed forces rest camps established on February 7.[157]

The KNDO forces, which had for some days been concentrating near Insein, seized this key town. Over the next three months, they occupied almost all the major towns along the Rangoon to Mandalay Road and much of the Irrawaddy delta.[158] From peaceful political protest, the Karens began to resort to arms. With uncertain results, their revolution was going to last for more than half a century, with many homes destroyed and thousands of lives lost.

The Karen state movement, which started with Dr. San C. Po in 1928 and continued through Saw Ba U Gyi in 1948, embraced peaceful negotiation as policy. Even Karen generals and military officials in the regular Burma Army were loyal to the government at a time when the country almost collapsed due to the mutinies in the Burma Army. Until the tragic Christmas Palaw massacre, Karen infantry units and Karen officers continued fighting communist rebellions for the Union of Burma. Yet, the Burmese government painted an ugly description of the Karen rebellion:

> KNDO leaders are generally men trained in the Judson College of the Rangoon University. Their entire cultural life in the University has been punctiliously segregated from the rest of the Burmans by the Missionary authorities of Judson College with the result that when out of College they find themselves out of place and difficult to fit in the general society. The growing sense of Nationalism ushered in by the War was caught on the mental atmosphere and created a rapid desire for a separate State of their own. When the vested interest whose prospects lie in the areas inhabited by Karens fan up this desire and turn it into an aspiration for an independent existence the Karen leaders lost sight of reality and became consumed with a blind desire for an independent Karen State.[159]

Of course, American missionaries gave the Karens Christian faith along with good education and national consciousness. However, the above statements were unfair to those Karen leaders who had struggled through a long political journey in their pursuit for a separate Karen state. The government statements only confirmed what Saw Ba U Gyi said: "The Karens were misinterpreted as the stooges of the British" and that "Burmese newspapers always mentioned the Karens indiscriminately." Probably, the traditional prejudice the Burmese government had toward the American missionaries and the Karens will continue as long as the Karens continue their fight for self-determination and national identity.

Notes

1. *Burma and the Insurrection* (Rangoon: Government of the Union of Burma, 1949), 51.

2. IOR: M/4/3023, The Karen National Union to the Prime Minister (via Governor of Burma); Hugh Tinker, Andrew Griffin, and S. R. Ashton, *Burma: The Struggle for Independence, 1944–1948: Compilation of Documents from Official and Private Sources*, vol. 2 (London: Her Majesty's Stationery Office, 1984), 2:417–19.

3. Tinker, Griffin, and Ashton, 2:418.

4. Ibid., 2:435, Resolution Passed by the Karen Council of Action, dated 22 February 1947.

5. PRO: FO 643/66 (51/GS/80/47), Note of a meeting of a Karen deputation with the Governor on Tuesday 25th February 1947; Tinker, Griffin, and Ashton, 2:437–38.

6. Tinker, Griffin, and Ashton, 2:447, Daily Intelligence Summary compiled by the Intelligence Branch of the CID, Burma, 5 March 1947.

7. Ibid., 2:448.

8. Ibid., 2:413; H. N. C. Stevenson to P. G. E. Nash, PRO: FO 643/66 (51/GSO/47 Pr. II).

9. Tinker, Griffin, and Ashton, 2:448.

10. IOR: M/4/3023, Bogyoke Aung San to General Secretary, Karen National Union; Tinker, Griffin, and Ashton, 2:444–46.

11. Ibid.

12. IOR: M/4/2677, Sir Hubert Rance to the Earl of Listowel, 1 May 1947; Tinker, Griffin, and Ashton, 2:501.

13. Smith Dun, *Memoirs of the Four-Foot Colonel*, Data Paper number 113 (Ithaca, NY: Cornell University Southeast Asia Program, Department of Asia Studies, 1980), xi, 10.

14. Tinker, Griffin, and Ashton, 2:449.

15. Ibid., 2:449–50.

16. Ibid., 2:450.

17. IOR: M/4/3023, Telegram from Sir Hubert Rance to Lord Pethick-Lawrence, 7 March 1947; Tinker, Griffin, and Ashton, 2:452.

18. Tinker, Griffin, and Ashton, 2:478.

19. Ibid., 2:452.

20. Ibid., 2:454, P. G. E. Nash to Sir Gilbert Laithwaite, including Thra Tha Hto's letter of March 12.

21. IOR: M/4/3023, President, Shwegyin Karen Association to Governor of Burma, March 10, 1947; Tinker, Griffin, and Ashton, 2:455–57.

22. Tinker, Griffin, and Ashton, 2:457.

23. Ibid., 2:919.

24. Ibid., 2:499.

25. Maung Sin Kyeh, *Bamapyi Chit Kayin Amyotha Kaung Saung Myar* (Bangkok: Pyidaungsu Kayin Amyotha Apweh Choke, 2003), 93.

26. Tinker, Griffin, and Ashton, 2:921.

27. Ibid., 2:628.

28. Ibid., 2:919.

29. Maung Sin Kyeh, *Bamapyi Chit Kayin Amyotha Kaung Saung Myar*, 93; also Tinker, Griffin, and Ashton, 2:501.

30. IOR: M/4/2854, Report of the Frontier Areas Committee of Enquiry: Chapter III, 24 April 1947; Tinker, Griffin, and Ashton, 2:485.

31. Tinker, Griffin, and Ashton, 2:629. See also letters of Marshall Shwin and four other Karens (all ex-Force 136) of Salween district, protesting against Saw Lu Lu's statement (2:512).

32. IOR: M/4/3025, Circular issued by Karenni Ministers (translation), Loikaw, 26 June 1947; Tinker, Griffin, and Ashton, 2:619.

33. Tinker, Griffin, and Ashton, 2:920.

34. Ibid., 2:xxviii (Tinker's introduction).

35. Ibid., 2:481.

36. Ibid., 2:493.

37. Maung Sin Kyeh, *Bamapyi Chit Kayin Amyotha Kaung Saung Myar*, 94.

38. Tinker, Griffin, and Ashton, 2:494.

39. IOR: M/4/3023, Sir Hubert Rance to the Earl of Listowel, 7 June 1947; Tinker, Griffin, and Ashton, 2:569.

40. Ibid.

41. Tinker, Griffin, and Ashton, 2:568.

42. Mahn Ba Zan received his early education from American Baptist Mission school in Myaungmya and higher education at Rangoon Judson College (1935–1937); see Pu Gee Doh, *Mahn Ba Zan Hnint Kayin Taw Hlan Yay* (*Mah Ba Zan and Karen Revolution*) (KNU publication, 1993), 43, 48.

43. Ibid., 76.

44. Dun, 70.

45. Martin Smith, *Burma: Insurgency and the Politics of Ethnicity* (New York: St. Martin's Press, 1999), 86.

46. Ibid., 569.

47. Edward M. Law Yone and David G. Mandelbaum, "Pacification in Burma," *Far Eastern Survey* 19, no. 17 (October 11, 1950): 182-87, quote on 184; also John F. Cady, *A History of Modern Burma* (Ithaca, NY: Cornell University Press, 1960), 589–90.

48. Dun, 70–71.

49. IOR: M/4/3023, Marshall Shwin to the Prime Minister (via Governor), President, Shwegyin Karen Association, 16 June 1947; Tinker, Griffin, and Ashton, 2:589–90.

50. Tinker, Griffin, and Ashton, 2:589, footnote.

51. Ibid.

52. PRO: FO 643/6651/GSO, Daily Intelligence Summary for 1 July 1947; Tinker, Griffin, and Ashton, 2:637.

53. *Sunday Times*, "Burma Cuts the Painter," 22 June 1947.

54. IOR: M/4/3023, Press Release: Karen National Union for Reuters, 25 June 1947; Tinker, Griffin, and Ashton, 2:610–12.

55. IOR: M/4/2678, Sir Hubert Rance to the Earl of Listowel, Rangoon, 29 June 1947; Tinker, Griffin, and Ashton, 2:633.

56. Tinker, Griffin, and Ashton, 2:591.

57. U Nu, *Saturday's Son* (New Haven, CT: Yale University Press, 1975), 134.

58. Tinker, Griffin, and Ashton, 2:xxxiii (Tinker's introduction).

59. Ibid.

60. Ibid., 2:722, footnote.

61. Ibid.

62. Ibid., 2:721.

63. Ibid., 2:722.

64. Ibid., 2:723.

65. Ibid., 2:725–26.

66. Ibid., 2:728, footnote.

67. Ibid., 2:730.

68. "A Karen State to include Karenni, Mongpai, Salween district, the Part II areas of Toungoo and Thaton, and the Pyinmana subdivision; (ii) The state to be on the same basis as the Shan State (cf. paras.159–173 of the latest draft Constitution), and so to have a State Council, a Minister in charge of administration and a wide measure of local autonomy," note by Sir Gilbert Laithwaite, Rangoon, 2 September 1947, Tinker, Griffin, and Ashton, 2:738.

69. Ibid., 2:739.

70. Ibid., 2:741, footnote, recorded by Latihwaite.

71. Ibid., 2:744–45.

72. Ibid., 2:746.

73. Ibid., 2:746–47, Thankin Nu to the Earl of Listowel.

74. Ibid., 2:749, speech by the Earl of Listowel to the Karen leaders, 8 September 1947.

75. Ibid., 2:750.

76. Ibid., 2:xxxv (Tinker's introduction).

77. The Constitution of the Union of Burma, sections 180, 181; see Tinker, Griffin, and Ashton, 2:544.

78. Constitution of the Union of Burma, sections 182–95.

79. Tinker, Griffin, and Ashton, 2:523.

80. 1947 Constitution of the Union of Burma, Article 1.

81. Maung Sin Kyeh, *Bamarpyi Chit Kayin Amyotha Kaung Hsaung Myar*, 96.

82. Ibid., 96; Dun, 82.

83. Maung Sin Kyeh, *Bamarpyi Chit Kayin Amyotha Kaung Hsaung Myar*, 96.

84. Dun, 82.

85. Maung Sin Kyeh, *Bamarpyi Chit Kayin Amyotha Kaung Hsaung Myar*, 96.

86. Dun, 83.

87. Ibid., 82.

88. Maung Sin Kyeh, *Kayin Bawa Dalay* (Rangoon: Padaytha Sar Bay, 1967), 217–18.

89. Dun, 82.

90. Ibid., 84.

91. Ibid., 82.

92. Ibid., 84.

93. Ibid.

94. Pu S'Kaw Ler Taw, *Ka Nyaw Ta Ber Hser Tar Si Soh Teh Soh* (KNU publication, 1992), 209.

95. Dun, 86.

96. Ibid.

97. Cady, 582–83.

98. Hugh Tinker, *The Union of Burma: A Study of the First Years of Independence* (London: Oxford University Press, 1957), 34–35.

99. Cady, 588–89.

100. PRO: WO 203/5240.

101. IOR: MSS Eur E 213/14, Aung San's letter to Mountbatten, dated 25 September 1945. See the whole letter in Angelene Naw, *Aung San and the Struggle for Burmese Independence* (Chiang Mai: Silkworm Books, 2001), 252.

102. For the text of this agreement, see Britain-Burma Defence Agreement, August 29, 1947, PRO: PREM 8/412.

103. Mary P. Callahan, *Making Enemies: War and State Building in Burma* (Ithaca, NY: Cornell University Press, 2005), 119–20.

104. Maung Aung Myo, *Building the Tatmadaw* (Singapore: Institute of Asian Studies, 2009), 211–12.

106. Callahan, 119.

106. Ibid., 120.

107. Tinker, 36.

108. Ibid.

109. *Nation*, 14 August 1948; see also Tinker, 37.

110. Cady, 589.

111. Nu, *Saturday's Son*, 168.

112. Cady, 590.

113. *Burma and the Insurrection*, 49.

114. Ibid., 49–50, Speech of Saw Ba U Gyi, at the Karen National Club, Mission Road, Ahlone Quarter, Rangoon, at 1 pm on Saturday, 9 October 1948.

115. Maung Sin Kyeh, *Bamarpyi Chit Kayin Amyotha Kaung Hsaung Myar*, 97.

116. *Burma and the Insurrection*, 51.

117. Maung Sin Kyeh, *Bamarpyi Chit Kayin Amyotha Kaung Hsaung Myar*, 98.

118. Cady, 501.

119. Tinker, 37.

120. Dun, 68.

121. Maung Sin Kyeh, *Bamarpyi Chit Kayin Amyotha Kaung Hsaung Myar*, 98.

122. Union of Burma, *Regional Autonomy Enquiry Commission Record* (Rangoon, 1951), 26.

123. Nu, *Saturday's Son*, 169.

124. Saw Ralph and Naw Sheera, *Fifty Years in the Karen Revolution in Burma, the Soldier and the Teacher*, ed. Stephanie Olinga-Shannon (Ithaca, NY: Cornell University Press, 2019). 65.

125. Callahan, 122–30.

126. Ibid., 127.

127. PRO: FO 371/69485, Brigadier Bo Let Ya, Special Commissioner, North Burma, Weekly Report for Week Ending August 28, 1948, cited in British Embassy, Rangoon, to Foreign Office, telegram, September 5, 1948.

128. PRO: FO 371/69485, January 8, 1949, Ambassador John Bowker, British Embassy, Rangoon, to Foreign Office, London, PRO FO 371/75661, telegram, September 7, 1948.

129. *Burma and the Insurrection*, 49–50.

130. Ibid.

131. Dun, 71.

132. Richard J. Aldrich, Gary D. Rawnsley, and Min-Yeh T. Rawnsley, eds., *The Clandestine Cold War in Asia 1945–1965: Western Intelligence, Propaganda, and Special Operations* (London and Portland, OR: Frank Cass, 2000), 136–37.

133. Ibid., 140.

134. *Daily Express*, September 18; *The Times*, September 20, 1948.

135. PRO: FO 371/75661, BSM to Burma, Rangoon, to Foreign Office, London, telegram, January 8, 1949.

136. Cady, 592.

137. Census Commissioner, *Census of India*, 1931, vol. 9, Burma, part 1, report by J. J. Bennison, Rangoon, 1933, map frontispiece, 190–91.

138. Cady, 592.

139. U Nu, *Towards Peace and Democracy: Translation of Selected Speeches* (Rangoon: Ministry of Information, 1949), 151.

140. Dun, 69.

141. Tinker, 38.

142. Ibid., 40.

143. Callahan, 128.

144. *Nation*, 22 December 1948.

145. Dun, 69.

146. Tinker, 39.

147. Dun, 69.

148. Ibid.

149. Tinker, 40.

150. *Nation*, 16 January 1949.

151. Tinker, 39.

152. Nu, *Towards Peace and Democracy*, 214–15.

153. Dun, 69.

154. Ibid.

155. Smith, 116; Callahan, 121, who further added that the PVO was not officially banned until July 19, 1951.

156. Special War Office Council Order, Appointments—Officers, March 17, 1949, no. 11/S/49, DR 1043, DSHRI, and Special War Office Council Order, Appointments—Officers, February 19, 1949, no. 6/S/49, DR 1042, DSHRI.

157. DSHRI, Administrative History, vol. 1, 821.

158. Tinker, 45.

159. *Burma and the Insurrection*, 35–36.

8
Sixty Years of Armed Struggle of the KNU

As the saying goes, "History is not grounded in facts; rather, it's the winners' interpretation of them that prevails." The Burmese government published its report of the Karen freedom movement with the title "The Karen Insurrection" and blamed American missionaries and Karen Christians. In reality, the uprising was not religious. Many Buddhist and animist Karens joined, while many Christian Karens opposed the rebellion. The American Baptist Foreign Mission Society's treasurer, visiting in 1948, ex-missionary American embassy staff members, and Methodist missionary Dr. E. Stanley Jones, who visited Rangoon on the eve of the rebellion, all tried to forestall the break. The American Baptist Mission in Burma's settled policy was not to participate in political affairs in any way. As Professor Cady claimed in his book, "The American missionaries deprecated the wartime feud from which the rebellion developed and were in no position in 1948–1949 to tell the KNU political leadership what they could or could not do."[1]

The Provoked Revolution

Throughout late 1948, Karen battalions and the KNDO defended the country from the Burmese Army deserters and communists, thus preserving the newly established Union of Burma's sovereignty. In addition, KNU leaders and General Smith Dun, supreme commander of the Burma Army, consistently cooperated with Prime Minister U Nu for peaceful co-existence between the Burmans and Karens. U Nu even made an agreement with KNU leader Saw Ba U Gyi for the KNDO to be employed directly under the command of General Smith Dun. So employed, the KNDO were to help the government in the Insein and Twante areas. The KNDO in Insein were allotted the neighboring areas like Hlegu, Taukkyan, and Hlawga for defense and garrisoning duties. By this arrangement, the regular forces would be able to strike at the communists, who were then the government's main threat. The KNDO was allowed to move freely with their military arms in the Insein district as well as in Twante. Unfortunately, U Nu did not make a public announcement of this agreement. When conflict started between the Burmese auxiliary police forces (Yebaw or Sitwandun), General Smith Dun requested U Nu to explain to the public, which he never did.[2]

Meanwhile, the Burmese press reported against the Karens by publishing the wildest stories about "Karen provocation."[3] The propaganda caused great alarm, and the Burmese community in Insein was armed to defend themselves against KNDO. Units of the Burmese auxiliary forces or Sitwundans were posted in Insein town to cope with possible KNDO attacks.[4]

As the tension began, Karen leaders worked hard to avoid misunderstandings between the Karens and Burmans in Insein. Saw Bellay, a Karen leader in Insein, explained how much caution was taken:

> On the eve of the Karen New Year which fell on the 29th December 1948 I went to the New Year's eve party given by General Smith Dun at his residence at Mingaladon. That night all the villagers and K.N.D.O. in Insein were strictly ordered, according to the decision of the meeting arrived by the Karen elders of Insein, not to celebrate the Karen New Year's Eve by firing shots on the New Year as was usually done in the past, as, by so doing, unnecessary alarm and commotion might be caused to the people in Insein. Church bells would be rung and midnight service would be conducted. I myself heard the order given to the K.N.D.O by their Commander, Maung Maung Than.[5]

Apparently, the Karen community behaved as instructed, but danger still followed. While the Karen congregation was in church, Saw Po Tu, a Karen police officer, reported, "At 12:00 midnight church bells were rung, adults and children alike came to the church and at about 12:30 whilst the congregation was in silent prayers, firing of rifles and automatic weapons was heard from the direction of the Technical Institute, Insein, followed immediately by two mortar shells, one of which dropped in Karen Quarters. The prayer had to be stopped as firing was also heard from [the] town area."[6]

With bullets continuing to fly over the Karen community without knowing who was responsible, the Karens became restless. To avoid any possible clash between the KNDO and Burmese levy forces, in January 1949, KNU leader Saw Ba U Gyi, together with Saw Bellay, had a meeting with Brigadier Ne Win (later General Ne Win), the then deputy supreme commander, the commissioner of police, and other officials from the Home Department. At that meeting, a reconciliation committee formed with seven members: Brigadier Ne Win, the inspector general of police, the chief secretary of the Home Department, the commissioner of police, Saw Ba U Gyi, Saw Tha Hto, and Saw Bellay.

The reconciliation committee's purpose was to settle a misunderstanding between the Burmese levies and the KNDO and to repatriate the KNDO of Insein to their respective homes. The committee also decided to form a reconciliatory subcommittee at Insein in an advisory capacity and to bring about a peaceful solution to the situation. This thirteen-member subcommittee was controlled by a police inspector, with four Karen leaders, four police officers (including a Karen, Saw Po Tu), and four Burmese levies. The four Karen leaders were Maung Maung Than (commander of the KNDO in Insein), Mahn Ye Lun (Thamaing), Saw Ba Than, and Saw Bellay.[7]

The second week of January 1949 was a fearful time for all residing in Insein, Gyogon, and Thamaing because of unpleasant incidents caused by the levies. On the morning of January 22, 1949, an armored car drove along Insein's main road, firing a long burst of Bren machine gun rounds into the Karen quarters.[8] The Karens residing along the Insein Civil Station Road reported on two or three occasions to Saw Po Tu that the levies patrolling that road not only abused them but also threatened to kill them saying, "You Karens will all be exterminated." The Karen United Military Police of Ywama also made similar complaints.[9]

The Burmese levies disturbed the Karen communities in several townships. One night, at about 10:00 or 11:00 pm, they fired at the Karen quarters in Thamaing for half an hour, using rifles, Bren guns, and mortars. In Gyogon, near Thamaing, two mortar shells were fired into the compound of a Karen businessman, Saw Benson, seriously injuring Mrs. McSimon, an assistant of Saw Benson & Company. Police officer Saw Po Tu visited these reported crime scenes to investigate. Area residents strongly suspected that the levies stationed at Kyaukwaing were the culprits because the camp was only a mile from Saw Benson's house. Additionally, Burmese levies killed a Karen at the Thamaing checkpoint in broad daylight while he was returning to his village from Rangoon, riding in a public passenger bus.[10]

During the last week of January 1949, it was reported that the Burmese levies were molesting Karen female travelers at Wanetchaung village, north of Insein. Saw Shwe Gyaw, a retired subedar-major, requested the police take action to prevent the levies from molesting Karen villagers. He reported that Karen female travelers were subjected to searches at the railway station while travelers of other nationalities were allowed to proceed without being searched. In addition, he reported to Insein police that fifteen village defense guns, including some that were licensed under his care, were confiscated by Burmese levies. Among the seized firearms were government firearms from the Insein police station. According to Saw Shwe Gyaw, Burmese levies fired into the Karen section of his village using all types of weapons including mortars.[11]

On January 24, Saw Po Tu encountered two armored cars stopped at a road junction with mounted guns pointed towards the Karen villages of Nanthagon and Taungthugon. As a police officer and member of the Insein reconciliation subcommittee, he told them that the government was taking steps to clear up the status of the KNDO.[12]

Due to the Burmese levies' mounting assaults on the Karen community, General Smith Dun went to Prime Minister U Nu requesting a meeting with Saw Ba U Gyi to clarify the position of the KNDO, which he had arranged with Ba U Gyi. U Nu agreed to meet Saw Ba U Gyi and Saw Bellay on January 31 at noon. Before the meeting took place, Burmese military rolled into the Thamaing Karens with armored cars, tanks, mortars, and guns. Saw Bellay noted, "Smith Dun's request had fallen on deaf ears."[13]

The January 31, 1949, attack on the Thamaing Karen quarters ignited full-scale war between the Karens and the Burmese government. The Burmese levies surrounded the village at dawn and fired into it with all their weaponry, including three mortars, causing several casualties to the Karen villagers. As the Burmese levies fired on the Karen quarters, Saw J. Poo Nyo, a retired frontier service officer who was then the Karen affairs officer and who was living in the attacked zone, phoned General Smith Dun and reported the situation. General Smith Dun replied that he would call U Nu to intervene as he himself did not know who was responsible and who had given the order to fire on Thamaing.[14] In his memoir, without mentioning the name Ne Win, Smith Dun said his "deputy" ordered the attack.[15]

Under KNU leaders' orders, the KNDO did not retaliate until the Burmese levies stormed the Karens in Thamaing. Burmese military troops rolled in with armored cars, tanks, mortars, and guns to join the levies. By noon, units of the regular Karen army joined to defend the Karens, under the belief they were fighting the ill-disciplined levies who had attacked the Karen quarters without proper authority from the government.[16] As fighting flared, other KNDO troops joined. The violence spread to Insein, only ten miles from the Burmese government's general headquarters. The battle of Insein lasted for three months and twenty-one days.[17]

As the events unfolded and until the last moment, Saw Ba U Gyi and other KNU leaders tried to meet with U Nu to wholeheartedly participate in the reconciliation committee arrangement for peace. Without being prepared for war, the situation had pushed the Karens to fight the government. While holding Insein, the KNU continued to annex Prome, Toungoo, Meiktila, Maymyo, Mandalay, and almost all the towns and villages in the delta region. General Smith Dun proudly proclaimed, "Most fortunately the Karen leadership had made it clear and plain that they were not fighting the Burmese people but the Burmese Government who had lost their respect and confidence with their deeds of shame."[18] In the KNU-occupied areas, Burmese civilians were not massacred or slaughtered as the BIA did to the Karens in 1942, just seven years prior.

VICTORY AND DEFEAT

During the three months of the so-called battle of Insein, the KNDO briefly took control of Mingaladon airport, removing guns from three Spitfires standing on the runway. The road to Rangoon lay open, and KNDO units pushed as close as four miles from the city. By this time, the PVO joined pro-government militias, including army regulars, Sit-wundans, and Gurkha troops to fight against the KNDO. At this critical moment, Saw Ba U Gyi and KNU leaders sought military support from other Karen forces, particularly the three battalions of the Karen Rifles.

Seemingly, the three Karen battalion commanders were confused as to whether to maintain their loyalty to the government and wait for orders from their supreme commander General Smith Dun or join the KNDO and defend their people. According to one report, on the first day of the battle, Saw Ba U Gyi made wireless contact with the 2nd Karen Rifles in Prome asking for help. However, their officers hesitated, refusing to believe that the supreme commander of the Burma Army, General Smith Dun, had been replaced by Ne Win. It took several days to call in their troops from outlying districts where most were still on operations against the communists. In this vital breathing space, the government moved promptly, disarming the 3rd Karen Rifles stationed in Maymyo and Mandalay.[19]

In response, the 2nd Karen Rifles gathered their troops, but in marching to Insein, they made a tactical mistake. Instead of traveling as advised through the Henzada district where local KNDO units were in control, they went via the main road towards Insein. On the open road near Nattalin, they came under aerial attack from the Burmese air force. The strike did not cause many casualties, but many of the 2nd Karen Rifles surrendered along with their regimental commander. The remaining troops scattered, with some making their way into Insein while others headed eastward across the Pegu Yomas highland towards Toungoo.[20]

The commander of the 1st Karen Rifles in Toungoo, Colonel Min Maung, was pushed into a dilemma when the local units of the KNDO asked him to join them and fight the government. The Burmese military, not having specific information from Toungoo at that moment, presumed that the 1st Karen Rifles had seized control of Toungoo and joined the KNDO immediately on January 27.[21] Lieutenant Sergeant Saw Yankee,[22] who was assigned by Colonel Min Maung to take charge of the wireless communications service to the 1st Karen Rifles, provided firsthand experience of that period. He was on his way to Rangoon but stalled in Toungoo, due to the fact that local units of the KNDO overran the city on the nights of January 25 and 26. The next day his friend, Captain Zaw Pe of the 1st Karen Rifles, met him and reported that he made a truce with the Karen national forces, but the 1st Karen Rifles were still loyal to the government and had not joined the Karen nationalist movement.[23]

During that period, the defense minister of Burma, Bo Let Ya, came to the 1st Karen Rifle headquarters in a Spitfire fighter aircraft and met with Colonel Min Maung, who reported on the situation in Toungoo. Bo Let Ya promised to supply arms, ammunition, and other supplies, which the 1st Karen Rifles had requisitioned. Colonel Min Maung waited, but soon the wireless communication was severed. During these days, local KNU leaders came daily, requesting Colonel Min Maung join the Karen movement without success. Saw Yankee said:

> Despite manifestations of continued loyalty to the Union Government, all wireless links with the 1st Karen Rifles were suddenly cut off. As a person-in-charge of signals, I personally called up the Tactical Headquarters at Pegu, which was our control station in the network. I used the assigned call signal as well as my person name in calling. As a result, some responses were received. . . . They told me that all had been explicitly ordered not to communicate with the 1st Karen Rifles nor to respond to its call because 1st Karen Rifles had gone over to the Karen rebels. This wireless exchange was made in the hearing of the C.O., the adjutant Captain Kyaw Nyein and some other officers of the 1st Karen Rifles.[24]

Colonel Min Maung was reluctant to rebel against the government because his future and his officers' and men's futures were at stake. He was aware that his battalion alone would have to take on the Burma Army because the 2nd Karen Rifles had been crushed. The 3rd Karen

Rifles had been disarmed and interned in camps in Maymyo. The 3rd Karen Rifles' commanding officer, Colonel Saw Di Htoo, was away in the Pakokku operations area with one of his companies. The Burmese government ordered him back to Maymyo to be disarmed and interned.

Meanwhile, without Colonel Min Maung's consent, Captain Zaw Pe took his company stationed at the Sittang Club in Toungoo and headed for Insein.[25] At Nyaung Le Bin, Lieutenant Colonel Saw Moody, commander of the 2nd Burma Rifles, disarmed Zaw Pe and his men of all weapons except sidearms carried by officers. Their vehicles were confiscated, but the soldiers were allowed to walk back to Toungoo.[26] This incident is yet another proof of the loyalty of Karen military leaders to the established Union of Burma. If Colonel Saw Moody's 2nd Burma Rifles and Colonel Min Maung's 1st Karen Rifles cooperated and joined the KNU movement, Karen history could have turned differently.

While Colonel Min Maung hesitated, the officers and men of the 1st Battalion became restless and eager to join the freedom fighters. The situation suddenly changed in mid-February when Captain Nawng Seng of 1st Battalion Kachin Rifles met with Colonel Min Maung.[27] Captain Nawng Seng told Colonel Min Maung that he was assigned by General Ne Win to retake Toungoo, but he did not want to fight the Karens. He reasoned that the Karens, together with American missionaries, brought Christianity to the Kachins. Karen teachers were the first educators the American missionaries brought to teach the Kachin to read, write, and reckon.[28]

He offered to fight on the Karen side and suggested a lightning strike on upper Burma where there were fewer government troops. The Kachin and Karen forces could strike a blitzkrieg on Maymyo, liberate the Karen personnel detained in the military detention camp, re-arm them, and bring them back to Toungoo. Thus strengthened, the combined force could invade lower Burma. Nawng Seng's eloquent presentation fired enthusiasm in the officers in the mess hall of the 1st Karen Rifles, culminating in operational plans being drawn up with dates and times set to invade upper Burma.

After Nawng Seng returned to his headquarters to prepare for the joint operation, Colonel Min Maung invited local KNU leaders to his headquarters and announced that he had decided to come over. Without giving away his real military objective for cooperating with the Kachins, he announced that he would very soon strike at the enemy and that he needed men and material to invade Burmese-held areas. He demanded that KNU leaders transfer to his command all officers and men in the

KNU's armed wing, known as the Karen National Defense Organization (KNDO). The KNU leaders gladly accepted his demand.

Colonel Min Maung immediately reorganized the Karen battalion. The thousand or so KNDOs were organized into a battalion of five companies. This new battalion, together with the 1st Karen Rifles and the yet to materialize 1st Kachin Rifles, were formed into a brigade and named the Toungoo Brigade.[29]

The operation called Objective Maymyo began to advance from Toungoo as one motorized column and one train column. Nawng Seng's Kachin company of the 1st Kachin Rifles joined the Karen motorized column at Swa. The combined Karen and Kachin troops first seized Tha Wut Hti. From there, the 1st Kachin Rifles and some of the 3rd Kachin Rifles attached to the 1st Kachins joined the convoy completing the Toungoo Brigade. Lieutenant Colonel Zaw Gaung, the commanding officer of the 1st Kachin Rifles, and a few officers who refused to cooperate with Nawng Seng were disarmed and kept under custody by Nawng Seng's associates. They eventually were sent by truck to Toungoo.[30] By February 20, the Toungoo Brigade seized Pyinmana, Tatkon, Yamethin, Pyaw Bwe, Meiktila, Thazi, and Nyaung Yan without serious resistance.

The opportunity for turning the communist enemies into friends happened in Pyinmana. The Toungoo Brigade won the trust of various anti-government elements such as the Communist Party Burma, the Red Flag Communist Party, and the People's Volunteer Organization. As mentioned before, these leftist Burmans considered the Karens as pawns of the British, fighting the government to restore British colonial rule in Burma. Credit must be given to political officer U Saw Lon's negotiation skills. When the Karens captured Pyinmana, U Saw Lon met with Bo Tar Yar, the Communist Party Burma (CPB) leader, and convinced him that all Karens aspired for was their own unique state. He explained that armed struggle was forced upon the Karens by the government. Following the talk, the village of Pyinmana plus some captured Italian and Japanese rifles and a few 12-gauge shotguns were transferred to Bo Tar Yar and the CPB. Since the CPB had never been able to capture Pyinmana, they agreed not to fight the KNU troops. In handing over the town of Pyinmana and subsequently others, the Karens were admitting they could not afford to leave troops to do garrison duty in towns they overran. They had to rely on anti-government elements to keep lines of communication open to Toungoo. The Toungoo Brigade also gave away Tatkon, Yamethin, Pyaw Bwe, and Thazi to the CPB, the Red Flag

Communists, or the PVO, whichever had a strong presence in town, to win their goodwill and friendship.[31]

Regarding the Karen-communist alliance of the time, the AFPFL government was probably correct in saying that "[T]hey made unholy alliance with the Communist insurgencies in Taungoo, Meiktila, Myingyan, Mandalay, and Maymyo." But the AFPFL was absolutely wrong in claiming "the KNDOs co-operated fully with both Red and White Flag Communist insurgents to further their interest of a separate State: that . . . they never co-operated with the Government for the suppression of Communist insurrection when it started in March 1948."[32]

One unexpected opportunity for the Karens occurred in Meiktila. When the motorized column arrived at Meiktila, Captain F. Terry, who had come over from the government side, reported to Brigadier Min Maung that two DC3s carrying government troops were expected to land at Meiktila airstrip at 10:00 am. The government in Rangoon had no knowledge of the fall of Meiktila for two reasons. One reason was poor wireless communication, and another reason was that Meiktila fell so quickly that the defenders did not have the opportunity to send information to Rangoon or Maymyo about the impending capitulation. Not knowing the situation, the two DC3s, which had taken off from Rangoon, unwittingly continued their flight to Meiktila. Brigadier Min Maung immediately dispatched a reception party to the airstrip to welcome the arriving government troops. When the Dakotas landed, the reception party disarmed the sixty passengers, put them on lorries, and sent them to the Meiktila jail as prisoners of war.[33]

The pilots and crew of the DC3s were taken to brigade headquarters. They were ordered to take a new batch of passengers to Maymyo, discharge their human cargo, and return to Rangoon. The DC3s were foreign-owned and foreign registered. The government chartered them to transport troops to Meiktila. The pilots were foreigners. The brigadier assured the pilots that he did not intend to commandeer the aircraft or to press them into *Kawthoolei* service. The crews' cooperation in the urgent transport of troops to Maymyo would facilitate their early and safe return to Rangoon. The brigadier assured them that they could fly to Rangoon from Maymyo.

Thus informed, the two DC3s carried two platoons of troops, one Kachin platoon under Colonel Nawng Seng and one Karen platoon under Major Saw Oo, to Anisakan, the airstrip at Maymyo. Assuming Bo Let Ya was on board, the commander of the North Burma subdistrict (NBSD) himself and most of his staff officers were waiting at the airstrip. Once the DC3s touched down and stopped, Kachin and Karen troops spilled out of the aircraft, overpowered the reception party, arrested them, and drove immediately to the NBSD headquarters. Under coercion, the NBSD commander, by telephone, ordered all units in Maymyo to surrender. Maymyo was taken on February 21, 1949, without a shot being fired. All Karen detainees were liberated and re-armed.[34]

The communication breakdown in the Burmese government system allowed the Karens to fly their troops and annex Maymyo without having to fight. As stated before, the Burma signal army personnel were mostly Karens, and when Karen personnel were detained or went underground, the Burma Army wireless communication suffered significant disruption.

The Kachin-Karen troops on the Rangoon-Mandalay Road were halted at Myit Nge, where government troops had destroyed the rail and road bridges. As they fought the enemy, a company of men under Captain Ba Shine from Maymyo rushed down to Mandalay for support. The two columns joined forces outside Mandalay, and on March 12, Mandalay fell. However, since Mandalay was not the area that the KNU asked for the Karen state, it was transferred into the hands of the communist insurgents. A Mandalay command named *Naww* (which means "palace") was established. A Karen major, John Hla Shin, was appointed commander of Naww. Lines of communication were established between Meiktila-Mandalay-Maymyo. Nawng Seng, Saw Oo, Ba Shine rejoined the brigade in Meiktila. The Toungoo Brigade gained another company when Brigadier Min Maung sent a task force by train to Pakokku and brought back Colonel Di Htoo, commander of the 3rd Karen Rifles, and his men.[35] Colonel Di Htoo was another Karen commander who was not in favor of the rebellion and loyal to the government.[36]

The Kachin-Karen forces, which had won every battle so far, began to decline in the fortunes of war. The Toungoo Brigade expected that the liberated Karens would join them. Many did join, but a significant number of senior officers, including General Smith Dun, refused, yet another indication that many Christian Karens preferred reconciliation and peace.[37]

The return journey to Toungoo was not easy. The Karens had to fight for weeks with the government forces that recaptured Thazi. The CPBs, Red Flag Communists, and the PVOs, who became their allies on their way north, turned against the Karens due to the atrocities committed by the renegade Karens in Toungoo. They destroyed the railroads and bridges and blocked the roads with trees across the roadways. After the Karen engineers cleared these roadblocks and repaired the road, the brigade finally reached Tatkon.

While the convoy, dependents, and camp followers were at Tatkon, the vanguard of the column, with U Saw Lon, went to Pyinmana. Again, through U Saw Lon's negotiation with Bo Tar Yar, a temporary truce was made. The CPBs agreed to let the convoy transit through Pyinmana on condition that all vehicles exited out of Pyinmana before 6:00 am and that no vehicle was to stop in Pyinmana. Any vehicle which stopped in Pyinmana and vehicles which were still in Pyinmana after 6:00 am would be seized by the CPBs as spoils of war, and the passengers would be detained as prisoners of war. Immediately after the agreement, the convoy with three hundred or so vehicles rolled past Pyinmana and reached Toungoo after three days. The trip was a half-day journey under normal circumstances.[38]

On their march back to Toungoo, the brigade brought along with them the Burmese prisoners of war, including Colonel Maung Maung and Major Thein Doke, who were initially detained in the Toungoo jail. Later, they were placed in a house in Bawgali Gyi village, where the Bawgali Gyi church's pastor and congregation fed them and looked after them. The POWs were not seriously detained but rather had free run of Bawgali Gyi. The Karens assumed that the POWs were so deep inside their territory that it would be impossible for them to escape. In 1951, they were rescued by a special task force. The rescued Colonel Maung Maung later became head of the Burma Army's military planning staff. It was said that Colonel Maung Maung returned the good deed that the pastor of Bawgali Gyi had done to the Burmese POWs.[39]

CEASEFIRE AGREEMENT AND NEGOTIATION

While the Toungoo Brigade's Objective Maymyo advanced in upper Burma, more towns in the delta and Tenasserim fell to the KNDOs. With several other major towns and cities under the control of the communists, the map of the Union of Burma was divided into different zones of the multi-insurgencies. As such, the international media described U Nu's AFPFL government as the Rangoon government. They asked for negotiations with the KNU forces which provided their strongest opposition. On March 14, 1949, the AFPFL government made an announcement that included the terms and conditions for the surrender of arms, amnesty for fighters, and the formation of a protection committee of fourteen negotiators.[40] Included in this committee were Burmans in whom the Karens had confidence, such as Sir Ba U, Justice E Maung, and Professor Hla Bu, former principal of Judson College. Other Karen leaders who did not join the rebellion, like Saw Lu Lu, Saw Aung Pa,

Mrs. Ba Maung Chain (daughter of Sir San C. Po), and Rev. Ah Mya, were also on the committee.[41]

According to S'Kaw Ler Taw, on April 4, 1949, the British ambassador, Mr. Boker, along with Indian ambassador Mr. Rauf, Pakistani ambassador Mr. M.D. Ali, and Anglican Bishop West, went to Saw Ba U Gyi. They brought with them an invitation letter from U Nu for peaceful negotiations. In his letter, he said that he and Ba U Gyi had a good understanding, but the fight started because their followers disobeyed them. To restore peace and unity, he wanted Ba U Gyi to meet him and negotiate. During this time, KNDO troops were short of weapons and ammunition, and the expected relief from the 2nd Karen Rifles had not yet arrived. It was an uncertain situation for an effective military campaign.[42] Ba U Gyi and the KNU leaders replied that they would meet with the government, provided the British ambassador would guarantee the settlement terms. A compromise was reached after the Commonwealth ambassadors of Great Britain, India, and Pakistan urged the Karens to negotiate under a guarantee of safe passage.[43] Several missions to the Karen headquarters were made, mostly by Mrs. Ba Maung Chain, to urge Ba U Gyi and his colleagues to negotiate. The Karens eventually agreed to meet with the government.[44]

Saw Ba U Gyi, Mahn James Tun Aung, and Saw Bellay went to Rangoon, where the negotiation with U Nu and his team, General Ne Win, Bo Khin Maung Galay, U Min Aung, and U Chan Tun, began. U Nu gave a warm welcome and told Ba U Gyi that he had already formed a protective committee for the establishment of the Karen state. According to his peace terms, it was not necessary for the KNDO to surrender all their weapons—only some tanks and heavy ammunition.[45] On April 5, 1949, Saw Ba U Gyi and General Ne Win signed a provisional treaty that granted amnesty to Karen troops who had joined the rebellion and allowed Karen civilians to keep weapons for their own protection.

Saw Ba U Gyi had to obtain his comrades' assent, and the final signing of the agreement was arranged for April 8. When he met with KNDO commanders, Saw Hunter Tha Hmwe and Mahn Ba Zan adamantly refused to accept the terms and put forward a condition tantamount to an armistice between equal governments. Included were demands for an immediate general ceasefire in Burma and government acceptance of the right of all insurgent organizations to hold any territories they occupied for the duration of the peace talks. These conditions were not acceptable to U Nu and Ne Win.[46] Many believed that Ba U Gyi was willing to sign the peace treaty but his KNDO leaders, specifically Saw Hunter

Tha Hmwe, Mahn Ba Zan, and Saw Aung Sein, were against him.[47] Consequently, on May 21, 1949, the full-scale war resumed, which has now continued for more than half a century.

Kawthoolei Government in Toungoo

Understanding the Karens in Insein needed assistance, General Min Maung reorganized the Toungoo Brigade and made plans for Operation Rangoon. Major Thet Wah was made brigade major. He was formerly of the Burma Engineers, as well as an ex-Royal Air Force signaler and wireless operator who parachuted into Burma to work behind the Japanese lines during World War II. Major Kyaw Nyein was responsible for taking over the Toungoo rear command headquarters. Colonel Nawng Seng was made operation commander.[48]

With the plan to take Pegu on April 26 and Rangoon on May 1, 1949, the Toungoo Brigade headed for Insein. They had their first serious battle with the 2nd Burma Rifles, after which Nyaunglaybin and Daik-U were captured. Both sides suffered losses, including Karen Captain Saw Charming Taw, who was killed. The next engagement was with the 5th Burma Rifles at Paungdawthi. The Karen-Kachin forces were able to fight the enemy from both front and back causing the Burmans to flee. The insurgents captured three abandoned armored cars and a jeep, which previously belonged to Lieutenant Colonel Chit Myaing, the commanding officer of the 5th Burma Rifles, who managed to escape.[49]

Despite successes on the field, the men in the ranks were beginning to suffer battle fatigue. Their morale was ebbing as they repeatedly engaged the enemy. There were no fresh troops to relieve them. However, the commanders prepared to attack Kadok, about seventy miles north of Rangoon. The government forces were well prepared and launched mortar bombs on the Karen troops. Eventually, the Karen forces had to withdraw, sustaining extensive casualties including Captains San Tun and San Shwe Htoo.[50]

Coincidental with the unsuccessful assault on Kadok came the news that Insein, the Karen stronghold north of Rangoon, had fallen. Since April, government forces had begun to capture KNDO positions around Insein town bit by bit. By May, the town had grown increasingly desperate without new relief. On May 22, 1949, after a 112-day siege, the KNDO quietly pulled back across the Hlaing River and slipped away into the countryside.[51] General Smith Dun's analysis was brief but clearly described the future of the KNU movement after Insein: "Insein was held and then given up—not surrendered—and evacuated by all armed forces when it became evident that supplies would not last. This small force marched hundreds of miles to join their main bases and headquarters at Toungoo in the North and their delta headquarters in the West."[52]

On their march north to Toungoo, the Karen troops captured the Burmese operational document entitled Operation Aung San, which clearly indicated the intention of the Burmese government to eliminate the Karens first and then other hill people. Having that knowledge, they decided "not to lay their necks down for the slaughter, nor their women to dishonor."[53]

Once Insein fell, the Toungoo Brigade had to consider whether to go it alone or withdraw and consolidate what it had gained. The Toungoo Brigade decided to withdraw and consolidate. To go it alone with fatigued and dispirited men would be a slaughter. General Min Maung reorganized his troops and formed a new brigade at Nyaung Lay Bin, called in Karen *Kler Lwih Htu*.[54] The establishment of a Karen state in KNU-controlled territory between Toungoo and Daik-U was declared on May 20, 1949.[55]

Saw Ba U Gyi and his entourage arrived at Toungoo, and an emergency meeting was called for June 14 in the hall of Saint Luke High School. Attendees included members of the central committee of the KNU who came with the chairman, the local KNU leaders from Toungoo, Thaton, and Nyaunglebin, heads of departments, town elders, plus army and police officers. Representatives from the delta were missing. Saw Ba U Gyi explained that the armed conflict was not the making of the Karens. In fact, he said, the Karens were not at all ready for an uprising, as they did not have enough men who could fight, nor enough weapons and resources to rise against the government. The government, he said, planned and instigated the armed conflict so it could rid the army command of all Karens and replace them with Burman officers. The Karens, he said, would have lost more and gained nothing of consequence if he had agreed to the terms and conditions of surrender offered by the government after seven days of negotiations during the temporary cessation of hostilities in Insein. The government forces, he said, had in breach of the agreement of truce moved their troops to strategic points, which they had not been able to take during the active fighting. There was, he said, no other way than to continue fighting. He called upon all true Karens to unite and fight the enemy.[56]

Following the meeting, the birth of the Kawthoolei government was celebrated in Papun with fanfare, a military parade, public gathering, fluttering flags, and speech making at the Maidan ground. KNU chairman Saw Ba U Gyi became the prime minister; Pa'O U Hla Pe, foreign minister; Saw Po Maung, home minister; Kaw Kasa Shwe Lay, defense minister; Kaw Kasa Tura Oo, finance; Saw Sein Tin, agriculture and forestry; Padoh Ba Tun, education; and Saw Johnson D. Po Min, transport and communication.[57] The self-proclaimed state of Kawthoolei was announced on the Radio Kawthoolei station, which Mr. Bruce, a Canadian radio technician, set up for the Kawthoolei government.[58] Several foreign radio stations including All India, BBC, Pakistan, and Australia radio stations broadcast the formation of the Kawthoolei government,[59] but no country accorded recognition of the new state.

The next day, the armed forces of Kawthoolei were renamed the Kawthoolei Armed Forces (KAF), and General Min Maung was confirmed as its general commander. It was restructured into two divisions along the lines of the KNDOs. General Min Maung became defense minister, and Kaw Kasa Shwe Lay was reassigned as commander of the Toungoo Brigade. Two army commands were set up, namely, the eastern command and the delta command. General Min Maung headed the eastern command, and under his command were Toungoo, Karenni, Nyaunglaybin, Moulmein, and Thaton brigades. Commander of the delta command was General Sein Hmone with four brigades under his leadership. The 1st Brigade was under Colonel Kyaw Mya Than and included the areas around Nyaungdon, Pantanaw, and Danuphyu. The 2nd Brigade was under Colonel Bo Pu and included Bassein and Myaungmya. Colonel Thein Aung led the 3rd Brigade, which included the Hanthawaddy and South Maubin areas. The 4th Brigade was assigned to Colonel Ba Thaw and covered the Henzada and Thayawaddy districts. By the end of 1949, a 5th Brigade was formed under Colonel Taw Meh Pa and Colonel Aung Sein.[60]

The Kawthoolei government, established on June 14, operated its administration through radio communication between the KAF units from the Bassein district in the western delta to Loikaw and Myawaddy in the eastern hills. Many began to feel that the civilian administration could not function while the revolution was in process, and thus, the military should hold the power. In September 1949, a Civilian Affairs Service-Kawthoolei or CAS-K, called a Kawthoolei Military Administration (KMA), was established. It was based on the postwar British Burma CAS (B) system, in which many Karen officers had served. Accordingly, Saw Ba U Gyi became the commander-in-chief. General Min Maung was renamed general officer in command and U Saw Lon as military secretary in the new KMA. All the previous civilian officials were given military titles to serve in the areas they were assigned. Several civil administrators became military officials without military experience, which caused casualties when they had to participate in battle. Some corrupted and misused their powers in the local areas they administered. S'Kaw Ler Taw opined that Kawthoolei Military Administration divided the leaders and demoralized many Karens, who decided to leave the movement and surrender to the Burmese government. Some of these Karens even offered their service to the government by revealing secret passages to the Karen areas.[61] As the events unfolded, by 1950, the KNU had lost all the territories they occupied in 1949, including their headquarters in Toungoo.

The Death of Saw Ba U Gyi and the Formation of Kawthoolei Governing Body (KGB)

The Civilian Affairs Service-Kawthoolei (CAS-K) military administrative system of the government seemed to be ineffective and caused the decline of the KNU movement. Alternatively, Professor Cady hypothesized another possible scenario. He said that many members of the European community at Rangoon believed that the Karens had been provoked into rebellion, and the Karen insurgents received encouragement from private British sources who were friendly to the Karen cause. However, the KNU's politically ambitious demands and their resort to overt violence denied them the support expected from many friends.[62] They considered the KNU's political demands unreasonable, and the violence of the KNDO destabilized the country.

Meanwhile, relations between U Nu's government and London improved. The Labour government spokesman refused to dictate to the Burma government how it should use arms purchased from Britain and insisted that the military mission was advisory and technical only.[63] In May 1949, a proposal surfaced that the United Kingdom, India, Pakistan, and Ceylon set up a coordinating committee at Rangoon. This group, functioning under the direction of the resident ambassadors, was to propose measures for aiding U Nu's government in restoring order. The Labour government decided in June to provide Burma with ten thousand rifles to replace those taken by mutineers, and it continued to resist Conservative pressure to make such aid conditional on Burmese concession to British interest or possible reaffiliation with the Commonwealth.[64]

In addition to military aid, the British government helped rebuild Burma's economy by distributing to British firms the sum of 10 million pounds for damages in Burma during the course of the war.[65] General Ne Win and Foreign Minister U E. Maung's visit to London and the United States in July and August 1949 resulted in both military and financial aid. After a series of negotiations, the government of Burma received a Commonwealth loan of 350 million rupees from New Delhi in December.[66] On September 13, 1950, Burma signed the Technical Aid Agreement with the United States, calling for expenditures during the current year of some 8 million dollars.[67] With these various aid programs, the Burmese government became well-equipped with resources to build up its armed forces with modern weaponry to launch attacks on its multicolored rebellious groups.

After recapturing all the previously Karen-occupied towns in lower Burma, government air raids started on Toungoo in January 1950. Then in February, the Karen lost Daik-U, Pyondasa, and Nyaunglaybin. By March 1950, the Karens withdrew from their headquarters in Toungoo. As they withdrew, the 2nd Brigade, formerly the Toungoo Brigade, set up headquarters at Pathichaung, milestone 13, from whence branched the roads to Thandaung and Mawchi. General headquarters moved to Mawchi, but chief of staff General Min Maung remained with the 2nd Brigade. Mawchi was not considered safe to set up a headquarters since the government forces had recaptured Loikaw and Bawlake, which were on Mawchi-Taunggyi Road. President Saw Ba U Gyi and some ministers proceeded to Papun to set up offices.[68]

The Karen Congress was held July 17–19, 1950, at Papun, where representatives from the delta, Toungoo, Papun, Thaton, Moulmein, Tenasserim, Karenni, and even Mon attended. Those at the congress included Saw San Key, S'Kaw Ler Taw, and Mika Rolly from the delta; General Min Maung, Saw Paul Paw, and Alfonzo A. Soe Myint from Toungoo; and Captain Toora Oo and Captain Aung Thaung from Nyaunglebin. On the meeting's first day, Saw Ba U Gyi explained three ways of gaining independence: by the government giving it voluntarily as a gift, by defeating the enemy through warfare, or by force of internal and international circumstances.[69]

During the next day's meeting, on July 18, a clash between the delta and Toungoo leaders ensued. The former wanted the reassignment of the KNU, but the military leaders in the Toungoo area wanted to continue with the emergency CAS-K. Delta leader Saw Sankey proposed the reassignment of the KNU, while A. Soe Myint, commander of the Lion Force Battalion of Thandaung-leythoo in northern Toungoo, strongly opposed it. After an intense argument, Saw Sankey withdrew his motion. The congress secretary S'Kaw Ler Taw opined that the goal of the congress failed because of the failure to re-establish the KNU. On the third day, the congress agreed on several matters, including the following:

1. The transfer of KNU headquarters from Mawchi to Papun,
2. The restructuring of the KAF Thaton Brigade into two brigades, west side of Salween as Thaton Brigade and east side of Salween as Papun Brigade (also Light Brigade) under the command of Brigadier Ta Ka Paw,
3. The development of political training courses,
4. The development of cooperative systems in the villages,
5. The appointment of Saw San Key as personal assistant to president Saw Ba U Gyi.[70]

After the congress, Saw Ba U Gyi delineated the following four principles of the Karen revolution:

For us, surrender is out of question,
The recognition of the Karen state must be complete
We shall retain our arms.
We shall decide our own political destiny.[71]

The information was sent to Kawthoolei Radio, which was temporarily stationed in Mawchi. For three days, from July 31 to August 2, 1950, Saw Ba U Gyi's legendary "four principles of the Karen Revolution" was broadcast in Karen, Burmese, and English languages. These four principles became Ba U Gyi's greatest legacy for successive Karen leaders to cling to as the policy for the Karens' resistance movement.[72]

Before he was able to implement or even explain the details of his four principles, Saw Ba U Gyi was killed along with his colleague, Saw Sankey, on August 12, 1950, by the Tatmadaw troops. They were on their way to the Thai border, camping near Toe Kaw Koe village, twenty-five miles from Kawkareik town. The Burmese army learned of Saw Ba U Gyi's movements through Karen informants living in that village. Saw Ba U Gyi and the men who died with him were on a mission to meet gunrunners to negotiate the purchase of arms and ammunition. The Burma Tatmadaw took Saw Ba U Gyi's body to Moulmein and put it on public display on August 14, where local and international journalists came to observe the deceased.[73] On August 16, at 7:30 am, Saw Ba U Gyi's body was taken by military boat and buried at sea.[74] Although there is no grave, every year on August 12, Karen communities around the world gather and celebrate their Karen national Martyr's Day, in honor of the death of their hero, Saw Ba U Gyi.[75]

In contrast to the Burmese government action, on August 23, 1950, former British governor Reginald Dorman-Smith remembered Saw Ba U Gyi in these words in *The Times*: "Saw Ba U Gyi was no terrorist . . . I, for one, cannot picture him enjoying the miseries and hardships of a rebellion. There must have been some deep impelling reason for his continued resistance. . . . The major tragedy is that Burma is losing her best potential leaders at far too rapid a rate."[76]

Saw Ba U Gyi's death left the Karens leaderless. To select his replacement, his wife, Mrs. Ba U Gyi (Monita Zan), and General Min Maung called an emergency meeting in Ler Kha Loo village in Mawchi on September 21, 1950. Karen leaders Pa'O Hla Pe from Thaton, J. Poo Nyo, Saw Paul Paw, Saw Po Nyaw, S'Kaw Ler Taw (delta), Captain Mika Rolly, Captain Htwe Kyaw, and Captain S. Thein attended the meeting. The presidency was offered to several, including Pa'O U Hla Pe, General Min Maung, and Mrs. Ba U Gyi (Monita Zan), but all refused for good reasons. Pa'O Hla Pe was in Shan state commanding the combining forces of Karen, Kachin, Karenni, and Pa'O troops and occupied Taungyi from August to December 1950.[77] Finally, J. Poo Nyo was nominated and accepted the presidency but resigned in a few days.[78]

The search continued. To resolve the matter, General Min Maung called a meeting on January 9, 1951, at Lumbu village near Toungoo. Unfortunately, the delta representatives were unable to attend due to the government troops recapturing the areas along the way to Papun. Because of the missing representatives, they decided not to elect a new president but to replace the leadership post with an executive committee called Kawthoolei Governing Body (KGB). It comprised six leaders of six military zones: Captain Saw Lon (Taungoo), Marshall Shwe (Nyaunglaybin), Pu Bwe Htaw or U Po Toe (Thaton), Saw Lorry Po Kee (Moulmein), S'Kaw Ler Taw (delta), and Captain Johnny Htoo (Takabaw zone).[79]

Here again, Pa'O Hla Pe was nominated as chair of the KGB, and since he was still in the Shan state, the information was sent by telegram. He refused and suggested they appoint General Min Maung. General Min Maung also refused, giving the reason that he was a military man with no knowledge of administrative affairs. Then he sent a telegram to Saw Hunter Tha Hmwe, who was still in the delta, to come to Papun and accept the chairmanship. Saw Hunter Tha Hmwe became the KGB executive committee chairman, adopting the traditional title of Kaw Kasa Hunter Tha Hmwe.[80]

The KGB headquarters was at Papun, but its chairman, Hunter Tha Hmwe, was in the delta region. When the KGB's first meeting was held on April 4, 1951, Hunter Tha Hmwe sent S'Kaw Ler Taw to represent him as the chairperson. The meeting resolutions included the declaration of KGB and the continuation of the military administration. The policy of Kawthoolei under the KGB government was, in S'Kaw Ler Taw's own words, "Nationalism based on Democracy in one word." Embracing their ancestors' ancient traditions, the KGB claimed that their policy was based on five major principles: Truth, Purity, Brotherhood, Co-operative Living, and Loyalty.[81]

It took almost eight months to replace Saw Ba U Gyi. Thus, the Karen revolution was without a real political leader to make key decisions. Due to a lack of strong political leadership and central coordination, major operations were poorly planned and executed. The KCB could not establish effective civil administration in the area they occupied. Although Papun was the capital of the KGB, the surrounding region that it shared with the border of Thailand was underdeveloped. Nevertheless, until 1951, the KGB still controlled the majority of Karens who resided in the countryside, in both the eastern hills and the delta region.

Unlike the eastern Karen hills, the delta had large villages with abundant food supplies and human resources for the Karens to fight for long-term success. The government, therefore, focused on recapturing Karen-controlled delta-area towns. In February 1952, Ne Win's Tatmadaw launched a major operation, bombing by planes and raiding by gunboats and tanks against the KAF's No. I Brigade under General Kaw Htoo at Kyaw Mya Than in the Tharrawaddy district sixty miles north of Rangoon. As one of the strongest KAF forces, the Karens' resistance was fierce and the government troops suffered. In retaliation, the Burmese Army burned Karen villages and destroyed paddy fields. Their scorched-earth tactics forced KAF general Kaw Htoo to order the main body of troops to pull back into the Pegu Yoma.[82]

Using the same strategy, the government launched offensive attacks to the southwest against the Kawthoolei Allied Forces No. 7 brigade in the Bassein district and the No. 2 brigade around Myaungmya. Like before, the KAF had initial success and captured several government tanks, but eventually KAF troops had to withdraw. Several leaders, including Saw Hunter Tha Hmwe and Mahn Ba Zan, fled for their lives.[83] The KAF troops retreated into the dense forest, some into Pago Yoma and some into Arakan Yoma, where the remote jungle and swampland prevented strangers like government troops from reaching.

The territorial losses in the delta were followed by mass surrender to the Burmese government. The Karen people living in the long-term war zone suffered too much to continue to support and supply the KAF troops. The corruption and the criminal actions of KAF commanding officers were additional reasons delta residents lost respect for KAF leaders. S'Kaw Ler Taw admitted that brigade commanders in the delta operated like warlords. Due to a lack of coordination and cooperation among the leaders, their military operations were not effective in fighting against government troops. Some KAF leaders left the movement and surrendered, including Bo Pu, commander of KAF's 2nd Brigade, along with some of the ranks who gave up to the Burmese forces along with their arms and weapons in late 1952.[84]

Like delta Karens, eastern area Karens also returned to the government, particularly educated Karens and ex-civil servants. In early 1953, the Lion Force, under Kawthoolei Allied Force's 2nd Brigade at Peinthilar, surrendered. The force's commander was Lieutenant Colonel Alphonso Pé (later A. Soe Myint). U Saw Lon and KGB members of the district went over with the Lion Force. The Highland Battalion, under the 4th Brigade led by commanding officer Lieutenant Colonel Nah Moo, also surrendered. The Highland Battalion's second in command, Major Bo Mya (later KNDO general), was unhappy with the situation. He and most of the officers and men returned to the 4th Brigade, where he became the battalion's commanding officer.

Since Saw Ba U Gyi's death, there were unsettled issues due to the lack of effective leadership. With Hunter Tha Hmwe, KGB head, still in the delta, S'Kaw Ler Taw had to manage on his behalf in the Papun headquarters. KAF commanders behaved like warlords and with local territories demarcated between them. Rivalries between the KNDOs and British-trained Karen Rifles sometimes led to armed clashes. Involvement in banditry was yet another problem. For example, the 1st Battalion, under Lieutenant Colonel Lynton (Lin Htin), which acted as a mobile force, held a group of university students from a train at Thaton for ransom.[85] The KNU's main resources of revenue also fell after government troops recaptured Thaton in May 1953 and Mawchi mines on November 22, 1953. Encountering these political, military, and economic problems, Karen leaders started to find better tactics for their revolution.

The Influence of Communism and the KNU's Second Phase Program

A political policy change started with Mahn Ba Zan, who developed relations with the CPB and signed an agreement with CPB politburo member Thakin Zin in May 1952 at Tharbaung, Bassein district. The so-called Zin-Zan agreement was initially to establish an effective cease-fire, a committee to discuss common problems, and a joint operations committee to coordinate future political and military campaigns.[86] After a series of meetings with CPB leaders, Mahn Ba Zan was inspired by Mao Zedong's leftist ideology of class characteristics. With increasing numbers of educated Karens, ex-civil officers, and career military officers surrendering, Mahn Ba Zan, Hunter Tha Hmwe, and their officers believed they could rely only on the working class. These leaders met at Weythaung village in the lower delta, on June 9, 1953, to strategize for the revolution. They agreed that the Kawthoolei military administration was ineffective and set about developing an effective revolutionary policy that would gain mass support.[87] Following the CPB model, they formed a new Karen National United Party (KNUP) as the vanguard party to take the political leadership role. The KNU, as the revolution's backbone, would remain as a mass organization. In September 1953, the KNUP was formally inaugurated at a conference at Gayetau village, Maubin district, and the delta KNUP cadre training classes began.[88]

For full-scale implementation of the new political policy, the KNU National Congress was held November 23-25, 1953, in Papun. As nominated by representatives, Saw Tha Din (S'Kaw Thu Kho) presided over the three-day congress.[89] There, the KNUP establishment was approved. The congress decided that the KGB administration would be dismantled, and a new KGB cabinet installed with almost all the same people. Hunter Tha Hmwe would serve as president with S'Kaw Ler Taw as vice president and head of foreign affairs.[90] Other major items from the congress included the release of a memorandum to the Thai government announcing the formation of the Kawthoolei Governing Body Cabinet. The congress also formally notified its neighbor that the KNU would be seeking United Nations recognition for a Kawthoolei Free State adjoining the Thai border.[91]

Before these leaders could implement their agendas, government forces raided Papun on December 8. Three Spitfire fighter aircraft, together in formation and singularly taking turns, launched rockets, dropped bombs, and strafed with machine cannon and machine guns until their ammunition was exhausted. The air raid lasted forty minutes.

(My brother and I, the author, when I was four years old were at school during the raid. The teacher sent us and other children to the trench and prayed for our safety.) The cause of the air raid was the Chinese Kuomintang (KMT) troops with whom the KNDO had made an alliance in 1952. In need of foreign aid, the KGB in Papun sent S'Kaw Ler Taw, Mika Rolly, and Saw Ohn Pe to meet with KMT General Li Mi. The KMT troops were in Monghsat in the northern Shan state, where an airstrip had been built that sported regular service for bringing arms and other supplies from Formosa (Taiwan). The KMT needed safe passage along the Salween River through the Karen area to cross over to Thailand, from whence they would go to Formosa. During the meeting, General Li Mi asked the Karen delegation to support the KMT troops passing through the Karenni state into Toungoo and the Thaton hills and to support the capture of Moulmein, which would open a way to the sea. They negotiated with the Karens and promised to help the Karens take Ye Lo Maing in Tenasserim and leave their weapons after crossing over into Thailand. General Li Mi offered to supply the KNU with small arms and ammunition immediately. The Karens agreed to these terms. Unfortunately, the Kuomintang did not live up to their promise.[92] The Burmese government chased out the KMT forces as they retreated. At the time of the air raid, there were Chinese KMTs in the jungles of eastern Papun, but they were unhurt.[93]

After the air raid, Papun was deserted for a few months. The Karens also lost Pathichaung on the Toungoo-Thandaung Road, along with Pasaung, Kemapyu, and Mawchi on the Taunggyi-Mawchi Road. Government forces set up outposts at Thandaung and at strategic points along the Toungoo-Mawchi Road. Meanwhile, KNU leaders prepared to reform the administration based on a new ideology. In 1954, relationships between the KNU and CPB progressed with more communication and better coordination. General Min Maung sent his military officers to CPB officials for cooperation in the anti-AFPFL government movement. Plans were discussed and programs for cooperation were drawn up.

In the delta, the vanguard party of the Karen revolution military, the KNUP led by Mahn Ba Zan, set up political platforms to improve contacts with farmers and workers from all nationalities, including the Mon, Karenni, Pa'O, and even the Burmans. Some admitted that their land reform programs and agricultural co-operatives in KNDO-controlled villages, where CPB and KNUP forces overlapped, were quite successful and that relations between KAF troops and local villagers improved. They even received support from local Burman villages.[94]

The Karen Revolutionary Council (KRC)

Preoccupied with the military maneuvering in the delta, Karen movement leader Hunter Tha Hmwe arrived at Papun, the headquarters in the eastern division in Karen hills in January 1955. Immediately on his arrival, he held a preliminary but informal meeting with leaders in the eastern Karen command, including Mrs. Ba U Gyi, General Min Maung, S'Kaw Ler Taw, Padoh Lorry Po Kee, Padoh We Re Gyaw, Padoh Mahn Thein Maung, Padoh Po Nyaw, and U Ohn Pe Nyunt.[95] These participants agreed to hold a Karen national congress to pursue Hunter Tha Hmwe's plans and reform ideas for the future revolution.

On January 15, 1955, the first national congress was held. All agreed to dismantle the Karen Governing Body and replace it with a new administration, the Karen Revolutionary Council (KRC). The old KGB was gone, and the new KRC came into existence with nominated representatives from all the KNU's military brigade districts in the delta and eastern divisions. Under Hunter Tha Hmwe's presidency, Mahn Ba Zan and General Min Maung became vice presidents 1 and 2. S'Kaw Ler Taw was named general secretary with Padoh Mahn Thein as deputy secretary. To settle unfinished issues, particularly the implementation of the administrative and military reforms and the selection of yet unfilled department heads, they decided to meet again on June 10, 1955.[96]

In the meantime, the Burmese government attacked Papun. On March 27, 1955, the capital city fell.[97] Hunter Tha Hmwe withdrew to Maw Ko, which was twenty miles away from Shwegyin town, and made it his headquarters. There, the KRC's first national congress was held on June 10, 1955. The KRC cabinet was fully established with the following leaders as heads of each department:

1. Saw Hunter Tha Hmwe, president and head of foreign affairs

2. Mahn Ba Zan, vice president and head of political affairs

3. General Min Maung, vice president and head of defense

4. S'Kaw Ler Taw, general secretary and head of administration

5. Mahn Thein Maung, deputy general secretary for administration

6. Padoh We Re Gyaw, head of home affairs

7. Mrs. Sankey, head of the communication department (the only woman in the KRC cabinet)

8. Padoh Su Maw Lwee, head of agriculture, forestry, and economic

9. Padoh Ba Htun, head of social welfare

10. Padoh Po Nyaw and Padoh Maw Re, head of finance

11. S'Kaw Wah Koh (Saw Po Chit), head of justice

In addition, for better coordination and cooperation among the executives, four committees, political, military, economic, and social, were also formed.[98] Hunter Tha Hmwe acclaimed the KRC's establishment as the "Second Phase Program" of the Karen nationalist movement. Following the plan, the KRC established three major camps.

1. The military headquarters was at Hsaw Bwe Der, a village off the Papun-Kyauk Hnyat road, and under the command of General Min Maung.

2. Kaw Kasa Hunter Tha Hmwe established residence at Hke Pah Htah, later called Say Baw Beh.

3. The third camp was west of Maw Ko, under the charge of S'Kaw Ler Taw and other KRC officials.[99]

Immediately after the congress, political training began with one hundred trainees. Wireless communication continued with the CPB. In late June, a wireless message from the CPB's office invited two KRC representatives to meet for future conversations. The KRC president sent S'Kaw Ler Taw and Padoh Su Maw Lwee to meet with the CPB executive committee at Kyaukkyi. At the meeting, both sides explained their agendas for future approaches to the revolution and agreed to call a meeting with all anti-Burmese government armed forces. The gathering was to be named "Unity Meeting of All Revolutionary Forces," and both sides agreed to share the expenses for the planned congress.[100]

Following the agreement in late June, Karen leaders invited various national resistance groups for said meeting. However, due to an aggressive attack near their headquarters, the CPB requested a postponement. They had to fight ten thousand Burmese government troops known as Operation Aung Marga. Finally, in March 1956, the KRC and CPB representatives met again in Shwegyin, but they agreed to delay discussions until the KNUP leaders, Mahn Ba Zan and Thakin Zin, were available. Near the end of March 1956, just a few days before Mahn Ba Zan arrived, the Mon, Pa'O, and Karenni leaders arrived at Say Baw Beh camp. These leaders previously worked with Saw Ba U Gyi and were willing to cooperate with the Karens. The meeting was held without CPB leaders. On April 4, 1956, the four nationalities signed an agreement to form the Democratic Nationalities United Front (DNUF). The four signatories were Mahn Ba Zan (Karen), Naing Tun Thein (Mon), Sayama Naw Thein Mya (Karenni), and Bo Khin (Pa'O) [101]

From the first KRC national congress, Karen nationalist movement leaders began to accommodate CPB's leftist ideology. The second KRC congress, held June 26–July 11, 1956, at the KRC's camp in Maw Ko in the Shwegyin district, turned the Karen revolution into a new epoch. The meeting had 150 participants, 80 Karen observers, and 70 KNU delegates, including several Mon, Pa'O, and Karenni representatives. Hunter Tha Hmwe, as KRC president, gave an opening address describing the effort of the KRC government in developing the economy, which included teak and mining businesses for the well-being of the people. He spoke of the village cooperative system in a very positive way, acknowledging the success of the KNUP's agrarian reforms. S'Kaw Ler Taw's speech detailed the seven-year Karen revolution journey. Mahn Ba Zan's message acclaimed the progress of the KNUP's Second Phase Program in the delta.[102]

Except for one or two members, the Karen Revolutionary Council's executive committee included the same people from the KRC's first national congress. The congress declared these four political goals:

1. For the Karens: To obtain an independent Karen state.

2. For the national minorities: To obtain independent states for each national group.

3. For the Union: To set up a new People's Democratic Federal Union based on the right of self-determination for every national minority.

4. For socialism: As the final goal, to march toward the establishment of a socialist state, which will provide peace and prosperity of human beings.[103]

Their main enemy, they claimed, was "imperialism and feudalism," and their immediate major target was the AFPFL government. The KRC declared that the working class was their "strength," but the peasants, who were the backbone of the revolution, would be their main source of strength. However, they must keep their "temporary alliances" with the intellectuals, government employees, businessmen, and national bourgeois. With these sources of strength, the four political goals would be obtained through armed struggle and agrarian revolution.[104]

After the congress, the KRC reorganized into four divisions: Kawthoolei People's Council, Kawthoolei People's Military Council, Kawthoolei People's Justice Court, and the Kawthoolei Administrative Body. The KRC government established special agendas in nine entities: political, national minorities, anti-government forces, economy, military, enemy territory, public affairs, religion, and foreign policy. In political matters, the Karens would look to the KNUP as the vanguard party and the KNU as the mass organization. Regarding the military, the Kawthoolei armed forces were restructured into three divisions—the Karen National Defence Organization (KNDO), the Kawthoolei People's Guerrilla Force (KPGF), and the Kawthoolei People's Liberation Army (KPLA).[105]

Without mentioning communism in any of the meeting minutes, all the terms and condition statements signified that the KRC's second congress transformed the KNU from so-called imperialist stooges into communist radicals. The newly elected executive committee, which the congress confirmed, was predominantly KNUP members dominating the KRC's supreme executive body. Tainted with Marxist and Leninist ideologies, these men campaigned in Karen camps to convert Karens to communism and the Karen freedom movement into a class struggle.

One could wonder why Karen leaders, almost all devout Christians, supported the KNUP's formation, which echoed leftist ideology. S'Kaw Ler Taw, KNUP's general secretary, explained that, in 1947, the Karen national organizations, the KNA, BKNA, KYO, and KCO, joined to form the KNU to forge national unity. But the foundation of the KNU was not firm and did not reach all levels of society. Therefore, "to reach the lowest level and to be deeply rooted amongst the Karen people we needed to form an elite party, [the KNUP]."[106] Interestingly, Mahn Ba Zan himself seemed to believe that his KNUP's approach was based on Jesus Christ's teaching. His son, Robert Zan, also a Karen freedom fighter, remembered a conversation with his father during which his father talked about his reliance on the Bible. When his father heard that Robert Zan was reading Marxism, Leninism, Stalinism, Maoism, and Darwinism, his father told him that, as a revolutionary, one should be equipped with both left and right political ideologies but choose only the ideas that would benefit the Karen revolution. Mahn Ba Zan warned his son to read the Bible, which he relied on as the best guiding principle in leading the Karen revolution. Referring to Luke 14:13, Mark 10:23, and Matthew 5:44, Mahn Ba Zan said, "Before Marxism and Leninism, Jesus Christ was the exemplary leader, teaching how to treat the poor and the enemy."[107] Unfolding events in the subsequent years would reveal the truth of these claims and the success and failure of the KNUP leaders.

Following the second KRC conference guidelines, training courses were conducted to equip local and regional officers with knowledge of the Second Phase Program. The first training course was in the Kyauk-kyi district, where one hundred participated. The majority represented the Nyaunglebin and Toungoo districts, with some coming from the Papun district. Mahn Ba Zan lectured on contemporary affairs and revolutionary strategies. S'Kaw Ler Taw discussed the Karen revolution's Second Phase Program. Mahn Sha Pale taught on the topics of party and agrarian policy, while Thra Pla Say reviewed the party organization for participants.

The first training session went well, but the second was not as successful. The second training session was in Meh Waing, some ten miles west of Narkokkhi, a village situated on the Bilin-Papun Road. Representatives from Thaton and Papun, including the 5th Brigade commander Bo Soe, Bo Ye Htoo, and Bo Soe Tint, attended the training. KRC executive members General Ohn Pe, Padoh Pu Ler Moo, Padoh Po Nyaw, and Mrs. Sankey were also among the two hundred attendees. During one training session, Mahn Shan Phale gave a talk on agrarian policy, describing the Kyaiktiyo monastery in Thaton in derogatory terms. He also talked about discrimination against women and criticized the abusive nature of men in the community. Since many of the 5th Brigade men were Buddhists, they felt insulted, and Bo Soe and his 5th Brigade delegates left the lecture. Mahn Ba Zan and Thra Pla Say tried to talk to them, but they refused to return. The conflict with the commander of the 5th Brigade, with more than twelve hundred men under arms, led to the cancellation of the remaining training courses.[108]

Unfortunately, prior to this conflict, Bo Soe had a long history of being a thorn in the Karen nationalist movement. He was a Burmese Buddhist without much enthusiasm for Karen nationhood. Approximately half of his followers were Burmese or Indian.[109] Unlike the earlier KNDOs, his men were heavily armed, and they lived off "territory," a selected area of land which was forced to yield a regular levy of blackmail. Travelers and merchants had to pay tolls and protection money. Several rackets, including opium smuggling, were given a trial to see if they might be profitable.[110]

There had also been clashes in the military, particularly between Bo Soe and General Tah Ka Paw, commander of No. 2 Division. These clashes led to the eventual murder of Tah Ka Paw by Bo Lin Htin. Bo Soe ordered Lin Htin to cross over to the east bank of Salween and kill Tah Ka Paw. Lin Htin had previously killed Wilkes, commanding officer of a battalion stationed along the Salween River between Kamamaung and Myaingale. Bo Soe accused Tah Ka Paw of planning a surrender. Tah Ka Paw's men under the 4th Brigade had suffered killings before. Only the 7th Brigade under Johnny Htoo escaped the atrocity. They were on the other side of the Dawna Range. The interfactional fighting was not only between Bo Soe's and Tah Ka Paw's men but also between Bo Soe's men. While playing peacemaker, Bo Soe himself was assassinated by his protégé Maung Bo, also called Myo Aung.[111] After Bo Soe's death, Lin Htin became commander of the 5th Brigade in 1957. This interfactional fighting greatly weakened the Karens. The Karens not only lost good leaders like Tah Ka Paw but also good junior leaders and many men.

Since Papun's fall, KRC headquarters operated from remote hill areas. Meetings were held in camps that government troops could not reach easily. Shortly after the KNUP's second national congress, members Mahn Sha Pale, Thra Pla Say, and Bo Tin Oo met with Thakin Zin, Thakin Mya, and Bo Pone Kyaw at Pana Kweeta in the Kyaukkyi district. They agreed to upgrade the joint operations committee of the Zin-Zan agreement into a new joint military committee. Consequently, maps were drawn for military operations.[112] On January 30, 1957, the joint CPB/Karen Peoples' Peace Forces attacked Pegu and Pyuntaza on the main Rangoon-Mandalay Road. By blowing up bridges and mining the railways, they halted all through traffic to Mandalay and Moulmein. For the next two years, such operations continued, particularly in the Sittang valley. After General Ne Win's takeover of power in November 1958, combined Karen/CPB forces attacked Paungdawthi, the railway stations at Daik-u and Nyaunglebin, and destroyed bridges along the rail lines.[113] These KNUP combined military operations upset the public, while the alliance with the radical leftists divided KNU leaders.

The major negative impact of the KNUP/CPB alliance could be found in the inner circle at the KRC's headquarters. Just after the KRC's second national congress in 1956, President Hunter Tha Hmwe tried to set up an underground Karen embassy in Bangkok to seek foreign aid. He sent a delegation, and he later joined them for a series of meetings with Thai, American, Central Intelligence Agency, South East Asia Treaty Organization, and KMT officials. He discovered in Thailand, however, that the KNU's adoption of the Second Phase Program was being treated with concern. The US containment policy perceived the declaration of a free state of Kawthoolei as a majestic communist strategy, orchestrated by China, to overrun Southeast Asia by declaring "autonomous nationality regions" across the southeast Asia mainland. Once he found out that western officials disapproved of the KNU's relationship with the CPB, Hunter Tha Hmwe warned the KRC, "Unless we change our line we will get no help. The quickest way to get help will be to drive out the left leaders."[114] Unfortunately, leftist leadership in the KNUP paid no attention to his request. Hunter Tha Hmwe's frustration with the KNUP grew. The relationships between the KNUP and the president became increasingly bitter by 1959.

The Defection of Hunter Tha Hmwe and the Change of Leadership

From the beginning of armed struggle in 1949 until 1956, the Kawthoolei state was divided into two divisions, the eastern division (the territory between Thailand and Rangoon-Mandalay railroad) and the delta division (the territory between Hlaing River and Bay of Bengal). A third division, the Pago Yoma division, was added on April 16, 1956. Until 1956, the eastern division was under the KNU central governing body's direct rule.

For military plan implementation, Brigadier General Ohn Pe arranged a meeting at Mei Sei Tah in 1957. All eastern division military commanders and KRC executive members attended. Unfortunately, due to an unexpected Burmese military operation in the area using ground infantry forces and bombs from three planes, they moved to another location called Yo Po Lait. Despite the invasion, the meeting sucessfully reached decisions. Accordingly, the eastern division was divided into three military zones: Zone 1 included 1st and 2nd Brigades under Colonel Truman, Zone 2 included 5th Brigade under Colonel Lin Htin, and Zone 3, 6th and 7th Brigades under Colonel Tin Oo (Tah Eh).[115]

In 1958, while the eastern division congress met in Mei Lay Leh, five government planes attacked the area, killing two nearby villagers. The leaders were transferred by boat to Tin Ban Wa (Paww Paw Tah), the 5th Brigade's headquarters. They soon had to move again, when they learned that Burmese government troops were heading towards the 5th Brigade. As predicted, government troops attacked, buildings were burned, and district administration officer Padoh Edward Bway Taw was killed. The eastern division moved again, settling in Mae Tha Loh, where the meeting was held, and leaders reelected. Until 1963, these leaders served in the same posts except for chief of staff General Min Maung, who was killed in a battle with government troops in 1961.

According to the common military structure deputy chief of staff Saw Kaw Htoo was to take General Min Maung's post. However, President Hunter Tha Hmwe assigned General Ohn Pe in charge of the combat operations center and General Kaw Htoo as commander of the eastern command in General Ohn Pe's place. From 1961 to 1963, the commander of the eastern command post changed rapidly from General Kaw Htoo to General Htaw Meh Pa to General Ba Shine.

While President Hunter Tha Hmwe was planning in the eastern division, Mahn Ba Zan's KNUP was also progressing with the leftist establishment in the delta. In the revolution's early days, the delta division was under General Sankey's charge, with seven brigades and twenty-five battalions. After the development of the Second Phase Program at the second KCR congress, the Karen People's Liberation Army (KPLA) was established, consisting of three brigades commanded by Bo Kyin Pe (Ko Doe). The congress also inaugurated the Kawthoolei People's Guerrilla Force (KPGF), formed with seven battalions in the delta. The delta division's president was Mahn Pan Htan (Saya Sein Han), with General Sein Hmone as commander and Colonel Mya Maung as deputy commander of the guerrilla force.[116]

Arrangements were made to hold the first KNUP congress in December 1958 with KNUP members from the delta and Pago Yoma invited to the eastern division headquarters at Say Baw Beh. Before the meeting began, however, they had to move to another location, when they learned that Burmese government troops were approaching. The meeting finally began in January 1959 at Po Tah village, where a draft constitution for the KNU was proposed with a new hierarchy. The KNUP was envisioned at the top as the "elite party of the Karen revolution," with an elected political and military council representing all KAF military brigade areas to supervise party policy administration. The KNU was deemed a "mass organization" and at the bottom of the organizational chart with the KRC as the central governing body for handling day-to-day affairs. Among other proposals at the meeting that President Hunter Tha Hmwe could not accept was the one that said, "For the peace of the country, the KNUP was to meet and negotiate with the AFPFL government." Acknowledging the congress's majority vote, Hunter Tha Hmwe had to accept it. At the end of the first day's meeting, Hunter Tha Hmwe told the crowd that they could continue as they desired, but he had to leave for his meeting at the 7th Brigade.[117] Apparently, that was a clear indication of the rift between the KRC president of the eastern division and the KNUP military from the delta and Yoma divisions.

Another matter that further divided Hunter Tha Hmwe from the KNUP was the National Democratic United Front (NDUF)'s formation in May 1959. As previously mentioned, in 1952, Thakin Zin and Mahn Ba Zan created the Zin-Zan agreement for joint military operations against the AFPFL. For that purpose, in April 1956, the DNUP formed with Mon, Pa'O, and Karenni resistance leaders, but CPB leaders were unable to attend due to the Tatmadaw's presence in the CPB's territory. In 1958, the Democratic Nationalities United Front (DNUF) ceased to exist with the surrender of Pa'O and Mon leaders. CPB leaders continued to discuss with Karen leaders how best to upgrade their cooperation. The negotiations were slow due to the reluctance of anti-communist Karen Christian leaders. The mass surrender of Pa'O and Mon forces, however, devastated KNU leaders and pushed them into a military alliance with the CPB. Thus, on May 19, 1959, the NDUF emerged after the representatives of the KNUP, New Mon State Party (NMSP), and CPB signed an agreement to establish a joint military alliance.[118] Mahn Ba Zan, S'Kaw Ler Taw, and General Kaw Htoo (head of the KNUP's military bureau) represented the KNU government, but President Hunter Tha Hmwe and several Karen Christian leaders rejected the formal relationship with the CPB. The disapproval seemingly had no effect on Mahn Ba Zan and the KNUP. As one of the signatories of the NDUP's formation, Mahn Ba Zan signed the agreement as the KNUP representative, not on behalf of the KNU.

After the formation of NDUF, the CPB and KNUP coordinated military operations across lower Burma quite successfully in the delta, strengthening Mahn Ba Zan's control over the Karen nationalist armed struggle. In January 1960, a two-hundred-strong delta Karen guerrilla force ambushed a train north of Moulmein, killing seventeen passengers including several police and government officials.[119] During this period, Burma was under General Ne Win's military caretaker government, and several insurgent forces surrendered after negotiation with the Tatmadaw. Just before transferring power back to U Nu's government, Ne Win's caretaker government secretly offered to meet with KNU leaders in Rangoon in early 1960. The initiative came from Brigadier Aung Gyi, the army vice chief of staff, who contacted the KNUP's delta president Bo Kyin Pe (Ko Doe) and the KAF's delta guerrilla force commander Mahn Mya Maung via letter in January.[120]

In early February 1960, General Kaw Htoo and S'Kaw Ler Taw flew by helicopter from Papun and joined Kyin Pe in Rangoon for peace talks with Tatmadaw leaders. On the Tatmadaw side were Aung Gyi, Aung Shwe, and the army's main spokesman, Colonel Maung Maung, whom the KNU briefly held in custody in 1949 in Toungoo. In addition, several junior officers were also present at these meetings, which lasted ten days. S'Kaw Ler Taw remembered their tone as "surprisingly conciliatory. They spoke as military officers about to hand over power." The Burmese leaders used expressions like "ending the civil war." But for the Karen delegation, the implication was clear that by making an agreement now, the KNU's position would be immeasurably strengthened before the politicians took over again in Rangoon. On the specific question of the Karen state, Tatmadaw leaders gave the impression of a willingness to redraw and redefine the territorial borders but maintained that they had no power to discuss constitutional matters. A new Karen state, they said, could be agreed upon only once the KNU had entered the legal fold. In the meantime, they were prepared to accept KAF troops and local KNDO militia, estimated by S'Kaw Ler Taw at twenty thousand men, into a reformed Karen Rifles and a special police reserve. The Karen delegation rejected this because the phrase "only after entering the legal fold implicated the surrender of the KNU" was considered by the Karen leaders as against Saw Ba U Gyi's four principles. In compromise, the Tatmadaw team suggested only the token handing over of "one gun and one pistol" as a symbolic gesture of reconciliation. After ten days of discussion, the peace talks ended without reaching any agreement, and the Karen delegation returned home.[121]

By this time, President Hunter Tha Hmwe, who initially supported his longtime colleague Mahn Ba Zan's KNUP, became extremely critical of the KNUP's Marxist-Leninist strategy. His public criticism against Mahn Ba Zan's NDUP began in April 1960 when he formed the Nationalist Liberation Alliance (NLA) with three nationalities, Karen, Shan, and Karenni. At the meeting, he explained that this new alliance would be quite different from the CPB-backed NDUF and would not contain a "Burman" component. His proposed plan included annexation of the entire east and southeast of Burma by simultaneous ethnic national uprisings. He was convinced that, by this tactic, they would get foreign support.[122] Apparently, after 1960, Hunter Tha Hmwe in the eastern division and Mahn Ba Zan's KNUP in the delta division made their own decisions in the areas they each controlled.

The third Kawthoolei national congress held in April 1963 at the Karen Revolutionary Council's Ka Hsaw Wah camp in the hills north of Papun was the first full KNU congress since the adoption of the Second Phase Program in 1956. But it became the first breakup in the Karen nationalist movement. During this time, the KNUP domination of the KNU organization in the delta was complete. With the arrival of KNUP delegates from the delta, the KNUP held its own second congress on the eve of the beginning of the third congress. Fifty-eight delegates attended, representing all the KNU districts in the delta, Pegu Yoma, and eastern division. In his eastern division, Hunter Tha Hmwe's faction was split, with half being KRC men and half being KNUP men. Before the congress started, Hunter Tha Hmwe foresaw his defeat because of the domination of the KNUP majority.

Despite the overwhelming KNUP delegation at the congress, Hunter Tha Hmwe proposed to repeal the ideological basis of the Second Phase Program and the abandonment of the KNU's "anti-imperialist line." He further insisted that the congress look to the west for allies and aid. Concerning the definition of the "enemy" of the Karen people, Hunter Tha Hmwe wanted the "Burmans," but the KNUP preferred "Burman Chauvinism," a term Hunter Tha Hmwe considered synonymous with communist ideology. For Hunter Tha Hmwe, all Burmans should be considered the enemy, but the KNUP argued that only the ruling Burmans were the enemy. The KNUP's policy was anti-imperialism based on the strength of the people. Thus, the revolution was a class struggle along with a nationalist movement. Hunter Tha Hmwe's policy was to fight for national aspiration first. Only after victory, plans for the people's welfare would follow. He argued that both left and right ideologies had weaknesses and strengths, but the anti-imperialist campaign would alienate wealthy people—and their support for the revolution was essential.[123] Except for a dozen KRC members, the remaining delegates, including Bo Mya, who later became the president of the KNU, rejected Hunter Tha Hmwe's proposal.[124] Citing the reason that his political principles and those of the KNUP were in opposite directions and beyond reconciliation, at the April 20 afternoon meeting Hunter Tha Hmwe spoke of dividing the governing areas into two. The eastern division would be under his KRC and the delta division under the KNUP. He left the meeting abruptly along with eleven members of the KRC, who followed him to the west and set up a camp in the area under the command of Colonel Lin Htin's 5th Brigade. S'Kaw Ler Taw of KNUP and Mika Rolly of Hunter Tha Hmwe's faction were sent to persuade Hunter Tha Hmwe's return, but he adamantly refused.[125]

General Ne Win's revolutionary government in Rangoon was aware of deep disagreements within KRC leadership and launched attacks during March and April. The split occurred in mid-April 1963, and the first offer for negotiation came on June 11. To discuss the proposals, the KNUP sent a delegation to talk with KRC leaders, still staying with Lin Htin near Thaton. At first, Hunter Tha Hmwe refused but later agreed to peace talks. On August 16, 1963, his KRC delegation of five, Saw Ba Htun, Saw We Re Kyaw, Colonel Truman, and Khun Ba Htwe arrived at Kyaukkyi town in Toungoo district, from whence they were to be airlifted to Rangoon for peace negotiations. At Kyaukkyi, a crowd of three thousand and performances of songs and dances welcomed them. They joined the worship service at Kyaukkyi Baptist Church, after which a military helicopter took them to Rangoon.[126] Hunter Tha Hmwe's KRC delegation explored Rangoon, which they had not seen since 1949. They additionally visited Karen churches and the Karen Theological Seminary in Insein.[127] During their Rangoon stay, a function was held for the KRC delegation at Alone Barrington School, at which the secretary of the Rangoon Karen Christian Association, Mahn Sein Hsay, joined the occasion, praying and singing hymns together with the delegation. KRC's minister, Saw Ba Htun, gave a talk, encouraging the Karen audience to wear Karen traditional dress, to keep united, and to strive for gaining the Karen state.[128]

Meanwhile, Mahn Ba Zan's KNUP delegation of eight was joined by NDUF members,[129] who arrived in Toungoo in September, on their way to the peace talks in Rangoon. They were greeted by two thousand people. Before they were given a lift to Rangoon, Mahn Ba Zan delivered two speeches in the Toungoo Karen Church about their political goals and the purpose for the peace talks. Burmese media acknowledged the delegation's arrival in Rangoon and reported on the entertainment of five hundred Karen ladies dancing and singing plus Christian pastors' praying for successful peaceful talks.[130] All these activities indicated imminent success for the peaceful agreement that the Karen community inside Burma wanted.

Optimism dwindled as the KNUP and NDUF finished within three months and left without agreement. However, the KRC leaders continued the talks, and a preliminary agreement was reached for a ceasefire and establishment of a war-free zone. The Burmese newspaper *Kyaymon* (*The Mirror*) reported on February 28, 1964, that the ceasefire agreement was quite effective. Commander Lin Htin and his staff members, Bo Aye, Shwe Aue, Bo Jolay, Major Myo Wai, Bo Wai Htoo, and Saw Maung Aye of the 5th Brigade, terminated all their military actions. After six months of negotiations, the final peace treaty was signed on March 12, 1964. The KRC agreed to drop demands for the right of secession. In return, General Ne Win's revolutionary council government agreed to title the Karen state by the nationalist name Kawthoolei. Additionally, he agreed to introduce machinery whereby the controversial proposal to enlarge Kawthoolei to include the Karen-majority areas of the Irrawaddy and Tenasserim division could be considered. Furthermore, to safeguard the interest of Karens living outside these areas, KRC officials would now be appointed to sit on the revolutionary council's security and administrative committee in each district. And the KRC would take part in writing Burma's new constitution. The government appeared to make a significant number of concessions to the Karen cause. Although it was short-lived, journalist Martin Smith was correct in claiming "it was the only political settlement ever agreed between the Ne Win's regime and any of Burma's insurgent organizations."[131]

After signing the peace treaty, Hunter Tha Hmwe delivered a speech in the Karen language on the Burma Broadcasting Service radio station on March 22. In his opening speech, he praised God for his fifteen-year journey in the Karen revolution. Then, he gave his analysis on the political strategy and leadership during those years. He divided the Karen revolution into four phases: 1949–1952 (pro-west or rightist), 1952–1960 (leftist), 1961–1964 (God's path based on the Old Testament), and from 1964 onward to Christ's path by perfecting God's path. He stressed that the first period of the pro-west policy was not God's path, and thus, Saw Ba U Gyi and San Key were killed on their way to get aid from the westerners. Neither the attempt to get aid from the Chinese Kuomintang nor his effort to build an embassy in Bangkok to get support from the west were God's path because they led only to misunderstanding and conflict among leaders. Hunter Tha Hmwe continued that the second phase, the leftist program from 1953 to 1960, was worse than the rightist phase. Initially, the program appeared to be good, but eventually abuse of power by some leaders such as seizing people's lands by force created suffering and dissension.[132]

With "rightist and leftist eccentricities" dividing the KNU leaders in the past, Hunter Tha Hmwe referred to the Bible as the only way to peace. He claimed the KRC had been following "God's path" since 1960, and the Old Testament had shown the way to "the Karen national revolution," while the New Testament had shown the way to live our life. He proposed an analogy by comparing Aung San who had led the Burmese national revolution and Ne Win who was now carrying out the social revolution.[133] A few weeks later, he went further, declaring full confidence in the Burmese Way to Socialism, and added, "This program is not something new to us. We Karens have practiced this kind of program since the days of our ancestors."[134]

The peace treaty signing was celebrated as a successful event. Only a handful of senior KNUs, like KRC ministers Saw Ba Htun and Padoh We Re Kyaw and military commanders General Ohn Pe, Colonel

Lin Htin, and Colonel Truman, followed the agreement. Less than 10 percent of all Karen forces are estimated to have surrendered. In fact, the agreement was short-lived. In February, just before the peace treaty signing, KRC troops attacked KNUP headquarters at Kaypu village north of Papun. The raid claimed the lives of thirteen KNUP followers, including Ohn Pe Nyunt and early members of KNDO. The KNUP/ KAF combined troops led by Bo Mya retaliated and attacked the area near Thaton, which was under Lin Htin's control. They burned down a number of villages.[135] Regrettably, Ne Win's government made no progress on constitutional changes as agreed to in the treaty. A few months later, KRC supporters returned to their old camps in the hills. Hunter Tha Hmwe himself sent Mika Rolly back to resume contact with the KNU and his former insurgent allies.[136]

Hunter Tha Hmwe's departure from the eastern division paved the way for General Bo Mya to be the Karen freedom movement's future leader. Immediately after Hunter Tha Hmwe left the Ka Hsaw Wah congress in 1963, the rest of the forty delegates continued the meeting and installed a new cabinet, with Mahn Ba Zan as president, General Kaw Htoo as vice president, S'Kaw Ler Taw as secretary, and two assistant secretaries, Bo Kyi Pe (Ko Doe) and General Mya Maung. General Bo Mya was designated as military commander of the eastern division.

During 1964, General Mya began his own military reorganization of the eastern division. He appointed a number of hill Karens, such as Colonel Taw Hla and Saw Gladstone, to senior positions. In April 1965, he called a meeting to explain the problems and difficulties of the revolution. He proposed strategies and policies related to the revolution and warned his leadership team to be careful using political terms, particularly the "socialist" political line. Since he was told that the decision for such a proposal could be determined only at the national congress, he tried to contact KNUP chairman Mahn Ba Zan and ask him to call a national congress. Unhappy with Mahn Ba Zan's long delay in taking action, General Mya held a meeting of the eastern division without the KNUP leaders and formed a new Karen National Liberation Council (KNLC).[137] Without elections, he filled senior administrative posts with two anti-communist hill Karen policemen, Saw Po Han and Benny Htoo, as minister of justice and minister of defense. Surprisingly, KNUP chairman Mahn Ba Zan and a party of four other senior KNUP officials crossed over and joined the new KNLC. In July 1967, Mahn Ba Zan sent his resignation letter to the KNUP, declaring he was to achieve national unity with the KNLC.[138] This action completed the design of a new era of the Karen nationalist movement under General Bo Mya's leadership.

General Bo Mya and the Renaissance of the KNU

The Karen revolution during the 1960s and 1970s revealed a clear picture of the power struggle between Karen leaders in two major political arenas—the western division (delta) with a pro-communist leaning and the anti-communist eastern division. Until 1963, Bo Mya showed pro-leftist leanings by siding with Mahn Ba Zan and KNUP. However, later in his conversation with Martin Smith, he claimed, "We, as a nation that believe in God, consider communism as Satan's tool."[139] Bo Mya's change of political leaning, according to some colleagues, was due to his conversion to Christianity after he married a Seventh-day Adventist Karen woman. Smith further claimed that, of all the KNU's predominantly Christian leaders, Bo Mya's political statements were the most deeply filled with reference to Christianity. The situation that convinced Bo Mya to abandon the KNUP's leftist stance stemmed from his meetings with political dissidents who tried to escape from General Ne Win's crackdown after his coup in March 1962. Those who came to Bo Mya's general headquarters talked openly about their anti-communist approach and positively about the pro-democracy movement. Among others, former vice chief of staff of the Burma Army, Brigadier General Saw Kyar Doe, who fled Burma and met with Bo Mya in 1965, urged the KNU to sever all associations with the communists.[140]

The introduction of General Ne Win's Burmese Way to Socialism after the coup in 1962 facilitated Bo Mya's rise to power. The nationalization of all economic sectors resulted in a shortage of essential goods inside Burma, making black-market trade the only source of supply. All kinds of consumer goods, textiles, machinery, spare parts for vehicles, and even medicines were smuggled illegally into the country from neighboring countries, especially from Thailand. From Burma, jade, rubies, teak, minerals, and cattle were smuggled out. From 1963, black-market trade with Thailand thrived, particularly along the KNU-controlled Thai-Burma border, which provided fast access to Moulmein and the delta. Bo Mya set up a series of toll gates through which goods were transported. The first was in Phalu, south of Mae Sot in 1964, in the 6th Brigade area. Soon, another gate at Wangkha in the 7th brigade area north of Mae Sot followed.[141] Like the Karens, the Mon, Karenni, and Shan rebels also set up toll gates along the Thai-Burma border of 1,304 miles, but Bo Mya's Wangkha seemed most profitable. After a few years, the daily taxes collected at Wangkha alone reached the sum of one hundred thousand Thai baht. Since the tax was collected at the rate of 5 to 10 percent on incoming and outgoing merchandise, the circulation per day at Wangkha was estimated between one to two million baht.[142] Meanwhile, the food and goods shortage inside Burma led to unrest in Rangoon in 1974. The government could not take serious action to halt the border trade. A scholar correctly claimed that although Burma's government "finds the black market troublesome, it recognises Burma's need for it."[143]

The Tatmadaw's preoccupation with the war against the CPB in central and northeast Burma allowed Bo Mya's eastern division to exploit the border black market. Thai authorities did not hinder Karen rebel business. Facing threats from Mao's Chinese communism and the impact of the Vietnam War, Thai authorities tolerated the Karen rebels. They viewed the Karens as a Foreign Legion, guarding their borders and preventing links between the Burmese and the Thai communists. The growing border trade provided Bo Mya ample resources to purchase US arms, ammunition, and other supplies. The rag-tag Karen guerrillas started to look almost like a regular army with smart uniforms, steel helmets, and officers' insignia.[144] Black-market trade was one of the major catalysts in promoting Bo Mya to emerge as the most powerful field commander of the Karen revolution.

Fully furnished with updated weaponry, the 6th and 7th brigades in the eastern hills became very strong through 1965. Another advantage was that all the original generals were gone. The original KNU commander-in-chief, General Min Maung, had died in action in 1961. General Ohn Pe went along with Hunter Tha Hmwe and surrendered in 1964. Without other strong military rivals, General Bo Mya's road was clear to challenge the KNUP's leaders. He quickly took advantage of the situation. As a first step, he convened a meeting with eastern division leaders and KNUP leaders where he explained his new policy for the Karen revolution. Unfortunately, his proposed amendment for political terms was not implemented. Then, in the beginning of 1966, he ordered that all KNUP troops and officials stationed in the eastern division leave immediately and transfer back to the KNUP's main base in the delta and Pegu Yoma.[145] The ultimatum from the eastern division commander left no choice for the KNUP leaders, but a new KNUP general headquarters was set up immediately at the foothills of southern Pegu Yoma, while maintaining a mobile KNUP force in the hills above Kyaukkyi.

After the KNUP's departure, Bo Mya moved by setting up a new political administration called the Karen National Liberation Council (KNLC), filling all the senior official positions with anti-communist hill

Karens. The KNU's military wing was also renamed the Karen National Liberation Army (KNLA).[146]

Initially, the KNLC emerged only as the KNUP's rival governing entity. But soon, Bo Mya overpowered the KNUP, once Mahn Ba Zan returned to the eastern headquarters. In 1968, despite ideological differences, Bo Mya and Mahn Ba Zan agreed to establish a new governing body called the Karen National United Front (KNUF) at To Do Plaw on the northern Moei River. As claimed by their KNLA representative, Colonel Marvel, the original idea was to reconcile their differences into a temporary front until they could agree to a future path.[147] Later in 1985, the KNU's education department head, Saw Ba Lone, explained the situation to Martin Smith: "After 20 years we found we had to use the simplest system to approach our people. If the political discussion was too complex, our people could not always understand. Especially we found the CPB-KNUP discussion had not worked. The traditions and culture of the Karen people are very simple. Saw Ba U Gyi recognized this. His four principles are based upon the concept of national unity."[148]

Among many important decisions, the agreement to return to a political platform based on Saw Ba U Gyi's four principles of the Karen revolution was most remarkable. The KNUF's decision to maintain the KNUP's anti-imperialist and anti-feudalist line was rejected by several KNLC leaders including defense minister Benny Htoo.[149]

Mahn Ba Zan became KNUF chair, and Bo Mya was named KNLA chief of staff. Although the military remained firmly under Bo Mya's control, KNUP leaders held important administration positions and began to work on the reformation of the KNU. From that time, the name KNU, Karen National Union, reemerged in the Karen revolution policy documents. According to the new arrangement, there were seven administrative districts: Thaton, Toungoo, Nyaunglebin, Tavoy-Mergui, Dooplaya, Pa'an, and Papun, with economic, agricultural, forestry, mineral, health, and education departments in each. In theory, these were centralized with each reporting to the KNU's general headquarters on the northern Moei River. But in practice, especially in finance, each had to learn to be self-sufficient.

Like the reforms in administration, the KNLA was reorganized with the five main brigade areas: No. 1, Thaton; No. 2, Toungoo; No. 3, Nyaunglebin; No. 6, Dooplaya; and No. 7, Paan with regular KNLA units and KNDO village militia in each. In addition, several special battalions under Bo Mya's personal control were set up: No. 20 in Papun district; No. 101 at the important trading post of Kawamura; and No. 10

in Tavoy-Mergui, which had previously been a disputed area between the KNUP 6th brigade and various local Karen militia. With an army that grew to ten thousand well-armed combatants, the new KNU movement in the east made a decisive entrance into insurgent politics in the country.[150]

The new KNUF movement, with its impressive military strongholds along the Thai border, attracted other anti-government forces, including former Prime Minister U Nu, who formed the Parliamentary Democratic Party (PDP) to overthrow General Ne Win by force. U Nu was General Ne Win's prisoner from 1962 to 1966, but upon release, he formed the PDP while in London on August 29, 1969.[151] Having knowledge of the KNUF's territorial control in the area for operations deep into Burma, U Nu met with Mahn Ba Zan and Bo Mya in Bangkok during 1969 and 1970. U Nu and U Law Yone's anti-communist approach gained support of the Karens and the National Mon State Party. On May 25, 1970, the three set up a united front identified as the National United Liberation Front (NULF) to fight Ne Win's Rangoon-based military government.[152] By joining the NULF, the Mons had broken away from the leftist NDUF.

The NULF cooperation agreement was signed in Bangkok by U Nu for the PDP, Mahn Ba Zan for the KNU, and Nai Shw Kyin for the NMSP. The alliance was short-lived due to the Mons' exit, after U Nu refused their demand for the right of secession. Karen leaders resolved to abandon the NULF at their ninth KNU congress. Nevertheless, the KNUF won short-term benefits from this alliance, including a down payment of four million Thai baht from the PDP and the promise of arms supplies to follow. The most gratifying aspect of the NULF to Karen leaders was the first indication, after twenty years of harsh warfare, of genuine international recognition for their largely forgotten struggle. They were invited to open a liaison office in Bangkok, and during 1970–1973, a KNUF team headed by Colonel Marvel worked openly in the city.[153]

Meanwhile, in Pegu Yoma, the KNUP cooperated closely with the CPB, but almost all CPB units in Henzada in the delta region eventually surrendered. On October 9, 1969, S'Kaw Ler Taw, KNUP general secretary, met with Thakin Zin and Bo Kyin Pe in the Pegu Yomas to settle these differences. Although the KNUP acknowledged the Red Flags as a true revolutionary force, they accused the CPB of negligence in its attention to building the NDUF. Particularly, the KNUP emphasized the fact that the revolution in Burma should be conducted under proletariat leadership. However, that did not mean that the NDUF, the Karens, or any other minority people would accept the CPB's leadership. According to KNUP general secretary S'Kaw Ler Taw, the KNUP sent three secret delegations to China in 1968–1969 to study Maoist ideology and to investigate developments in communist China. This action was in response to many leaders' growing doubts about the CPB. During these visits, they stood by their basic principle of keeping the KNU's demand for self-determination, which was the common goal of other minorities joining the National Democratic United Front (NDUF). The purpose of these preliminary teams, the KNUP claimed, was to prepare the way for the KNUP delegation led by S'kaw Ler Taw. They planned to talk with Chinese officials and CPB leaders including their former Kachin ally, Naw Seng, who at that time led the resistance movement from China.[154]

The CPB's policy toward ethnic nationalities was first discussed with Than Tun shortly before his death in 1968. CPB leaders passed a new agreement at their meeting in the Pegu Yomas on January 21, 1971. In it, Thakin Zin declared a new union would be based on equality after the national democratic revolution was completed and the people's common enemy, Ne Win's military regime, was overthrown. The exact details of the system would have to be worked out after victory, but in principle, the CPB agreed to these goals:

1. The Burmans shall have a separate state like the Kachin, Karen, Kayah, Chin, Shan and others;
2. The New Union of the Socialist Republic of Burma shall be voluntarily established from the states of the nationalities;
3. There shall be state governments and the central federal government.[155]

Meanwhile, in 1969, Mahn Ba Zan resigned from his chairmanship in both the KNUP and NDUF. He affirmed that by this time, there were two organizations with two different policies in the Karen revolution.[156] In early 1970, the NDUF had disintegrated, but the KNUP continued to cooperate with the CPB. In their efforts to get Chinese aid, in December 1970, the KNUP sent a thirty-seven-man delegation, known as the Dawna team, to CPB headquarters in the northeast. Due to battles with Burmese government troops, the team finally arrived at Panghsang, the CPB's new headquarters on the Chinese border, in October 1973. The vice chairman of CPB, Thakin Ba Thein Tin, gave S'Kaw Ler Taw and the Shan leaders a lavish dinner party, telling them that the Chinese Communist Party (CCP) was already aware of their mission.

In mid-December 1973, the team crossed into China and, upon S'Kaw Ler Taw's request, a conference was set up with CCP officials at Sumao province. During these meetings, the CCP clarified that they gave full military support to the CPB, recognizing it as the only legal workers' party in Burma. Thus, any aid or help the KNUP wanted must be requested through the CPB. Ba Thein Tin promised to provide everything they needed, on condition that they accept the CPB's political leadership. S'Kaw Ler Taw reminded Ba Thein Tin of the agreement between the KNUP and CPB's Thakin Zin in 1968, but Ba Thein Tin and the leaders at Panghsang all denied any knowledge of the treaty.[157]

The KNUP refused to accept the terms offered by the CPB and returned, carrying back some AK-47s and other rifles given to them. After detouring through the northern Shan state war zone for over a year, the team arrived back in May 1975, where they discovered that the KNUP base in Pegu Yoma had collapsed. During the absence of S'Kaw Ler Taw and his team, government troops escalated their attacks in the KNUP-CPB bases in the delta and Pago Yoma. The Tamadaw's *Pyat lay Pyat* (Four Cuts), a counterinsurgency program designed to cut the four main links (food, funds, intelligence, and recruits) between insurgents and families, had proven devastatingly effective. The CPB-KNUP troops fled from their base. KNUP chairman Kaw Htoo died from heart disease in 1972, and his chosen successor, Bo Kyin Pe, was killed in action. The Burmese government captured two members of the KNUP central committee, Saw Tun Aye and Saw Mya Yin. The fatal blow was the loss of Saw Jack,[158] who was killed in an ambush near Ngaputaw. The last remnants of KNUP units eventually evacuated to the eastern mountains. Beginning with 600 men under arms at the beginning of the final offensive, just over 100 KPLA soldiers made the final journey into the Nyaunglebin hills. They were united with another 150 KNUP troops and officers, including Bo San Lin and S'Kaw Ler Taw, who returned from China in May 1975.[159]

The KNUF headquarters in the west ceased to exist while Bo Mya's bases along the Thai border became important meeting points for arms dealers and traders. His bases at Wangkha, Phalu, Maw Po Kay, and Three Pagoda Pass secured the towns along with clusters of villages scattered in the forest around the KNLA defense lines. The Karen leaders decided to reuse the name Karen National Union and draw a new KNU constitution. However, it was only when the ninth KNU congress convened in September 1974 at Bee Hee Lu on the Moei River that new KNUF reforms were officially sanctioned. In the first of a new ten-article list on the aims and objectives of the KNU, the need for a Karen

Vanguard Party or the KNUP was dropped: "The KNU is the sole organ for the development of the Karen national cause, the elite of the Karen national revolution. The KNU is the highest organ for all Karen people and represents all Karen people."[160]

The KNU's aim was reaffirmed as a "national democratic revolution" and among others, article 4 stated that "patriotism is our sole ideology, We will never accept dogmatism." The national congress would be the KNU's supreme legislative body and would elect the KNU president, the general secretary, their deputies, and a ruling central committee of twenty-five persons. Four administrative departments were set up with the party organization under the KNU president. There would be standing departments for justice and the military. A sixteen-member central executive committee would provide day-to-day administration.[161]

The reform process continued in 1975, when the last KNUP headquarters collapsed and the KPLA remnants came to KNLA territory in the east. With the unhappy news brought by S'Kaw Ler Taw, all KNUP survivors decided to dissolve the KNUP and incorporate with the KNU. To accommodate the KNUP's experienced party leaders, the KNU central committee increased to thirty-three members. Some were given senior positions: Mya Maung as mining minister, Soe Aung as agriculture minister, S'Kaw Ler Taw as propaganda chief, and San Lin as vice president.[162] During this period, Bo Mya made an important move, calling a meeting on May 10, 1976, at the KNU's new general headquarters at Manerplaw. The attendance of thirteen insurgent groups set the record as the largest meeting of insurgent leaders ever held. As a result, the KNU became a founding member of the National Democratic Front (NDF) with eight other nationality forces.[163] In 1988, the NDF became the only ethnic minority front to have a significant impact on the course of the civil war in Burma. Manerplaw thus became the hub of both the military and political democracy movements. However, at that moment in 1976, the NDF was not their priority since Bo Mya and the KNU leaders were preoccupied with their own political reforms and movement for the Karen revolution's third phase.

The third phase movement appeared to be the change in leadership of the KNU. Despite apparent cooperation, Bo Mya was uncomfortable with Mahn Ba Zan's political terms. Although Mahn Ba Zan had clearly dropped his intention of moving on to Mao's second stage of a people's democracy by the 1970s, he publicly praised the Chinese government's high-priority support for minority rights. He expressed hope that Burma's minorities might win future Chinese political support. He saw an emerging triangular conflict between the CPB, the Rangoon government, and the national minorities. He warned that the KNU would ally with whichever side accepted the essentials of the KNU-NDF's program.[164]

That was unacceptable to Bo Mya. Contradicting this interpretation, he now insisted that a clause in the KNU's 1974 interim period policy documents that asserted "any country" could give aid to the KNU be amended to specify that the KNU would accept aid only from capitalist nations. An emergency central committee meeting was called at Bo Mya's house near Manerplaw on August 10, 1976. A day-long argument continued, which concluded with the resignation of Mahn Ba Zan in which he accepted the role of honorary KNU adviser. Bo Mya, the KNLA chief of staff, became the president. In addition, he assumed two other portfolios of ministers of foreign affairs and defense.[165] The new leadership with their policy change ushered in a new era of Karen revolution.

By 1978, Bo Mya exhibited his true anti-communist stand. A platoon of ex-KNUP soldiers from the 14th battalion, led by Saw Paul, defected from the KNLA to join the CPB. They were allowed to pass through territory controlled by a left-wing faction of the Karen National People's Party on its way north. This enraged Bo Mya so much that he ordered the battalion's immediate disbanding and sent KNLA troops into the Kayah state to help KNPP leadership quell the pro-CPB movement.[166] In this scenario, Bo Mya simultaneously displayed his strong anti-communist policy and staged his absolute domination of the KNU movement.

The Imminent End of the Karen Revolution

The Karen political organization, the KNU, and its military wing, the KNDO, began the revolution against the AFPFL government in 1949 when peaceful negotiations failed. During the movement, the name Karen National Union was often overshadowed by successive political organizations. When Bo Mya came into power, he resuscitated the name of the original political organization, the KNU. The original military arm ceased to exist, and the KNLA emerged in its stead. Unlike the initial state of the movement, where the political and military held different portfolios, Bo Mya assumed both roles as president of the KNU and commander-in-chief of the KNLA. Mahn Ba Zan's death in 1982 left Bo Mya with all power to conduct the affairs of the KNU "liberated Karen State" until he stepped down as president in 2000.

Bo Mya's anti-communist policy relieved Thai fears about its western border where the threat of the Communist Party of Thailand was strong. Having right-wing Karen leaders with KNLA forces along its western border, the Thai government closed its eyes to Bo Mya's cross-border trading businesses. From his general headquarters at Manerplaw near the junction of the Moei and Salween rivers, Bo Mya made political decisions, most of the time, with his closest advisers in a five-man standing committee. Noticeably, the KNU under Bo Mya's leadership was strongest in the 1970s and 1980s, due to monopolizing black-market trade on the Burma-Thailand border.

Up to 1984, Bo Mya ruled his "liberated Kawthoolei State" stretching from the Maw Daung Pass to the Toungoo hills. He established KNU government departments, hospitals, clinics, and hundreds of village schools that served seven main KNU administrative districts. These included five high schools in which most of the teachers were university graduates, including the children of KNU veterans, secretly brought up by relatives in towns inside Burma. Eventually, these high schools were forcibly moved to refugee camps in Thailand. The main medium of education was S'gaw Karen, but in the valleys to the west, Pwo Karen was used for the Pwo villagers. Burmese was also taught alongside English and Thai as a "foreign language."[167]

The KNLA operated as a parallel administration inside Kawthoolei. In several areas, it was the real administration, relaying messages and making quick day-to-day decisions depending on the state of fighting. In the secure rear areas, a string of permanent KNLA strongholds were built in strategic military positions, usually close to forest trade roads leading towards the Thai border. The traders themselves, amongst whom were agents of the Burmese military intelligence services traveling in disguise, were kept at a safe distance. In these KNLA bases, Karen nationalist festivals and holidays were celebrated: Revolution Day (January 31), KNU Day (February 5), and Martyr's Day (August 12). The camps came alive with military parades, traditional Don dancing, and theater performance in Karen national costumes.[168]

At all KNU bases, there were churches and the strong influence of Christianity among senior KNU leadership. Virtually everyone on the KNU central committee was a practicing Baptist. Of the others, most were Seventh-day Adventists, including Bo Mya and his assistant, Dr. Marta. Even so-called Buddhists, like Vice President San Lin, took full part in the regular Christian festivals and celebrations. The predominance of Christian leaders was also reflected in the district administrations. A Buddhist monk, Mahn Htila, who was one of the senior KNU administrators, announced his intention to convert to Christianity. However, at the village or township level, most officials were

Buddhists or animists. In the military, Buddhist recruits were in the majority, and many frontline KNLA units were entirely Buddhist or Buddhist-animists.[169]

Many of Bo Mya's pronouncements became increasingly interwoven with Christian sentiment, and the KNU judicial system revealed a distinctly Old Testament view of Christian morality. There were strict prohibitions against alcohol and premarital sex. In theory, the death penalty for adultery existed, though this was not a modern imposition. Unlike their neighboring hill peoples in the region, most Karen subgroups and animists have traditionally kept strict intra-village sexual mores. Freedom of religion is, however, one of the most important articles of KNU faith. Accordingly, there were Buddhist temples or shrines and even Muslim mosques in KNU territory. The Christian churches mostly operated independently of the KNU. Despite obvious difficulties, churches tried to work on both sides of the battle lines, sending Karen missionaries trained at Bible schools in Kawthoolei throughout southeast Burma.[170]

The surrender of several hundred of the Communist Party of Thailand's army, on December 27, 1982, caused a fatal blow to Bo Mya's Kawthoolei Liberated State. With the communist threat over, the crucial role that the Karens, Mons, and other ethnic groups from Burma had played for Thailand security also came to an end. Taking advantage of the new situation, Ne Win's government launched a massive operation against Karen camps in early 1984. After a few days of fierce fighting, Mae Tha Waw, a Karen stronghold along the Moei River, fell on January 28. The operation continued to Maw Pokay, Klerday, Wangkha, Phalu, and other camps.[171] For the first time in history, the Burmese government directly controlled a portion of the Thai border.

The Burmese foothold attained in KNU territory led them to turn their attention to severing financial ties, supply lines, and KNU connections to the local civilian population. This was part of continuing a decades-long policy of the Four Cuts. Unlike the Four Cuts campaign in central Burma, the Four Cuts campaign in southeast Burma during the years of 1984–1990 was even more brutal as "the *Tatmadaw* behaved like a marauding, conquering army. It was branded as racial cleansing as there was a definite racial focus in how the attacks were organized. The attacks were strongly ethnic in character and were carried out by predominantly Burman officers against Karen, Karenni and Mon villagers."[172] Because of the 1975 Four Cuts campaign, more than two thousand Karens from the Toungoo, Nyaunglebin, and Thaton districts crossed over the Salween River, seeking refuge at a place called Pha

Leh (meaning "wide space"), which is in Thailand's Mae Sariang township near the Burma border. A group of Christian missionaries looked after these refugees, and a committee called the Refugee Committee was formed with Bo Mya, Pu Ler Say, Pu Benny Gyaw (later married to the widow of Saw Ba U Gyi), Pu Marble, Pu Kor Htoo, Pu Yo Shu, and Pastor Robert. Other support also came from the Catholic Church of Thailand, Thai Baptist Mission Fellowship, and World Vision. The camp moved several times, from Pha Leh to U Da Hta in 1977, then in 1979 to Phoo Mya Lu. Between 1980 and 1983, the Swedish Pentecostal Church headed by Rev. Don Olafson supported the refugees. After Mae Tha Waw's fall in 1984, the population of refugees reached nine thousand. The Refugee Committee was reorganized and renamed the Karen Refugee Committee, with Pastor Robert as its chairman, Pu Ler Moo and Mahn Steela as vice chairmen, and K'Neh Mee as secretary.[173]

Until 1984, the government forces raided the Karen areas during the dry season but usually retreated during the monsoon season. This changed in 1984 when Burmese troops entered a large ethnic corridor near the Thailand border and some ten thousand Karen refugees were forced to stay in Thailand for the whole year. "The refugees thought that the soldiers would leave before the next monsoons. And then [the refugees] would just go home . . . ," but that was not to be the case.[174] Besides, the refugee population was going to increase due to the political upheaval in 1988, which began with the students' peaceful demonstration in March.

Under military administration, Burma's rich natural resources were mismanaged for years. The economy suffered and eventually collapsed in 1987, precipitating the student-led demonstrations of 1988. Demonstrations initially began on March 13, when Maung Phone Maw, a young student at Rangoon Institute of Technology in Insein, was shot dead by police. Enraged by police brutality, on March 16 more university students joined the demonstrations. As they marched along Inya Lake, military forces blocked the road. The so-called Lon Htein security forces threw tear gas into the crowd, beat the students with clubs, and tossed several of them into waiting trucks.[175] Within days, hundreds of students were killed, but protests continued with more civilians joining demonstrations. To suppress the demonstrations, the Burmese government closed all schools and universities and banned public gatherings.

Despite the curfew and shootings, the anti-government movement intensified to the extent that the Burma Socialist People's Party (BSPP) chairman, General Ne Win, announced his resignation on July 23, 1988. His chosen successor was Brigadier General Sein Lwin, who had chased and killed Saw Ba U Gyi in 1950. Sein Lwin declared martial law on August 3. Nevertheless, people rushed back to the streets, calling for the restoration of multiparty democracy, which became the main rallying slogan of the 1988 democracy movement.

Advised by an astrologer that "four eights," August 8, 1988 (8-8-88), would be an auspicious number for their movement, a mass demonstration was set for that day. Thousands of people took to the main streets of Rangoon and other cities, chanting anti-government slogans and demanding democracy. Sein Lwin sent out his troops in every city. The troops opened fire on the crowd, making every city the scene of a blood bath. In Rangoon alone, the death toll was estimated at more than three thousand, including children. His notorious bloody massacres of demonstrators made Sein Lwin resign on August 13. To appease the people, the government appointed a civilian leader, Dr. Maung Maung. However, the demonstrations continued to gain momentum.[176]

During this period, the most active organization was the All Burma Federation of Students' Union (ABFSU), which was formed on August 28, 1988, having around fifty thousand students in membership.[177] Once the BSPP leaders stepped down, old politicians and retired military leaders, whom General Ne Win ousted, began to form political parties. These parties demanded the immediate resignation of the BSPP and the formation of an interim civilian government to organize a new election. Among others, Aung San Suu Kyi, the daughter of Aung San, the architect of Burma independence, who happened to be attending her ailing mother in Burma, was persuaded to join the movement. On August 26, she spoke to a rally of five hundred thousand on the slopes of the Shwedagon Pagoda. Since then, she became the icon of the Burma democracy movement, leading the National League of Democracy (NLD), which was officially formed on September 24, 1988.[178]

After these events, the military leaders rebranded themselves the State Law and Order Restoration Council (SLORC) and declared martial law. On June 18, 1989, the SLORC renamed the country to Myanmar. In July, they announced that a national election would be held in 1990. Yet, the campaign movements were suppressed. In 1990, the SLORC held multiparty elections, but when the NLD won more than 80 percent of the seats in parliament, the SLORC would not cede power. Instead, the SLORC put Daw Aung San Suu Kyi, the leader of the NLD, under house arrest for what would eventually become nearly two decades.

Since students started the demonstrations, they were the first victims of the government's military response. Many fled to the border and took refuge in KNU territory. After its formation in late August 1988, the ABFSU sent a secret delegation to the KNU headquarters.[179] These student groups joined the KNU and other ethnic freedom fighters in their struggle for democracy. It was the first alliance between ethnic and pro-democracy movements. Offices were established at the KNU headquarters at Manerplaw, and more than thirty small "student" camps were established along the border.

As the NLD movement extended into the KNU territories, the KNU headquarters at Manerplaw was invigorated as the democracy movement's main political base. The KNU-sponsored ethnic insurgent alliance, the National Defense Front (NDF), which was established in 1976, played a huge role at the headquarters in Manerplaw. In 1984, Bo Mya and the NDF agreed to change their position from one of principled secessionism (the advocacy for outright independence) to a demand for substantial autonomy within a proposed Federal Union of Burma.[180] Since then, this policy of a future federal union has become the KNU's political objective. They have negated the military government's accusation of KNU scheming to wreck the union.

The KNU's leadership in the NDF, with the new political objective of a federal union, made it convenient for all anti-government groups to join the KNU in Manerplaw and establish alliances. The first among these was the Democratic Alliance of Burma (DAB), formed in 1988 along with the KNU, NDF, and several pro-democracy groups. After the SLORC military government blocked the 1990 general elections, a dozen NLD members of parliament-elect fled to Manerplaw. In 1992 in Manerplaw, they formed the National Council of the Union of Burma (NCUB). Its members included all the anti-government groups, and Bo Mya was named the joint head of the new NCUB. Aung San Suu Kyi's cousin, Dr. Sein Win, was the leader of the NLD members of parliament-elect at Manerplaw. For a moment, "the activist claimed that there were two capitals in Burma: Yangon and the KNU headquarters at Manerplaw."[181]

Certainly, this was the high point of the KNU and Bo Mya's leadership. Manerplaw had become the hot spot in Southeast Asia as the center of the pro-democracy movement. Unfortunately, the situation soon changed when the SLORC tried to revamp its image from warmonger to peacemaker. The military offensives against ethnic minority movements forced thousands of Karen to be displaced into Thailand. During the eighteen months of heavy fighting between 1989 and 1990, the number of refugees in Thailand grew to more than forty thousand.[182]

When the world began to condemn these atrocities, the SLORC tried to restore its reputation by offering anti-government groups ceasefire proposals in 1989. By 1994, agreements were reached with several groups, including the United Wa State Army, Shan State Army, the Kachin Defense Army (KDA or the ex-KIO 4th Brigade), Pa'O National Organization, Palaung State Liberation Army, and even the KNU's closest ally, the New Mon State Party.[183] In 1992, the SLORC offered the KNU the same ceasefire proposal, but the negotiation failed. In 1994, the SLORC sent a Karen team to Manerplaw as mediators led by the Anglican Archbishop, Andrew Mya Han. This group disbanded after two unsuccessful trips. Next, a six-member Karen Peace Mediator Group (KPMG) facilitated "confidence-building" meetings for the KNU and SLORC between 1995 and 1997.[184] Included on this team were Professor Tun Aung Chain, ex-KNU leader Saw Alfonzo (A. Soe Myint), Saw Henson Tardaw, Saw Richard, Kun Myat, and Rev. Mar Gay Gyi (general secretary of Myanmar Baptist Convention).

The negotiation for peace was slow, but the road to war was swift. From 1994, the KNU lost not only its allies but also its headquarters at Manerplaw. The Karen National Liberation Army's Brigadier General Ralph blamed U Thuzana, a Karen Buddhist monk, for using propaganda and exaggerating the differences between Karen Christians and Karen Buddhists, who had been hitherto living in harmony. But he admitted that the problem originated in the misdemeanors of some KNLA officers in the villages in Hlaingbwe township in Pa'an district in 1992. Lieutenant Charles and San Lom Gyi went to villages recruiting soldiers by force, and the parents had to pay money get back their children. While such misconduct against the villagers kindled resentment, the KNLA leaders failing to remove these officers created more hostility.

Serious conflict exploded in 1994, when the KNLA leader refused the request of U Thuzana, a Karen Buddhist monk, to build a pagoda at his base in Myaing Gyi Ngu village. The KNLA leaders explained to U Thuzana that they could not allow him to build the pagoda because the land in question was strategically important for their operations. They were still fighting on this battlefield. During that period, the SLORC's general secretary, General Khin Nyunt, visited U Thuzana by helicopter and told him that the Christian Karens were oppressing Buddhist Karens. General Nyunt said the Burmese government would support him building new pagodas as he wished once they could clear the area. Initially, the monk did not support the idea, but eventually, he started talking, which divided Christian and Buddhist villagers in the community.[185]

Proclaiming his prophecy that by building fifty pagodas, peace would be restored for the Karens, U Thuzana began construction of the first "peace pagoda" at Thu Mweh Hta, at the confluence of the

Salween and Moei rivers, a few miles north of Manerplaw. He had approximately two thousand Karen families living around his monastery who followed his teaching and believed he had supernatural powers. Concerned about the Tatmadaw's potential attack using the pagoda, the local KNLA commanders ordered it dismantled.[186]

As tensions grew, in November 1994, Bo Mya called a meeting to settle the issues between the Buddhist and the Christian Karens, but U Thuzana did not show. Since other Karen monks joined the meeting, Bo Mya asked everyone to speak frankly and discuss the issues to avoid misunderstandings and provide accurate information if needed. U Thuzana's absence discouraged one of the monks to the extent that he started crying, saying that "this will lead to Karens fighting Karens."[187] Unfortunately, the situation was soon out of control. In December, a group of disaffected Buddhist Karen soldiers mostly from KNLA's 102nd Battalion deserted their frontline position and joined U Thuzana. On December 21, 1994, the monk and his soldiers established the Democratic Karen Buddhist Association (DKBA), consolidating a major split in Karen insurgent ranks. Within a few days, they made an announcement of the formation of the DKBA, led by ex-KNDO Sergeant-Major Kyaw Than. The Tatmadaw units supplied the DKBA with military and logistic support as the government military agents incited disaffection with the KNU.[188] The DKBA's defection weakened the KNU and led to Manerplaw's fall.

With the DKBA agreeing to a ceasefire with the SLORC, the Tatmadaw acted quickly. On December 10, 1994, Burmese government forces attacked the KNU at Manerplaw. By January 26, 1995, the capital city of Karen's virtual country was taken by the Burmese troops after the KNU burned and abandoned it.[189] Since the remaining bases of the KNU territory also fell, the KNLA retreated north into the Papun hills and south to join the 6th Brigade in the lower Karen state. The KNU's original goal of building a Karen state became uncertain. On March 24, 1995, the KNU began peace talks with the Burmese government. By April 28, 1996, delegates from the KNU met in Moulmein to continue negotiations.[190]

There were seven talks in all between Moulmein and Rangoon. At one point, a ceasefire seemed close, but the SLORC made six conditions for the KNU to accept, and the KNU hardened its negotiations. On the eve of January 1997, Bo Mya rejected the terms in a letter taking issue with two demands. The two objectionable demands were that the KNU should join "the legal fold" and should agree to "lay down arms."[191] These terms were rejected because Bo Mya and his advisors felt that the

State Peace and Development Council (SPDC), the new name for the rebranded SLORC, demanded an admission of surrender.

By February 1997, the SLORC commenced an offensive on any remaining KNU areas and had immediate success due to one KNU battalion's defection. This defection, in conjunction with the DKBA's breakaway, dropped KNU morale.[192] Between 1995 and 1998, the DKBA instigated a dozen attacks on KNU-controlled refugee camps in Thailand, killing more than twenty people.[193]

Since the 1995 fall of Manerplaw, the KNU was significantly weakened. But the old leaders held faithfully to Ba U Gyi's four principles, especially "surrender is out of the question." Meanwhile, the younger generation began to assume leadership with some having the desire to end the armed conflict and negotiate with the SPDC while others did not. In December 2003, a group of KNU leaders (Padoh Soe Soe, Mahn Johnny, Htoo Htoo Lay, David Taw, and 7th Brigade commander Brigadier General Htein Maung) went to Bangkok, Thailand, to start ceasefire talks with the SPDC leaders. Then, on January 16, 2004, General Bo Mya, who had stepped down as KNU chairman in 2000, along with a KNU delegation of twenty, went to Yangon and continued the negotiations. On January 18, a ceasefire agreement, known as a gentleman's agreement, was reached verbally. The apparent cordial relationships at that moment between the SPDC and KNU leaders was evident when General Khin Nyunt (SPDC secretary 1) attended Bo Mya's seventy-seventh birthday celebration on January 21 at the Karaweik Hotel in Yangon. Unfortunately, the ceasefire negotiation came to a halt when General Khin Nyunt was forced to resign in October 2004.[194]

Meanwhile, General Bo Mya's physical and mental health deteriorated. His influence began to wane, leading to internal conflicts and fractional groups among the Karens. In June 2006, representatives from KNLA 7th Brigade met in Myawaddy with Tatmadaw Colonel Myat Htun Oo and discussed the possibility of Bo Mya traveling to Yangon to resume the gentleman's agreement. A few days later, Pastor Timothy Laklem and Bo Mya's son, Colonel Ner Dah Mya, met in Bangkok with Colonel Tin Soe, the Burmese military attaché. The plan was to arrange a trip for Bo Mya to Yangon for medical treatment. Initially, Bo Mya agreed to cooperate, but he finally refused on the planned day of his departure in July 2006. Despite his refusal, KNLA 7th Brigade commander, Brigadier General Htein Maung,[195] continued to meet with Colonel Myat Htun Oo. On July 30, 2006, they issued a joint statement with Colonel Ner Day Mya, denouncing KNU leadership and beginning a separate ceasefire negotiation.[196]

Bo Mya's death in December 2006 unleashed Htein Maung and his colleagues for further negotiations. After several meetings with Lieutenant General Thein Sein (SPDC secretary 1) and Major General Ye Myint (head of the military affairs department), Htein Maung made a peace agreement with the SPDC on January 16, 2007. Following the peace agreement, he formed the National Union/Karen National Liberation Army Peace Council (KNU/KNLA PC) with 7th Brigade soldiers and family members. Colonel Ner Dah Mya was named as secretary 1. The SPDC granted them a 20 km x 2 km stretch of land along the border behind Mae La refugee camp in Thailand and a new base at Toh Kaw Koe, site of the death of Saw Ba U Gyi, near Kawkareik.[197]

Htein Maung's defection was a blow to the KNU in that he and his members provided the Tatmadaw with important information about the KNU. By April, the KNU lost their last major controlled bases between Mae Sot and Mae La due to the joint military attacks by the Tatmadaw, DKBA units, and the KNU/KNLA.[198] Despite the territory loss, under the leadership of KNU hardliners in Mae Sot, like General Secretary Mahn Sa and Joint General Secretary David Takabaw, the KNU continued as the oldest and the only legitimate Karen ethnonationalist group. When the SPDC handed over its office to a quasi-civilian government led by the ex-general Thein Sein in 2011, followed by the National League for Democracy (NLD) entering the elections in 2012, the Karen National Union agreed to a ceasefire with the new government.

The long-term warfare and the increased Burmese government military offensive caused great damage to the Karen villages in the KNU-controlled border areas. Even after the military government and the KNU entered an informal ceasefire in 2004, the human rights abuses did not lessen and even got worse for the Karens. The SPDC demanded that the villagers who stayed must do hard labor improving infrastructure and being porters for SPDC supplies. Farmers suffered greatly when forest fires intentionally started by the SPDC destroyed rice crops and cardamom plantations.[199] The armed Burmese troops raided and destroyed unarmed Karen villages. The rape and sexual violence against women, forced labor, religious persecution, and torture, in combination with the litany of other human rights abuses committed in Burma with near complete impunity, constitute crimes against humanity.[200] Reports of these human rights abuses have led many to view the period starting in November of 2005 until 2011 as the worst against the Karens since the mid-1990s. Possibly, it was an attempted genocide.

Back in the 1980s, Karen refugees formed new villages just inside Thailand that were absorbed into the landscape. But as time went on, refugees were rounded up. By the turn of the century, refugee camps were shifted and integrated into seven large camps along the Thai-Burma border: Mae La, Umphiem, Noh Poe, Mae Ra Ma Luang, Mae La Oo, Ban Don Yan, and Htam Him. The refugee population increased to 120,000. In addition to Karens, the camps included Mons, Arakan, Burmese Shan, Pa'O, and Indians with a mixture of religious beliefs— Buddhists, Muslims, animists, and Christians. However, there was no official recognition of Karen refugees by the host country since Thailand was not a signatory of the UN declaration on "Refugees."[201]

Life in these camps was unstable, but it allowed Karen history to be passed from one generation to the next. Camp life also provided a venue to nurture nationalist sentiments among the Karens. Refugees received reasonable educational support in camps beginning with nursery education to kindergarten to secondary education, which ended at tenth grade. No higher education was provided in the refugee camps. In Mae La camp alone, more than four hundred youths yearly graduated from the tenth grade. Some received further studies abroad, but not more than one hundred students per year.[202] Conversely, it is from these camps that refugees have taken steps toward a brighter future where they can perhaps support the Karen revolution from international locations.

Notes

1. John F. Cady, *A History of Modern Burma* (Ithaca, NY: Cornell University Press, 1960), 596.

2. Smith Dun, *Memoirs of the Four-Foot Colonel*, Data Paper number 113 (Ithaca, NY: Cornell University Southeast Asia Program, Department of Asia Studies, 1980), 71.

3. Hugh Tinker, *The Union of Burma: A Study of the First Years of Independence* (London: Oxford University Press, 1957), 40.

4. Dun, 72.

5. Ibid., Saw Bellay's testimony. His name is spelled Saw Belly in other books.

6. Ibid., 75., Saw Po Tu's testimony.

7. Ibid., 72, 74. From the statements of two Karen leaders, Saw Bellay, customs officer, and Saw Po Tu, police officer. These were their statements when they were asked by the Burmese government to give explanation as to why they should not be charged and prosecuted as rebels.

8. Ibid., 72.

9. Ibid., 76, Saw Po Tu's testimony.

10. Ibid.

11. Ibid.

12. Ibid., 77.

13. Ibid., 73.

14. Ibid.

15. Ibid., 53–54.

16. Ibid.

17. Ibid., 77.

18. Ibid., 70.

19. Martin Smith, *Burma: Insurgency and the Politics of Ethnicity* (New York: St. Martin's Press, 1999), 138.

20. Ibid.

21. Ibid. Colonel Min Maung did not join the KNDO until Captain Nawng Seng came to him in February.

22. Saw Yankee Myint Oo, my father.

23. Angelene Naw, *Memoirs of a Karen Soldier in World War II: Saw Yankee Myint Oo* (independently published, 2020), 14. This is the memoir of my father.

24. Ibid., 14–15.

25. Zaw Pe's fiancée in Maymyo was raped by Burmese soldiers. She was the bridesmaid of my mother.

26. Naw, 15–16.

27. Smith, 138. General Ne Win ordered the 1st Kachin Rifles down from Pyinmana to retake Toungoo and selected Nawng Seng, holder of the British Burma Gallantry Medal, to lead the first attack.

28. Naw, 16.

29. Ibid., 17.

30. Ibid., 18.

31. Ibid., 26.

32. *Burma and the Insurrection* (Rangoon: Government of the Union of Burma, 1949), 31.

33. Naw, 18.

34. Ibid., 20.

35. Ibid., 21–25.

36. He secretly passed the information of the operation plan of General Min Maung through the Chin battalion, which declared its neutrality in the conflict between the Karens and Burmese when the Karen seized Meiktila (interview with former KNDO personnel who were with General Min Maung during the incident).

37. Smith, 139.

38. Cady, 593.

39. Naw, 28.

40. Smith, 139.

41. *Burma and the Insurrection*, 52–53.

42. Pu S'Kaw Ler Taw, *Kayin Taw Hlan Yay Thamaing*, ed. Saw Maung Maung and KNU Central Committee (KNU publication, 1992), 146.

43. Tinker, 43.

44. Ibid.

45. Ler Taw, *Kayin Taw Hlan Yay Thamaing*, 146.

46. Tinker, 46. In his biography, Mahn Ba Zan claimed that when Ba U Gyi came back with the document he and Hunter Tha Hmwe argued. The terms required that the Karens were to surrender, but they could not accept it. Ba U Gyi suggested that he signed the paper as the KNU leader, but Mahn Ba Zan could go and negotiate as the KNDO commander. On May 5, Mahn Ba Zan had a meeting with the AFPFL government. After his return, the new counterproposal was signed by Colonel Aung Sein and sent to the government. Pu Gee Doh, *Mahn Ba Zan Hnint Taw Hlan Yay (Mah Ba Zan and Karen Revolution)* (KNU publication, 1993), 114.

47. Richard Butwell, *U Nu of Burma* (Stanford, CA: Stanford University Press, 1963), 167.

48. Naw, 28–29.

49. Ibid., 30–31.

50. Ibid., 31.

51. Smith, 140.

52. Dun, 70.

53. Ibid.

54. Naw, 34.

55. *The Times*, 21 May 1949.

56. Naw, 36–37.

57. Ler Taw, *Kayin Taw Hlan Yay Thamaing*, 105. Some leaders used the traditional title *Kaw Kasa*, which means "Lord of the Land" in S'gaw Karen language.

58. Naw, 37.

59. Ler Taw, *Kayin Taw Hlan Yay Thamaing*, 106; Reuters, June 16, 1949.

60. Ler Taw, *Kayin Taw Hlan Yay Thamaing*, 106. In 1951 two more brigades were formed; 6th Brigade in Pegu Yoma under Brigadier Seaplane and 7th Brigade in central delta area under Brigadier Myo Chit, alias Mahn Nyo.

61. Ibid., 106–9.

62. Cady, 596.

63. Parliament, House of Commons, *Debates*, vol. 461 (February 14 and 23, 1949), 764, 1854; vol. 462 (March 7, 1949), 792-95. Hereafter cited as PD, C.

64. PD, C, vol. 464 (May 6 and 11, 1949), 1444–46, 1828–30; vol. 466 (June 24-27), 43–44, 749–50.

65. *Manchester Guardian*, May 13, 1949; *Statesman*, June 24, 1949.

66. Cady, 598.

67. Ibid., 607–8.
68. Naw, 38–41.
69. Ler Taw, *Kayin Taw Hlan Yay Thamaing*, 111.
70. Minutes of the Kawthoolei Congress, 17-19 July 1950; see Ler Taw, *Kayin Taw Hlan Yay Thamaing*, 111 (in Burmese), Pu S'Kaw Ler Taw, *Ka Nyaw Ta Ber Hser Tar Si Soh Teh Soh* (KNU publication, 1992), 245 (in Karen).
71. Ibid.; also Maung Sin Kyeh, *Bamarpyi Chit Kayin Amyotha Kaung Hsaung Myar* (Bangkok: Pyidaungsu Kayin Amyotha Apweh Choke, 2003), 188.
72. Ibid.
73. *Myanma Alin* (newspaper), August 15, 1950, 2.
74. *Bama Khit* (newspaper), August 22, 1950, 1.
75. Ler Taw, *Kayin Taw Hlan Yay Thamaing*, 111.
76. *The Times*, 23 August 1950.
77. Saw Ralph and Naw Sheera, *Fifty Years in the Karen Revolution in Burma, the Soldier and the Teacher*, ed. Stephanie Olinga-Shannon (Ithaca, NY: Cornell University Press), 2019, 50.
78. Ler Taw, *Kayin Taw Hlan Yay Thamaing*, 112.
79. Ibid., 112–13.
80. Ibid., 113. He adopted the traditional title of Kaw Kasa.
81. Ibid., 115.
82. Smith, 148.
83. Ibid., 149.
84. Ler Taw, *Kayin Taw Hlan Yay Thamaing*, 117.
85. Naw, 44.
86. Pu Gee Doh, 87.
87. Ler Taw, *Kayin Taw Hlan Yay Thamaing*, 117.
88. Smith, 151.
89. Ler Taw, *Kayin Taw Hlan Yay Thamaing*, 119. Later he left the KNU movement due to the influence of communism.
90. Ibid., 121. General Min Maung continued to be head of the defense department. Saw We Re Gyaw, Saw Ba Htun, and Saw Toray were assigned as department heads of finance and revenue, education and health, and secretary of Kawthoolei state, respectively.
91. *Bangkok Post*, April 12, 1954.
92. Smith, 153, his interview with Pu S'Kaw Ler Taw, January 14, 1985.
93. Naw, 44–45.
94. Smith, 153.
95. Ler Taw, *Kayin Taw Hlan Yay Thamaing*, 133.
96. Ibid., 123.
97. Tinker, 55–56.
98. Ler Taw, *Kayin Taw Hlan Yay Thamaing*, 124.
99. Ibid., 125.
100. Ibid.
101. Ibid., 126.
102. Ibid., 127.
103. Ibid., 128.
104. Ibid.
105. Ibid.
106. Smith, 216, his interview with Pu S'Kaw Ler Taw.
107. Pu Gee Doh, 168–69.
108. Ler Taw, *Kayin Taw Hlan Yay Thamaing*, 129.
109. *Nation*, January 27, 1955.
110. *Nation*, January 30, 1955.
111. Naw, 47.
112. Ler Taw, *Kayin Taw Hlan Yay Thamaing*, 129.
113. Smith, 184.
114. Ibid., 213.
115. Ler Taw, *Kayin Taw Hlan Yay Thamaing*, 132.
116. Ibid., 134.
117. Ibid., 136.
118. Ibid., 139.
119. *The Times*, January 12, 1960.
120. Ler Taw, *Kayin Taw Hlan Yay Thamaing*, 147.
121. Ibid., 147; Smith, 186.
122. Smith, 214.

123. Ler Taw, *Kayin Taw Hlan Yay Thamaing*, 141-43.

124. Saw Bo Mya, *Kyundaw Bawa Pyatthan Hmu Asit Ahman* (Yangon: Nay Yee Yee Sar Oak Taik, 2014), 81.

125. Smith, 216.

126. *Attauktaw* (newspaper), August 16, 1963.

127. *Botataung* (newspaper), August 19, 1963; *Myanma Alin*, August 20, 1963.

128. *Botataung*, August 31, 1963.

129. Mahn Ba Zan, S'Kaw Ler Taw, Bo Kyin Pe, Bo Than Aung, Major Tamala Baw, Major Mya Maung, Than Lwin, Saw Tun Kyaw.

130. *Working People's Daily*, October 13, 1963.

131. Smith, 217.

132. Maung Sin Kyeh, 153–54.

133. *Forward*, April 7, 1964.

134. *Forward*, April 22, 1964.

135. Ler Taw, *Kayin Taw Hlan Yay Thamaing*, 145.

136. Smith, 218.

137. Ler Taw, *Kayin Taw Hlan Yay Thamaing*, 152.

138. Smith, 283.

139. Ibid., 282.

140. Ibid., 284.

141. Bertil Lintner, *Burma in Revolt: Opium and Insurgency since 1948* (Chiang Mai: Silkworm Books, 1999), 222.

142. Chao Tzang Yawnghwe, "Politics of Burma and Shan State: Effects on North Thailand and Thailand," *Political Science Review* (September 1982), 132.

143. Ronald D. Renard, "The Karen Rebellion in Burma," in *Secessionist Movements in Comparative Perspective*, ed. Ralph R. Prendas, S. W. R. de A. Samarasinghe, and Alan B. Anderson (New York: St. Martin's Press, 1990), 107.

144. Lintner, 223.

145. Ler Taw, *Kayin Taw Hlan Yay Thamaing*, 152.

146. Smith, 285.

147. Ibid., 286.

148. Ibid., his interview with Saw Ba Lone of the KNU's education department, December 26, 1985.

149. Ibid.

150. Ibid., 287–88.

151. Josef Silverstein, *Burma: Military Rule and the Politics of Stagnation* (Ithaca, NY: Cornell University Press, 1977), 118. U Nu made the announcement while he was in London on August 29, 1969.

152. Lintner, 275.

153. Smith, 287–88.

154. Ibid., 326.

155. *The Guardian*, August 18, 1968; *Forward*, May 15, 1969.

156. Pu Gee Doh, 151.

157. Smith, 326-28.

158. He was the former naval officer who had mutinied with his vessel at the beginning of the revolution in 1949 to lead the KNDO attack on Bassein.

159. Smith, 259–67.

160. *Policy and Rules and Regulations of the Karen National Union* (KNU publishing, 1974). These regulations, approved by the 1974 congress, were published in both Karen and Burmese languages. They became a handbook for KNU teachers and administrators throughout Kawthoolei. See Smith, 297.

161. *Policy and Rules and Regulations*.

162. Smith, 295–96.

163. Other founding members were Arakan Liberation Party, the KIO, KNPP, the Kayan New Land Party, the Lahu National United Party, the Palaung State Liberation Party, Pa'O National Organization, and the Shan State Army. See Smith, 294.

164. Ibid., 298.

165. Ibid., 288.

166. Ibid., 296.

167. Ibid., 391.

168. Ibid., 393.

169. Ibid.

170. Ibid., 393–94.

171. Lintner, 328.

172. Smith, 397.

173. *Karen News Collection*, "Profile of the Karen Refugees" (Mae Sot: Karen Refugee Committee, 2009), 23–24.

174. Sandy Barron, *Between Worlds: Twenty Years on the Border* (Chiang Mai: Burmese Border Consortium, 2004), 16.

175. Whitney Stewart, *Aung San Suu Kyi: Fearless Voice of Burma* (New York: iUniverse, 2008), 50.

176. Ibid., 50–52.

177. Smith, 7.

178. Stewart, 56–57.

179. Smith, 11.

180. Ashley South, *Ethnic Politics in Burma: States of Conflict*, Routledge Contemporary Southeast Asia (London: Routledge, 2008), 40.

181. Saw Ralph, 6 (Martin Smith's introduction).

182. Smith, 408.

183. South, 122, table 5.1.

184. N. Ganesan and Kyaw Yin Hlaing, eds., *Myanmar: State, Society, and Ethnicity* (Singapore: Institute of Southeast Asia Studies, National University of Singapore, 2007), 222.

185. Saw Ralph, 93–94.

186. South, 57–58; Mikael Gravers, "A Saint in Command? Spiritual Protection, Justice, and Religious Tensions in the Karen State," *Independent Journal of Burmese Research* 1, no. 2 (2018): 87–89.

187. Saw Ralph, 95.

188. South, 58.

189. Lintner, 476.

190. Ibid., 477.

191. Smith, 449.

192. Saw Ralph, 94.

193. South, 58.

194. Bo Hmu Gyi San Bwint, *Ah Myo Tha Pyan Lei Siyoneyay* (*Nyein Chan Yay Hmattaing Myar*) (Yangon: La-woon-bya Sarbei, 2016), 143–44; in Burmese. The author is a retired colonel.

195. Ibid.

196. South, 65.

197. Ibid.

198. *Free Burma Rangers*, April 20, 2007.

199. "Internal Displacement and Protection in Eastern Burma" (Bangkok: Thailand Burma Border Consortium, 2005), 36.

200. *Burma Human Rights Yearbook 2007*, edited and published by the Human Rights Documentation Unit, National Coalition Government of the Union of Burma, September 2008, i.

201. *Karen News Collection*, "About Karen Refugees in the USA" (in preparation of World Refugees Day, 2009), 24.

202. Ibid., 26.

9
Christianity and the Karen Identity in the Twenty-First Century

> As for the Karen heritage, . . . "As a nation, we have at least eight," and proceeds to present them "in order of merit and value." They are: the knowledge that there is a God, the Divine Being; high moral and ethical standards; honesty; simple, quiet, and peaceful living; hospitality; language; national costumes; and aptitude for music.[1]

As the strongest and longest armed opposition group against several successive Burmese governments in one of the longest-running conflicts in the world, the Karen National Union's armed struggle has received the attention of historians, political scientists, and journalists. Millions of people were further made aware of the movement through the American action movie *Rambo (January 2008)*, directed by Sylvester Stallone. In the film, Rambo (Stallone) leads a group of mercenaries into Burma to rescue Christian missionaries who provide medical aid to a village inhabited by the Karen people. The film portrays mercenaries as directly involved in the KNU movement.[2] Seperately, and with no association with mercenaries, through the humanitarian work of the Baptist missionary organizations and the international human rights organization Christian Solidarity Worldwide, people from Australia, the United States, and the United Kingdom indirectly provided for the needs of Karens living in villages around those war-torn zones. A British Christian journalist and human rights activist, Benedict Rogers, after visiting the area, wrote:

> The Karen legend that a young white brother would come across the ocean to bring the lost book and to help them has proven to be true. Not only did Adoniram Judson come carrying the Bible, but he has been followed by many others. Major Seagrim . . . followed Judson's step. So too have men like James Mawdsley . . . Dr. Martin Panter, and politicians such as Baroness Cox, Lord Alton and Congressman Joseph Pitts. They have all helped in different ways, making sacrifices of various types to help the Karen in their time of need.[3]

The Karen people's story could never be told without including Christian missionaries. A plethora of stories of the KNU's separatist movement and the sufferings of the Karen refugees on the Thai-Burma border traveled throughout the world of literature and into movie theaters. Easy access was allowed to the KNU-controlled and Kawthoolei liberated zones, so that scholars, journalists, and even adventurers were able to explore the areas and spread information on the KNU, lifestyle, and suffering of the Karen people.

Furthermore, the scarcity of scholarly work, especially by outsiders, and about the Karens living inside Burma, made it impossible to know who the Karens truly are. The Ne Win government's isolation policy beginning in 1962 prohibited foreign scholars, journalists, and researchers from accessing Burma to study the Karen people. The government policy of censorship also discouraged many local scholars from writing about the actual Karen work and lives. The study of Karen nationalism or nationalist movement were sensitive fields for Karen scholars to address because they could lose their job (thus, their only source of income and survival as a citizen of Burma). Publications about Karen people came out sporadically through the government program only after thorough censorship. A scholar from Northern Illinois University correctly stated, "Research and other scholarly pursuits regarding the Karens have largely shifted to the Thai Border and refugee camps."[4]

In the 1970s, studies of Karens were conducted solely among the Karen people in northern Thailand. Hamilton (1976), Anderson (1976), Cooke, Hudspith, Morris, Lehman (1979), Keyes (1979), Kunstadter (1969), Iijim (1970, 1979), Ron Renard (1980), Hinton (1975), and Rajah (1984) became leading scholars of the Karen people. This resulted in misinformation, like Rajah's claim, "In almost every work the Karen are virtually 'tribal' subjects of anthropological study."[5] Anthropologist Peter Hinton even raised the question, "Do the Karen really exist?" concluding that the Karens do not have a common identity and that the "Karen identity was inauthentic because it was made real by colonialism."[6] By contrast, Keyes commented, "The vast majority for whom the term Karen is appropriate live in Burma and it is from Burma that the first studies of the Karen come."[7]

The first thorough study of Karen people inside Burma appeared in the twenty-first century, when a Karen scholar, Ardeth Maung Thawnghmung, published The "Other" Karen in Myanmar. Regarding her book title, she emphasized, "Conventional studies . . . which focus predominantly on the Karen insurgency and Karen refugees, have largely ignored the existence of these 'quiet' Karen—who I refer to . . . as the 'other Karen.'"[8]

The lifestyle of the Karens living inside Burma was hidden from the outside world. Many assume they also endure a dangerous life and thus are trying to flee the country and become refugees. The following is one such interpretation as the author compares the lives of the Karens in Burma and Thailand: "The Karens who moved into the regions of Burma controlled by the KNU to escape the direct oppression by the military government until recently lived in relative freedom compared with those still in government-controlled areas."[9]

The military government's severe persecution and repressive measures on the Karen people in Burma is undeniable. Rural Karen villagers face human rights abuses daily, including rape, killings, forced relocation, displacement, and land confiscation. However, such abuses are not common to Karens living in major cities, although they regularly experience less obvious discrimination. In fact, several Karen leaders who did not join the Karen revolution in 1949, and some who joined but surrendered afterward, became parliamentary members in the AFPFL government. Even during the BSPP period, several Karens, including former Karen military commanders, became parliamentary members. Except for a few, these Karen leaders were true Karen nationalists who preserved Karen cultural and national identity while working for Karen rights and privileges within the government framework.

This chapter's opening statement depicts the KNU's bold claim of Karen heritage, which included eight features. Even without thorough studies, the four major features of the mentioned Karen heritage—belief in the Divine Being (Christian faith), S'gaw Karen language, Karen national costume, and music—are noticeable in the KNU-controlled zone. Under Bo Mya, speaking S'gaw Karen and attending Karen language chapel were required in the KNU educational system.[10] One could question if Karens living inside Burma, or the "other Karens" as named by Ashley South and Ardeth Maung Thawnghmung, could claim that they, too, hold to this heritage. It seems necessary to revisit the work of Karen leaders and the experiences of these Karens since the time KNU left the Burmese legal political scene.

The Karen People from Burma to Myanmar

As discussed earlier, many Karen leaders did not expect to wage war against the AFPFL government. Notably, other Karen leaders did not participate in the fight, not because they lacked nationalist sentiment, but for a variety of reasons. Members of the KNU's central committee, including Thra Tha Hto, were arrested in the Ahlone Karen quarter. Saw Tha Din and Saw Po Chit were arrested in Moulmein.[11]

As a devout Christian, Mrs. Ba Maung Chain (Irene Po), daughter of Sir San C. Po, preferred to preserve peace instead of hostility and war. She advised Ba U Gyi to accept the peace treaty with the AFPFL government and opposed armed resistance. Mahn Ba Zan remembered that she urged him to agree with the peace treaty signed by Saw Ba U Gyi and to work with the government for the formation of the Karen state.[12] She tried to persuade many young Karens that their community would be better served if they learned trades and professions rather than adhering to their vow not to cut their hair until the Burmese had been defeated.[13] Another strong Christian leader and peacemaker, Saw Pu, lived in Myaungmya and negotiated to end hostilities with the government.[14]

KYO leader San Po Thin, who hitherto cooperated with the government, was the special commissioner of Bassein in January 1949 but was arrested later on suspicion of attempting to form a private army. During this period, thousands of Karen civilians were sent to camps arranged by the government. Although government records showed that they set up forty refugee camps for Karens who lost their homes during civil wars, most of them were forced into these camps without consent. Rangoon University campus and Judson College campus were among the six locations set up as refugee camps in Rangoon.[15]

U Nu's AFPFL government established the Karen Affairs Council in 1948 under section 181 of the constitution in anticipation of the creation of a Karen state (chapter 6). During that period, three main Karen political parties emerged: the Union Karen League (UKL), with former KYO leaders Mahn Win Maung and Aung Pa as president and vice president respectively; the Union Karen Organization (UKO) led by Dr. Hla Tun; and the Karen Congress (KC), led by Thra Ba Than, Saw Po Thein, and Saw Norton Bwa. Both UKL and UKO were allies of AFPFL whereas the KC represented the KNU but did not go underground and later broke with the KNDO.[16]

In 1951, the AFPFL government and UKL promoted legislation to create a Karen state, which was to consist of the Salween district and any adjacent areas that might vote for inclusion after peace was restored.[17] Unfortunately, for this concession, the number of Karen members of Parliament in the Chamber of Nationalities was reduced from twenty-four to fifteen and in the Chamber of Deputies from twenty to seven. Additionally, separate Karen institutions in Burma proper were gradually abolished.[18]

When the 1951 election approached, the UKL invited Mrs. Ba Maung Chain to join the league. She was elected and became the first governmental minister for the Karen state. The strength of the parties in the Karen State Council was as follows: UKL twenty-one seats, UKO nine seats, and Karen Congress seven seats. Mrs. Ba Maung Chain assisted hundreds of Karen soldiers, though some were brought to trial and others were discharged from the service. However, realizing she was the constant center of various party maneuvers, she resigned after one year in office. UKL vice president Aung Pa became the minister of the Karen state.[19] The Karen state came into existence by law in December 1951 (Constitution Amendment Act, 1951), but by June 1, 1954, only three of its constituent townships, Hlaingbwe, Pa-an, and Thandaung, were controlled by the Karen state government. On July 1, 1955, Kawkareik and Kya-In townships passed from military to state rule. Only the Salween district was left under the military government. All the constituent states are deficit areas, and the Karens were virtually without any resources save for central contributions. The administration was headed by a special commissioner, Thra Donation, who was a political leader turned official. Indeed, the whole state government was a makeshift of "territories" run by political bosses. The Karen state ministry in Rangoon could, under these circumstances, only plan for the future.[20]

Despite these developments, the Karen state was denied the right of secession from the Union of Burma by section 181 (10) of the Constitution Amendment Act. Before General Ne Win's 1962 military coup, Karen politicians stood as AFPFL candidates in the general election in addition to their roles in the Karen state. In May 1955, UKO chief Dr. Hla Tun became minister of the Karen state, and Aung Pa assumed the health portfolio in the central government. By 1956, the UKL and UKO no longer existed due to the abolition of seats reserved for Karens in the national parliament. Later, former UKL members participated in the general election as AFPFL representatives. Mahn Win Maung, former KYO and UKL leader, renounced Christianity for Buddhism to become the Union of Burma's president from 1956 to 1960.[21] Mahn Win Maung, a graduate of Judson College in Rangoon, could not profess Christianity for his political success in the Union of Burma. In 1962, he was arrested and imprisoned by Ne Win. He was later released on November 13, 1967.[22]

Karen Leaders and Karen Community Development
Inside Myanmar

Since independence from Britain in 1948, the Karens in Burma, and all other citizens of Burma, have endured several government systems changes. During the first decade under AFPFL, they experienced a parliamentary system. The next two decades were under Ne Win's Burmese Way to Socialism with the Burmese Socialist Program Party's one-party government. From 1990 to the end of the twentieth century, the nation was under military rule. Despite various terms and names since Ne Win's coup in 1962, Burma has been under a military regime. Any opposition to that regime was either persecuted, driven underground, or forced into revolt.

Until 1958, education in the Karen state inside Burma was under the Directorate of Karen Education, which counted 586 primary schools, 17 middle schools, and 2 high schools (excluding Karen Christian private schools).[23] The Karen education department was responsible for promoting Karen literature and culture plus developing the academic curriculum. All this was done in the Karen language for Karen students. The education system allowed Karen students to take their exams in the Karen language up to the tenth grade.

However, all publicly sponsored teaching and learning in Karen ceased after 1959, when the Ne Win caretaker government abolished the Directorate of Karen Education. Nevertheless, some Karen leaders, who became parliamentary members, university professors, and government officials in the Union of Burma and in Ne Win's Burma Socialist People's Party (BSPP), continued to work for Karen language and culture preservation and promotion.

Mahn Ba Hsaing was a Karen leader remembered for his contribution to the Karen people's development. He was the Karen Affairs Minister (1949–1950) but was elected a member of parliament in the Union of Burma and eventually became chairman of the Union of Burma parliament. That ended when he was arrested by Ne Win during the 1962 coup. After his release, he focused on social and cultural services, especially the promotion of Karen language and culture. His colleague, Thra Tha Hto, a KNU veteran, was imprisoned from 1949 to 1951 during the civil war. Later, in 1967, when Ne Win's government formed the National Unity Advisory Group, he became one of its thirty-three members. At the seventieth meeting of the advisory group, he proposed the development of a Karen language and culture government program.[24] He and Mahn Ba Hsaing led the formation of the Karen Cultural

Committee in Rangoon, and for several years they alternately served as the chairman of the Rangoon Karen New Year celebration committee. They frequently published articles about Karen social and cultural affairs. Before he died in 1980, Mahn Ba Hsaing wrote an article for the 1980–1981 Karen New Year celebration in Rangoon entitled "Research on the Karen New Year."[25]

Before his house arrest, ex-KNU leader Saw Hunter Tha Hmwe actively promoted Karen language and culture. Upon his suggestion, General Ne Win changed the name Karen state to Kawthoolei for a few years, but later Karen leaders rejected the change. He also researched Karen cultural heritage and produced a thirteen-month Karen calendar.[26] In 1967, he and P'doh Ba Tun led a Karen cultural conference at Bassein College attended by five hundred participants including BSPP members, military officers, faculty members, and other civilians.[27]

On the pretext of recognizing national ethnic groups, the BSPP elaborated the Union Day (February 12) celebration by inviting thousands of representatives to attend with each national ethnic group (Chin, Kachin, Karen, Mon, Shan, Kayah, and Rakkhine) with their flags hoisted with the BSPP flag. Karen state leaders, along with leaders from other national ethnic groups, addressed the crowd. Each national group dressed in their traditional costumes, and traditional dances were performed. Karen students formed national associations in colleges and universities. Karen faculty actively helped with cultural activities, which included Karen language, Karen traditional dances, newsletters, and the annual Karen students' magazine. In 1969, all the universities in Rangoon joined and held the twenty-second Union Day celebration in the Rangoon University Convocation Hall.[28] These activities continued unless the universities were closed due to political upheavals. In 1972–1973, I taught Karen-language classes organized by the Bassein College Karen Students' Association as a part of the Karen faculty of the college.

During the 1988 upheaval, a Karen National Democracy and Peace Lover Group was formed with nine Karens who chose Saw Richard as president, Dr. Saw Simon Tha as vice president, and Saw Jubilee San Hla as secretary. The purpose was to prepare for general elections if the democratic movement became successful. The group sent the president of Burma, Dr. Maung Maung, a letter asking him to grant democracy, annul the one-party system, and form an interim government so general elections could be held.[29] This effort was to no avail due to the transfer of power to the military and the rule of the State Law and Order Restoration Council (SLORC).

In 1989, the Karen National Congress for Democracy (KNCD) was founded as a political party by Saw Harry Si with mostly Christian membership. The party participated in the 1990 general elections but did not win any seats. The KNCD formed a close alliance with Aung San Suu Kyi's National League for Democracy. The SLORC declared it an illegal party, although no arrests were made.[30] The Union of Karen League (or the old KYO) survived as a legal political party led by Saw Tan Aung into 2007. A well-known Karen activist, Alan Saw U, claimed, "The Karen leaders in Myanmar have projected the idea of transferring the armed struggle in the battlefield to the political struggle."[31] Many highly educated Karens in high positions are involved in peacemaking between the military junta and KNU.

In the Karen attempt to transfer energy from the battlefield to political struggle, leaders have focused on humanitarian and community development through social, educational, and healthcare programs. Dr. Simon Tha and his wife, Dr. Rebecca Ya, are both leaders in social and community development for Karens. In June 1994, with other Karen leaders, they formed the Karen Development Committee (KDC), which I joined at the first meeting. In 1997, the KDC opened a medical clinic in Insein and named it for a symbol of the Karen nation, Kwe Ka Baw. This small clinic has developed into a thirty-bed hospital. Dr. Simon Tha and his team travel to treat the sick in remote Karen villages. Since he was a member of the go-between peace team, his travels to the KNU battle zones were overlooked. As he is a neurosurgeon accepted into the Fellowship of Royal College of Surgeons (FRCS) from the UK, military generals relied on his skills, and several family members were his patients. Dr. Rebecca Ya is a graduate from Harvard and worked as director of World Vision in Myanmar.

History professor Tun Aung Chain, a retired director of the Myanmar Historical Commission, is another prominent Karen leader who is also a Harvard graduate. He is from a devout Christian family and is highly respected by both the secular and religious communities. His grandfather, Saw Maung Chain (father-in-law of Karen minister Mrs. Ba Maung Chain), was in the earliest group of Karens who came to study in the United States in the late nineteenth century. Professor Tun Aung Chain's younger sister, Dr. Anna May Say Pa, was president of Myanmar Theological Seminary and founder of the bachelor of arts in religious studies (BARS) program at MIT. Professor Tun Aung Chain was moderator and deacon of the Judson Church on the Yangon University campus for many years. He presided over the Karen New Year

Celebration Committee in Yangon, delivering important speeches on these occasions. Tun Aung Chain was a member of the Karen Peace Mediator Group (KPMG), trying to negotiate peace with Bo Mya and KNU leaders since 1995. In April 2002, when the KPMG convened the first Karen Forum on Development at Pa'an in the Karen state, Professor Tun Aung Chain delivered the opening speech.

Another significant Karen leader is a committed Baptist Christian, Saw Tun Aung Myint (known in the Karen community by his Karen name, Hsar Tu Gaw), son of the last KNA president, Saw Ba Maung. He served in the Burma navy from 1964 to 1988 and was promoted to the rank of lieutenant colonel. After retiring from the navy, he continued to hold senior-level positions and received several government awards for his outstanding performance. He was always active in the Karen community, including chair of the Karen New Year's Celebration Committee. He published a Karen-language booklet about the history of the Karen New Year including a Karen poem that he composed. The poem, or hta, praises the greatness of God's love for the Karens. He participated in the 2010 general elections and became the Karen affairs minister in Rangoon.[32]

These Karen leaders are committed Christians with strong nationalistic sentiments, but instead of encouraging the armed struggle, they keep good relationships with the authorities to restore peace and promote Karen culture through education, healthcare, and community development. However, the activities for the development of the Karen language and culture were very limited except in the Christian community. Since the government made Burmese the official language, many young Karens in the cities could not read or write the Karen language. Only those who live near Karen churches and attend Sunday school and summer Bible camps continue to read and write in the Karen language. Since only 30 percent of Karens are Christians, promotion of Karen cultural heritage remains challenging.

On the bright side, after the 2012 KNU peace negotiations, the government relaxed its travel policy. This allowed Karens from all over the world to return and visit relatives and friends. This has set the stage for the Karen culture to gain momentum. Because of Karen visitors, the Karen New Year celebrations now have larger crowds. These traveling Karens have purchased Karen cultural arts and crafts as souvenirs, thus creating a bigger demand for items such as the Karen flag, Karen drums, and traditional dresses. Karen cars are decorated with stickers that display the Karen flag and Karen slogans. Previously inconceivable commercial billboards in the Karen language have sprouted on the main roads of big cities and towns. The business in Karen arts and crafts has boomed because of the reunion of the Karens inside Myanmar.

Reunification has an important impact on the Christian community and the Karen Baptist Convention. Renovation of old churches, construction of new churches, and development of new mission fields have been accomplished through the contributions of Karen churches and individual members outside of Myanmar. In 2013, when the Karen Baptist Convention (KBC) celebrated its centennial anniversary, many diaspora Karens sent donations and joined the celebration. Worldwide, Karen Baptist churches, including those in Australia, the United States, Singapore, Sweden, and Thailand, sent their greetings to the KBC. Rev. Dr. Roy Medley (general secreatary of ABCUSA), Rev. Stanley Murray (area director for Southeast Asia/Japan), and Rev. Dr. Reid Trulson (executive director of International Ministries), sent letters of greeting and congratulations.[33] The great celebration affirmed the growth of this Karen Christian organization inside Myanmar. In fact, without the KBC, the Karen language would cease to exist in Myanmar today. One could often wonder how the KBC managed to grow under the notoriously harsh military rule.

The Karen Baptist Convention, Christian Education, and Karen Cultural Heritage

As previously mentioned, the Burmese government was biased against Christianity, so Judson College was viewed as an anti-Burmese government institution. After independence, the American Baptist Mission negotiated to reopen the college and started assembling a new lecturing staff. However, it gradually became obvious that the AFPFL government was strongly opposed to the idea of a separate Christian college. First, Judson College was done away with as a separate teaching institution. Then, the American Baptists were compelled to relinquish control over the Judson hostels that provided housing for students. Only Judson Church and the parsonage were left under Baptist control. Thus, the mission planned to build a new Judson College at Moulmein with an emphasis upon science, sociology, and business administration. As the cabinet approved, new buildings were erected, and an opening date of July 1, 1952, was announced. However, at the last minute, the cabinet reversed its earlier decision and took over the newly completed buildings.[34]

In 1974, General Ne Win stepped down from his military position and assumed the presidency of Burma under a new constitution.

Professor Robert Taylor studied the new constitution thoroughly and claims that, although the seven states named Kachin, Kayah, Karen, Chin, Mon, Rakhine, and Shan existed, "the 1974 constitution made it absolutely clear that the sub-states of the Union possess no political or administration sovereignty or autonomy."[35] Christian education was further destroyed after General Ne Win implemented his Burmese Way to Socialism. All private enterprises, including trading companies and banks, hospitals, and schools, were nationalized. All Christian missionary schools and hospitals were confiscated.

However, Ashley South explored the diverse social groups under military rule and discovered that, among the few institutions in Burma not directly controlled by the state, the *sangha* and Christian churches remained among the most powerful sectors of civil society.[36] This privilege allowed the Karen churches to conduct their services in the Karen language, and the KBC, which initially started in 1913 by the name of S'gaw Karen Conference, has become the major organization in preserving the Karen language and cultural identity. Even before the 1931 name change, Karen high schools were established under the support of the KBC in Tavoy, Rangoon, Bassein, Henzada, Toungoo, Shwegyin, and other towns. At the time of the centennial celebration of Ko Tha Byu in 1929, there were seven hundred Karen high schools in Burma.[37]

In 1962, just before Ne Win's nationalization, 195 primary and secondary schools with a student enrollment of 14,962 and 11 Bible schools enrolling 408 students related to the S'gaw Karens were under the KBC umbrella. Additionally, the Pwo Karen Baptists had a separate entity, the Pwo Karen Conference (PKC), which later became the Pwo Karen Baptist Convention (PKBC). In 1962, the Pwo Karens reported 55 primary and secondary schools with 4,624 students and 1 Bible school with 31 students.[38] The Judson Students' Aid Fund and Old Students' Karen organizations were formed in the 1950s to help Karen students by providing loans and aid. Until then, there were groups of Karen Baptists not affiliated with the KBC, among which the largest was the Self-Supporting Karen Baptist Home Mission Society with about 4,000 members. There were also thousands of Karen Anglicans and additional thousands of Karens in the Roman Catholic Church in Burma. It was estimated that there were 100,000 Karen Baptist Christians. Tallied together, the total Christian population was approximately one-sixth of the total Karen population in Burma.[39]

During World War II and the civil war in 1949, many Christian Karen villages, churches, and schools were burned and destroyed. In 1949, anti-Christian squatters occupied and destroyed the greatest S'gaw

Karen compound in Bassein, one of the outstanding mission stations of the world at that time. The Karens lost their oldest and the most prestigious Karen high school (established in 1858 as Bassein Sgaw Karen Normal Industrial Institute) and the church that was dedicated to Ko Tha Byu. Karen schools and churches, including the theological schools in Insein, suffered heavy losses. Despite the losses, after the AFPFL government gained control in 1952, Karens worked hard to rebuild their churches and schools.

In 1959, when Ne Win ruled as the caretaker government, the unlawful residents were evicted, and Karens regained their Bassein compound. Immediately, the Bassein Karens began to reconstruct the campus and were able to build forty structures including a new brick church. In Insein, the Karen Theological Seminary and Karen Women's Bible School were rebuilt. The seminary celebrated its centennial even though the party was overdue by almost five years.[40]

These reconstruction projects went well without interference because the KBC operated as a legal religious organization in the Union of Burma. In early 1950, KBC leaders decided to make the KBC a legal organization in the new Union of Burma. They applied and received the "Certificate of Registration of Societies" No. 12 (1951–1952) from the government of the Union of Burma.[41] At that time, Rev. Saw Be was KBC president, and the general secretary was Rev. Htun Shein Narku. From 1952 to 2013, forty-eight presidents and seven general secretaries worked for the KBC, including Rev. Dr. Clifford Kyaw Dwe, who had the longest tenure, serving more than thirty years (1961–1992).[42] He received his master of religious studies from Andover Newton Theological Seminary in 1957 and later was awarded an honorary doctorate from the Karen Baptist Theological Seminary. The KBC and all its affiliated Christian associations and churches have freedom unless they are involved in anti-government activities.

In the early 1960s, the KBC worked with a staff of seven: general secretary, treasurer, youth secretary, women's secretary, director of Christian education, cashier-accountant, and a typist. In 1960, under the KBC, there were 13 Karen Baptist Associations, 843 churches, 90,390 members and 1,097 pastors and mission workers.[43] Under the military government, the KBC continued to hold annual conventions, conduct training for pastors, Christian education for youth and women, plus publication and other evangelical activities. The Judson Students' Aid Fund and Old Students' Karen organizations, which were KBC affiliations, helped Karen students by giving loans and aid. Official reports show progress:

In 1988, the KBC had 17 Karen Associations and 1,265 churches with 163,208 baptized members.

By 2013, it increased to 20 associations, 1,758 churches, and 274,110 baptized members.[44]

By 2020, the KBC had 1,865 churches and 303,142 members.[45]

Since Karen churches conduct services and Sunday school classes in the Karen language, the numerical growth of churches and members signify that the S'gaw Karen language is widely used. As during the KNU era, Karen heritage prevails in the Karen Baptist communities inside Myanmar.

On the other hand, the KBC lost all its Karen schools after the government confiscated the private schools in 1964. Because they were religious institutions under the KBC, Karen Bible schools and the Karen Baptist Theological Seminary (KBTS) escaped government control and continue to offer courses in the Karen language. The KBC's mission statement says, "The KBC is committed to strive for oneness of the Karen Baptist Churches, and working together in Church planting, holistic development of the Church leaders and church members . . . through meeting, training, publishing of literature."[46] This statement outlines the tasks for its affiliated associations and the directors of its fourteen departments. Three departments, specifically Christian education, publications, and youth work, bear the main load in preserving Karen language skills.

In 2013, the KBC had 14 Bible schools with 282 teachers and 1,537 students.[47] Three additional Bible schools were not KBC-affiliated.[48] The KBC takes pride in its oldest theological institution, located in Insein since 1894. The Karen Baptist Theological Seminary started as the Karen Theological Seminary for male students only in 1845. In 1897, the Karen Women's Bible School was founded in a different location. The two schools jointly offered the diploma in theology program by 1973 and introduced the bachelor of theology program (BTh) in 1982. By the end of the 1985–1986 academic year, the two schools merged into one under the name of Karen Baptist Theological Institute. It is now the Karen Baptist Theological Seminary. KBTS has offered master of arts in religion (MAR) and master of divinity (MDiv) since the 2002–2003 school year. In addition, a liberal arts program has been added, offering business and communication courses.[49]

Its vision statement claims, "The KBTS commits itself to prepare and nurture Karen men and women to become leaders in Christian ministries and Karen organizations." Today the seminary offers five programs: bachelor of theology, master of arts in religion (missiology), master of divinity, master of theology, and church music program. Many of the principals and faculty members obtained their degrees from US institutions.[50] The first native principal of the Karen Theological Seminary, Dr. Chit Maung, directed the seminary from 1945 to 1967. He obtained his first BA degree from Judson College, a BL from Rangoon University, and doctor of divinity (DD) from Newton Theological Seminary in Boston. The last two former principals, Dr. Doh Say (1992–1996) and Dr. Hsa Mu Taw (1998–2014), received doctorates from Fuller Theological Seminary in California.[51] Thra Solomon Ophetoo, in 2018, returned to KBTS after being awarded a doctor of philosophy (PhD) in theological anthropology from Lutheran School of Theology in Chicago.

Having several faculty members with terminal degrees from institutions in the US and other countries, and with the addition of the liberal arts program in 2002, KBTS is one of the most prestigious higher academic institutions in Myanmar. Though S'gaw Karen is the language of instruction at the KBTS, English is required for business, music, and community health courses in the liberal arts program and master's-level classes. The government colleges and universities in Myanmar offer courses only in Burmese, except for English classes. KBTS trains Karens and other indigenous groups to acquire sound scriptural knowledge and equips them with musical skills to share the Good News in their ministries.

KBTS had an enrollment of 853 students in 2013.[52] It sits on Seminary Hill in Insein next to the Myanmar Institute of Theology (MIT), where the majority of faculty, staff, and students are Karen Christians. MIT has a Karen Student Association, which was formed in 1999 and publishes an annual magazine with articles in S'gaw, Pwo, and English.[53]

A 1973 Karen graduate from MIT, Saw Simon, earned his doctor of theology in the Philippines in 1987. He founded the Bible school in Mae La refugee camp in 1990 with 34 students. As the school grew, in 1996 a bachelor of arts course was introduced, offering secular subjects including political science, history, economics, education, and English. In 2002, his school had 233 students and 20 faculty members. He received the Human Rights Award from the Baptist World Alliance in 2000, recognizing his evangelical and educational efforts in the Burma-Thai border area. The Human Rights Award was introduced in 1990. Since it is offered once every five years, Dr. Simon became the second recipient after the first winner, former US president Jimmy Carter in 1995.[54]

Rev. Dr. Yaha Lay Lay La, another Karen MIT graduate (1983), contributed to the development of the Karen Christian community and

Karen cultural identity at a global level. He received his doctor of ministry (DMin) from Eastern Baptist Theological Seminary (now Palmer Theological Seminary) near Philadelphia. From 1997 to 2014, while working as a professor at KBTS, he formed the *Klo Kweh* Karen music team; developed the Nargis Rehabilitation Care Center; and initiated the Dr. T. Thanbyah Christian Institute (TCI) plus the Karen Arts and Science Institute (KASI). He traveled internationally to help establish the KBC-Norway and the KBC-USA. He took his Klow Kweh music team to other countries to perform at Karen churches and Karen communities, raising funds for new buildings, churches, KBTS, and TCI.[55]

TCI received support from various Karen Christian communities around the world. In 2015, a Sydney community group in Australia consisting of academics and other professionals formed the Friends of TCI Committee to provide knowledge and expertise toward curriculum development and linkages to wider institutes. P'doh Mahn John Roc, founder of the Friends of the TCI, visited TCI in January 2016 and commented, "The university had made great progress in such a short time." He reflects the true Karen Christian lifestyle: "Students, who live in male and female dormitories, carry out a number of chores, including firewood gathering, wood chopping, working in the garden and helping with cooking and preparing meals on a roster basis. There are two recreational courts and musical instruments for use by students to relax and enjoy and choir groups they can join."[56]

Another important department of the KBC to preserve the Karen language is that of publications. When the socialist government confiscated all Karen schools, Karen textbooks vanished from the school curriculum, and Karen-language publications stopped. Knowing the language would cease to exist without books, KBC leaders encouraged the Department of Publication to print Christian books, Sunday school lessons, magazines, and educational materials in the Karen language. KBC's Go Forward Press (*Lei Hsu Nyar*) became instrumental in printing almost all Karen language books.

The KBC monthly magazine, *Go Forward*, was affirmed at the KBC annual meeting in 1950 at Cool Chapel in Rangoon. Subsequently, that December, one thousand copies of the first eight-page issue were published. The consecration service of the KBC printing press was held on September 21, 1951, at Thra Rawley Dee's residence at Insein Seminary Hill, where several American missionaries joined the occasion. Thra Rawley Dee was the first editor of the KBC press. When he retired, the press was moved to the Karen Theological Seminary on June 5, 1953. Thra Marku Shwe Zan was the editor when Dr. Chit Maung, principal of the Karen Theological Seminary, laid the foundation of the press on March 3, 1957.[57]

The publication department has faced several challenges dealing with government censorship. Every publication in Karen had to be translated into Burmese for censorship approval. Copies of the proposed publication in the original language and in Burmese were submitted to the censorship board for approval. The process took months to get approvals for publications. On April 9, 2003, the government issued an order that the Go Forward Press must stop all operations and close. The reason was that the press published a book, *Big Mountain*, that did not yet have permission to print due to pending censorship. A month later, on May 20, the press was allowed to reopen.[58]

Another problem was distribution delays for published books due to the government post office system. Books were sometimes lost in transit. Despite these challenges, KBC publications progressed under the socialist government. The *Go Forward* monthly magazine, originally printed in eight pages, increased to thirty-two pages and from one thousand copies to five thousand copies in 1978.[59]

KBC publications focused on four areas: pastors, youth, women, and children. Sunday school lessons for children and *Endeavor Magazine* are published every three months. Faculty members of KBTS, MIT, and many Bible schools wrote most of the books and articles. Rev. Dr. Clifford Kyaw Dwe, the longest-serving KBC general secretary, authored several books and articles, including the history of the KBC. In 1993, KBC started to work toward publishing a new Karen Bible using current Karen terms. It was followed by a study guide for learning the new Bible and was completed in 2013.[60]

In addition, Go Forward Press publishes manuals and reports of the KBC and KBC-affiliated associations and their meetings. They serve as the printing arm for Karen student associations from the theological schools, universities, colleges, and other government-approved Karen organizations. In 2013, the publication department reported an increase in the publication of various materials including magazines, cooperation programs, calendars, brochures, and pamphlets.[61] Since the peace negotiations with the KNU in 2012, the government has relaxed some red tape on all minority groups in Myanmar, and the Karen language is used more freely inside Burma than previously.

Another important department under KBC that played a crucial role in promoting Karen culture and heritage is the Department of Youth Work, mostly known as Christian Endeavor (CE). Formed in 1955, CE provides several youth programs to nurture spiritual and intellectual growth, including weekly worship services, summer Bible study camps, songs, music contests, debates, sports tournaments, and other humanitarian activities. Along with these programs, CE published quarterly magazines, youth weekly worship guidebooks, Bible lessons for youth and children, prayer books, songbooks, and other educational books.[62] Because of CE program participation at church, Karen youth have a strong command of Karen language. The church-related activities of Christian Endeavor have helped young people develop a lasting commitment to God's work and have elevated their morality and confidence.

The KBC's Department of Youth arranges summer Bible camp programs in various associations. Most camps are ten days long, though some are longer. Along with Bible teaching, programs include church music and other educational topics like health and communication skills. The training instructors are pastors, KBTS faculty, university faculty, doctors, and nurses. Summer Bible camps' closing ceremonies are held with concerts and song competitions in choir, quartet, trio, duet, and solo, where not only CE youth but also church pastors, leaders, choir members, and their families participate.

Most CE members from Nanthagone Karen Baptist Church, my home church in Insein, attended the summer Bible camp organized by the Rangoon Karen Baptist Association. Many were inspired by the instructors who were viewed as spiritual and intellectual role models, motivating the campers to pursue even more knowledge. Our church Sunday school teacher, Thramu Gilda Htwe, was the Rangoon University librarian. She earned a graduate degree from a UK institution in 1959. Her teaching influenced our thoughts and actions throughout our lives. Many Karen church members who attended Sunday school and CE camps earned university degrees and accepted high government positions. Naw Helen Pe, who was once our CE vice president, received scholarships and earned two master's degrees, one in English language teaching from Warwick University in the UK in 1988 and the other in public administration from Harvard University in 2002.

The Karen Bible teachers in these summer camps emphasized the importance of the Karen language. In 1974, two close friends from my church went to the summer Bible camp. They studied together for the exam to be evaluated by their lecturer, Rev. Doh Say, who later became the principal of Karen Baptist Theological Seminary. One of these campers got first and the other got second, but when the one who got second compared the answers on both exams, she argued that her answers were all correct, like those of her friend. They both went to see the teacher and learned the one who got second made several spelling mistakes whereas her friend had only one. Even after thirty years, they talk about it whenever they reminisce about their experience at the youth summer Bible camps.

In 2002, the Karen Baptist Convention's CE developed a humanitarian program that supported youth in need including the disabled, drug addicted, and AIDS patients. To nurture a new generation of Karen leaders, CE started the first Myanmar Karen Youth Conference in 2001, from April 26 to 30, at Myaungmya; 571 Karen youth from all over Myanmar participated. CE decided to hold this youth conference every three years. Thus, the second was held in 2004 (April 21-25), the third in 2007, and the fourth in 2010. All these conferences were presided by Rev. Dr. Ya Ha Lay Lay La with other pastors and KBTS faculty delivering lectures and coordinating discussions. The second conference had the highest attendance of a thousand due to the location that housed the famous Karen Prayer Mountain, called *Naw Bu Baw*, in Thandaung. The subjects discussed in these conferences encouraged participants to embrace God's Word, be brave and courageous in doing God's work, and strive for unity, peace, and the growth of Christianity. In addition to hymns and gospel music, newly composed songs were taught at these conferences.[63] Attendees made new friends living in other areas of Myanmar who shared their language and these common learning experiences.

The KBC's work with youth encouraged young Karens to read the Bible, participate in Christian evangelical movements, praise God with songs and music, and serve in humanitarian and community development. It also sharpened their Karen-language skills and created wider social networks for Karens. The combination of Christian education, Karen-language publications, Christian Endeavor's summer Bible camps, youth conferences, and other functions in Karen local churches play a huge role in maintaining Karen cultural heritage in the Karen Christian community. Indeed, the Karen Baptist Convention is the major pillar in promoting and preserving the Christian-oriented Karen identity in Myanmar.

The Karen Exodus and the Extension of a Christian-Oriented Karen National Identity

In 1989, Anders P. Hovemyr, author of *In Search of the Karen King*, claimed there were two schools of thought in writing Karen history. One school consisted of the nineteenth- and early twentieth-century studies carried out almost exclusively by missionaries. The other school contained modern studies from 1950 onward carried out by ethnologists and anthropologists.[64] Twenty-first-century developments suggest that the writing of Karen history should either move to a new school of thought or return to the first one—the missionaries and Christian scholars. This review of the past would renew the pioneering efforts of the nineteenth-century American missionaries with a greater appreciation of their legacy as it expands across the globe. Understandably, such scholarship cannot be accomplished without exploring the Karen diaspora communities and their evangelical movements.

The story of Karen evangelical movements expanding outside of Burma must begin with the Karens in Thailand. From 1828 to 1865, missionaries and pastors made three trips to Thailand, but they had to return due to malaria or being robbed along the journey. In 1872, American missionary Chapin Carpenter and two Karen pastors, Thra San Po and Thra Aye Baw, reached Thailand and discovered 63 Karen villages. In December 1880, the Burma Baptist Convention (BBC) sent Thra Maung Klo, Thra Shwe Mya, and Thra Sa Kay to Chiangmai, where they successfully established a church. A year later, the BBC sent Rev. Webster to survey the work in Thailand, and on his way, he baptized seventy people and established three more churches. Again in 1884, Thra Mya Gaw, a Thai Karen, began his study of the Bible at the Karen Seminary in Burma. He graduated in 1888 and returned to Thailand, serving as a pastor at the Ban Nawk Church, thirty miles north of Lampang. During 1900–1907, Karen missionaries from Burma left Thailand. Because of a request from Karens in Thailand, the BBC appointed Rev. En Nay Dee Wah to lead the work among the Karens there.[65]

After independence, the Burmese government restricted Karen missionaries' movement, yet several Karen pastors crossed over the border quietly through KNU-controlled areas. Pastor Winai, who lived his entire life in the KNU liberated zone until 1971, studied in the Karen seminary in Insein and later founded a Karen church in Maesot, Thailand, in 1994.[66]

As the churches in Thailand grew, the Thailand Karen Baptist Convention (TKBC) was established in 1955 in Chiang Mai.[67] From its headquarters, TKBC arranged conferences, published Karen Christian literature, and sent evangelists to expand the mission field inside Thailand. The KBC in Burma and the TKBC in Thailand jointly organized conferences, especially for women and youth. The latest statistics show that Thailand Baptist Karen Convention has 219 churches with 41,566 members. The current president is Snit Wongnitisthaporn, and the general secretary is Prateep Dee.[68]

In Thailand, Roman Catholic missionaries developed educational opportunities for Karens in the rural hill regions. They represented the Karen language using Roman letters. In 1955, priests of the French Betharram Congregation founded the Mae Pon School in the Karen hills of northern Thailand with Father Joseph Seguinotte as the founding leader. Over the years, Mae Pon school developed a curriculum for children who, in addition to attending the obligatory Thai government school, wanted to learn the Karen language. A student named Pav Di from Mae Pon earned a doctorate in 2007 in social science from Chiang Mai University. He has worked as the regional director of the Indigenous Knowledge and People's Network (IKAP) and the Inter-Mountain People's Education and Culture in Thailand Association (IMPECT).[69]

On October 22, 2021, the Baptist World Alliance (BWA) delivered a welcoming message to four Baptist groups including the Kawthoolei Karen Baptist Convention (KKBC) churches. The BWA introduced its new member the KKBC as follows: "Born out of the oppression and persecution of ethnic minorities in Myanmar in the early 1980s, KKBC formed in 1983, and is comprised of Internally Displaced Persons living on the border. . . . The KKBC was accepted as a member of the regional fellowship, the Asia Pacific Baptist Federation, in February of this year."[70]

Noticeably, the KKBC is in the KNU area on the Burma-Thai border. Therefore, the members are from the conflict-affected Karen population. Beginning in 1975, about two thousand Karen people from Toungoo, Nyaungleybin, and the Thaton district fled to Thailand to escape the military government of Burma's repressive measures. The government's Four Cuts policy caused more internal displacement, and the refugee population grew each year. By 1984, after the fall of Mae Tha Waw, the population had increased to nine thousand.

Despite the January 2004 informal ceasefire agreement, a reduction in military clashes, and ongoing negotiations between the Karen National Union and the State Police and Development Council, human rights abuses continued in the Karen state. In Thandaung, civilians were forced to repair military outposts. Cultivation of rice fields was restricted by a ban on overnight travel and orders to stay away from designated villages. In the Papun area, military operations along the east side of the Yunzalin River destroyed the road between Kyaukkyi and Saw Hta during March and April 2005. To support local troops, the SPDC and DKBA continued forced labor, extortion, and land confiscation, thus depriving villagers of their livelihood. Fear of land mines caused many villagers to flee. Thus, the internally displaced population

(IDP) in the Karen state alone was 89,900; in Mon state 49,700; and in Pegu 21,300.[71] In August 2008, the Karen Refugee Committee reported there were 120,821 refugees in seven camps.

Formed by these internally displaced persons, Kawthoolei Karen Baptist Church membership fluctuated, especially after 2007, because the United Nations High Commission on Refugees (UNHCR) relocated many refugees to various host countries. Currently, under the chairmanship of Rev. Robert Kaytoe and general secretary Saw Peacefully Thomas, the KKBC has 18,208 members in 87 churches. KKBC's international communication liaison, Saw Wado, claimed that joining the Baptist World Alliance would build the KKBC and help them to navigate a holistic mission for the border community, "both in Thailand and in Myanmar—globally for Jesus Christ."[72]

In fact, the KKBC was first founded in 1984 by Rev. Saw Htoo. He was from Shwegyin and studied at the Karen Theological Seminary. He established the first Kawthoolei High School in Kwee De Koh village in the eastern hills in 1951; the Karen Mission Middle School at Myat Yen in 1956; and the Blut Doh Lu Karen Mission High School in 1960. After Saw Htoo fled to the KNU-controlled zone, he started two Bible schools, one in Blut Doh Luh Kyaukkyi in 1970, and then Kawthoolei Karen Bible School in Kyaukkyi in 1983. He worked with Harry Klein, who was the son of American missionary Edward Norman Harris (Shwegyin Karen Mission founder and author of *A Star in the East*, published in 1920). Embracing his father's legacy, he worked with Rev. Saw Htoo in the conflict-affected Karen hills. Rev. Saw Htoo wrote several articles including the KNU Bulletin 1 in November 1985, and the reports for the Karen Refugee Committee from 1984 to 1986.[73]

Rev. Saw Htoo's daughter, Naw Plahset, married the son of Saw George Kacher (Ka-CHER), who founded the first Karen and Burmese Christian fellowship in the United States in 1977. This is now known as the First Burmese Baptist Church of San Francisco. George Kacher's grandfather, Saw Ka Sa, was the first Karen missionary who studied in America and joined the American missionary in the Shwegyin Karen area in the eastern hills. George Kacher was a graduate of Judson College in Rangoon but later went to engineering school. He received a government scholarship to study military engineering in the UK, but when he came back in 1949 during the Karen rebellion, he was arrested and imprisoned for a year. In 1958, at the age of thirty-eight, he married Naw Thelma, the daughter of the treasurer of Bassein Karen Baptist Association.

Then in 1968, he sent his application to work in the US after he learned that the US government offered jobs for people in Burma. After struggling through troubles imposed by the Burmese government, he and his family arrived in Chicago on May 5, 1971. By then, he had five children, the eldest aged thirteen. He did not find a proper job in Chicago and thus traveled to California. Finally, in San Francisco, he settled with his family and attended the Park Presidio Bible Church. Through his sponsorship, Mrs. Kacher's brothers and sister and their families arrived in the US. Since Mrs. Kacher's mother could not follow the sermon in English, Saw Kacher and his family invited friends from Burma to start Sunday worship at his house.

In 1975, they launched house worship and fellowship in Burmese, rotating from one house to another. In addition to George, those leading the services were Shirley Chow, Mrs. April Shan Lone, Saw Nelson Dwa, U San Mya, and Daw Mya Thin. George Kacher, who served as worship leader at Park Presidio Bible Church, asked permission for his group to hold weekly worship at the church. On October 10, 1977, they received permission. Sadly, he died of a heart attack on October 18, just a week later. On the arrival of pastor emeritus Shwe Hlaing Dwa from Burma in October 1980, the fellowship had its first trained pastor. Known as the First Burmese Baptist Church of San Francisco (FBBC), today under the leadership of senior pastor Rev. Yi Shey Latt, all ethnic groups from Burma join as members.[74]

Mrs. Thelma Kacher's siblings—Miller Aung, Taylor Aung, Yoe Aung, Keller Aung, and Elma Aung—moved to Bakersfield, California, and started a Sunday worship service with Karen friends already living there. They rotated from one house to another calling themselves the Karen Baptist Fellowship. On October 30, 1983, after the worship service at Saw Taylor Aung's house, they discussed building a church in Bakersfield. Three years later, on July 3, 1986, they received the legal documents certifying the church as a 501c3 not-for-profit.[75] The Karen Baptist Fellowship emerged as the first Karen church in the US and was established by the descendants of devout Karen Christians from Bassein. The church members regularly support other churches and mission fields in Burma. Naw Lu Baw Keller, president of the church, wrote in their church history book: "Our desire for our children is that when they hear their parents and elders worshipping God in their native language, they will understand and retain their native language. In addition, future generations after generations will have the opportunity to hear the spoken Karen language, where they descend from, their ethnicity, and their cultural identity."[76]

The Bakersfield Karen Church is a haven for all Karen pastors and scholars visiting America, especially those who came to study at Fuller

Theological Seminary. Long before the arrival of refugees from the camps, US Karens gathered every year in Bakersfield to celebrate Karen New Year. About 250 people attended when I joined the celebration in December 1984.

By founding the first Karen church, Thelma Kacher's siblings plus the Aungs' descendants and friends developed the first Karen community in the US. Like conventional migrants, they entered the country by applying for jobs available to them. There was not much hope for increasing the number of Karen people or churches in the US when all the job applications had to go through the socialist government of Burma that embraced an isolationist policy.

However, through the Federal Resettlement Program of the US government, many Karens started to arrive in 1990. In 1984, 20,000 Karen refugees lived in nine camps along the Thai side of Moei River. The Consortium of Christian Agencies (CCA), a group of several religious relief organizations, provided aid to the Karen refugees in these camps. Contributions also came from Relief International (formerly International Christian Aid), the Catholic Office for Emergency Relief and Refugees, plus other relief groups. Medical supplies were provided by *Medecins sans Frontières* (Doctors without Borders). All food and relief were distributed through the Karen Refugee Committee (KRC), an organization established by the Karen themselves. As of March 1990, 26,547 Karen refugees were in the twelve camps inside Thailand, and 32,000 internally displaced Karens were spread in various locations along the border.[77]

The first group of Karen refugees arrived in the US in the late 1990s from Thai cities such as Bangkok or from a special camp in Thailand called Manee Loi. Due to the September 11, 2001, attacks, admission of refugees slowed. From 2006, the US government started to open the door wider, allowing Karens from various Thailand refugee camps the option of coming to the US. On February 7, 2006, Anastasia Brown testified to the international relations committee of the House of Representatives, "Today I recommend four steps that the US should take to address the needs of the Burmese refugee population so that durable solutions can be found to their plight."[78] She continued to explain that in 2006, more than 450,000 refugees resided in Thailand. Of those, 142,917 live in nine camps along the Thai-Burma border, most of which are of Karen and Karenni ethnic groups. It was decided these refugees could be resettled in the US during the 2005–2006 fiscal year.[79]

From 2006 to 2009, 53,406 refugees left their camps and resettled in Australia, Canada, Denmark, Finland, Ireland, the Netherlands,

Norway, New Zealand, Sweden, and the United States, with the largest crowd numbering 49,451 (see a chart online).

The State Department coordinates resettlement policy and manages overseas processing, cultural orientation, and transportation to the US. Refugees were allocated among the ten national voluntary agencies that operate throughout the US. Around 90 to 95 percent of Karen people from the refugee camps are Christian. Recognizing the strong Baptist background of the Karens, American Baptist International Ministries and National Ministries prepared to assist the Karens in the resettlement process and to help integrate the new Karen arrivals into their local Baptist congregations and denominations. In 2006, they appointed Duane and Marcia Binkley, a missionary couple who worked in Thailand for many years and spoke S'gaw Karen. Regarding their mission responsibilities the Binkleys wrote,

> We (Marcia and Duane) will remain as Missionaries on special assignment with International Ministries of the American Baptist Churches USA (IM-ABC/USA) jointly appointed as Field Personnel with the Cooperative Baptist Fellowship (CBF) as follows:
>
> Within the ABC, we will work in coordination with the joint International Ministries' (IM), National Ministries' and Office of the General Secretary's task force formed to respond to the influx of refugees from Burma to America.
>
> In Thailand . . . we will remain members of the Thailand Baptist Missionary Fellowship, and will partner and link . . . Thailand Karen Baptist Convention and the Kawthooley Karen Baptist Convention.
>
> Our mission is to act as agents to connect the Karen people arriving in the U.S. with ABC and CBF related churches and the wider Baptist community, while finding ways to allow the Karen to remain connected with each other within America and around the world.

The Binkleys traveled extensively, providing resources for US churches on the background of Burma and the Karens, introducing the newly arrived Karens to the ABC/CBF churches available in their areas, and advancing the connections between the ABC and CBF with the churches in the refugee camps and the IDPs in Burma. Rev. Florence Li, national coordinator of Asian Ministries for the American Baptist Home Mission Societies, worked with the Binkleys helping the newly established Karen churches communicate with the American Baptist churches in the United States. Through their efforts, several Karen churches were formed by the time 12,800 Karens settled in thirty-three states across the US in 2007.[80]

Another US organization that plays a significant role in connecting the American Baptist heritage to the Karen Christians in Burma is the Friends of Burma (FOB). In 1985, Dr. Neil and Diana Sowards of Fort Wayne, Indiana, founded the FOB, dedicating their support for the Christians of Burma. Dr. Soward's parents, Erville and Genevieve, served in Burma as missionaries for more than thirty years. A scholarship program was established in their name and administered by the Myanmar Baptist Convention. In addition to scholarships, the FOB helped various projects of the Karen Baptist Convention (KBC), such as the healthcare clinic, Karen Baptist Convention staff housing, KBTS library, Nyaunglybin Bible school, and the Pathein S'gaw Karen Baptist Association, to mention a few. FOB also gave grants to the Pa'an Mawlamyine Karen Women Association (PKWA) in the Karen state to buy materials for a Karen traditional manmade weaving machine—a loom.[81] Since Karen traditional dresses carry Karen national identity, by supporting the Karen traditional weaving industries the FOB has perpetuated the Karen national identity.

The first group of Karen refugees was relocated in Indiana, Minnesota, and upstate New York in the late 1990s. Concerned for new arrivals in their city of Fort Wayne, Indiana, the Sowards volunteered their services, personally attending to refugee needs. As of 2007, about one thousand arrived in Fort Wayne, with few English skills and many medical problems. Diana drove her car more than eight hundred miles each month taking Karens to various appointments. Dr. Sowards purchased a rundown house for a widow with eight children and fixed it up so that her monthly outlay would be within her means.[82]

Following the Karen ministries in the US, the FOB reported the following in its June 2008 newsletter:

> The Karen Baptist Church of Western Chicago, now celebrating a one-year anniversary, reaches Karens, many of whom travel a considerable distance to attend each Sunday to join in the fellowship which has grown to about 80. In Moline, Illinois, a worship service in the Karen language has been started with about 30 to 50 in attendance. New families are arriving every week so the potential for growth is great. They currently worship with the First Baptist Church of Moline.
>
> Phoenix, Arizona continues to be a site of great activity with Burmese refugees. June 7th Burmese pastors from around the United States gathered to develop continuing support for each other and new

churches that are forming as refugees continue to flow into the U.S. Twenty Karens attended the ABC Mission Conference in Cincinnati, Ohio. They are net-working and hope to develop a Karen Baptist Convention within the American Baptist Convention within two years. They are also developing a nation-wide Karen Women's Association.[83]

The first Karen church in Illinois, the Karen Baptist Church of Western Chicago, formed in May 2007, became a member of the American Baptist Churches of Great River Region through the arrangement of its director, Dr. Cheryl Henson.[84] The North Shore Baptist Church in Chicago helped the Karen refugees who arrived in 2007 by arranging space for a separate Karen worship service. Two years later, in 2009, the Karen North Shore Baptist Church was established, with Rev. Roger Poe Nyunt as pastor.[85]

In Phoenix, Arizona, when Karen refugees arrived in 2007, two members of the FOB, Adam Maung and his wife, Tansy Kadoe, who lived in Phoenix since 2000, volunteered their services for resettlement programs and for Sunday worship in the Karen language. With the arrival of Pastor Tha Hgay, who was a KKBS graduate and ordained since 1995, they establish the Arizona Karen Baptist Church.

Rev. Tha Hgay had been the executive secretary for Bliek-Tavoy Kaw Thoo Lei Karen Baptist Convention for five years, and served as chairman for fifteen churches organized under Zone 1. Having much experience serving churches, he wanted to unify the Karen Baptist Churches in the US. After visits with Rev. Florence Li and Mr. Duane Binkley in Phoenix, and with their encouragement, he made a concerted effort for the formation of the Karen Baptist Convention-USA (KBC-USA).[86]

KBC-USA's formation moved faster than expected. Twenty-four Karen pastors and leaders met in June 2008, at a conference arranged by National Ministries of ABCUSA and held at the Dallas Chin Baptist Church in Texas. The two-day conference on October 21–22, 2008, featured a list of dignitaries including Florence Li, Richard Harris, Rev. Ni, Rev. Mang Tiak, Dr. Angelene Naw, and Duane Binkley. Rev. Dr. Roy Medley, general secretary of the ABCUSA, delivered the message "Back to the Future'" at the closing worship celebration.[87]

After closing worship, the Asian American Baptist Conference embraced major leaders of the Burmese/Karen diaspora in the US. The meeting took forty-five minutes, where all the leaders of the Karen churches unanimously agreed to join ABCUSA. In April 2009, the executive board of the KBC-USA was formed with Rev. Tha Hgay as the president, Rev. Hsa Mu as the vice president, Rev. Ler Htoo as the general secretary, and Rev. Aye Aye Thaw as assistant secretary.[88]

Thus, on April 28, 2009, the Karen Baptist Churches-USA was founded with ninety-one member churches and twenty-six hundred members. As an Associate Ministries Organization of American Baptist Churches USA, it has partnerships with ABCUSA, Global Karen Baptist Fellowship, Karen Baptist Convention, Kawthoolei Karen Baptist Churches, and the Thailand Karen Baptist Convention. KBC-USA is organized into seven regions: West Coast, East Coast North, East Coast South, Central North, Central South, Midwest North, and Midwest South. The KBC-USA has arranged many programs, including global and local Karen conferences plus training and workshops for women and youth. In 2015, KBC-USA assisted local Karen Baptist churches and leadership training while starting Karen-language Bible schools awarding a diploma in theology and a certificate of theological study.[89] These activities of the KBC-USA have rejuvenated the American Baptist tradition and strengthened the Christian-oriented Karen national identity.

On July 21, 2009, KBC-USA held its first general meeting at Fort Wayne, Indiana, where the committee members for the seven regions of the KBC-USA were selected. Since then, the general meeting has been held annually: 2010 in St. Paul, Minnesota; 2011 in San Francisco; and 2012 in Denver, Colorado. In 2013, the four Karen churches in St. Paul hosted the celebration of the two hundredth Judson anniversary where Karen pastors, church leaders, and laymen from all around the world joined the celebration.[90] The KBC-USA also arranges Karen youth programs each year. Because of the Judson two hundredth anniversary celebration, during 2012 and 2013, many Karen Christian leaders and pastors from Burma and Thailand visited the Karen churches in the US and provided training and workshops.

As of July 2015, 64,759 Karen refugees have resettled in the US plus an additional 11,619 Karenni. Since these numbers were only the refugees from the Thailand camps prior to 2015, and excluding other Karens from Burma, the total Karen population in the US could be far more than 70,000.

Among the earliest arrivals in Minnesota was Robert Zan, son of KNU leader Mahn Ba Zan. As the first Karen refugee settlement in the US with a leader in the KNU tradition, the Karen New Year and Martyr's Day became great celebrations. A Karen Reunion 2003 (North America) was held in the First Baptist Church of St. Paul, Minnesota, August 8-10, 2003. Robert Zan's speech on August 10 reminded the Karen people of Ba U Gyi's principle that "surrender is out of the question" and to strive hard to maintain the Karen national identity. Zan recapped the SLORC General Maung Aye's proclamation in 1997 that "in twenty years you will be able to find Karen people only in a museum." He then warned the Karens of the importance of courage and unity to preserve their Karen national identity. Karens from Australia, Canada, Thailand, and Singapore joined the reunion. Two daughters of Saw Ba U Gyi were among the crowd of more than five thousand.[91]

According to the Minnesota human resource record, 7,285 Karen refugees settled in the state from 2003 to 2015. The Karen Organization of Minnesota, which was formed in 2003, claims that there were more than 17,000 Karens in Minnesota.[92] With the majority living in St. Paul and Maple Wood, Karens gather there yearly to celebrate the Karen New Year. St. Paul is considered the largest and fastest-growing Karen population of any city in the US. The first Karen church was established in St. Paul in 2000 and the latest one being Sinai Church in Willmar. At present, there are eighteen churches in Minnesota with Hosanna Karen Baptist Church as the largest having 750 members.[93]

Upstate New York metropolitan areas including Buffalo, Rochester, Utica, Rome, and Albany have the second-largest Karen community in the US with some that came earlier than 2006. The New Year celebration of 2006 was held at Tabernacle Baptist Church in Utica with the performance of Karen Don dance.[94] Although it was celebrated inside a church, many non-Christian Karens and several Karen Buddhist monks joined the celebration. It is estimated that in 2015, there were five thousand Karens in Albany[95] and fifty-five hundred in Buffalo in 2016.[96] In 2017, the Karen community of Syracuse bought a Polish-American bar and converted it into the Syracuse Karen Baptist Church. The newspaper reported that the club was sold in the spring to the next generation of Syracuse newcomers, Karen refugees. The Karen Baptist Church of Syracuse bought the brick building on Teal Avenue for $120,000. The church has a congregation of three hundred. Since 2006, Syracuse has welcomed twenty-four hundred refugees of Karen descent.[97]

Omaha, Nebraska, has the third-largest Karen community. Karen refugees first arrived in the Omaha area in 2005. The next year, Rev. Kaw Khu initiated the Karen Society of Nebraska while working with Lutheran Family Services, Inc. The society's current executive director, Pa Naw Dee, moved to the US in 2008 and is listed as a co-founder on the society's website. Tha Ther Moo, president of the Karen Society of Nebraska's Omaha chapter, said more than five thosand Karen people now live in Omaha, with more than eight thousand Karen statewide in Nebraska.[98]

Nebraska Karens celebrated the fifty-ninth Karen National Martyr's Day (August 15–16, 2009) with Karen traditional dance and songs, sports, and food festivals. The mayor of Omaha, Jim Suttle, honored the ceremony with an opening speech after Rev. Chrysler Gay Su said the opening prayer. The ceremony included the presentation of a Karen student from Omaha, Saw Lor, who received the Gates Scholarship that year. Karen youth soccer teams from twelve states competed on the pitch with a crowd of around three thousand in attendance.[99]

Karens began arriving in the Kansas City area in the heartland of the United States in 2007 and 2008. They were well received through the local Jewish Vocational Service that had helped local congregations find housing and employment for these new neighbors. American Baptists reassigned Karen-speaking missionaries Duane and Marcia Binkley from the Karen refugee camps in Thailand to the Kansas City area where they served the growing Karen population before moving to Arkansas. Four Baptist churches in the Kansas City area are now enriched by the addition of these Karens. Led by three trained pastors, Grace Karen Baptist Church meets weekly with a full program of worship and language studies. Emmanuel Karen Baptist Church and Kansas City Kansas Baptist Christian Church plus the Hosanna Karen Baptist Church provide similar ministries to more than one thousand Karens who currently live in the Kansas City area. Central Baptist Theological Seminary has established a doctor of ministry program with MIT in which students from Myanmar and students from America study cross-culturally in the world of the other. Several Karens each year are in Kansas City benefiting from this academic program.[100]

At present, 105 Karen churches are affiliated with KBC-USA and about 30 to 40 additional Karen congregations with a total population of about thirty-five thousand.[101] Christianity plays an important role in the life of most Karen Americans, and church attendance is generally high. Since churches tend to be the focal point of the Karen community where many activities and organizations are based, many Buddhists and non-Christian Karens sometimes attend church to participate in community events with Christian counterparts.

As events unfold, the Baptist tradition paved the way for Karens to conveniently build faith-based communities in various parts of the US. The growth of the Karen churches and their coordinating activities comprise the realization of the Karen culture and identity. In addition to Baptist churches, the enhancement of the Karen national identity can be observed through other Karen associations and organizations formed in the US.

1. Karen Organization of Minnesota, KOM

2. Karen Culture Organization of Minnesota, KCOM

3. Karen American Community Foundation, KACF

4. Karen Organization of San Diego, KOS

5. Karen Organization of America, KOA

6. The Karen Society of Nebraska

7. Karen Culture Organization in USA, KCO[102]

These associations and organizations conduct a series of cultural events including Karen New Year celebration, Karen and Burmese language classes for children and youth, Karen cultural dance preservation through scheduled practice and performances, plus cultural presentations to schoolteachers and the public. The activities of these organizations in the US extend their efforts to promote Karen national identity.

In 2020, the KOA arranged an international essay competition for young writers to commemorate the Karen Martyr's Day seventieth anniversary. The essay competition focused on Saw Ba U Gyi's three strategies that he outlined for the Karen struggle to succeed. Among the forty-seven papers submitted, the three winners were first prize to Saw Klo Kwe Moo from Kham University, Oslo, Norway; second prize to Ehler Tha Win from the University of Washington, Seattle, US; and the third prize to Saw Blut Doh Say from University of Chamber of Commerce in Bangkok, Thailand. Mr. Phil Thornton, one of the judges, said that the writing of the young Karens was thought-provoking and covered important issues for the Karens' current political struggle. He commented, "Many of the essays identified weaknesses in the KNU's approach to the National Ceasefire Agreement process. Others questioned the KNU's political structures and its capacity to handle negotiations with the Burma military use of tactics that locked Karen into ineffective positions."[103] Fortunately, they were all outside the orbit of the Burmese military and so had full freedom to promote their political and cultural movements through the network of their newly formed associations and organizations.

The Karen cause in the US was brought to the silver screen in 2017 with the motion picture *All Saints* starring John Corbett, Barry Corbin, Cara Buono, and Nelson Lee. The true story of Karens settling in Smyrna, Tennessee, and revitalizing the All Saints Anglican Church received favorable reviews from critics and good ratings from moviegoers. The movie created awareness of these new refugees who came to the States.

The historic American Baptist missionary expression of Christianity made the US the major player in helping the Karens promote their Karen culture and their Christian-oriented national identity. It confirmed what Mikael Gravers claimed more than a decade ago: "Religion has a crucial role in the Karen self-presentation as their cultural foundation and in their national identity."[104]

Between 2006 and September 2017, a total of 109,402 refugees from the camps on the Thai-Burma border were resettled in thirty countries, with the greatest number in the United States; others settled in Australia, Canada, Denmark, Finland, Ireland, New Zealand, Norway, Sweden, the Netherlands, and the United Kingdom.[105] Despite the lack of religious ties, almost all these countries, especially Australia and Canada, offered sanctuaries for the Karens to build Karen churches and expand Karen cultural movements.[106]

The worldwide Karen diasporas have different approaches to nationalist movements, with some advocating armed struggle and others calling for dialogue on social justice and political reform. In the end, all the Karen national celebrations signify the Christian orientation of this coveted national identity. The Karen New Year originated from the efforts of Karen Christian parliamentary members. The Karen national anthem was composed by Karen Christian pastors. The Karen flag hoisted in all these occasions was designed by Karen Christian artists. As the Karen language that Jonathan Wade invented is continually used around the world and the Bible that Francis Mason translated into that Karen language is still read in Karen churches, a Christian-oriented Karen national identity will not fade in the next century. Many Americans may not recall their early foreign missionaries' names, but Karen Christians will continue to honor the names Judson, Mason, Boardman, and Wade for making a Karen nation among the world's civilizations.

Notes

1. Saw Moo Troo and Mika Rolley, *Karens and Communism, and Karens Fight for Peace* (N.p.: Kawthoolei publication, n.d). See also Ananda Raja, "Ethnicity, Nationalism, and the Nation-State: The Karen in Burma and Thailand," in *Ethnic Groups across Boundaries in Mainland Southeast Asia*, ed. G. Wijeyewardene (Singapore: ISEAS, 1990), 114.

2. *Soldier of Fortune: The Journal of Professional Adventurers* (April 1984; March 1990).

3. Benedict Rogers, *A Land without Evil: Stopping the Genocide of Burma's Kern People* (Oxford, UK, and Grand Rapids, MI: Monarch Books, 2004), 211; published in conjunction with Christian Solidarity Worldwide.

4. Karla Findley, "History of Burmese Karen" (unpublished paper, 2015).

5. Rajah, 118.

6. Peter Hinton, "Do the Karen Really Exist," in *Highlanders of Thailand*, ed.John McKinnon and Wanat Bhrusksasri (Kuala Lumpur: Oxford University Press, 1983), 155–66.

7. Charles F. Keyes, ed., introduction in *Ethnic Adaption and Identity: the Karen on the Thai Frontier with Burma* (Philadelphia: Institute for the Study of Human Issues, 1979), 8.

8. Ardeth MaungThawnghmung, *The "Other" Karen in Myanmar: Ethnic Minorities and the Struggle without Arms* (Lanham, MD: Lexington Books, 2012), 30.

9. Yoko Haymi and Susan M. Darlington, "The Karen of Burma and Thailand," in *Endangered Peoples of Southeast and East Asia: Struggles to Survive and Thrive*, ed. Leslie E. Sponsel (Westport, CT: The Greenwood Press, 2000), 149.

10. Ashley South, *Ethnic Politics in Burma: States of Conflict*, Routledge Contemporary Southeast Asia (London: Routledge, 2008), 41.

11. Pu Gee Doh, *Mahn Ba Zan Hnit Kayin Taw Hlan Yay (Mah Ba Zan and Karen Revolution)* (KNU publication, 1993), 79.

12. Ibid., 116.

13. Hugh Tinker, *The Union of Burma: A Study of the First Years of Independence* (London: Oxford University Press, 1957), 75.

14. Pu Gee Doh, 79.

15. Union of Burma, Parliamentary Report, vol. 8, no. 10 (June 20, 1949) (Rangoon: Government Printing, 1949), 290 (in Burmese).

16. Tinker, 74.

17. Ibid., 75.

18. *Nation*, June 29 and October 6, 1951.

19. Tinker, 75–76.

20. Ibid., 159.

21. Ibid., 76.

22. *New Light of Burma*, November 13, 1967.

23. Maung Sin Kyeh, *Bamapyi Chit Kayin Amyotha Kaung Saung Myar* (Bangkok: Pyidaungsu Kayin Amyotha Apweh Choke, 2003), 138.

24. Union of Burma, Seventieth Advisory Board Meeting Report (type printing copy, April 10, 1969), 19–20.

25. Maung Sin Kyeh, 140.

26. Ibid., 155.

27. *New Light of Burma*, October 13, 1967, 16.

28. Sa Maung Maung Kyi, *University Karen Students' Magazine* (1970), 4-6 (in Burmese).

29. P'doh Jubilee San Hla, "Ah Ye Gyon Ga Nyi Nyod Kya Me," *Kayin Kyay Hmone Magazine* (Yangon: Karen New Year Celebration Committee, 2019), 105–10.

30. South, 184.

31. N. Ganesan and Kyaw Yin Hlaing, eds., *Myanmar: State, Society, and Ethnicity* (Singapore: Institute of Southeast Asia Studies, National University of Singapore, 2007), 221.

32. Angelene Naw, interview with Karen Affairs Minister Tun Aung Myint, December 14, 2012.

33. *The History of Karen Baptist Convention 1913–2013* (Yangon: 100 Year Celebration Committee, 2013). The first seven pages are without page numbers; in the Karen language.

34. Tinker, 203.

35. Robert H. Taylor, *The State in Myanmar* (Honolulu: University of Hawaii Press, 2009), 305-6.

36. South, 176.

37. *History of the Karen Convention*, 10.

38. Maung Shwe Wa, *Burma Baptist Chronicle*, ed. Genevieve Sowards and Erville Sowards (Rangoon: Burma Baptist Convention, 1963), 268.

39. Ibid., 325.

40. *History of the Karen Baptist Convention*, 13. This seminary was established in Moulmein in 1845 by Dr. J. G. Binney. In 1859, it was first moved to the Vinton compound in Ahlone, Rangoon, then to 143 St. John Road, the Burma Baptist Convention compound, in 1864, before moving to Insein in 1894.

41. Ibid., 60.

42. Ibid., 199–201.

43. Rev. Clifford Kyaw Dwe, *The Work of the Karen Baptist Convention: Its Progress in Burma, 1828–1978* (Rangoon: Go Forward Press, 1978), 44.

44. *History of the Karen Baptist Convention*, 159.

45. Karen Baptist Convention website, kbcm1913.org.

46. Ibid.

47. *Annual Report to the Karen Baptist Convention, 96th General Conference*, November 27 to December 1, 2013 (Rangoon Association), 9.

48. *History of the Karen Baptist Convention*, 159.

49. *Karen Baptist Theological Seminary Pamphlet* (Insein: Seminary Hill, January 2018); Angelene Naw, interview with the principal, Dr. Lwai Say Wah, July 2019.

50. Ibid.

51. *History of the Karen Baptist Convention*, 193–94, 197–98.

52. *Annual Report to the Karen Baptist Convention*, 13.

53. Myanmar Institute of Theology, *Karen Students Association Annual Magazine, 2009–2010* (Yangon: Go Forward Press, 2010).

54. Rogers, 175–76.

55. Angelene Naw, interview with Rev. Dr. Ya Ha Lay Lay La, July 14, 2019.

56. P'doh Mahn John Roc, "TCI by Friends of TCI," *TCI Annual Magazine* 1 (2018–2019), 36–38.

57. Clifford Kyaw Dwe, 64–65.

58. *Report of the Karen Convention*, vol. 3, 1992–2002 (Rangoon: Go Forward Press, 2003), 28–30.

59. Ibid., 65.

60. *History of the Karen Convention*, 79.

61. *Annual Report to the Karen Baptist Convention*, 4.

62. *Report of the Karen Convention*, 46–47.

63. *History of the Karen Baptist Convention*, 96–98.

64. Anders P. Hovemyr, *In Search of the Karen King: A Study in Karen Identity with Special Reference to 19th Century Karen Evangelism in Northern Thailand* (Uppsala: University of Uppsala, 1989), 65.

65. Rogers, 53–54.

66. Ibid., 36–37.

67. Robert E. Johnson, *A Global Introduction to Baptist Churches* (Cambridge: Cambridge University Press, 2010), 266.

68. Baptist World Alliance, Thailand Karen Baptist Convention, baptistworld.org.

69. Pia Jolliffe, *Learning, Migration, and Intergenerational Relations: The Karen and the Gift of Education*, Palgrave Studies on Children and Development (London: Palgrave Macmillan, 2016), 64, 67–69.

70. Baptist World Alliance, "Baptist World Alliance Welcomes New Members," www.baptistworld.org.

71. *Internal Displacement and Protection in Eastern Burma* (Bangkok: Thailand Burma Border Consortium, 2005), 36–37.

72. Baptist World Alliance, baptistworld.org.

73. Naw Mu Yeh, *Life Journey of Pu Thra Saw Htoo* (Yangon: Go Forward Press, 2019; also Angelene Naw, interview with Plahset, daughter of Thra Saw Htoo, September 10, 2020.

74. Angelene Naw, interview with Thelma Kacher; also, the website of First Burmese Baptist of San Francisco. September 15, 2020.

75. *The History of Karen Baptist Fellowship Church, Bakersfield* (N.p.: private publication, n.d.), 26.

76. Ibid., 23.

77. Robert Court, "The War Is Growing Worse and Worse: Refugees and Displaced Persons on the Thai-Burma Border," issue brief (Washington, DC: The US Committee for the Refugees, May 1990), 7–11.

78. *Human Rights in Burma: Where Are We Now and What Do We Do Next?*, "Statement of Director MRS/USCCB, House of Representatives—Serial #109-147," February 7, 2006, 61–63.

79. Ibid., 63.

80. OPE BKK Report, August 2007.

81. *Friends of Burma* newsletter, spring 2009.

82. Ibid., spring 2008.

83. Ibid., fall 2008.

84. With the encouragement of Dr. Jerry Cain and through the connection of Dr. Richard Clossman, my son, Dominic Po, and I developed the church to be affiliated with the American Baptist Churches-Great River Region.

85. Sources from Cecilia Poe Nyunt, wife of the late Rev. Roger Poe Nyunt.

86. The current pastor, Tha Hser, and the five hundred church members have their worship service at Pastor Stan Crews's Monte Vista Baptist Church. Adam Maung is the grandson of Rev. Dr. Chit Maung, the first local national president of the Karen Theological Seminary. See the website akbc.us.

87. Conference paper, October 21-22, 2008 (I participated as a workshop leader).

88. Courtesy of Rev. Tha Hgay's son. He sent me his father's handwritten notes in the Karen language.

89. Board of General Ministries Reports: BGM Item 6—Reports of Ministry 1202:6/16; see the website, abc-usa.org.

90. Courtesy of Rev. Tha Hgay's son (his late father's notes).

91. I was a speaker at the conference and attended this Martyr's Day ceremony and have a copy of Robert Zan's speech. SLORC General Maung Aye made that statement while treading on a Karen flag.

92. Karen Organization of Minnesota, https://www.mnkaren.org/.

93. Courtesy of Sa Ba Taw, assistant pastor of Zion Karen Baptist church in Albert Lea, Minnesota.

94. Heather MacLachlan, "The Don Dance: An Expression of Karen Nationalism," *Voices: The Journal of New York Folklore* 32 (Fall-Winter 2006), 5.

95. Matthew McKibben, "Albany's Karen Community Celebrates New Year," *The Daily Gazette*, January 12, 2015.

96. Jerry Zremski, "Tribes from a Divided Land Settle in Buffalo," *The Buffalo News*, October 21, 2016, https://buffalonews.com/news/local/tribes-from-a-divided-land-settle-in-buffalo/article_948fb094-251b-53f2-a6dd-2e74b2dbbe11.html.

97. Marnie Eisenstadt, "From a Bar to a Baptist Church: Syracuse's 'Klub Polski' Is Sold and Remade," Syracuse.com. October 3, 2017, updated January 4, 2019, https://www.syracuse.com/living/2017/10/from_a_bar_to_a_baptist_church_syracuses_klub_polski_is_sold_and_remade.html.

98. Doug Meigs and Manger Baw, "Finding Refuge in Omaha: The Karen Community's Perseverance through War, Displacement, and Pandemic," *Omaha Magazine*, February 15, 2021.

99. At the official opening ceremony, I was given the opportunity to read the greeting message of the KNU General Tamala Baw in Karen and in English.

100. Courtesy of Dr. Jerry Cain.

101. Courtesy of Rev. Dr. Ler Htoo.

102. For information about the groups in this list, see https://karenamerican.org/; https://karensandiego.org/; http://www.karenksn.org/.

103. See https://karenamerican.org/about.

104. Mikael Gravers, "The Karen Making of a Nation," in *Asian Forms of the Nation*, ed. Stein Tonnesson and Hans Antlov (Richmond, Surrey, England: Curzon, Nordic Institutes of Asian Studies, 2000), 249.

105. See https://www.theborderconsortium.org/where-we-work/camps-in-thailand.

106. The development of Karen churches and cultural organizations in these countries is included in the online materials.

Glossary of Burmese and Karen Terms

Burmese

Adipati	leader (Führer), head of state
Anashin Mingyi	dictator king (Dr. Ba Maw's assumed title)
Athins	societies
Bama	Burman or Burmese ("Burman" as used herein refers to the majority ethnic group)
Bo	military commander
Bogyoke	supreme commander (military general)
Dacoit	robber, brigand
Dobama Asiayone	"We Burmans' Association"
Lakh	100,000
Ma	form of address to Burmese girl
Maung	form of address to Burmese boy
Min	prince or king
Myo-oak	township officer
Myo-thu-gyi	township headman
Myo-sa	a junior prince or ruler
Pongyi	Buddhist monk
Sawbwa	hereditary prince or regent in the Shan and Karenni states
Saya	teacher
Sayadaw	abbot of Buddhist monastery
Sitwundan	irregular government militia in late 1940s
Tat	army, militia
Tatmadaw	Burmese Army
Thakin	lord or master
Taungya	hill cultivation
Thugyi	village headman

U	form of address to adult Burman male
Wun	high government official
Wungyi	royal minister of state
Wunthanu	nationalism
Yebaw	comrade
Ywa	village (in Burmese)
Zayat	rest house

Karen

Daw Kalu	the whole race (the Karen ethnic group)
Hta	poem
Htee	water
Kasa	lord or master
Kaw Kasa	head of state in Karen (Saw Hunter Tha Hmwe's assumed title)
Kawthoolei	country of Karen people
Mahn	form of address to Pwo Karen adult male
Naw	form of address to S'gaw Karen female
Pee	grandmother (also form of address to Karen female leader)
Pu (Hpu)	grandfather (also form of address to Karen male leader)
Pywa-Ka-nyaw	Karen people (also meaning people)
Saw	form of address to S'gaw Karen male
Sawke	traditional Karen headman
Thra	teacher or pastor (male)
Thramu	teacher or preacher (female)
Ywa (ah)	God (in Karen)

Bibliography

Archival Documents

IOR: L/R/5/207. Burmese Press Abstract. No. 43 of 1939.

IOR: M/3/1735. General Secretary, AFPFL to the Secretary of State for Burma (through HA Force 136).

IOR: M/4/2601.Thakin Thein Pe Myint. Burma Patriotic Front (AFO) and the Communist Party of Burma.

IOR: M/4/132. SAC (Misc.) 13th meeting. 23 June 1945.

IOR: M/4/2805. Record of Meeting on Frontier Areas. 7 February 1947.

IOR: M/4/2807. Director, Frontier Areas Administration to Governor.

IOR: M/4/3023. The Humble Memorial of the Karens of Burma to His Britannic Majesty's Secretary of State for Burma.

IOR: M/4/3023. Karen Claims: Note by L. B. Walsh Atkins, Burma Office. 13 February 1947.

IOR: M/4/3023. Sir Hubert Rance to Lord Pethick-Lawrence. 7 March 1947.

IOR: MSS Eur. C. 13. Buchanan, Dr. F. *Journal of Progress and Observations during the Continuance of the Deputation from Bengal to Ava in 1795 in the dominion of the Barmah Monarch.*

IOR: R/8/20. Thakin Than Tun, General Secretary, AFPFL to Lord Louis Mountbatten (through HQ Force 136).

PRO: FO 371/69485. British Embassy, Rangoon, to Foreign Office. Telegram. September 5, 1948.

PRO: FO 643/66 (51/GSO/47Pt 1). Minutes of a Mass Meeting of the Karen Central Organization Held for Three Days, 1-3 October 1945, at No. 2 U Loo Nee Street, Kemmendine, Rangoon.

PRO: FO 643/66 (51/GSO/47 Pt I). Sir Herbert Dunkley to Sir Reginald Dorman-Smith.

PRO: FO 643/66 (51/GSO/47 Pt I). Sir San C. Po to Sir Reginald Dorman-Smith.

PRO: FO 371/75661. Bowker, Ambassador John, British Embassy, Rangoon, to Foreign Office, London. Telegram. September 7, 1948. Bo Let Ya, Brigadier, Special Commissioner, North Burma. Weekly Report for Week Ending August 28, 1948.

PRO: FO 371/75661. BSM to Burma, Rangoon, to Foreign Office, London. Telegram. January 8, 1949.

PRO: FO 371/69485. January 8, 1949.

PRO: WO 203/5239. Headquarters of Camp, Supreme Allied Commander, Southeast Asia.

PRO: WO 203/5240. Leaders' Conference, 16-18 August 1945. Reported by Thakin Than Tun.

Official Government Publications

Annual Report on the Administration of the Province of British Burma for the Year 1875–1876. Rangoon: Government Printing.

Bennison, J. J. *Census Report of Burma*, 1931, Pt. I. Rangoon: Government Printing, 1933.

British Burma Gazetteer. Vol. I. Rangoon: Government Printing, 1880.

Burma and the Insurrection. Rangoon: Government of the Union of Burma, 1949.

Burma Legislative Proceedings of the First House of Representatives. Vol. 2, no. 5. Second session, fifth meeting. Monday, 23 August 1937.

Burma Round Table Conference Proceedings. London: His Majesty's Stationery Office, 1932.

Census Commissioner. *Census of India*, 1931. Vol. 11, Burma.

Census of India, 1911. Vol. 9. Rangoon: Government Printing, 1912.

Constitution of the Union of Burma, 1947. Rangoon: Government Printing, 1948.

Frontier Areas Committee of Enquiry. Rangoon: Government Printing, 1947.

Furnivall, J. S., and W. S. Morrison. *Insein District Gazetteer.* Vol. A. Rangoon: Government Press, 1914.

Great Britain. Burma Reforms Committee, Record of Evidence. 3 vols. London, 1922.

———. Government of India Act, 1919.

———. House of Commons *Parliamentary Debates.* Fifth series. Vol. 97 (1917) col. 1695–1696.

———. House of Commons. *Sessional Papers.* Vol. 30 for 1920 (cmd. 746).

Human Rights in Burma: Where Are We Now and What Do We Do Next? Statement of Director MRS/USCCB, House of Representatives—Serial #109-147. February 7, 2006.

India Office Archives. India Secret Proceedings. Vol. 180 (1852). Reported by H. Godwin. May, June 9 and 22, and August 23, 1852.

India Statutory Commission. Vol. 11: *Memorandum Submitted by the Government of Burma to the Indian Statutory Commission.* London: His Majesty's Stationery Office, 1930.

Jamieson, P. E. *Burma Gazetteer, Amherst District.* Vol. A. Rangoon: Government Printing, 1913.

KNDO Insurrection. Rangoon: Government Printing, 1949.

Symes, Michael. *An Account of an Embassy to the Kingdom of Ava, Sent by the Governor-General of India, in the year 1795.* London: W. Bulmer and Co., 1800.

———. *Journal of His Second Embassy to the Court of Ava in 1802.* London: George Allen & Unwin, 1955.

Tenasserim (Burma) Office of the Commissioner. "E. A. Blundell to Sec. to the Sudden Board of Ft. William, December 9, 1839." *Selected Correspondence of Letters issued from and received in the Office of the Commissioner Tenasserim Division for the Years 1825–26 to 1842–1843.* Rangoon: Superintendent, Government Printing and Stationery, 1929.

Tinker, Hugh, Andrew Griffin, and S. R. Ashton. *Burma: The Struggle for Independence, 1944–1948: Compilation of Documents from Official and Private Sources.* Vol. 1. London: Her Majesty's Stationery Office, 1983.

————. *Burma: The Struggle for Independence, 1944–1948: Compilation of Documents from Official and Private Sources.* Vol. 2. London: Her Majesty's Stationery Office, 1984.
Union of Burma. Parliamentary Report. Vol. 8, no. 10. June 20, 1949. Rangoon: Government Printing.

Newspapers and Periodicals

Attauktaw. August 16, 1963. (in Burmese)
Bama Khit. August 22, 1950. (in Burmese)
Bangkok Post. April 12, 1954.
Baptist Missionary Magazine. 1824, 1833, 1834, 1837, 1871.
Botataung. August 19, 1963; August 31, 1963. (in Burmese)
Burma Issues. Vol. 16, nos. 6, 7, and 10.
Burma Issues. Vol. 18, no. 1.
Friends of Burma Newsletter. Spring 2008; spring and fall 2009; spring and fall 2010.
Forward. April 7, 1964; April 22, 1964; May 15, 1969.
Free Burma Rangers. April 20, 2007.
Great Britain, Burma Reforms Committee, Record of Evidence. 3 vols. London, 1922.
The Guardian. August 18, 1968.
Soldier of Fortune. April 1984; March 1990.
Karen News Collection. 2009. (Karen Refugees in the USA, World Refugees Day 2009)
Kyay Mon. February 13, 1963. (in Burmese)
Manchester Guardian. May 13, 1949.
Myanma Alin. August 15, 1950; August 20, 1963. (in Burmese)
Nation. August 14, 1948; June 29, 1951; October 6, 1951; January 6, 1954; January 27, 1955; January 30, 1955.
New Light of Burma. October 16, 1945; October 13, 1967; November 13, 1967.
Pyidaungsu. February 13, 1963. (in Burmese)
The Burman. 27 September 1946.
The Times. May 31, 1945; June 22, 1947; September 20, 1948; May 21, 1949; January 12, 1960.
Statesman. June 24, 1949.
Working People's Daily. October 13, 1963.

Secondary Sources

Aldrich, Richard J., Gary D. Rawnsley, and Min-Yeh T. Rawnsley, eds. *The Clandestine Cold War in Asia 1945–1965: Western Intelligence, Propaganda, and Special Operations.* London and Portland, OR: Frank Cass, 2000.
Allen, Louis. *Burma, the Longest War, 1941–1945.* London: Phoenix Press, 2000.
Anderson, Courtney. *To the Golden Shore: The Life of Adoniram Judson.* Boston: Little, Brown, 1972.
Annual Reports, American Baptist Foreign Mission Society, 1852.

Annual Reports, American Baptist Foreign Mission Society, 1856.

Annual Report to the Karen Baptist Convention, 96th General Conference. Rangoon Association. November 27 to December 1, 2013.

Aung San. "Burma's Challenge." In *The Political Legacy of Aung San*, edited by Josef Silverstein. Southeast Asia Program series, no. 11. Ithaca, NY: Cornell University Press, 1993.

Ba Maw. *Breakthrough in Burma: Memoirs of a Revolution, 1936–1946*. New Haven, CT: Yale University Press, 1968.

Ba Than. *The Roots of the Revolution: A Brief History of the Defence Services of the Union of Burma and the Ideals for Which They Stand*. Rangoon: Director of Information, 1962.

Barron, Sandy. "Twenty Years on the Border." Bangkok: Burmese Border Consortium, 2004.

Burma Human Rights Yearbook 2007. Human Rights Documentation Unit, National Coalition Government of the Union of Burma. September 2008.

Burma Intelligence Bureau. *Burma during the Japanese Occupation*. October 1, 1943.

Butwell, Richard. Communist Liaison in SE Asia, United Asia. 1954.

———. *U Nu of Burma*. Stanford, CA: Stanford University Press, 1963.

Cady, John F. *A History of Modern Burma*. Ithaca, NY: Cornell University Press, 1960.

———. *Contacts with Burma, 1935–1949: A Personal Account*. Athens: Ohio University Southeast Asia Series 61, 1983.

Callahan, Mary, P. *Making Enemies: War and State Building in Burma*. Ithaca, NY: Cornell University Press, 2003.

Carpenter, Chapin Howard. *Self-Support, Illustrated in the History of the Bassein Karen Mission from 1840–1880*. Boston: The Franklin Press, 1883.

Chatterjee, Sumil Kumar. *Felix Carey: A Tiger Tamed*. Calcutta: Hoogly Chatterjee, 1991.

Christian History and Biography 90 (Spring 2006).

Collis, Maurice. *Last and First in Burma (1941–1948)*. London: Faber and Faber, 1938.

Colquhoun, Archibald Ross. *Amongst the Shans*. London: Field & Tuer, 1885.

Committee on Survey of the Northern Baptist Convention. *Second Survey of the Fields and Work of the Northern Baptist Convention*. Presented in Denver, Colorado, June 17, 1929. New York: Northern Baptist Convention Board of Missionary Cooperation, 1929.

Crawford, John. *Journal of an Embassy from the Governor-General of India to the Court of Ava in the year 1827*. London: Henry Colburn, 1829.

Cross, E. B. *Journal of the Oriental American Society* (1854).

Crosthwaite, Charles. *The Pacification of Burma*. London: Edward Arnold, 1912.

Deniker, Joseph. *The Race of Man*. London: Walter Scott, 1900.

DeSai, Walter Sadgun. *History of the British Residency in Burma, 1826–1840*. Rangoon: University of Rangoon Press, 1939.

Dun, Smith. *Memoirs of the Four-Foot Colonel*. Data Paper number 113. Ithaca, NY: Cornell University Southeast Asia Program, Department of Asia Studies, 1980.

Eddy, Daniel C. *Heroines of the Church*. Boston: H. Wentworth, 1866.

Furnivall, J. S. *Colonial Policy and Practice: A Comparative Study of Burma and Netherlands India*. Indian Office Archives, Home Department (Upper Burma) series, vol. 2303 (1888). New York: Macmillan; Cambridge: Cambridge University Press, 1948.

———. *The Governance of Modern Burma*. New York: Institute of Pacific Relations, 1958.

———. *An Introduction to the Political Economy of Burma*. Rangoon: Burma Book Club, 1938.

Fytche, Albert. *Burma, Past and Present*. Vol. I. London: C. Kegan Paul & Company, 1878.

Ganesan, N., and Kyaw Yin Hlaing, eds. *Myanmar: State, Society and Ethnicity*. Singapore: Institute of Southeast Asia Studies, National University of Singapore, 2007.

Gilmore, David. "The Karen Traditions." *Journal of the Burma Research Society* 1, part 2 (1911).

Gravers, Mikael. "The Karen Making of a Nation." In *Asian Forms of the Nation*, edited by Stein Tonnesson and Hans Antlov, 237–69. Richmond, Surrey, England: Curzon, for the Nordic Institutes of Asian Studies, 2000.

———. "A Saint in Command? Spiritual Protection, Justice, and Religious Tensions in the Karen State." *Independent Journal of Burmese Scholarship* 1, no. 2 (August 2018).

Gutzlaff, Karl Friedrich August (Charles). *A Sketch of Chinese History, Ancient and Modern*. New York: J. P. Haven, 1834.

Hall, D. G. E. *Burma*. London: Hutchinson's University Library, 1950.

———. "Felix Carey." *Journal of Religion* 12, no. 4 (October 1932): 473–92.

Harvey, Godfrey E. *British Rule in Burma, 1824–1942*. London: Faber & Faber, 1946.

Haymi, Yoko, and. Susan M. Darlington. "The Karen of Burma and Thailand." In *Endangered Peoples of Southeast and East Asia, Struggles to Survive and Thrive*, edited by Leslie E. Sponsel, 107–153. Westport, CT: The Greenwood Press, 2000.

Hinton, Peter. "Do the Karen Really Exist?" In *Highlanders of Thailand*, edited by John McKinnon and Wanat Bhrusksasri, 155–168. New York: Oxford University Press, 1983.

History of Hanthawaddy. Burmese manuscript. India Office Library Catalogue. No. 3505.

The History of Karen Baptist Fellowship Church, Bakersfield. N.p.: private publication, n.d.

Hovemyr, Anders P. *In Search of the Karen King: A Study in Karen Identity with Special Reference to 19th Century Karen Evangelism in Northern Thailand*. Uppsala: University of Uppsala, 1989.

Howard, Randolph L. *Baptists in Burma*. Philadelphia: Judson Press, 1931.

Internal Displacement and Protection in Eastern Burma. Bangkok: Thailand Burma Border Consortium, 2005.

James, Sharon. *My Heart in His Hands: Ann Judson of Burma*. Darlington, Durham, England: Evangelical Press, 2012.

Johnson, Robert E. *A Global Introduction to Baptist Churches*. Cambridge: Cambridge University Press, 2010.

Jolliffe, Pia. *Learning, Migration and Intergenerational Relations: The Karen and the Gift of Education*. Palgrave Studies on Children and Development. London: Palgrave Macmillan, 2016.

Jones, John Winter, and George Percy Badger, eds. *The Travels of Ludovico de Varthema: in Egypt, Syria, Arabia Deserta and Arab Felix, in Persia, India and Ethiopia, A.D. 1503–1508*. Translated from the original Italian edition of 1510. London: Printed for the Hakluyt Society, 1863.

Judson Chapel Golden Jubilee. Rangoon: Thamee Hnit Tha Press, 1983.

Judson, Emily Chubbuck [Fanny Forester]. *Memoir of Sarah B. Judson, Member of the American Mission to Burmah*. New York: L. Colby and Company, 1848.

Karen Baptist Theological Seminary Pamphlet. Insein: Seminary Hill, January 2018.

Keyes, Charles F., ed. *Ethnic Adaption and Identity: The Karen on the Thai Frontier with Burma*. Philadelphia: Institute for the Study of Human Issues, 1979.

Kirby, S. Woodburn. *War against Japan: The Official History of the Second World War*. Vol. 4: *The Reconquest of Burma*. London: Her Majesty's Stationery Office, 1957–1969.

Knowles, James D. *Memoir of Mrs. Ann H. Judson, Late Missionary to Burmah*. 4th ed. Boston: Lincoln & Edmands, 1831.

Koschorke, Klaus, Ludwig Frieder, Mariano Delgado, and Roland Spliesgart, eds. *A History of Christianity in Asia, Africa, and Latin America, 1450–1990: A Documentary Sourcebook*. Grand Rapids, MI: Eerdmans, 2007.

Langham-Carter, R. R. *Old Moulmein (1875–1880)*. Moulmein: Moulmein Sun Press, 1947.

Laurie, W. F. B. *Our Burmese Wars and Relations with Burma*. 2nd ed. London: W. H. Allen & Co., 1885.

Lewis, James Lee. "The Burmanization of the Karen People: A Study in Racial Adaptability." Unpublished Master of Arts Dissertation Presented to the Department of Practical Theology, University of Chicago, 1924. (microfilm)

Lintner, Bertil. *Burma in Revolt: Opium and Insurgency since 1948*. Chiang Mai: Silkworm Books, 1999.

Logan, James Richard. "On the Ethnographic Position of the Karens." *Journal of the Indian Archipelago and Eastern Asia* new series 2 (1858): 364–90.

Luther, Calista V. *The Vintons and the Karens: Memorials of Rev. Justus H. Vinton and Calista H. Vinton*. Boston: W. G. Corthell, Mission Rooms, 1880.

MacLachlan, Heather. "The Don Dance: An Expression of Karen Nationalism." *Voices: The Journal of New York Folklore* 32, nos. 3-4 (Fall-Winter 2006): 26–32.

Mahn, P'doh, John Roc. "TCI by Friends of TCI." *TCI Annual Magazine* 1 (2018–2019), 36–38.

Marshall, Henry I. *Burma Pamphlets No. 8: The Karens of Burma*. New York: Longmans, Green & Co., 1945.

———. *The Karen People of Burma: A Study in Anthropology and Ethnology*. Columbus: The Ohio State University, 1922.

——— . *On the Threshold of the Century: An Historical Sketch of the Karen Mission, 1828–1928*. Rangoon: American Baptist Mission Press, 1929.

Mason, Ellen Huntly Bullard. *Great Expectations Realized; or Civilizing Mountain Men*. Philadelphia: American Baptist Publication Society; New York: Blakeman & Mason; Chicago: Church, Goodman and Kenny, 1862.

Mason, Francis. *Burmah: Its People and Natural Productions*. London: Trubner & Co., 1860.

———. *The Karen Apostle: or Memoir of Ko Thah-Byu, the First Karen Convert, with Notices Concerning His Nation*. Boston: Gould, Kendall and Lincoln, 1861.

———. "Saw Quala, the Second Karen Convert." *Missionary Magazine* 36 (1856).

Maung, Maung. *Burma in the Family of Nations*. Amsterdam: Djambatan, 1958.

———. *Burma and General Ne Win*. Mumbai: Asia Publishing House, 1969.

McKibben, Matthew. "Albany's Karen Community Celebrates New Year." *The Daily Gazette*, January 12, 2015.

McMahon, A. R. *The Karens of the Golden Chersonese*. London: Harrison, 1876.

Meigs, Doug, and Manger Baw. "Finding Refuge in Omaha: The Karen Community's Perseverance through War, Displacement, and Pandemic." *Omaha Magazine*, February 15, 2021.

Minutes of the Kawthoolei Congress. 17-19 July 1950. KNU publication.

Mitsuru, Sugii. *Minami Kikan Gaishi (An Unofficial History of the Minami Organization)*. Rangoon, n.d.

Moffett, Samuel. *A History of Christianity in Asia*. Vol. 2. Maryknoll, NY: Orbis Books, 2005.

Morrison, Ian. *Grandfather Longlegs: The Life and Gallant Death of Major H. P. Seagrim, G.C., D.S.O., H.P.* London: Faber and Faber, 1947.

Moscotti, Albert D. *British Policy and the Natioinalist Movement in Burma, 1931–1937*. Honolulu: University of Hawaii Press, 1974.

Myanmar Institute of Theology. *Karen Students Association Annual Magazine, 2009–2010*. Yangon: Go Forward Press, 2010.

Myo, Maung Aung. *Building the Tatmadaw*. Singapore: Institute of Asian Studies, 2009.

Naw, Angelene. *Aung San and the Struggle for Burmese Independence*. Chiang Mai: Silkworm Books, 2001.

———. *Memoirs of a Karen Soldier in World War II: Saw Yankee Myint Oo*. Independently published, 2020.

Nu, U. *Burma under the Japanese*. Edited and translated with introduction by J. S. Furnivall. London: Macmillan; New York: St. Martin's Press, 1954.

———. *From Peace to Stability: Speeches from August 1949 to April 1951*. Rangoon, 1951.

———. *Saturday's Son*. New Haven, CT: Yale University Press, 1975.

Overseas Processing Entity, Bangkok (OPE BKK) Report. August 2007.

An Outline of the History of the Catholic Burmese Mission from the Years 1720–1887. Compiled by the Head of the Mission. Rangoon: Hanthawaddy Press, 1887.

Pearn, Bertie Reginald. *A History of Rangoon*. Rangoon: American Baptist Mission Press, 1962.

———. *Judson of Burma*. London: Edinburgh House Press, 1939.

Phayre, Arthur Purves. *History of Burma*. London, 1885; reprint, Bangkok: Orchid Press, 1998.

Po, San C. *Burma and the Karens*. London: Elliot Stock, 1928.

Po, Thyra. *Sir San C. Po, C.B.E., M.D., A Karen Pioneer*. Yangon: Privately printed, 2008.

Raja, Ananda. "Ethnicity, Nationalism, and the Nation-State: The Karen in Burma and Thailand." In *Ethnic Groups across Boundaries in Mainland Southeast Asia*, edited by G. Wijeyewardene, 102–33. Singapore: ISEAS, 1990.

Ralph, Saw, and Naw Sheera. *Fifty Years in the Karen Revolution in Burma, the Soldier and the Teacher*. Edited by Stephanie Olinga-Shannon. Ithaca, NY: Cornell University Press, 2019.

Renard, D. Ronald. "The Karen Rebellion in Burma." In *Secessionist Movements in Comparative Perspective*, edited by Ralph R. Premdas, S. W. R. de A. Samarasinghe, and Alan B. Anderson, 93–110. New York: St. Martin's Press, 1990.

Robbins, Joseph Chandler. *Boardman of Burma: A Biography*. Philadelphia: Judson Press.1940.

Robert, Court. "The War Is Growing Worse and Worse: Refugees and Displaced Persons on the Thai-Burma Border." Issue Brief. Washington, DC: The US Committee for Refugees, May 1990.

Robert, Dana L. *American Women in Mission: A Social History of Their Thought and Practice*. Macon, GA: Mercer University Press, 1997.

Rogers, Benedict. *Burma: A Nation at the Crossroads*. London: Ryder Books, 2012.

———. *A Land without Evil: Stopping the Genocide of Burma's Karen People*. Oxford, UK, and Grand Rapids, MI: Monarch Books, 2004. Published in conjuction with Christian Solidarity Worldwide.

Sakhong, Lian Hong. *Religion and Politics among the Chin People in Burma (1896–1949)*. Uppsala: Studia Missionalia, 2000.

Schmidlin, Joseph. *Catholic Mission History*, Techny, IL: Mission Press, 1933.

Scott, Sir George. *Burma*. London: Alexander Moring Ltd., 1911.

Shwe Wa, Maung. *Burma Baptist Chronicle*. Edited by Genevieve Sowards and Erville Sowards. Rangoon: Burma Baptist Convention, 1963.

Silverstein, Josef. *Burma: Military Rule and the Politics of Stagnation*. Ithaca, NY: Cornell University Press, 1977.

———. *Burmese Politics: The Dilemma of National Unity*. New Brunswick, NJ: Rutgers University Press, 1980.

———, ed. *The Political Legacy of Aung San*. Southeast Asia Program series, no. 11. Ithaca, NY: Cornell University Press, 1973.

Singh, Surendra Prasad. *Growth of Nationalism in Burma, 1900–1942*. Calcutta: Firma KLM Private Ltd., 1980.

Slim, William. *Defeat into Victory: Battling Japan in Burma and India, 1942–1945*. London: Cassells and Company, 1956.

Smeaton, Donald Mackenzie. *The Loyal Karens of Burma*. London: Kegan Paul, Trench & Co., 1887.

Smith, George. *The Life of William Carey, D.D.: Shoe Maker and Missionary*. London: John Murray, 1885.

Smith, Martin. *Burma: Insurgency and the Politics of Ethnicity*. New York: St. Martin's Press, 1999.

Snodgrass, John James. *Narrative of the Burmese War*. London: John Murray, 1827.

Soothill, William Edward. *A History of China*. 1929. New York: Contemporary Books, 1951.

South, Ashley. *Ethnic Politics in Burma: States of Conflict*. Routledge Contemporary Southeast Asia. London: Routledge, 2008.

St. John, Wallace. "Chronicle." *Judson Chapel Golden Jubilee*. Rangoon: Thamee Hnit Tha Press, 1983.

———. *The Baptist Investment in Burma*. Unpublished manuscript in the library of St. Paul's Church, 1945.

Stewart, Whitney. *Aung San Suu Kyi: Fearless Voice of Burma*. New York: iUniverse, 2008.

Tadaw, Saw Hanson. *The Karens of Burma: A Study in Human Geography*. London: University of London, 1961.

Taylor, Robert H. *The State in Myanmar*. Honolulu: University of Hawaii Press, 2009.

Thawnghmung, Ardeth Maung. *The "Other" Karen in Myanmar: Ethnic Minorities and the Struggle without Arms*. Lanham, MD: Lexington Books, 2012.

Thompson, Virginia, and Richard Adolf. *Minority Problems in Southeast Asia*. Stanford, CA: Stanford University Press, 1955.

Tinker, Hugh. *The Union of Burma: A Study of the First Years of Independence*. London: Oxford University Press, 1957.

Torbet, Robert G. *Venture of Faith: The Story of the American Baptist Foreign Mission Society and the Women's American Baptist Foreign Mission Society, 1814–1954*. Philadelphia: Judson Press, 1955.

Tun Aung Chain. "The Early Church." *Judson Chapel Golden Jubilee*. Rangoon: Thamee Hnit Tha Press, 1983.

Union of Burma. *Regional Autonomy Enquiry Commission Record*. Rangoon, 1951.

———. *Seventieth Advisory Board Meeting Report*. Type printing copy. April 10, 1969.

Vance, Christie. *Into All the World: Four Stories of Pioneer Missionaries*. Uhrichsville, OH: Barbour, 2004.

Wayland, Francis. *A Memoir of the Life and Labors of the Reverend Adoniram Judson, D.D.* Vols. 1 and 2. Boston: Philips, Sampson and Company, 1853.

Willson, Arabella Stuart. *The Three Mrs. Judsons*. Missionary Series. Edited by Gary W. Long. Springfield, MO: Particular Baptist Press, 1999.

Wilson, Horace Hayman. *Documents Illustrative of the Burmese War with an Introductory Sketch of Events of the War and an Appendix*. Calcutta: Government Gazette Press, 1827.

Winston, W. R. *Four Years in Upper Burma*. London: C. H. Kelly, 1892.

Wyeth, Walter Newton. *The Wades: Jonathan Wade, D.D., Deborah B. L. Wade, A Memorial*. Philadelphia: Published by the author, 1891.

Yawnghwe, Chao Tzang. "Politics of Burma and Shan State: Effects on North Thailand and Thailand." *Political Science Review* (September 1982).

Yeh, Allen, and Chris Chun, eds. *Expect Great Things: William Carey and Adoniram Judson, Missionary Pioneers*. Eugene, OR: Wipf & Stock, 2013.

Yeh, Naw Mu. *Life Journey of Pu Thra Saw Htoo*. Yangon: Go Forward Press, 2019.

Yone, Edward M. Law, and David G. Mandelbaum. "Pacification in Burma." *Far Eastern Survey* 19, no. 17 (October 11, 1950): 182–87.

IN THE KAREN LANGUAGE

100 Year History of the Karen Baptist Convention 1913–2013. Yangon: Karen Baptist Convention, 2013.

Aung Hla. *The Karen History*. Rangoon: self-published, 1939.

Ba Tu, Thra. *Karen Baptist Churches in Bassein and Myaungmya, 1837–1961*. Insein: Seminary Press, 1963.

Cultural Committee of CE 2000 for Christ, comp. *Kha Na Kee Kato Kanyaw Ta-hset-ta-la Ahlit Heet Khar* (*Culture Handbook*). Yangon: Karen Baptist Convention, 2000.

Dwe, Thra Clifford Kyaw. *Karen Baptist Convention*. Rangoon: Go Forward Press, 1978.

———. *The Work of the Karen Baptist Convention: Its Progress in Burma, 1828–1978*. Rangoon: Go Forward Press, 1978.

The History of Karen Baptist Convention 1913–2013. Yangon: 100 Year Celebration Committee, 2013.

Lit Tha We Ka Sa Ywa (*Karen Hymnbook*). Karen Baptist Convention, 1972, 2006, 2018.

Karen Folk Songs. N.p.: private publication, n.d.

Pu S'Kaw Ler Taw. *Ka Nyaw Ta Ber Hser Tar Si Soh Teh Soh*. KNU publication, 1992.

Report of the Karen Convention. Vol. 3. 1992–2002. Rangoon: Go Forward Press.

Report to the KBC, 96th General Conference. 2013.

Thesaurus of Karen Knowledge, Native Karen Dictionary. Vol. 2. Written by Sau Kau-Too and compiled by J. Wade. Tavoy: Karen Mission Press, 1848.

Thra Kalaw Lah, Thramu Naw Mya Aye, and Thra Ku Kuh, comps. *Karen New Year*. Publication of Karen New Year Celebration Committee, 2019.

Thanbyah, T. *Karen People and Development*. Rangoon: American Baptist Mission Press, 1906. Republished by Global Karen Baptist Fellowship, 2010.

———. *The Karens and Their Persecution, 1824–1854*. Rangoon: American Baptist Mission Press, 1904.

Troo, Saw Moo, and Mika Rolley. *Karens and Communism, and Karens Fight for Peace*. N.p.: Kawthoolei publication, n. d.

Oo Zan, P'doh Tha Bwar. *History of the Baptist Mission among the Karen in Burma*. Rangoon: Go Forward Press, 1961.

IN THE BURMESE LANGUAGE

Doh, Pu Gee. *Mahn Ba Zan Hnint Kayin Taw Hlan Yay* (*Mah Ba Zan and Karen Revolution*). KNU publication, 1993.

Hla, P'doh Jubilee San. "Ah Ye Gyon Ga Nyi Nyod Kya Me." In *Kayin Kyay Hmone Magazine*. Yangon: Karen New Year Celebration Committee, 2019.

Hla, Loo Htu U. *Thadin-sarmyar Pyaw-pya-thaw Sit Pyee-sa Bamar-Pyi*. Vol. 1. Rangoon: Gyi Bwa Yay Press, 1969.

Kyeh, Maung Sin. *Kayin Bawa Dalay*. Rangoon: Padaytha Sar Bay, 1967.

———. *Bamarpyi Chit Kayin Amyotha Kaung Hsaung Myar*. Bangkok: Pyidaungsu Kayin Amyotha Apweh Choke, 2003.

Kyi, Sa Maung Maung. *University Karen Students' Magazine*. 1970.

Mya, Saw Bo. *Kyundaw Bawa Pyatthan Hmu Asit Ahman*. Yangon: Nay Yee Yee Sar Oak Taik, 2014.

Nyar, U Pyin. *Kayin Yar Zawin*. Rangoon: Zwe Sar Pay, 1929.

Pu S'Kaw Ler Taw. *Kayin Taw Hlan Yay Thamaing*. Edited by Saw Maung Maung and KNU Central Committee. KNU publication, 1992.

Taing Yin Thar Yin Kyaymu Yoya dalay Tonesan Myar. Government printing, 1967.

Tatmadaw Thamaing (1824–1945). (*History of the Armed Forces*), vol. 1. Rangoon: Myawaddy Press, 1996.

Tetkatho Sein Tin. *Saw San Po Thin Attopatti* (*The Biography of Saw San Po Thin*). Rangoon: Chin Dwin, 1974.

Thakin Tin Mya. *Petsit Taw Hlan Yay Hnit Taing Seh Taing* (*Fascist Revolution and Ten Commands*). Rangoon: Thiha Yadana Sarbei, 2010.

Thutaythana Ye Baw. *Ye Baw Thone Kyeik Hnint Ba Ma lut lat ye Tat Ma Taw Sit Kyaung Myar* (*The Thirty Comrades and the Military Campaign Routes of the Burma Independence Army*). Rangoon: Ye Baw Yargyaw, 1975.

Websites

ABC [Australian Broadcasting Corporation] News. "Karen Refugees Make $40m Contribution to Nhill Economy in Victoria's Wimmera Study Finds." April 23, 2015. https://www.abc.net.au/news/2015-04-24/study-reveals-refugees-boosting-nhill-economy/6417620.

American Baptist Churches USA. "Board of General Ministries Reports: BGM Item 6—Reports of Ministry 1202:6/16." https://www.abc-usa.org/wp-content/uploads/2012/06/BGM-Item-6-Ministry-Reports.pdf.

Arizona Karen Baptist Church. https://akbc.us.

Australian Government Department of Home Affairs. www.homeaffairs.gov.au/mca/files/2016-cis-myanmar.

———. "Myanmar-born Community Information Summary." https://www.homeaffairs.gov.au/mca/files/2016-cis-myanmar.PDF.

Australian Karen Foundation. https://australiankarenfoundation.org.au/about_us_17.html.

Australian Karen Organization. https://www.ako.org.au.

Baptist Union of Victoria. https://www.buv.com.au/good-news-stories.

Baptist World Alliance. "Baptist World Alliance Welcomes New Members." October 22, 2021. https://baptistworld.org/?s=Baptist+World+Alliance+Welcomes+New+Members.

Eisenstadt, Marnie. "From a Bar to a Baptist Church: Syracuse's 'Klub Polski' Is Sold and Remade." Syracuse.com, October 3, 2017. https://www.syracuse.com/living/2017/10/from_a_bar_to_a_baptist_church_syracuses_klub_polski_is_sold_and_remade.html.

Farrugia, Lynn, Renato Delcioppo, Lah May Wah, Lei Thoo, Hse Nay Paw, and Ku Ku. *Working with Karen Immigrant Students: Teacher Resources.* Canadian Multicultural Education Foundation and Alberta Teachers' Association. January 2015. https://www.cmef.ca/wp-content/themes/cmef /pdf/CMEF-ATATeacherResourceKarenStudents.pdf.

First Baptist Church of San Francisco. https://firstsf.com.

First Karen Baptist Church of Regina. https://firstbaptistregina.ca/new-friends -in-christ/nfic-karen-church/.

Friends of Burma. http://friendsofburma.org.

Immigrant Services Society of British Columbia. https://issbc.org/wpcontent /uploads/2018/03/9__Karen_Refugees_After_Five_Years_in_Canada _CS.pdf 24/. Accessed October 12, 2021.

International Organization for Migration (IOM) UN Migration. www.iom.int /news.

———. April 28, 2017. www.iom.int/news/australian-assistant-minister-visits -thai-myanmar-border-re. Accessed October 10, 2021.

Karen American Communities Foundation. https://karenamerican.org/.

Karen Baptist Churches of Canada. https://www.canadacompanyregistry.com /company?utm_source=karen-baptist-churches-of-canada.

Karen Baptist Convention. https://kbcm1913.org.

Karen Canadian Community. "About KCC." https://karencanadiancommunity .wordpress.com/about.

———. "Karen Canadian Community Was Established in 1999 at Thunderbay, Ontario." October 19, 2012. https://karencanadiancommunity.wordpress .com/2012/10/19/.

———. "News and Events." https://karencanadiancommunity.wordpress.com /events-news/.

Karen Organization of Minnesota. https://www.mnkaren.org/.

Karen Organization of San Diego. https://karensandiego.org/.

Karen Society of Nebraska. https http://karenksn.org/.

Kearney, Mark. ABC Central Victoria [ABC News]. "Karen Refugees Boost Regional Victoria's Economy, New Study Finds," September 24, 2018. https://www.abc.net.au/news/2018-09-25/karen-refugees-boost-bendigo -economy/10299948.

James North Baptist Church. "Interview with Klosay." February 1, 2021. https://www.hughson.ca/news/interview-with-klosay.

Thailand Karen Baptist Convention. Baptist World Alliance. https:// baptistworld.org/?s=thailand+karen+baptist+convention.

Zremski, Jerry. "Tribes from a Divided Land Settle in Buffalo." *The Buffalo News.* October 21, 2016. https://buffalonews.com/news/local/tribes-from -a-divided-land-settle-in-buffalo/article_948fb094-251b-53f2-a6dd-2e74 b2dbbe11.html.

Index

Karen National Anthem

Saw San Ba –Lyrics

Music – Saw Tha Aye Gyi

၁. ယပှၤကလုာ် ယဲဧၢ, ပှၤလၢအဂ့ၢ်ကတၢၢ်, ယအဲၣ် ဒိၣ် နၤ,

နအဲၣ်တၢ်တီတၢ်လိၤ, တမုံၤနအဲၣ်တူၢ်လိာ်,

နတၢ်အဂ့ၤကိးမှိ, ယအဲၣ် ဒိၣ် နၤ.

၂. ကစၢ်အပှၤကလုာ်, ပှၤကွၢ်လၢ်ယွၤတဖု, နဘၣ်ဆိၣ်ဂ့ၤ,

တၢ်နးတၢ်ဖှိၣ်ဘၣ်နၤ, နကဲကုၢ်ပှၤဘၣ်ဆၣ်,

ဒ့ ဝါပှၤအုၣ်ခီၣ်တၢ်, စၢ်ယွၤဆှၢက့ၤ.

၃. ပပၢ်အယွၤစၢ်ဧၢ, ပတၢ်မုၢ်လၢ်လၢပျၢၤ, ပဘါထီၣ်နၤ,

ဒ်သိးကကဲပျၢ်ဘီၣ်, စိာ်တၢ်သးခုကစီၣ်,

တုၤလၢကိးထံကိးကီၢ်, ဆိၣ်ဂ့ၤက့ၤပှၤ.

English Translation

1. My people all my own, the best in all the land,
   I love you much.
   For you love righteousness, and you serve guests with care,
   Your many good characters, I love you much.
2. People of gracious God, who hope and wait for God,
   you are so blessed.
   Through your suffering and pain, hardship of slavery,
   White brothers as savior, God sent to you.
3. Oh Lord, our Father God, our hope from ancient times, we
   worship you.
   To make new followers, and spread your great gospel,
   'til reach every country. Blessing, please grant.

September 15, 2022
English translation by Angelene Naw

THE Karen National Anthem

KAREN NATIONAL ANTHEM

Saw San Ba
Vigoroso

Saw Tha Aye Gyi

My peo - ple all my own, the best in all the
Peo - ple of graci - ous God, who hope and wait for
Oh Lord our Fa - ther God, our hope from an - cient

land, I love you much, for you love right - eous -
God, you are so blessed, through your suffer - ing and
times, we wor - ship you, to make new fol - low -

ness, and you serve guests with care, your
pain, hard - ship of sla - ve - ry, white
ers, and spread your great gos - pel, 'til

ma - ny good charac - ters, I love you much.
bro - thers as sa - vior, God sent to please you.
reach eve - ry coun - try, Bles - sing, please grant.

September 15, 2022
English translation by Angelene Naw
Score by Saw Kanyaw Hoo
Permission granted from the Karen Baptist Convention for use of anthem that was taken from the
Sgaw Karen Hymn and Tune Book by Raleigh Dee, published by The Baptist Board of Publications of
the Burma Baptist Convention, Hong Kong, 1963.